THE EFFECT OF MAN ON THE LANDSCAPE: THE HIGHLAND ZONE

The effect of man on the landscape: the Highland Zone

Edited by

J. G. Evans

Susan Limbrey

Henry Cleere

1975

Research Report No. 11

The Council for British Archaeology

ISBN 0 900312 27 0

PRINTED BY DERRY AND SONS LIMITED CANAL STREET NOTTINGHAM ENGLAND

Contents

PAGE

Editors' Foreword vii

List of Contributors vii

Highland landscapes: habitat and heritage 1
E. Estyn Evans

The role of climatic factors in environmental and cultural changes in prehistoric times 6
J. A. Taylor

Processes of soil degradation: a pedological point of view 20
D. F. Ball

Early agriculture and soil degradation 27
R. T. Smith

Soils and archaeology in Scotland 37
J. C. C. Romans and L. Robertson

The ecology and behaviour of deer in relation to their impact on the environment of prehistoric Britain 40
R. E. Chaplin

The intimate relationship: an hypothesis concerning pre-Neolithic land use 43
Pam Evans

Ungulate populations, economic patterns, and the Mesolithic landscape 49
P. Mellars

The ecological setting of Mesolithic man in the Highland Zone 57
I. G. Simmons

Neolithic and Bronze Age landscape changes in northern Ireland 64
A. G. Smith

The effect of Neolithic man on the environment in north-west England: the use of absolute pollen diagrams 74
Winifred Pennington (Mrs T. G. Tutin)

The evidence for land use by prehistoric farming communities: the use of three-dimensional pollen diagrams 86
Judith Turner

Habitat change in coastal sand-dune areas: the molluscan evidence 96
Penelope J. Spencer

Survival and discovery 104
J. B. Stevenson

The evidence of air-photographs 108
D. R. Wilson

Economic influences on land use in the military areas of the Highland Zone during the Roman period 112
W. H. Manning

Dry bones and living documents 117
L. Alcock

Comments on Professor Alcock's paper 123
R. E. Chaplin

The impact of landscape on prehistoric man 124
Frances Lynch

Summary and general conclusions 127
G. W. Dimbleby

Editors' Foreword

This volume contains papers given at a Conference entitled *The Effect of Man on the Landscape: The Highland Zone,* organized by the Scientific Research Committee of the Council for British Archaeology. The Conference was held in the University of Lancaster on 29, 30, and 31 March 1974. A second Conference to cover the Lowland Zone is planned for the autumn of 1975. In planning the Conference we were primarily concerned with the evidence for past landscapes—the latter being a broad term which we have taken to include soils, fauna, climate, and ancient monuments, as well as the more obvious aspects such as topography and vegetation—and the majority of papers are indeed concerned with the techniques of interpretation in one form or another. We also felt that, in order to preserve a degree of uniformity in what is a very diverse subject, the Conference should be restricted to the prehistoric and early historic periods.

As Professor Dimbleby mentions in his closing remarks, the Conference provoked much discussion on the very concept of the Highland Zone/Lowland Zone classification, clearly one which can be defined in various ways, and which is more applicable in some periods of the past than in others.

We would like to take this opportunity of thanking, on behalf of the CBA, all the contributors to the Conference and the Chairmen of the various sessions, Professor G. W. Dimbleby, Professor Gordon Manley, Professor R. J. C. Atkinson, Professor G. F. Mitchell, Professor C. D. Pigott, and Professor Leslie Alcock; Miss Beatrice de Cardi, Mr Peter Marchant, and other members of the staff of the CBA for their hard work in carrying out the successful administration of the Conference; and Lancaster University for the magnificent accommodation and hospitality.

Throughout this publication, dates based on radiocarbon assay are referred to as bp, bc, or ad.

List of Contributors

Professor Leslie Alcock. Department of Archaeology, The University, Glasgow G12 8QQ.

Dr D. F. Ball. The Nature Conservancy, Penrhos Road, Bangor, Caerns. LL57 2LQ.

Dr R. E. Chaplin. Netherfield, Upper Blainslie, Galashiels, Selkirkshire.

Professor G. W. Dimbleby. Department of Human Environment, Institute of Archaeology, 31–34 Gordon Square, London WC1H 0PY.

Professor E. Estyn Evans. Institute of Irish Studies, The Queen's University of Belfast, 42 University Road, Belfast BT7 1NJ.

Mrs Pam Evans. 8 Church Road, Penarth, Glam.

Miss Frances Lynch. Department of History, University College of North Wales, Bangor, Caerns.

Dr W. H. Manning. Department of Archaeology, University College, Cardiff.

Dr P. Mellars. Department of Ancient History, The University of Sheffield, Sheffield S10 2TN.

Dr Winifred Pennington (Mrs T. G. Tutin). Freshwater Biological Association, Ambleside, and School of Ecology, University of Leicester, University Road, Leicester LE1 7RH.

Mr L. Robertson. The Macaulay Institute for Soil Research, Craigiebuckler, Aberdeen AB9 2QJ.

Mr J. C. C. Romans. The Macaulay Institute for Soil Research, Craigiebuckler, Aberdeen AB9 2QJ.

Dr I. G. Simmons. Department of Geography, The University, Durham DH1 3LE.

Professor A. G. Smith. Department of Botany, University College, Cardiff.

Dr R. T. Smith. Department of Geography, The University of Leeds, Leeds LS2 9JT.

Miss Penelope J. Spencer. Department of Archaeology, University College, Cardiff.

Mr J. B. Stevenson. The Royal Commission on Ancient and Historical Monuments of Scotland, 54 Melville Street, Edinburgh EH3 7HF.

Dr J. A. Taylor. Department of Geography, Aberystwyth, Cardiganshire.

Dr Judith Turner. St Aidan's College, University of Durham, Durham DH1 3LJ.

Mr D. R. Wilson. Committee for Aerial Photography, University of Cambridge, 11 West Road, Cambridge CB3 9DP.

Highland landscapes: habitat and heritage

E. Estyn Evans

Synopsis

The division of Great Britain into Highland and Lowland Zones, which archaeologists associate with Sir Cyril Fox and which was first proposed by the geographer Sir Halford Mackinder in 1902, is inadequate for our purpose because it ignores Ireland, which is neither Highland nor Lowland. Like the other islands of the Atlantic fringe, it is characterized by extreme topographic fragmentation, resulting mainly from the high and persistent precipitation and the feeble evaporation which quickened the erosive processes. Since Highland Britain is also a region of high precipitation it can be included in a larger pluvial zone which would embrace Ireland and the Scottish islands. This definition leaves the author free to discuss prehistoric landscapes in the Irish uplands as well as in the Highland Zone. Once man enters upon the scene, the physical environment acquires a new dimension: the landscape is altered — enriched or impoverished — by the actions of its occupants, and their heritage is itself deeply affected in the process. Examples taken from Ireland suggest that the interaction of prehistoric societies with upland environments has long-lasting effects on both habitat and inhabitants.

I confess that in this gathering of specialists I am, as a geographer, something of a Jack-of-all-trades, professionally obliged and temperamentally inclined 'to keep one eye on nature and the other on man', conscious of knowing nothing very thoroughly but cherishing a faint hope that, as with mankind among the higher mammals, there may be some compensating gain in remaining unspecialized. A less kindly chairman might have introduced me as a magpie among birds or as a rogue among honest men, stealing scraps of information from them under the pretext of being able to assemble them into an intelligible whole. It would be rash and presumptuous for one who is not at the growing point or anywhere near the front line of current research to attempt to summarize present views on environmental change in prehistoric times. I will try rather to outline my approach to the problem and illustrate it by examples from Ireland. In trying to understand human motives and actions in prehistory, imagination and intuition should not be sacrificed on the altar of statistical techniques. We must ask ourselves not only what man did to the forest but also what the forest did to man and how this influenced his thoughts and actions. These things cannot be measured but should not for that reason be overlooked. In looking at prehistory I have tried to follow the advice of A. W. Brøgger (1940, 166): "to understand early cultures it is necessary to know something of life along the coast, in the forest and amid the mountains, on the land, the fields, the pastures".

A geographer can claim that we owe the terms *Highland* and *Lowland Britain* to another geographer, Sir Halford Mackinder, whose *Britain and the British Seas* (1902) was one of the first attempts to identify and analyse the physical and cultural regions of Great Britain. Mackinder saw the primary division into 'a more accessible east and a less accessible west' as making for variety of initiative and resulting interaction. I am not sure that we would all agree with the idea of the inaccessibility of the west in prehistoric times—I recall Stuart Piggott's reminder that the back door is also the tradesman's entrance—but the concept of a contact zone of cultural interaction and innovation is as valuable when applied to, let us say, the Early Bronze Age as it is to that late iron age which we call the Industrial Revolution and whose beginnings Miss Margaret Hodgen (1952) has so convincingly linked with the habitat and heritage of the contact zone between Highland and Lowland Britain.

Mackinder saw the many contrasts between south-east and north-west "with all the resultant differences, agricultural, industrial, racial and historical", as depending on a fundamental distinction in rock structure, and he lays stress on the associated climatic differences: "the climatic contrasts of Britain harmonize with its structure". This statement appears as No. 10 in his list of twenty conclusions. One is inevitably reminded of Cyril Fox's twenty-five propositions in *The Personality of Britain* (1932). I remember drawing attention to these similarities in a review—although Fox, of course, went far deeper into prehistory—but he subseqently told me that he had not read Mackinder or indeed the French geographer Vidal de la Blache when he wrote *The Personality*.

Let me at this point touch on the sub-title I have chosen for this opening address: "Habitat and Heritage". Cyril Fox (1932) applied the term 'personality' to the total physical endowment of Britain and its regions and traced its 'influence' on successive prehistoric cultures in his two zones. A geographer cannot see the environment as an absolute but looks on man and nature as interacting forces, constantly shaping each other. Once man comes on the scene—and for most of the Highland Zone this is not until Post-glacial times—the physical environment acquires a human dimension. Man's choice of action is affected not only by the nature of his habitat but also by actions he has previously taken and by the contacts he makes. His areas of concern, both territorially and culturally, are related to previous experience and to opportunities for cultural borrowal as well as to environmental opportunities. Between habitat and heritage there is a two-way traffic, and I think we would agree that this exchange must have increased greatly when man undertook forest clearance on any considerable scale.

Neither Mackinder nor Fox discusses how Ireland fits into the scheme of Highland and Lowland Zones, although it has generally been regarded as a detached, if somewhat eccentric, part of the Highland Zone. In fact, being Irish, it is predominantly lowland. There have indeed been suggestions that the south and east, on the British analogy, should be classed as the island's Lowland Zone, but a better case for cultural replacement could be made for the north-east, much of which is upland—and indeed the south-east is blessed with one of the largest of all the Irish mountain massifs, the Wicklow Mountains. What distinguishes Ireland topographically is the extreme fragmentation of its uplands. A similar juxtaposition of terrain of high and low relief characterizes the Western Isles of Scotland. It was, I believe, my revered teacher, H. J. Fleure, who first proposed that the westernmost fringes of Britain (together with Ireland) should be recognized as constituting a third, Atlantic, Zone, in some ways distinct from the Highland Zone of moorlands and glens (Fleure, 1951). Topographic fragmentation becomes more extreme as one approaches the open Atlantic, and Professor David Linton (1964, 125) attributes it to secular erosion, due not so much to the abundant precipitation as to "the persistence of the rain and the feebleness of the evaporation". Linton argues that "the true understanding of our landscape involves nothing less than the tracing of its history, in all its aspects, through the whole span of Tertiary time". Similarly, our understanding of the present cultural landscape involves the tracing of its history from the beginning of human occupation. In triggering off complex ecological changes, man's first attacks on the forest were of critical importance.

While recognizing differences between Highland and Atlantic Zones in prehistory—the fact, for instance, that the high proportion of relatively low-lying land (60–200 m) made so much of Ireland attractive to Neolithic farmers—I propose to include Ireland in the Highland Zone for the purposes of this paper. If one were to choose an environmental term that would embrace both regions, it would surely be the Pluvial Zone. Excessive precipitation, whether frontal or orographic, has set its mark on Highland Britain and Ireland throughout Tertiary and post-Tertiary time, and most conspicuously in the cold phases of the Quaternary, when ice erosion and deposition moulded most of the surface features we know today. In general, the widespread Post-glacial peat deposits record stages in the adjustment of vegetation to ill-drained landforms (cf. the drumlins) and to a pluvial climate, whether or no man had a hand in the formation of some blanket peats. Here I would pay tribute to J. W. Watson, who wrote a pioneer paper in 1939: "Under man's influence the landscape was made anew. From the first he seems to have liberated the bog, for where he first worked peats have most formed" (Watson, 1939, 153). Late- and Post-glacial adjustments of land and sea levels, moreover, brought raised beaches and extensive estuarine muds, attractive respectively to men and molluscs, and made the narrow belt where the Atlantic shores meet the Highland Edge a watery contact zone perhaps more important, in the Mesolithic and early Neolithic, than the contact zone between Highland and Lowland in Britain. Marine life in great abundance, fowl, fish, migratory fish (salmon and eels) and shellfish, multiplying under favourable Atlantic conditions, provided coastal and estuarine populations with unfailing, if monotonous, sources of food. It seems to me to be more than a coincidence that the two Irish locations most famous for their rich archaeological sites in the late Mesolithic and the Neolithic, the Bann and the Boyne, are also famous fishing rivers. It would certainly be true to say with Fluellen that "there is salmons in both". The lavish and conspicuous display of wealth evident in the great corbelled tombs of the Boyne valley recalls the megalomaniac efforts of the native salmon fishers of the British Columbian coasts to make the most of their seasonal surpluses in massive gifts and architectural display. Of course, this could be only part of the story, but such evidence as there is points to native Mesolithic roots for the material elements in the Boyne Culture, and there is the slender evidence of that eminently Mesolithic artefact, the coracle, uniquely surviving in Ireland among the salmon fishers of the Bend of the Boyne. The primary function of the Welsh coracle, too, as of the Scottish currach which died out in the 18th century, was salmon fishing. I shall come back to the Bann.

Another climatic characteristic of Atlantic coasts and Highland slopes is the prevalence of high winds, often of gale force, which have bent and shaped natural and cultural elements to their will, and influenced human behaviour in many ways. To observe or to expect the keeping of appointments by time or tide under these conditions would be folly. Or to take an example from material culture: the 19th century Donegal house, with its thatched roof shipshape and battened down with a mile of home-made rope, probably differed little from the ancestral Neolithic house. The ground plans, at any rate, of such Neolithic dwellings as have been recovered in north-west Ireland are almost precisely of the same shape and dimension.

Here I should like to recall an experience I had in Donegal one harvest-time. On a stormy October day I was helping a crofter to shear with a toothed sickle his quarter-acre of oats, growing among the stumps of fossil pine trees in black peaty soil that had lain under two metres of bog before it was cut away for fuel last century. I learnt how dependent the farmer is on the wind to harvest his late and meagre crops. " 'Tis wet", the crofter admitted when I commiserated with him on the weather, "but thank God 'tis windy". The tiny sheaves were loosely tied with thin bands (to facilitate drying) and laid with their butts to the wind: the elongated stooks of ten sheaves, with two 'hooders' atop, were also carefully aligned with the wind; when as I left him I expressed the hope that he would have a fine day for carrying the crop, the crofter replied: "the best harvest weather is a scourging wind that will 'cowp' the stooks and blow them into the haggard". As we worked I had the uncanny feeling that the plot we were in had lain on the edge of a prehistoric clearing, that the adjacent land had been cultivated in prehistoric times, and that "another ghostly wind was singing in a long-vanished forest above our heads" (Evans, 1968). In this environment, it seems to me, for the wind to be effective as a drying agent, clearings would need to be of considerable extent. I was not able to prove that my imagined clearing had been a reality—I looked in vain for prehistoric cultivation ridges—although peat-covered megaliths and traces of buried field walls were visible not far away. Clear proof of pre-peat cultivation, however, has been forthcoming in recent years, as we shall see, from Co. Mayo.

If I seem to be spending too much time in Ireland, it is not only because this has been my own fate but also because, since the last decade of the 19th century, Belfast has played a leading part in Quaternary research. Dr W. B. Wright dedicated his work on the Quaternary Ice Age (1914) to Dr Lloyd Praeger, "discoverer of the Post-glacial climatic optimum", and the discovery was made in the estuarine clays of Belfast. Following early pollen studies in Ireland by Dr Erdtman in 1924, an Irish Committee for Quaternary Research was set up in 1934 to further pollen-analytical work on the Irish bogs under the supervision of Professor Knud Jessen, research which was continued almost single-handed by Professor G. F. Mitchell from Dublin. In 1954 a joint appeal to the Nuffield Foundation by the Departments of Archaeology, Geography, and Botany at Queen's University, Belfast, resulted in the establishment of a Nuffield Quaternary Research Unit as an inter-disciplinary enterprise of which Dr A. G. Smith was leader and M. G. S. Morrison and V. B. Proudfoot his first assistants. It now has a fully equipped Palaeoecology Laboratory.

A topic of particular interest is the relationship between Mesolithic communities and the forest, and here we must return to "the fishy fruitful Bann" and to Adolf Mahr's perceptive (if also megalomaniac) presidential address to the Prehistoric Society in 1937, with its analysis of the River-ford or Salmon Culture (Mahr, 1937). He argued that salmon fishers would have made heavy demands on the forest for timber, and he interpreted many of the diverse mudstone artefacts associated with Irish river-fords as hammers, cleavers, and wedges for splitting wood. Alan Smith's pollen studies do indeed point to considerable changes in some Bann Valley woodlands in late Atlantic times, before the elm decline, although he is inclined to see these in terms of firing as a means of controlling grazing and food supplies such as hazelnuts (Smith, 1970, 89). Mr Peter Woodman tells me that the famous site at New Ferry, Co. Antrim, has yielded much new evidence and that a polished mudstone axe has been carbon-dated to *c.* 5500 bc. Further downstream at Mount Sandal, adjacent to a modern salmon fishery at the Cuts, he is excavating a rich Mesolithic site displaying microlithic tools, abundant fish bones, and houses or shelters marked by circles of postholes. From the island of Jura, too, there is new dating evidence of tanged points older than 7000 bc and the intriguing suggestion of eskimo-type hunters roving the shores of the western seas, under whose waters most of their relics probably rest (Mercer, 1974).

A puzzling feature, in Ireland at least, is the apparent absence of evidence for an upland version of the Mesolithic, or even for seasonal occupation of the uplands by lowland dwellers. Flint axes of Mesolithic forms are confined to rivers and coasts. Polished axes of hard stone, abundant everywhere, do not appear before the Neolithic, in response to a massive demand.

One of my most cherished field memories is the rediscovery, nearly forty years ago, of an exiguous exposure of bluestone (porcellanite) high on the steep face of Tievebulliagh (411 m) in Co. Antrim, which ancient woodsmen had discovered and exploited but which had escaped the notice of the Geological Survey. I have the feeling that such discoveries were made by acculturated native folk of Mesolithic ancestry rather than by Neolithic newcomers in a strange land. We have been conditioned by concepts and phrases such as the 'Neolithic Revolution' to expect, and therefore to find, change at the expense of continuity, and to underestimate the cultural achievements of the Mesolithic.

An aspect of the clearing of woodland that has interested me is the deep imprint it seems to have left on the succession of farmers and herders who came to occupy the clearings. It may be doubted whether in the beginning the cultivators used muck to promote fertility, but they almost certainly used magic. The success of their stone felling-axes probably owed much to their magical properties. I imagine there was much athletic competition as well as co-operation in the work of clearing trees, not only to make full use of the few dry weeks of spring which are one of the rare blessings of an Atlantic climate, but also because the vigour of the crops could be ensured by appropriately vigorous action in preparing the ground.

While not overlooking increasing continental influences from the Neolithic onwards, I find myself looking to the Mediterranean world and to north Africa for parallels to, or explanations of, many aspects of early Atlantic cultures. Apart from similarities in blood groups and in linguistic types, as illustrated for example in the structural pattern of the Gaelic tongue, there are in Ireland several recorded customs connected with cattle, such as bleeding them for food and 'blowing' them to induce a flow of milk, that have close African parallels (Evans, 1973, 48). The clearing of woodland in parts of Africa, although not complicated by the burning problem of a very short dry spell, is an occasion of intense activity, great rivalry, and high spirits. Among the Bemba of central Africa, for example, the formalized boasting and displays of daring by young men competing in lopping off branches not infrequently result in injury or death, which appear to be regarded as virtuous sacrifices. Up to 10 acres (4 ha) of forest are cleared and the wood burnt to provide ash for a 1-acre garden. The nature and magical properties of every variety of tree and plant are known to children as well as adults (Richards, 1939). Similarly, in the west of Ireland and in the Hebrides the varied properties of the few surviving species of trees and of the many shrubs, herbs, and weeds are well known and are traditionally put to multiple practical and magical uses. The idea of a convenient combined herbal cure lies behind the euphemistic term applied to cows' urine: 'all flowers' water'.

One of the most dramatic changes consequent on forest clearance was the spread and blossoming of herbaceous plants, flowers, and flowering shrubs—the appearance of buttercups and daisies, of docks, plantains, tormentil, the primrose, dandelion, and the familiar hedgerow flowers. Many of these are linked in folk belief, in Ireland at any rate, with the luck of the herd. So, too, are the flowering shrubs, especially the rowan and the may bush, whose creamy blossoms are believed to herald a full flow of milk, just as the yellow flowers of mayflower, primrose, and buttercup bring with them the promise of golden butter. The tradition dies hard in Ireland that to injure in any way a whitethorn that is self-sown (a lone thorn) is to court misfortune. These flowers and shrubs must have been familiar companions of our forebears ever since they made their first forest clearances and took to sedentary life, and with every fresh spring we find their scented beauty strangely evocative.

The Romantic poets of our Highland Zone were fascinated by these harbingers of spring. Here in Lancaster on the edge of the Lake Country one recalls that William Wordsworth wrote several poems to the lesser celandine, a flower which I associate with waste corners at the bottom of my garden, if not with fairies. Folklore links it with an affliction that is commonly regarded as a product of a sedentary life—haemorrhoids—and there is indeed an old and intimate association between man and the lesser celandine. Its country name is 'pilewort', and one has only to pull up a plant to see the homeopathic principle in its cluster of fleshy roots, which wither as they dry: presumably the magic is the medicine. Remembering the fame of the celandine as a pile-shrinker one might bring Wordsworth's poem to a painful end at the ninth word:

> "There is a flower the lesser celandine that shrinks . . ."

What most of our hill landscapes have in common, whether or not they are thinly draped in blanket bog, is their nakedness, although we know that they were once almost entirely wooded. Frequently, the only bushes one will see are those thorny enough to be avoided by grazing animals. Relics of the human past in the form of cairns, standing stones, cultivation ridges, old field walls, or banks, if not buried in peat are visible from afar and their presence is felt. The mountainy Irish refer to such landscapes as 'gentle', and the word applies particularly to the solitary whitethorns I have already mentioned. A friend collecting folklore in the Sperrin Mountains, Co. Tyrone, and prying too deeply into such elder faiths was given this advice: "Leave old thorns and priests alone; give them their dues and leave them alone". The cattleman, in this evergreen island, has had much to do with the making of the landscape. Free-range grazing in the hills in summer enabled the animals to obtain a greater variety of grasses and browse than would be possible in enclosed plots. Even in the arable infields the fences were temporary, and along the Atlantic coasts the tradition dies hard that field banks and walls are neglected or deliberately broken in winter to give livestock a free run of the townland. Unless protected in some other way, it is often only on steep stony slopes or on lake islands that woodland has had a chance of survival.

The swards of heavily grazed outfields in particular become fibrous and compacted, checking the vertical movement of water. On a moderate slope rain will run off as off a thatched roof, and this could cause waterlogging downslope. One would like to know the processes and the stages by which the loose humus of forest clearings gave way to *mor* humus and to unbroken swards which, while preventing soil erosion, brought their own problems. Lacking aeration soils would tend to become sour, while the sward would deteriorate under differential grazing, and it was the traditional wisdom of Highland and Atlantic farmers to break them up periodically. An ox-drawn coulter plough capable of cutting such swards seems to have reached Ireland at about the same time as Christianity, but even today small farmers will complain that they are "too tough for the plough". Traditionally selected portions of such outfields, in a long rotation, were stripped with flaying spades, foot ploughs, breast ploughs, or mattocks and cultivated in ridges. The peeled and piled turves were frequently burnt and their ashes spread, a custom which can be regarded as a continuation of prehistoric 'slash and burn' cultivation (Evans, 1958, 63). After a few years soils became leached and lost their fertility and the outfield reverted to pasture. From this practice of alternating grazing with short spells of cultivation the modern system of ley farming seems to have evolved. The mutual benefits of cowman and ploughman were as real in our far west as they were to become in Oklahoma:

> "Oh, the farmer and the cowman must be friends."

The ideal balance between animal and arable husbandry would have varied from one region to another and from one period to another, but over most of the uplands for long periods the cowman was king. I have suggested that the introduction and adoption of oats, probably in early Celtic times, helped to facilitate and standardize improved environmental relations (Evans, 1956, 231). Others might see the Early Christian period in a similar light. Among the older cereals the cultivation of wheat (presumably autumn sown) would have left the land exposed to leaching through the wet winter months. Not only were oats spring-sown but they were also food for man and, including the straw, for beast.

The most striking conclusion to be drawn from a study of agricultural history is the continuity of certain practices. In Ireland the cultivation ridge is as persistent as the cult of the thorn tree. Throughout the wet tropics the traditional method of growing crops in forest clearings among communities lacking the means of deep cultivation is in 'mounds' or 'hills' made by scraping up the loose soil. The lazy-beds of our Atlantic Zone would seem in origin to have been just such scrapings of soil in forest clearings. Obviously the process would be difficult once a sward had formed, especially on *mor* soils, but the cheesy humus below the sward can be cut horizontally with narrow or pointed spades and the severed sod overturned by leverage: a wooden ancestor of the Atlantic long-handled pointed shovel found at Satrup Moor, Schleswig Holstein, has even been dated to the late Mesolithic (Gailey and Fenton, 1970, 5). We note in passing that our word *palstave*, incorporating the element *peel*, derives from the Icelandic word for a narrow spade. That the severance of discrete sods was an efficient process by the late Neolithic is shown by the vast numbers used in constructing some burial mounds: the stripping of several acres of grassland, for example, would have been necessary to build New Grange, one of the Boyne tombs (O'Kelly, 1970–71).

Watching Connemara crofters making their lazy-beds, I have marvelled at the ecological propriety of ridge cultivation as proven by its high yields. One sees their traces on the hillsides almost everywhere in our Atlantic Zone and one can judge their age from their state of preservation. The face of old Ireland is wrinkled with their tracks. In the last few years they have been found singularly well preserved beneath blanket peat at Carrownaglogh under the Ox Mountains of Co. Mayo (Herity, 1971). Here at a height of about 150 m (500 ft), Michael Herity has uncovered many bundles of ridges within a 1·6-ha. (4-acre) enclosure. Both the enclosing wall and the ridges (*c.* 1·5 m wide) are very similar to examples nearby made in living memory. The ridges consist of a leached grey-brown soil with a thin iron pan resting on a sandy subsoil. Preliminary pollen studies by Dr J. R. Pilcher suggest that cereals had been grown in a clearing in mixed woodland that included ash but no pine, and that the succeeding grassland containing abundant plantain had given way to heather and blanket peat. A probable pollen date somewhat after 2000 bc (say 19th century bc) fits in with the date of some flint artefacts associated with the enclosing wall. In the same townland, a house which stood until recently against a bog face appeared almost as old as the bog itself. This apparently miraculous survival was probably erected in the 19th century AD (Danaher, 1954–5).

I must briefly refer to three other sites in North Mayo. At Ballyglass, Séan Ó Nuallaín discovered the foundations of a rectangular timber house partly underlying the front end of a court grave. Alongside, possibly but not positively contemporary, were fossil cultivation ridges buried deep below the level surface of old pasture land. Further west at Behy/Glenulra, a pre-peat complex examined by Seamas Caulfield included a transepted court grave, an apparently contemporary oval stone enclosure (carbon dated to 2510 ± 115 bc) which yielded Neolithic potsherds, and a series of rectangular walled enclosures, 150–200 m wide, and about 2·4 ha. (6 acres) in area, aligned in slightly curved parallel strips and traceable over a considerable area between 60 m (200 ft) and over 180 m (600 ft) above sea level. This is thought to be a planned and not a piecemeal enclosure system, and to point to sophisticated farm management designed to procure rotational grazing. Improving Irish landlords of the 19th century (AD) recommended rectangular fields of this shape and size as ideal!

The fourth site in Co. Mayo is 4 miles further west at Belderg, at a height of 36 m (120 ft). Here, Caulfield has uncovered a pre-peat complex comprising several small contiguous tillage plots and enclosing walls, all apparently dated by shouldered Neolithic pottery. The plots were marked by cultivation ridges under which in many places were found criss-cross ploughmarks. I would be inclined to see the ard-marks as indicating the breaking of the soil before hand-ridging, but Caulfield thinks the two processes could have been separated "by decades or even generations" (personal communication). Below the site, the stumps of oak trees (one carbon-dated to 1885 ± 85 bc) can be seen, while uphill to the west, at about 60 m (200 ft), pine stumps predominate (one dated to 2770 ± 85 bc).

I conclude with an example of positional geography which would have pleased H. J. Mackinder. The narrow seas between Great Britain and Ireland, lying near the centre of our combined Highland and Atlantic Zones, were well placed to become a cultural melting pot and centre of innovation in the 4th millennium bc (Waterbolk, 1968, 1100). North-east Ireland in particular, uniquely provided with flint supplies and with an abundance of salmon and eels, seems to have attracted cultural influences from Scandinavia and Iberia as well as from Great Britain and the continent.

REFERENCES

Brøgger, A. W. (1940). From the Stone Age to the Motor Age. *Antiquity,* 14, 163–181.

Danaher, K. (1954–5). Semi-underground habitations. *J. Galway Archaeol. Hist. Soc.,* 26, 75–80.

Evans, E. E. (1956). The ecology of peasant life in Western Europe. *In* Thomas, W. L. (ed.). *Man's Role in Changing the Face of the Earth.* Chicago: University Press; 217–239.

Evans, E. E. (1958). The Atlantic ends of Europe. *Advan. Sci.,* 15, 54–64.

Evans, E. E. (1968). Irish Harvest. *Ulster Folklife,* 14, 3–5.

Evans, E. E. (1973). *The Personality of Ireland: Habitat, Heritage and History.* Cambridge: University Press.

Fleure, H. J. (1951). *A Natural History of Man in Britain.* London: Collins. (Fontana edition, with M. Davies, 1971).

Fox, C. (1932). *The Personality of Britain: Its Influence on Inhabitant and Invader in Prehistoric and Early Historic Times.* Cardiff: National Museum of Wales.

Gailey, A. and Fenton, A. (eds.) (1970). *The Spade in Northern and Atlantic Europe.* Ulster Folk Museum.

Herity, M. (1971). Prehistoric fields in Ireland. *Ir. University Rev.,* Spring number, 258–265.

Hodgen, M. T. (1952). *Change and History.* New York: Viking Fund Publication No. 18.

Linton, D. (1964). Tertiary Landscape Evolution. *In* Watson, J. M. and Sissons, S. B. (eds.). *The British Isles: A Systematic Geography.* Edinburgh: Nelson.

Mahr, A. (1937). New aspects and problems in Irish archaeology. *Proc. Prehist. Soc.,* 3, 261–436.

Mercer, J. (1974). New C-14 dates from the Isle of Jura, Argyll. *Antiquity,* 48, 65–66.

O'Kelly, M. J. Newgrange. *Roy. Irish Acad. Annual Report,* 1970–71, 38.

Richards, A. I. (1939). *Land Labour and Diet in Northern Rhodesia.* Oxford: University Press.

Smith, A. G. (1970). The influence of Mesolithic and Neolithic man on British vegetation: a discussion. *In* Walker, D. and West, R. G. (eds.). *Studies in the Vegetational History of the British Isles.* Cambridge: University Press; 81–96.

Waterbolk, H. T. (1968). Food production in prehistoric Europe. *Science,* 162, 1093–1103.

Watson, J. W. (1939). Forest or bog: man the deciding factor. *Scot. Geogr. Mag.,* 148–161.

The role of climatic factors in environmental and cultural changes in prehistoric times

J. A. Taylor

Synopsis

Reconstructions of climatic changes in Britain since the last major glaciation have neglected the significance of meso- and micro-climatic deviations (for example due to altitude, aspect, ground conditions, etc.) in the Highland Zone. Despite the inadequacy of modern meteorological data for British upland terrain, the paper attempts, on the basis of available evidence, an extrapolation of the probable scale and timing of climatic oscillations at altitude over the past 12,000 years.

It emerges that climate change and culture change may be conceived on two separate but complementary wavelengths: first, the macro-scale framework embracing the millennia presents the backcloth and general chronology, but secondly, the actual changes at ground are governed by short-term periodicities in climate and weather, and a metachronous mosaic of environmental and cultural changes is generated. The paper argues finally that such changes may be fully comprehended only in ecosystematic terms, and locally and regionally rather than zonally or hemispherically.

This paper is composed of three sections: first, a review of the evolution and definition of the British Post-glacial climate; second, a delineation of the role of climate in environmental change; and third, a discussion of how climate and weather may have been related to environmental and culture changes in prehistoric times, with particular reference to selected evidence from three sites in Wales.

THE BRITISH CLIMATES

As Professor Estyn Evans implies in his opening paper, there is, and was, more than one British climate. The concentration of moorland and mountain in the west and north-west of our islands in a generally exposed maritime location, and the confinement of the major English lowlands to the south-east, overlooking the European mainland, gives immediate climatic connotation to the classical Highland Zone/Lowland Zone division which archaeologists have largely adopted. However, within the Highland Zone, the 'Atlantic Zone' (as first proposed by Fleure (1951)), clinging to the western littorals and normally west of the major watersheds, may be clearly differentiated within the 'Pluvial Zone', including Ireland, proposed by Evans. These distinctive sub-regional variations in climate within the Highland Zone of Britain are an intimate and dramatic expression of the effects of altitude and distance from the sea, especially the western seas, in an intensely maritime location. Without doubt they have constituted regular deviants from the standard Post-glacial macro-climatic succession of 'Boreal' and 'Atlantic' phases. They may be termed 'regional' climates in their own right; their antecedents were equally distinctive.

Macro-, meso-, and micro-climates

The term 'climate' normally refers to the macro-climate, which is based on standardized meteorological data and instrumental exposures, and imputes large areas and long time-periods. More locally and nearer or at ground, the concepts of meso- and micro-climates (i.e. below Stevenson screen level of 4 ft = 1·22 m) are more applicable, especially when studies of vegetation, soils, or agriculture, ancient or modern, are involved.

The chronic imbalance in the current distribution of meteorological stations in the United Kingdom (Fig. 1) means that there is an increasing shortage of primary climatological information (a) with increasing altitude above sea-level and (b) with increasing distance from the coast. Again, the relative abundance of macro-climatic data is in stark contrast to the extreme paucity of meso- and especially micro-climatic data. The pioneer and monumental contributions of Manley (1942, 1943, 1945, 1946, 1949, 1951, 1952, 1953, 1959, 1964, 1966, 1971) and of Pearsall (1950) to our perception of the British upland environment and its climate must be at once acknowledged. There are, however, severe problems in the unavoidable assumptions of arithmetic extrapolations across the contours, between high-altitude and low-altitude meteorological stations using, for example, screen temperatures or conventional rain gauge data. The use of the former, as Harrison (1973) has revealed, implies that temperature lapse-rates and ranges between ground and screen height are constant, which they are not. They vary not only with ground/soil/vegetation/land-use conditions and weather type but also, broadly, with increasing altitude and increasing latitude. Screen data also underestimate the range and extremes occurring in the micro-climatic layer near the ground and are not representative either of intra-forest conditions at, above, or below screen height. These qualifications apply especially to the estimation of temperature lapse-rates on the extensively wooded slopes of the prehistoric period, and of the temperature regimes of the colder mountain zones of the Highland Zone of Britain. Again, Rodda (1970) has explained that the conventional rain gauge used in Britain may underestimate rainfall occurring at ground by as much as 10%. That size of error represents a substantial amount of precipitation, especially when the high rainfalls of the Highland Zone (up to 2000 mm (78·7 in) and in places more than 2500 mm (98·4 in) on the average) are considered. Equally problematical is the

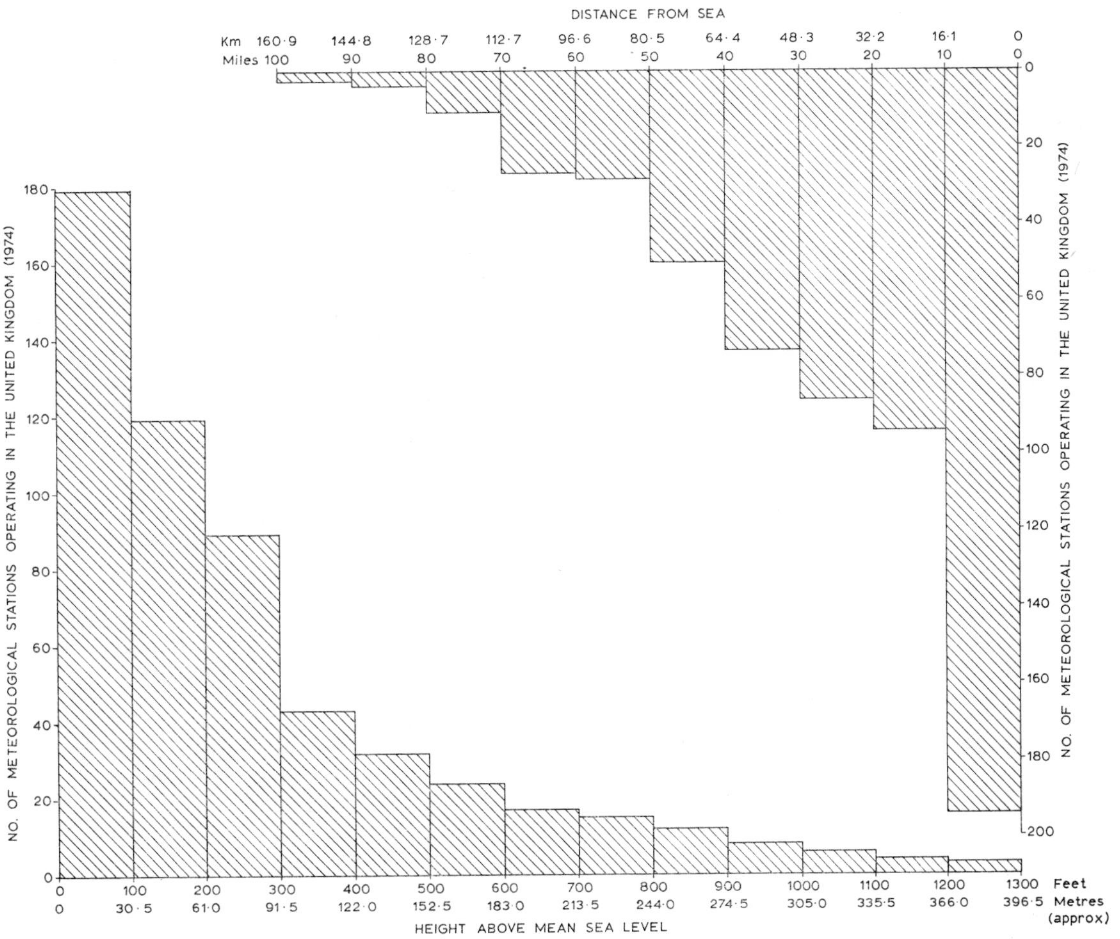

(a)

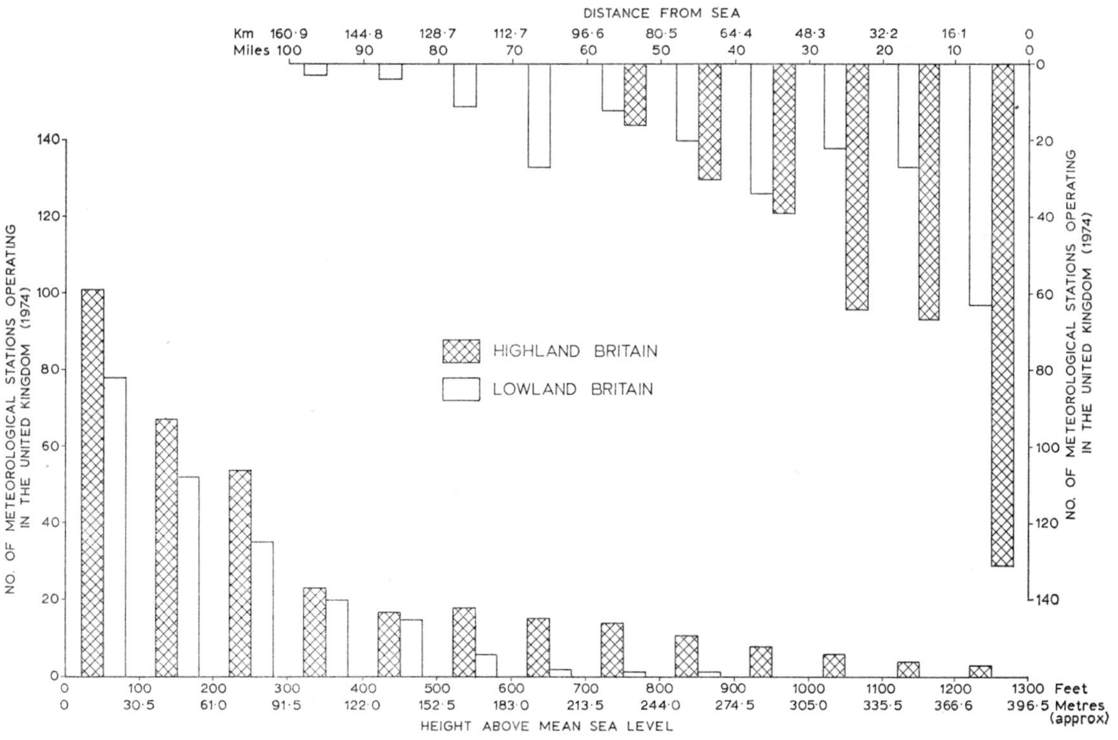

(b)

Fig. 1 Distribution of meteorological stations (1974) (a) in the British Isles as a whole and (b) in the Highland and Lowland Zones of Britain in relation to (i) altitude and (ii) distance from the sea (Compiled by Susan Llewellyn)

extensive adjustment of isohyets to contours in upland areas where the gauge cover is thin, and the uncritical assumption that climatic gradients with altitude are linear, or nearly so.

Climate at ground

In reality, climate at ground is as much, if not more, a function of terrain/soil/vegetation/land-use factors than an expression of the macro-climate. Taylor (1967) has shown experimentally for a coastal hill in Cardiganshire that a south-facing slope may be virtually half as warm again as a comparable north slope, although, of course, it will dry out more quickly. He has also revealed (1967) that the difference in climate at two points of identical elevation and only half a mile (0·8 km) apart on the south Lancashire plain, one on sand, the other on peat, could be equivalent to a difference in elevation of 700 ft (213 m) or a relative distance from the sea of about 200 miles (322 km). The scale of extreme variations in micro- and meso-climate is truly very great and has been underestimated, especially in view of (a) the extensive peat cover of much of upland Britain and the resulting hydrological and meteorological consequences and constraints and (b) the persistence of relatively cold climates and snow-cover in the Highland Zone during the Late-glacial period and in the early prehistoric periods, just after the end of Zone III, and also in the Atlantic and Sub-Atlantic periods when the dominance of maritime weather must have induced severe lapse rates and sharp changes in weather and climate with increasing altitude.

Altitudinal climatic gradients

Harrison (1974) concluded from a study of the ecoclimatic gradient between the coast of Cardigan Bay and the Plynlimon upland (his highest station was established at 450 m = 1476 ft OD), that there were greater altitudinal temperature differences and more marked seasonal periodicities at and in the ground than at screen level where inversions, as Oliver (1964) discovered for a similar study in South Wales, may reverse lapse-rates with a surprisingly high frequency. Harrison also discovered that the greatest altitudinal differences in *screen* temperatures occurred in *autumn* and *winter*, but that similar maximum differences for *soil* temperatures occurred in *summer*. Moreover, the altitudinal differences in *maximum* temperatures for the *soil* were *twice*, on average, those for the *screen*.

Clearly, the degree of wetness and peatiness of the ground and, in late autumn, winter, and spring, the presence or persistence of snow cover or frost are major controls of variations in micro-climate. Hare and Ritchie (1972) have put forward parallel arguments in a discussion of modern 'tundra' and 'Boreal' environments in Canada. They indicate the seasonal and local range of variation in albedo in environments where snow cover and organic terrain are so vast. Interestingly enough, whereas Manley (1951) has pointed out that the temperature variability in the Highland Zone is greater generally than in the Lowland Zone, Gregory (1964) has discovered that, for rainfall variability, the reverse in general applies. A veritable mosaic of climatic habitats emerges which may well provide a mirror for reconstruction of the early prehistoric environments of the Highland Zone, more particularly for the highest ground, above say 300 m (984 ft OD) and for Zones I–VI, inclusive, up to the impact of Neolithic and, later, Bronze Age man on the forest cover, the removal of which must clearly have vastly altered micro- and meso-climatic conditions at and near ground, especially as upland peats began to form.

Climatic effects of prehistoric forest cover

The presence of a virtually continuous deciduous forest-cover in Highland Britain for about 5000 years up to Neolithic times must have played a major role in the heat exchange and water cycle at ground, particularly in summer. The interception of both insolation and rainfall reduced available heat and moisture at ground. At the same time evapotranspiration back to the atmosphere would have been more efficient and generally at greater rate from the forest layer than from the succeeding moorland vegetation. Moreover, the soils beneath the forests are considered to have been richer in earthworms and less podzolic (probably 'brown earth' in general type) than under heath, and therefore less peaty and, except in hollows and on flats, less retentive of moisture. A more rapid and larger-scale return of moisture to the atmosphere than now is envisaged. The general effect of the forest-cover on temperatures within the forest environment must have been to retard and reduce ranges, both daily and annual, and to moderate exposure to wind, especially in summer but obviously less so in winter.

Consequently, the ancient woodlands offered ameliorated habitats, the forest edge and small clearings offering advantageous combinations of shelter and access for Mesolithic man—preferentially in summer (probably a season of many colours, notably greens and browns) rather than winter (probably a season of fewer colours, notably whites and dark browns).

In stark contrast, the peat cover which replaced the forests is the black legacy of the impact of several thousands of years of upland climate *directly* on the ground and its heath vegetation. A layer of peat or 'organic top' is an excellent natural store for water but its own inherently low heat conductivity together with its surface wetness and the wetness of its surface vegetation, bestow a very low thermal diffusivity on its soil environment. Thus the upland peats and soils with a substantial organic top are colder and later than even their elevation above sea-level would indicate.

Nevertheless, the peats act as natural, if potentially unstable, reservoirs and are clearly vital to the contemporary water balance of individual catchments. Wind exposure, which can be so severe at altitude without tree cover, and soil deterioration have severely reduced the bioclimatic and agricultural potential of the British moorlands as we see them today. Lapse-rates and weather gradients are severe, especially on maritime slopes and when polar maritime air dominates, as it does characteristically on the extreme north-western littorals (i.e. in north-west Scotland, west Scotland, northern and western Ireland, north-west England, and extreme north-west Wales) of the Highland Zone (Manley, 1945; Taylor, 1960; Taylor and Yates, 1967). Harrison (1973) reported, however, that variations in lapse-rates over a two-year period in western Cardiganshire were not correlated with variations in the frequency of the passage of polar maritime air over that area.

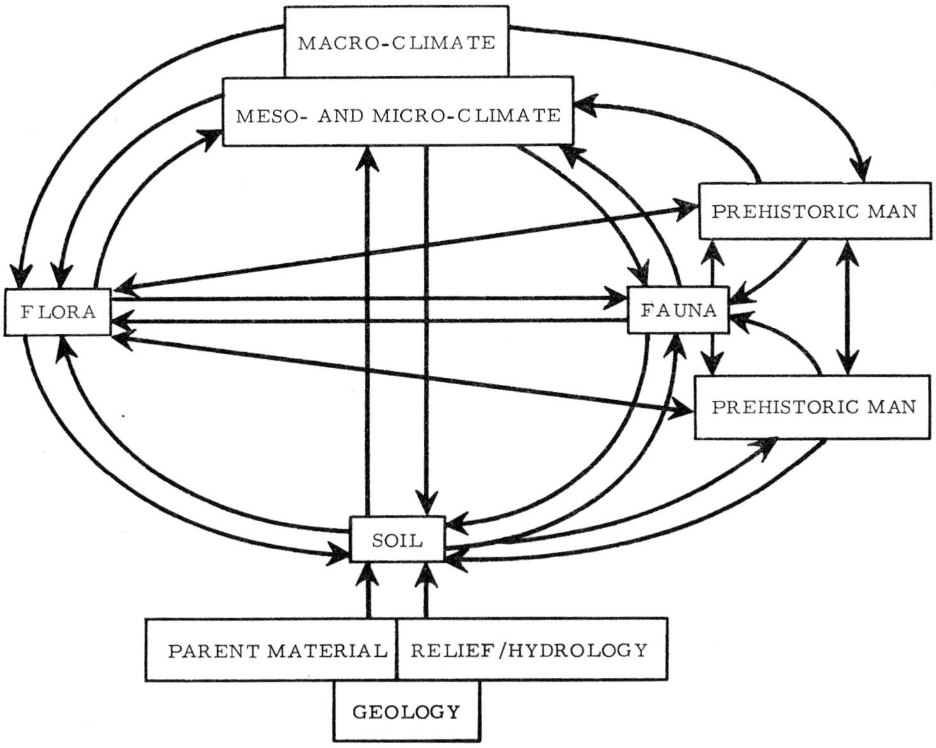

Fig. 2 A simple model of a palaeo-ecosystem

CLIMATE CHANGE IN THE HIGHLAND ZONE

Palaeoclimatological and palaeobotanical research

Manley (1953, 1964) and also Lamb (1965, 1966a, 1966b) have been the major architects in the recent reconstructions of the evolution of our climate. The pioneer vision of Brooks (1926-49) earlier this century had been a stimulant. Yet, almost a century ago, Blytt (1876) had introduced ideas in Norway on the use of fossil biological material to identify climatic swings. Later, in co-operation with Sernander (1908), the basis of the now conventional Atlantic/Boreal alternations in Post-glacial time was first consolidated. Subsequently, von Post (1916) launched pollen analytical research which later became established in Britain under Godwin (1956) for bog pollen and under Dimbleby (1962) for soil pollen.

Some assumptions in palynological research

Palynological research and its associated techniques have proceeded apace in the past thirty years or so in many centres in Britain but have on occasion been unable to resist a number of temptations. These are, in summary:

(i) to assume a regular relationship between macro-climate and vegetation or between man and vegetation to the neglect of other components of the ecosystem, notably the micro- and meso-climate, the soil, the fauna, and the terrain, all of which impose individually or collectively, local qualifications of macro-trends or relationships (Fig. 2). In fact, some of these components may *initiate* ecosystematic change on their own terms.

(ii) to apply Lowland Zone chronologies, based on largely English data, to adjacent sections of the Highland Zone, and in general to extrapolate too crudely over vast areas of inorganic terrain from widely spaced peat bogs, which in any event have had their own very specialized ecological history. This point has been developed elsewhere (Taylor, 1973) with reference to the premature superimposition of English and Irish chronologies on to Wales.

(iii) to concentrate too narrowly on one or two techniques of palaeo-dating without achieving the fullest possible integration of available data and interpretations. For example, whilst it is clear that bog pollen records are invaluable for calibration of the changing, more or less natural environments of pre-Neolithic periods but become confused and metachronous for subsequent periods, not least because of increasing human interference, nonetheless it is precisely in the post-5000 bp stages that soil pollen records (for upland moors and lowland heaths) become more legible and reliable, as R. T. Smith (1970) and Dimbleby (1962) have shown. The judicious selection of bog and soil sites in combination with available archaeological or historical sites offers a most versatile and revealing integration of techniques and evidence as work directed by Turner (e.g. Roberts *et al.*, 1973) has demonstrated, and as Walker's (1974) work is currently demonstrating in the Rhinogau of western Merioneth.

Regional climate change

It was A. G. Smith (1965) who pinpointed the idea of retardation of *regional* as distinct from national or continental change in palaeo-chronologies. An ecosystem will not respond to macro-climate change unless, first, a bio-climatic threshold is crossed by the change and, secondly, the ecosystem does not resist such an event on its own biological terms. Pearsall, writing in the same year (1965), also anticipated what may now be described as the *ecosystematic* approach to palaeo-habitats, when he referred to "a succession of geomorphological, pedological, vegetational and biological events . . . which were . . . conditioned by the average climate" (Fig. 2).

It is becoming increasingly apparent that the timing of the local or regional impact of a climatic change is more significant than the chronology of the climatic change itself. The concept of broad time zones marching across the continents is now being replaced by a vista of variable regional mosaics in which the discontinuities are merely phases or bands of least variation. Yet the changes now appear to have occurred more quickly than was previously thought. It is in this context that the Late-glacial and Post-glacial climatic oscillations may be re-assessed for the specific environments of the Highland Zone of Britain.

Past climates of the Highland Zone: some general principles

Before discussing the possible and probable nature and sequence of the Highland Zone's past climates, it is essential to venture a few points of general principle which will help to sketch the framework of factors that have variably affected the pattern and scale of climatic oscillations.

First, it may be justifiably postulated that, within the accepted concept of metachronous or sloping time zones, climatic changes were relatively *retarded* in the Highland Zone as compared with the Lowland Zone because up to the Boreal period (Zones I–VI inclusive), the probable truncation of the Gulf Stream off western Ireland (Manley, 1964) and the probable persistence of relatively low sea temperatures off western Britain (Lamb, 1966b) maintained a north/south or perhaps a north-west/south-east temperature gradient across Britain for most of the year, including much of the winter. The abundance of high ground rising generally in altitude northwards would further reinforce a pattern of retardation from south to north. From Atlantic times onwards, however, sea temperatures not only attained present-day levels but probably exceeded them. An advection of warmth via sea mass and air mass must have imposed a west–east thermal gradient in the winter half of the year to a greater extent than at present. West coast littorals must have been intensely mild—virtually winterless (and attractive to settlements, the flood risk apart)—but sharp lapse-rates occurred with increasing altitude. Fleure's 'Atlantic Zone' must have achieved its highest climatic identity at this stage (i.e. probably the late Atlantic), but tree lines did not reach their Post-glacial maximum till the succeeding, more continental Sub-Boreal period, when lapse-rates in general were less severe and westerly exposure was relatively reduced (Fig. 3).

Secondly, whilst the pattern of colonizations by plants, animals, and man may have followed the broad south-to-north or south-east to north-west directions of climatic amelioration, once the western seas had warmed, a second avenue direct from the south into the Highland Zone was presented which permitted earlier and more direct colonizations in the late Mesolithic and early Neolithic and beyond, some of them bypassing the Lowland Zone at certain stages. Relatively early evidence of *Alnus* and *Tilia* for sites on and overlooking the Dovey Estuary (Smith and Taylor, 1969; Taylor, 1973) suggests a southerly provenance.

Thirdly, it is possible that cold or cool, raw habitats survived after Zone III at the highest elevations or on exposed sites of northerly aspect or concave relief. It is equally possible that a modified Boreal-type woodland dominated by *Betula* survived through the optimum on the highest exposed plateau tops till the revertence of *Betula* on lower ground which marks the beginning of the Sub-Atlantic deterioration about 2500 bp. This thesis would suggest a diversified mosaic of new and old habitats at altitude between 10,000 and 2500 bp. At least, the application of the mixed oak/alder woodland climax to the Highland Zone is to be resisted, except perhaps on slopes and valleys of medium or steep angle and favoured aspect, where survivals of sessile oak woodland (through the post-5000 bp heath/podzol transformation of the higher plateaux) have been independently proposed by Smith and Taylor (1969) and Pennington (1974) herein.

Fourthly, recent research has made progress in explaining climate change in terms of critical periodicities of weather types or hazards. The individual or instant meteorological event rather than the long-term cumulative effect of a meteorological trend may now be envisaged as a cause of ecosystematic instability and change.

Fifthly, non-climatic and non-human factors may initiate ecosystematic changes and may precipitate local reversals of trends stimulated by the general macro-climatic trend. Soils in particular, as R. T. Smith and Taylor (1969) and others have shown, probably deteriorated naturally prior to the impact of Bronze Age man in west-central Wales, where it is most likely he encountered *secondary* woodland.

The climatic succession in the Highland Zone: the Late-glacial

Figure 3 attempts to summarize the possible shape and trend of Late- and Post-glacial climate changes for the Highland Zone of Britain. It has been derived and adapted mainly from the penetrating and successful reconstructions achieved by Lamb, Lewis, and Woodruffe (1966b), Lamb (1966a), and Manley (1964), supplemented from several other sources (Taylor, 1973). It incorporates evidence derived from the correction of radiocarbon dates (Godwin, 1970; Olsson, 1970).

As Pennington and Bonny (1970) and Taylor (1973) and others have foreshadowed, the accumulation of additional data for the Late-glacial will probably modify vastly the conventional Zone I–III subdivision, especially for environments such as those presented at that stage in Highland Britain. Shorter period oscillations and a chronic instability of both soil and vegetation (and presumably of culture, too) are indicated. Rainfalls and temperatures must have oscillated as they have done in medieval and modern times, comparably, in southern Greenland. Alternations of wet/raw and cold/dry phases have been postulated to explain the succession of periglacial slope deposits in West Cardiganshire, although there is continuing debate as to whether the periglacial climate referred is Late-glacial or the later part of the last 'Devensian' glaciation (Watson and Watson, 1967; Bowen, 1974). Wide fluctuations in rainfall would help to reconcile Lamb's earlier view (in discussion following Manley's paper, 1951) that Late-glacial precipitation was relatively low—as in the low-temperature regimes of the modern tundra—

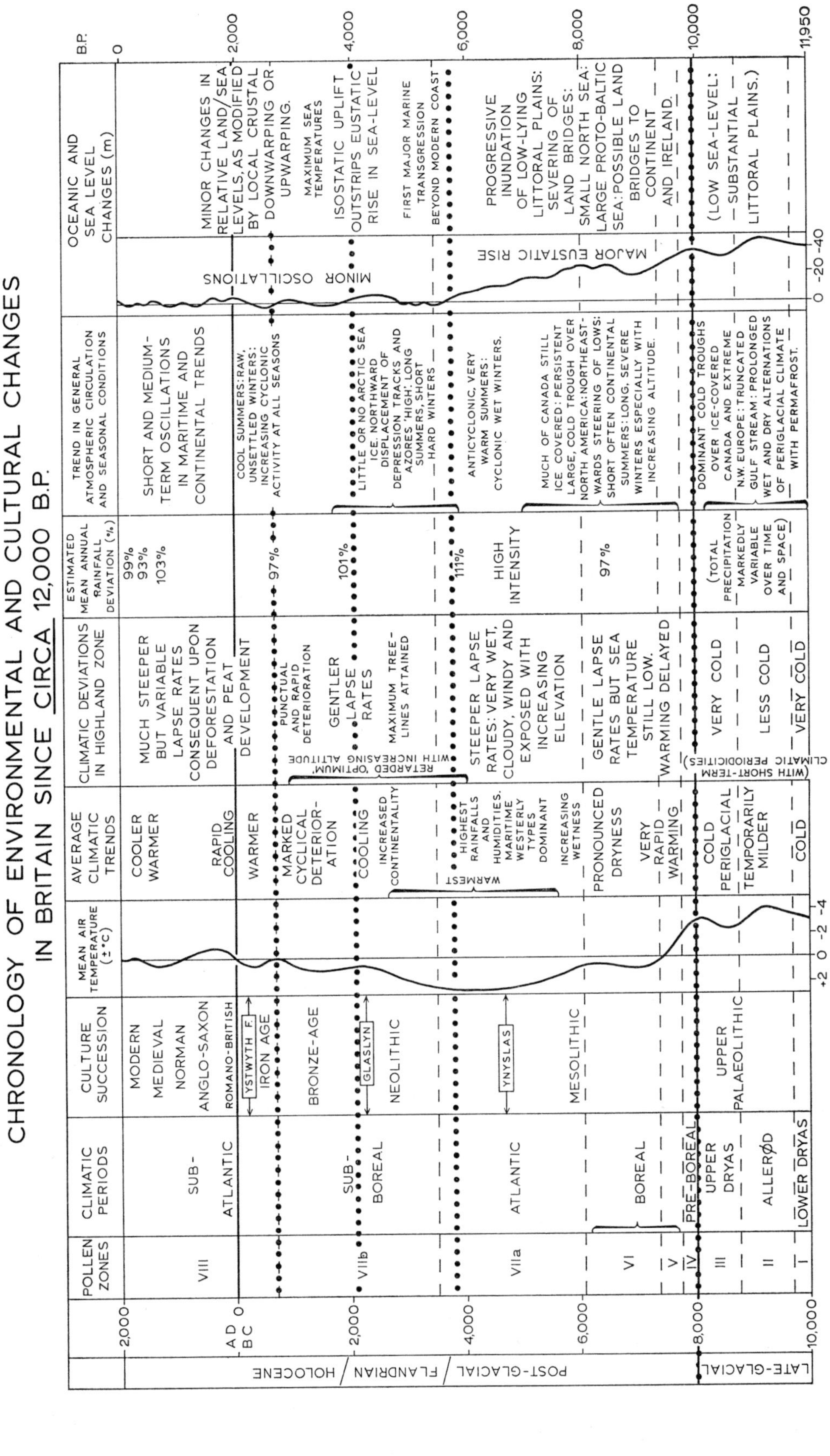

Fig. 3 *An attempted reconstruction of the chronology of environmental and cultural changes since* c. 12,000 *bp (Adapted from Lamb, Lewis, and Woodruffe (1966); Lamb (1966); Manley (1964); Godwin (1956 and 1970); Olsson (1970); Taylor (1973) and other sources)*

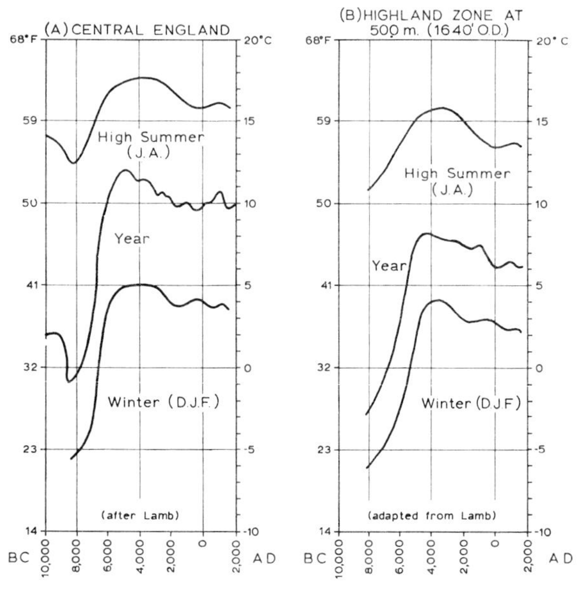

Fig. 4 Estimated *average air temperatures (A) in the lowlands of central England (= Lowland Zone) and (B) corrected for the Highland Zone at 500 m (1640 ft OD). Since* c. *12,000 bp (Adapted from Lamb, Lewis, and Woodruffe, 1966)*
Note: *The corrections in (B) are based on the estimated variations in the range of temperature lapse-rates with altitude as synthesized by Harrison (1974) for available data for Britain, Europe, and comparable environments. These range between 5·6°C and 7·6°C per 1000 m, and have been adjusted appropriately for 'Boreal' and 'Atlantic' phases, respectively*

and Manley's view that rainfalls of 50 in (1270 mm), 80 in (2032 mm), or even more could be envisaged at quite low altitudes. As Lamb *et al.* (1966b) subsequently explain, phases of high precipitation (snowfall or rainfall) in the Late-glacial could be attributed to the steering of storm tracks along sharp thermal gradients across the British Isles, probably in summer when the climate zones were more northerly in position.

Incidentally, it is likely that the rainfall averages (Lamb, 1966a) in Figure 3 for Zone VI onwards are on the conservative side, and shorter-cycle and larger-scale variations should be envisaged around the means at all stages.

A distinctive feature at the Late-glacial period was the very low sea-level and the emergence of wide littoral plains with the probable existence of land bridges to the continent and to Ireland. However, it was still much too cold for any rapid cultural advancement: this was the later stage of the Upper Palaeolithic (see also Figs. 3 and 5).

The Post-glacial climatic succession

On average the Boreal period was inaugurated by a sharp rise in temperature. Corrections to radiocarbon chronologies (e.g. Ferguson, 1970; Michael and Ralph, 1970; Godwin, 1970) as related to archaeological time scales, have been incorporated into Figure 3, and reveal an abbreviation of Zones IV and V, an earlier (*c.* 7600 bp) onset of the optimum and therefore its prolongation. This relative advancing of the general Post-glacial amelioration would be compatible with recent re-assessments of (a) the Mesolithic culture as having a more significant effect on the vegetation cover (A. G. Smith, 1970) than was previously supposed and (b) the Neolithic revolution as a cumulative rather than an instant culture change (Ucko and Dimbleby, 1969). It also follows that Highland Zone chronologies were probably less retarded also, if only relatively.

The pronounced dryness of Boreal period with long severe winters and short continental summers conjures up an image of today's 'taiga' zones of Canada and the USSR. At altitude, gentler lapse-rates were countered by low snowlines and prolonged snowy, frosty winters.

Just before 8000 bp the wetter and warmer Atlantic period commenced with high-intensity rainfalls, up to 11% on average above present-day levels according to Lamb *et al.* (1966b). Short-term variations could have included some years with rainfalls at 25% or even 50% above the average. Such years must clearly have involved repetitive storm rainfall and local flood hazards at selected Neolithic sites. Sea levels had risen progressively since about 10,000 bp, and around 5500 bp there is evidence that the sea transgressed the position of the modern coastline in many parts of Britain. The coincidence of persistent galeforce westerly winds, a rising sea level, and the highest tides, which was very possible in late Atlantic times, must have been a very severe hazard on western littorals, as was the combination of high tides and south-westerly gales in January 1974, particularly on the Welsh coasts.

About 5500 bp the more continental Sub-boreal period developed but with significantly higher temperatures than either the Boreal or the present-day, perhaps 1·0–1·5°C higher, initially more than 2·0°C higher than the present (Fig. 4). Tree growth at the highest altitudes would have been favoured, for example, in the Cairngorms (Manley, 1966), with an increased potential for expansion of settlement and agriculture to maximum elevations in the middle and later Neolithic and the early Bronze Age.

The cyclical but marked deteriorations into the Sub-Atlantic phase about 2650 bp were probably not delayed at altitude because of the sharpening of lapse-rates and increase in wind exposure as deforestation proceeded apace through the late Bronze Age and succeeding Iron Age. Unsettled raw winters and cool cloudy summers must have been frequent but cyclical and alternate with superior seasonal types of weather. As previously stated, the accumulation of hill peat after deforestation, particularly during the Sub-Atlantic, demoted the micro- and meso-climates of the uplands below their altitudinal rank. There is some evidence of rapid cooling in Romano-British times and of a climatic recession during the Dark Ages (Figs. 3, 4 and 5).

SELECTED SITE EVIDENCE

The third and final section of this paper will hinge its argument on palaeo-environmental evidence for three selected sites in west central Wales and will raise the fascinating issue as to how the behavioural environment of the late prehistoric times may be initially reconstructed and possibly comprehended. The sites (Fig. 6) are at (i) Ynyslas submerged forest (Atlantic period: Mesolithic), (ii) Glaslyn Sub-Boreal: Bronze Age), and (iii) Ystwyth Forest (early Sub-Atlantic: late Iron Age). They have been described and interpreted in detail elsewhere (Taylor, 1973). Suffice

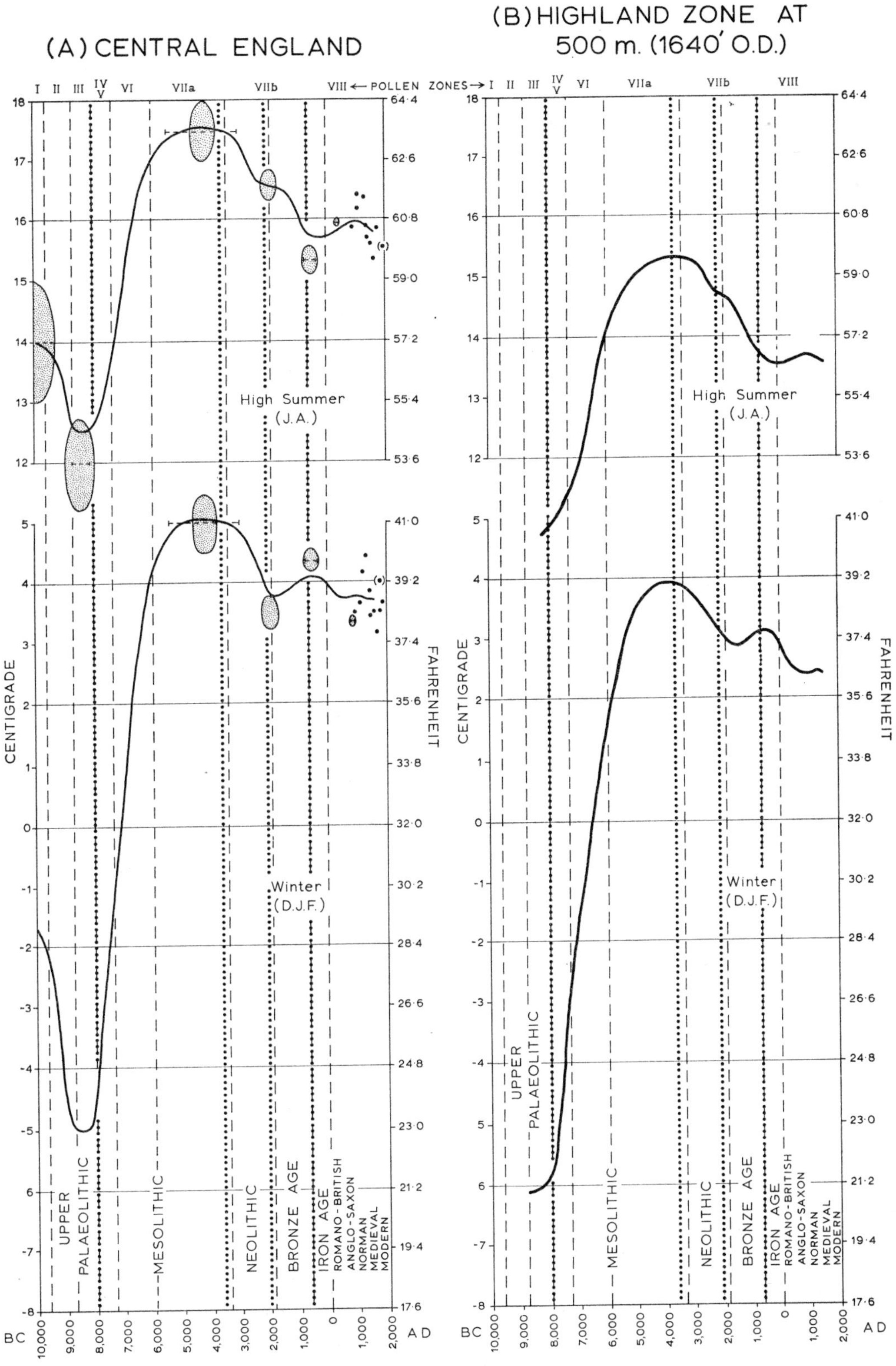

Fig. 5 *Average maximum and minimum air temperatures (A) in the lowlands of central England (= Lowland Zone) and (B) corrected for the Highland Zone at 500 m = 1640 ft OD since* c. *12,000 bp (Adapted from Lamb, Lewis, and Woodruffe, 1966)*

Note *(1) The temperature curves in (A) show the course of the* supposed *(or last millennium calculated) 1000-year averages. The dots in (A) refer to individual century averages. The dots in brackets refer to the period 1900–1965 (66 years). The shaded ovals indicate the approximate ranges within which estimates of temperature lie and 2σ error margins of dating (carbon-14 method) on either side of the most probable date. The horizontal lines through the ovals indicate the supposed duration of the epoch to which the 'observed' mean value applies*

Note *(2) (as for Note Fig. 4)*

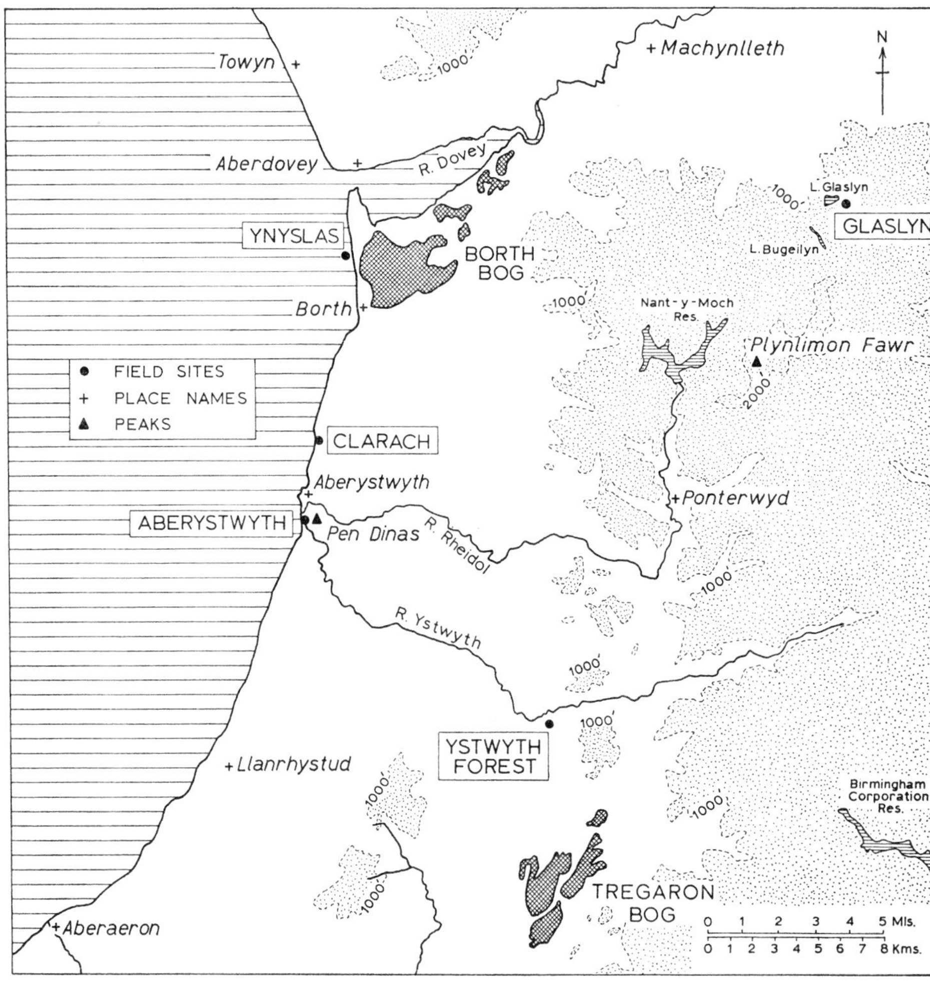

Fig. 6 General map of west central Wales showing location of field sites

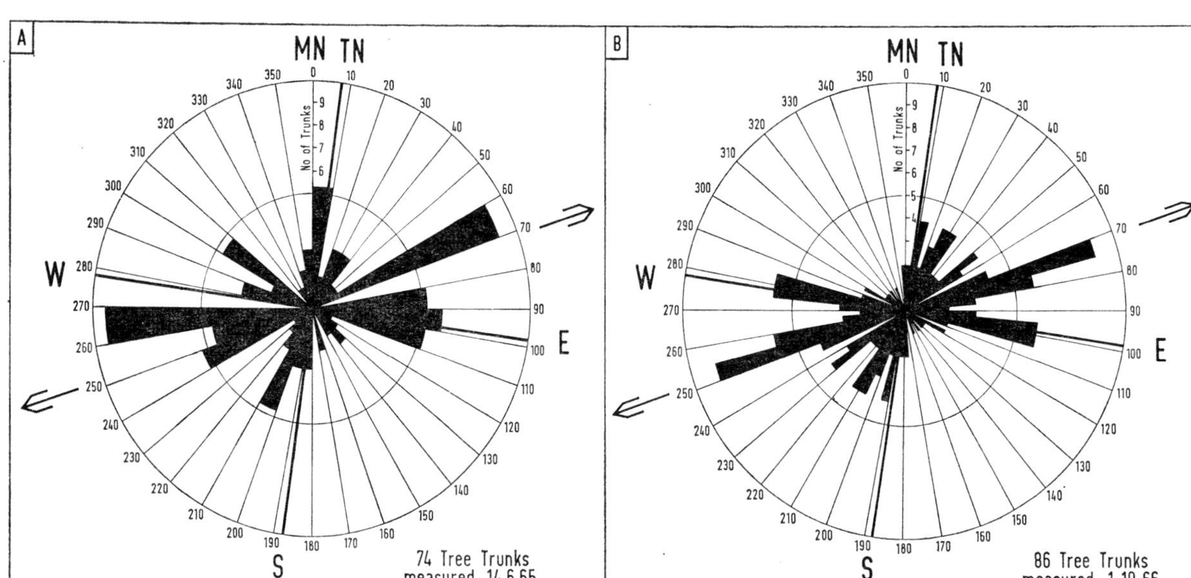

Fig. 7 Ynyslas submerged forest, Cardiganshire: orientation of collapsed trunks

it here to abstract points of palaeoclimatic and behavioural relevance.

Ynyslas

Godwin and Newton's (1938) first pollen diagrams for the submerged forest section off Ynyslas and for Borth Bog just to the east exhibited a relatively late pine-wood maximum, evidence of retardation. Much more enigmatical, however, is the abundant macro-remains of *Pinus,* both roots and trunks, not only at Ynyslas but also at Clarach, north of Aberystwyth (Taylor, 1973). The exceptionally powerful erosive effect of the recent (January 1974) gale-lashed tides on the coast of Cardigan Bay has been to expose evidence at the lowest tides of similar forest beds at Tan-y-bwlch just south of Aberystwyth, at the mouth of the Aeron at Aberaeron (Fig. 6), and at Newgale in Pembrokeshire apparently for the first time in living memory. At Ynyslas, however, many roots and lower trunks up to 0·2–0·4 m high are *in situ,* and the majority of the trees appear to have fallen under west–east stress (Fig. 7), suggesting strong winds, strong tides, or both, as being associated with what must have been a *rapid* collapse and inundation. Tree ring counts give answers repeatedly of between 70 and 80 years. At Clarach and Aberaeron cliffs in particular, the pollen record of fossil pine pollen is scanty compared with the macro-evidence. Radiocarbon datings for the Ynyslas basal peat and a *Pinus* root *in situ* in a comparable organic veneer at Clarach are as follows:

Ynyslas basal peat: 5898 ± 135 bp (Q. 352) (Godwin and Willis, 1961)
Pinus root at Clarach: 5970 ± 90 bp (NPL 113) (Taylor, 1973)

If a correction of + 750 years be applied (Olsson, 1970), dates emerge of 6648 ± 135 B.P. and 6720 ± 90 B.P., respectively, which are in the middle of the 'Atlantic' period when the major eustatic rise in sea level was rapidly inundating the once extensive plain of Cardigan, which is considered to have extended many miles westward in Late-glacial times (Taylor, 1973).

Thus, it may be postulated that the rapid submergence of the short-lived pine forests along the Cardigan coast probably involved a coincidence and probably a repetition of the following events:

(a) exceptionally high tides at a time of general rise in sea level

(b) strong and persistent westerly winds of gale force and continual bouts of heavy rain (which were very typical at this stage of the Atlantic period), causing ground saturation.

Primitive man's preference for sites in 'ecotones' (e.g. forest edge, riverside, coastal flat) may well have been exercised around the balmy Dovey estuary (Fig. 6) in late Mesolithic times, but to date only Aberystwyth harbour has yielded any evidence. Thomas and Dudlyke (1925) identified "a late Tardenoisian flint chipping floor" there with an estimated age of 5500 bp—very late Mesolithic. At the same time the tidal flood hazard at Ynyslas must have confronted prehistoric, as it did medieval and modern, man and environment. References to (a) the discovery in 1968 of an almost complete post-cranial skeleton of *Bos primigenius* (the aurochs) in the clay/silt just below the forest bed at Borth, and (b) the Welsh legend of the flooding of the "lowlands of Ardudwy" about AD 500 off the coast of Merioneth to the north and (c) the vexed question as to the natural origin or otherwise of the several 'sarns' or causeways which extend westwards in remarkably straight lines from the modern coast, cannot be resisted here. The resolution of some of these problems may be possible when current geological research into deposits on the floor of Cardigan Bay is completed (Dobson *et al.,* 1972).

Glaslyn

The northern shore of Lake Glaslyn (Fig. 6), 12·5 km north of Plynlimon at an elevation of 480 m (1575 ft OD) has been described as a Bronze Age hunting ground since the discovery of several barbed and tanged arrowheads (Houlder, 1969). Many flints have also been found near Lake Bugeilyn, 2 km to the south. This particular region of the central Wales uplands was, and still is, a zone of convergence of several mountain trackways in a number of directions. This may have facilitated access for Bronze Age colonizations in addition to the attraction of the area as a source of game and fish.

Again, this site constitutes a major ecotone with access to lake, forest, clearing, and moor and also to major trackways. Continuity of prehistoric settlements would be favoured on such sites, allowing flexibility and alternates to prehistoric man in his constant search for adequate and, if possible, varied sustenance as an insurance against unforeseen hazards and, if possible, a variety of environmental experience, not least on grounds of curiosity.

In July 1969 a basal peat from an eroding bog was sampled for radiocarbon dating, and from the full peat section of 1·2 m, additional samples generated the pollen diagram reproduced in Fig. 8 (Taylor, 1973). Teledyne Isotopes, New Jersey, dated the basal peat sample at 3870 ± 100 bp. Applying a correction of + 350 years, a final date of 4220 BP = 2270 BC is produced, which actually dates the peat and the associated elm decline (Fig. 8) to the very late Neolithic period and mid-Sub-Boreal climate phase when gentler lapse rates favoured high altitude settlement. Quoting the original paper (Taylor, 1973): "The view is now taken (Pears, 1972; Smith, R. T., 1972; Taylor, 1972) that the precise date of onset of upland peat formation for any locality must have depended on relief, hydrology, climatic exposure and the timing and intensity of human interference with the ecosystem".

The pre-peat buried soil yielded some *Lycopodium* and *Chamaenerion* pollen near its base and, a little later, *Caryophyllaceae,* suggesting an open phase which was probably early Sub-Boreal or late Atlantic when Frenzel (1966) suggests that a brief cold spell occurred in the Northern Hemisphere between about 3400 and 3000 bc. About 4000 bp and just before, an intermittent woodland was dominated by *Corylus, Quercus,* and *Alnus,* with subsidiary *Ulmus, Pinus, Betula,* and *Tilia.* Percentage arboreal pollen ranged from 15% to 35%, indicating relatively open and variably extensive woodland cover. (Percentages of 38–40%, however, would indicate virtually complete cover for sites of this altitude (R. T. Smith, 1970; R. T. Smith and Taylor, 1969; Tinsley and Smith, 1974)).

Just before the elm decline, the ferns had been quickly reduced (bad preservation could be a factor here) and

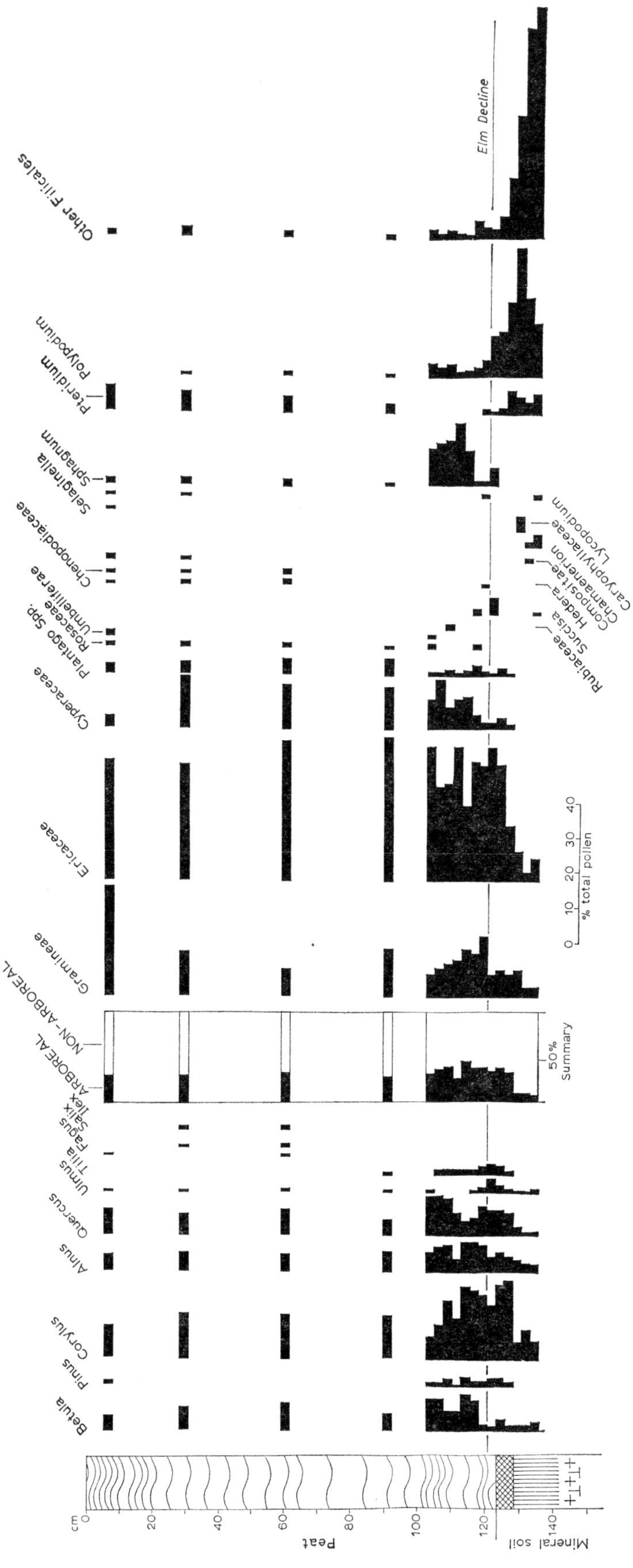

Fig. 8 Glaslyn: pollen diagram

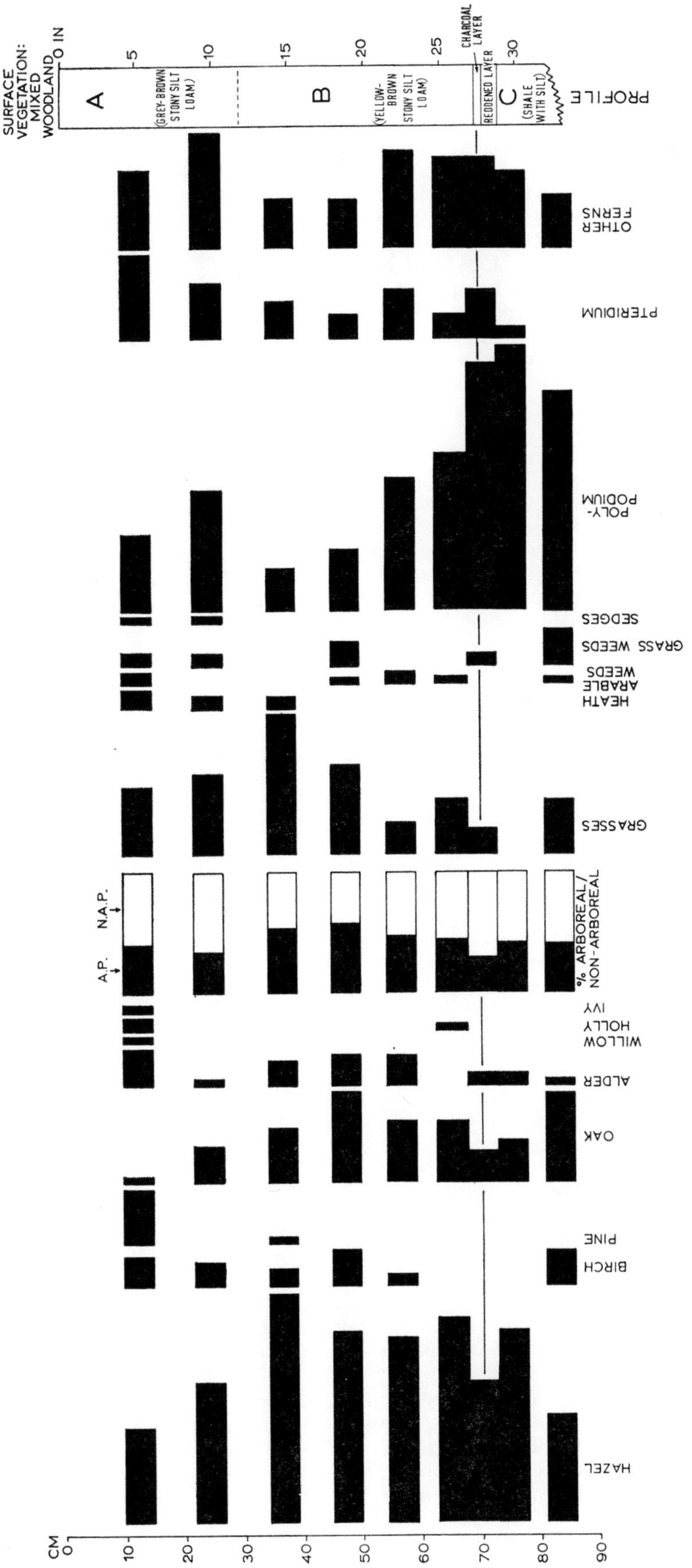

Fig. 9 Ystwyth Forest: pollen diagram

Ericaceae had expanded quite rapidly, and to a lesser degree, the grasses. After the elm decline, fluctuations in the proportion of arboreal pollen, and in particular of *Quercus, Corylus, Alnus,* and *Betula,* are compatible with periodic local clearances, which no doubt intensified in the Bronze Age and Iron Age in these regions.

Ystwyth Forest

The site (studied by Rudeforth, 1970) located at 137 m (450 ft OD) on a 12°, north-west, wooded slope 15 km south-east of Aberystwyth (Fig. 6). A charcoal band at 61-2 cm yielded a radiocarbon date of 2133 ± 110 bp (Q.814). If a correction of + 50 years be applied, a mid-Iron Age date of 233 ± 110 BC emerges. By this stage, lower slopes such as this one in the Ystwyth Forest (now planted by the Forestry Commission) were being burnt for charcoal or cleared for settlement and agriculture. The pollen diagram for the soil profile (Fig. 9) shows a marked discontinuity at the charcoal horizon which was obviously a residue of *in situ* burning because of the reddish colour of the horizon below it at 62–66 cm. Both tree and grass pollen fall, temporarily, at the charcoal horizon; *Quercus* and *Corylus* are reduced, so are *Polypodium* and grass and arable weeds; *Betula* disappears completely. Later on, *Corylus, Quercus,* and to some extent *Betula* recover, only to decline towards the top of the diagram. The *Pinus* pollen (which has penetrated to 46 cm in this loosely textured, colluvial soil) is modern, being derived from afforestation. To quote the original paper (Taylor, 1973):

> "The sequence of small peaks in arable weeds and then grass weeds is parallel to the sequence of mixed medieval farming and modern grass-dominated systems."

Like prehistoric man and nature herself, medieval man generated a localized mosaic of repetitive variations in his land-use (or landscape) patterns. Aided by a temporary climatic amelioration, he was able to colonize very high ground between 1150 and 1300 AD (Lamb, 1965) and expand agricultural limits. This phase of so-called 'high culture' is probably revealed by the fall in fern spores between 37 and 47 cm (Fig. 9) (Taylor, 1973).

Iron Age man chose to burn the forests on thickly wooded but accessible slopes (probably for the first time in many areas), like this one in the upper Ystwyth valley. By this time not only had he superior metal tools to tackle dense woodland but he must also have found the open, windy and, by then, peaty moorlands less attractive to his life-style. The slopes, lower hills, and valleys were his home.

CONCLUSION

In summary, it emerges that climate change and culture change may be conceived on two separate but complementary wavelengths. First, the macro-scale framework embracing the millennia presents the backcloth and general chronology, but, secondly, the actual changes at ground were governed by short-term periodicities in climate and weather and generated a metachronous mosaic of environmental or cultural responses. This is partly due to the inexorable march of palaeoecological research which is generating data and ideas at an increasingly accelerating rate. It is mainly due to the realization, from a variety of interdisciplinary sources, that the only valid way to comprehend environmental and culture change is in *ecosystematic* terms, and that such changes were in reality local and regional rather than zonal or hemispheric.

ACKNOWLEDGEMENT

The assistance of Dr R. T. Smith in the preparation and interpretation of the pollen diagrams included in this paper is gratefully acknowledged.

REFERENCES

Blytt, A. (1876). *Essay on the Immigration of the Norwegian Flora.* Cammermeyer: Christiania, Norway.

Bowen, D. Q. (1974). The Quaternary in Wales. *In* Owen, T. R. (ed.). *The Upper Palaeozoic and post-Palaeozoic Rocks of Wales.* University of Wales Press; 373–426.

Brooks, C. E. P. (1926). *Climate through the Ages.* London: Benn. (Last Edition, 1949).

Dimbleby, G. W. (1962). *The Development of the British Heathlands and their Soils.* Oxford Forestry Memoir No. 23.

Dobson, M. R., Evans W. E., Whittingham, R. J. and Wright, J. (1972). *The Geology of the Central and Southern Irish Sea.* Geology Department, University College of Wales (Aberystwyth) (Mimeo).

Erdtman, G. (1943). *An Introduction to Pollen Analysis.* USA: Waltham.

Faegri, K. and Iversen, J. (1950). *Textbook of Modern Pollen Analysis.* Copenhagen.

Ferguson, C. W. (1970). Dendrochronology of bristle cone pine, *Pinus aristata.* Establishment of a 7484-year chronology in the White Mountains of eastern-central California, U.S.A. *In* Olsson, I. U. (ed.). *Radiocarbon Variations and Absolute Chronology.* Nobel Symposium No. 12. Stockholm; 237–259.

Fleure, H. J. (1951). *A Natural History of Man in Britain.* London: Collins.

Frenzel, B. (1966). Climatic change in the Atlantic/Sub-Boreal transition on the Northern Hemisphere: botanical evidence. *In* Sawyer, J. S. (ed.). *World Climate from 8000 to 0 B.C.* London: Royal Meteorological Society; 99–123.

Godwin, H. (1956). *The History of the British Flora.* Cambridge University Press.

Godwin, H. (1970). The contribution of radiocarbon dating to archaeology in Britain. *Phil. Trans. Roy. Soc.,* A, 269, 57–75.

Godwin, H. and Newton, L. (1938). The submerged forest at Borth and Ynyslas. *New Phytol.,* 37, 333–344.

Godwin, H. and Willis, E. H. (1961). Natural radiocarbon measurements III *Radiocarbon,* 3, 60–76.

Gregory, S. (1964). Climate. *In* Watson, J. W. and Sissons, J. B. (eds.). *The British Isles: A Systematic Geography.* London: Nelson; 53–73.

Hare, F. K. and Ritchie, J. C. (1972). The Boreal climates. *Geogr. Rev.,* 62, 3, 333–365.

Harrison, S. J. (1973). An ecoclimatic gradient in north Cardiganshire, West Central Wales. (Ph.D. research, Geography Department, University College of Wales. Aberystwyth) (Private communication).

Harrison, S. J. (1974). Problems in the measurement and evaluation of the climatic resources of upland Britain. *In* Taylor, J. A. (ed.). *Climatic Resources and Economic Activity.* Newton Abbott: David and Charles; 47–63.

Houlder, C. H. (1969). Private communication. (see *Archaeol. Cambrensis,* 90, 153).

Iversen, J. and Troels-Smith, J. (1950). Pollen morfologiske definitioner og typer. *Danm. geol. Unders.*, IV, RK. 3, 8.

Lamb, H. H. (1965). The history of our climate: Wales *In* Taylor, J. A. (ed.). *Climatic Change as Related to Wales and its Agriculture.* Geography Department, University College of Wales (Aberystwyth); Memo No. 8, 1–18.

Lamb, H. H. (1966a). *The Changing Climate: Selected Papers.* London: Methuen.

Lamb, H. H., Lewis, R. P. W., and Woodroffe, A. (1966b). Atmospheric circulation and the main climatic variables between 8000 and 0 B.C.: meteorological evidence. *In* Sawyer, J. S. (ed.). *World Climate from 8000 to 0 B.C.* London: Royal Meteorological Society; 174–217.

Manley, G. (1942). Meteorological observations on Dun Fell. *Quart. J. Roy. Met. Soc.*, 68, 151–165.

Manley, G. (1943). Further climatological averages for the northern Pennines. *ibid.*, 69, 257–260.

Manley, G. (1945). The effective rate of altitudinal change in temperate Atlantic climates. *Geogr. Rev.*, 35, 408–417.

Manley, G. (1946). Variations in the length of the frost-free season. *Quart. J. Roy. Met. Soc.*, 72, 180–184.

Manley, G. (1949). The snowline in Britain. *Geogr. Annlr.*, 31, 179–193.

Manley, G. (1951). The range and variation of the British climate. *Geogr. J.*, 117, 43–68.

Manley, G. (1952). *Climate and the British Scene.* London: Collins.

Manley, G. (1953). The mean temperature of central England, 1698–1952. *Quart. J. Roy. Met. Soc.*, 79, 242–261.

Manley G. (1959). The Late-glacial climate of north-west England. *Liverpool Manchester Geol. J.*, 2, 188–215.

Manley G. (1964). Evolution of the climatic environment. *In* Watson, J. W. and Sissons, J. B. (eds.). *The British Isles: A Systematic Geography.* London: Nelson; 152–176.

Manley, G. (1966). Problems of the climatic optimum: the contribution of glaciology. *In* Sawyer, J. S. (ed.). *World Climate from 8000 to 0 B.C.* London: Royal Meteorological Society; 34–39.

Manley, G. (1971). The mountain snows of Britain. *Weather*, 26, 192–200.

Michael, H. N. and Ralph, E. K. (1970). Correction factors applied to Egyptian radiocarbon dates from the era before Christ. *In* Olsson, I. U. (ed.). *Radiocarbon Variations and Absolute Chronology.* Nobel Symposium No. 12. Stockholm; 109–120.

Oliver J. (1964) A study of upland temperatures and humidities in south Wales. *Trans. Inst. Brit. Geogr.*, 35, 37–54.

Olsson, I. U. (ed.) (1970). *Radiocarbon Variations and Absolute Chronology.* Nobel Symposium No. 12. Stockholm.

Pears, N. V. (1972). Interpretation problems in the study of tree line fluctuations. *In* Taylor, J. A. (ed.). *Research Papers in Forest Meteorology.* Aberystwyth: Cambrian News.

Pearsall, W. H. (1950). *Mountains and Moorlands.* London: Collins.

Pearsall, W. H. (1965). A discussion of the development of habitats in the Post-glacial. *Proc. Roy. Soc.*, B, 161, 293–294.

Pennington, W. and Bonny, A. P. (1970). Absolute pollen diagrams from the British Late-glacial. *Nature, Lond.*, 226, 871–873.

von Post, L. (1916). Om skogsträd pollen i sydsvenska torfmosselagerföljder (föredragsreferat). *Geol. För. Stockh. Förh.*, 38, 384.

Roberts, B. K., Turner, J. and Ward, P. F. (1973). Recent forest history and land use in Weardale, northern England. *In* Birks, H. J. B. and West, R. G. (eds.). *Quaternary Plant Ecology.* Oxford: Blackwells; 207–221.

Rodda, J. C. (1970). On more realistic rainfall measurements and their significance for agriculture. *In* Taylor, J. A. (ed.). *The Role of Water in Agriculture.* Oxford: Pergamon; 1–10.

Rudeforth, C. C. (1970). *The Soils of Northern Cardiganshire.* Harpenden (Soil Survey of Great Britain).

Sernander, R. (1908). On the evidence of Post-glacial changes of climate furnished by the peat mosses of northern Europe. *Geol. För. Stockh. Förh.*, 30, 465–478.

Smith, A. G. (1965). Problems of inertia and threshold related to Post-glacial habitat changes. *Proc. Roy. Soc.*, B, 161, 331–342.

Smith, A. G. (1970). The influence of Mesolithic and Neolithic man on British vegetation: a discussion. *In* Walker, D. and West, R. G. (eds.). *Studies in the Vegetational History of the British Isles.* Cambridge: University Press; 81–96.

Smith, R. T. (1970). *Studies in the Post-glacial Soil and Vegetation History of the Aberystwyth Area.* Unpublished Ph.D. thesis, Geography Department, University College of Wales (Aberystwyth).

Smith, R. T. and Taylor, J. A. (1969). The Post-glacial development of vegetation and soils in northern Cardiganshire. *Trans. Inst. Brit. Geogr.*, 48, 75–96.

Taylor, J. A. (ed.). (1960). *Hill Climates and Land Usage with Special Reference to the Highland Zone of Britain.* Geography Department, University College of Wales (Aberystwyth); Memo No. 3.

Taylor, J. A. (1965). Climatic change as related to altitudinal thresholds and soil variables. *In* Johnson, C. G. and Smith, L. P. (eds.). *The Biological Significance of Climatic Changes in Britain;* 37–50.

Taylor, J. A. (1967). Growing season as related to land aspect and soil texture. *In* Taylor, J. A. (ed.). *Weather and Agriculture.* Oxford: Pergamon; 15–36.

Taylor, J. A. (ed.). (1972). *Research Papers in Forest Meteorology.* Aberystwyth: Cambrian News.

Taylor, J. A. (1973). *Chronometers and Chronicles: A Study of the Palaeo-environments of West Central Wales.* Progress in Geography Vol. 5. International Reviews of Current Research; 248–334.

Taylor, J. A. and Yates, R. A. (1967). *British Weather in Maps.* Methuen.

Thomas, R. and Dudlyke, E. R. (1925). A flint-chipping floor at Aberystwyth. *J. Roy. Anthrop. Inst.*, 55, 73–89.

Tinsley, H. M. and Smith, R. T. (1974). Surface pollen studies across a woodland/heath transition and their application to the interpretation of pollen diagrams. *New Phytol.*, 73, 547–566.

Ucko, P. J. and Dimbleby, G. W. (eds.). (1969). *The Domestication and Exploitation of Plants and Animals.* London: Duckworth.

Walker, M. F. (1974). Private communication. (Research in progress at the Geography Department, University College of Wales, Aberystwyth).

Watson, E. and Watson, S. (1967). The periglacial origin of the drifts at Morfa Bychan near Aberystwyth. *Geol. J.*, 5 (2), 419–440.

Wodehouse, R. P. (1935). *Pollen Grains.* London.

Processes of soil degradation: a pedological point of view

D. F. Ball

Synopsis

The "pedological point of view" considers soils as complex natural bodies, evolving in response to the interaction of environmental factors. From this viewpoint, "soil degradation" is limited to physical loss of soil by erosion, but the general understanding of this term implies also development of soils less adapted to sustaining forest vegetation.

Soil types, their distribution, and the relevant soil-forming factors are reviewed for the Highland Zone. Podzolization, gleying, and peat formation are discussed as the major processes affecting Highland Zone soils. The influences of man on soils formed under the "natural" highland pedogenetic trends are considered from published views. It is concluded that for the British highlands generally man's intervention has only moderated or increased locally the inherent trends to leaching, increased acidity, podzolization, gleying, peat formation, and erosion, rather than changing completely the trends from one pedogenetic system to another.

INTRODUCTION

Of alternative approaches to my subject, I rejected strict limitation to technical discussion of key processes in favour of including these within a broader consideration of soils and soil-forming factors in the Highland Zone of Britain.

Two points in the title should be commented on. The 'pedological point of view' derives from the pedological approach to soil science. This considers soils as complex natural bodies, formed by the interaction of primary environmental factors through time, which are themselves an additional key control affecting, and being further modified by, the biological character of natural habitats and the exploitation of these habitats by man. The core of pedology is an attempt to understand the formative factors of soils (pedogenesis) and, by consideration of the morphology of the soil body, to subdivide the three-dimensionally varying thin and dynamic surface skin of the earth into meaningful classes.

The second point concerns 'degradation', which would be less widely used by pedologists than by others, such as agriculturalists. I appreciate the general consensus that degradation implies development of a soil less adapted to sustaining a forest vegetation and I will go along with that here. However, a pedologist would not consider that a natural sequence of soil change towards equilibrium with its environment was degradation in a pedological sense, and would limit this term to actual physical loss of soil due to erosion, if he used it at all.

Soils of the Highland Zone of Britain

These can, for our present purposes, be simply treated in terms of the seven major soil groups of a classification scheme (Ball, in press) based on conventional British practice and the terminology of Kubiena (1953), a scheme less extensive than that recently proposed for use in the British Soil Surveys (Avery, 1973). The basis for classifying soils into major soil groups and their sub-groups is the presence or absence in a soil profile of certain key horizon types. The definition of these horizons and the major soil groups is as follows:

Horizons

- O Horizon which, although it may contain some mineral admixture, is dominated by the organic fraction (loss-on-ignition values (equivalent to organic matter content) >30%).
- A Horizon at or near the soil surface consisting of an intimate mixture of organic and mineral material (<30% loss-on-ignition).
- E Horizon which occurs below O or A horizons and from which sesquioxides (Fe and Al) and/or clay have been removed.
- B Sub-surface horizon of mineral material, modified by physical, chemical or biological alteration so that it is differentiated by structure, colour, or texture from horizons above or below. Subdivisions include Bh and Bs horizons in which humic organic matter or sesquioxide levels respectively are high compared with horizons above and below.
- C Mineral material which has been little affected by pedological processes other than gleying (due to waterlogging). Includes Cr for fractured rock.
- R Unaltered rock that is too hard to dig.
- suffix gg Applied to any mineral horizon showing dominant structural or colour effects due to long-term waterlogging.
- suffix c Applied to any horizon containing residual calcium carbonate.

Major Soil Groups

(1) *Raw Mineral Soil* Soils lacking continuous lateral development of any master horizon other than C.

(2) *Ranker* Non-calcareous soils with O or A, and C (or R) horizons, but lacking B horizons. Incipient E horizons in some variants.

(3) *Calcareous Soil* Mineral soils with calcareous A and C horizons or with non-calcareous A and calcareous B and C horizons.

(4) *Brown Earth* Mineral soils of A, B (other than Bh or Bs), and C horizons.

(5) *Gley* Soils with horizons of gg type at or near the surface.

(6) *Podzolic Soil* Soils which include Bs and/or Bh horizons, generally but not always underlying an E horizon.

(7) *Organic Soil* Soils with no master horizons other than O present at depths less than 50 cm.

Soils in groups 2, 5, 6, and 7 are the most widely distributed in the Highland Zone. These may be treated as typical Highland Zone soils and, if one uses a circular argument, the Highland Zone can be defined as areas dominated by these soils. Clearly this involves essentially a climatic rather than altitudinal definition of highland. Soils of groups 3 and 4 can be considered as essentially 'lowland soils' which can occur in the Highland Zone whether one defines this altitudinally or climatically.

Factors influencing Highland Zone soil distribution

Environmental variables controlling the direction and rate of soil development (see e.g. discussions in Bunting (1965) and Fitzpatrick (1971)) are usually given, after Dokuchaev and the formulations of Jenny (1941), as: climate; geology; relief; time; and biotic influences. These last include man's activities, which I will consider separately later.

In outline, the major climatic influences on soil characteristics are temperature and rainfall, with wind and frost as important erosive factors. As Duchaufour (1965) noted, higher temperatures give faster rates of weathering of mineral components and decomposition of plant residues. Rainfall acts in soils of free drainage by its leaching effect and in soils of poor drainage by filling pore spaces with water, the scale of these effects depending on the effective water throughput after evaporation losses. The proportion of rainfall effective in pedogenetic terms is greater where lower temperatures cause less evaporation losses. The overall effects of high rainfall and low temperatures give pedogenetic trends of:

(1) in freely drained soils, the leaching of exchangeable nutrient ions, notably calcium, and a consequent lowering of soil pH and accumulation of non-incorporated humus at the surface to give, ultimately, the possibility of increased mineral breakdown and sesquioxide transport, and thus podzolic soil development;

(2) on poorly drained substrates, especially in sites of receiving drainage, the accumulation of peaty plant residues at the soil surface to give mainly peaty gleys and deep peats, with peaty rankers on hard rock in hill areas of very high rainfall.

The primary geological factors in soil development are the chemistry, mineralogy, and lithology of the rock types which form soil parent materials, either directly by weathering of rock *in situ,* or indirectly through their contribution to transported parent materials. Simplifying the picture in highland Britain and considering only outcrop rock *in situ,* at one end of the spectrum are rocks which remain virtually unaffected by Post-glacial weathering so that their ice-scoured and striated surfaces have been preserved over thousands of years, to support at most only the accumulated organic residues that build up shallow Peat Rankers. At the other extreme are those few rock types that weather sufficiently rapidly and/or are sufficiently calcareous to counterbalance the climatic leaching effect through their ability to supply freshly weathered mineral material or to sustain a high pH in overlying soil. These rocks thus carry, even in high rainfall localities, non-podzolized soils of Brown Earth or Brown Ranker types, or occasionally Calcareous Soils. Adjacent examples of these weatherability extremes are, for example, found on Snowdon, North Wales (Ball, Mew and Macphee, 1969). Between these extremes are rocks that weather sufficiently, though slowly, to form mineral soils which, however, are too poorly supplied with initial or replenishment calcium to prevent the onset of podzolization and/or peat accumulation.

Relief influences highland soils through the interaction of slope and climate, which affects their liability to erosion, and through its control on water run-off and percolation and hence on soil drainage.

The sharp distinction of one critical variable as an influence on pedogenesis is usually impossible since all interact, and in Britain this is particularly true of considerations of time as a factor in soil formation. It is often assumed that the time available for soil development has been about the same for all areas of highland Britain. This is not necessarily so, particularly on higher ground, where there is often evidence for both contemporary and relatively recent material disturbance and transport by land-slipping and by water, wind, and frost action, all providing fresh surfaces from which pedogenetic trends must re-start.

Where redistributed material initiates a fresh cycle of soil development, then typically the eroded and redeposited material has been derived from previous soils so that, although starting at a new zero time, the new profile develops in material already subjected to one or more weathering cycles. Inherited degrees of weathering, contaminating soil humus from previous cycles in the eroded soil, and the penetration of roots into buried profiles make it difficult in absolute terms to date the onset of development of the ranker soils formed in eroded material which locally cover relic well developed podzolic soils, for example in the Cairngorms (Metcalfe, 1950; Burges, 1951) and on footslopes of the hills of Rhum, Orkney, and Shetland.

Even in our small country, the Highland Zone extends over some 700 miles from Dartmoor in the south-west to Shetland in the north-east, and has also in Wales and the north a west to east rainfall gradient. At any single altitude within this range, even if geological and relief conditions are closely similar, clearly the climatic differences (as considered in the contribution by Mr Taylor) throughout the period of soil development would give a particular soil distribution for each individual area. Some aspects of regional differences in soil development are summarized in Table I.

The data in Table I are inadequate and too generalized for convincing quantitative interpretation but some points emerge. The altitude of the transition from the 'marginal' land zone dominated by Brown Podzolic Soils (an intergrade between Brown Earths and well-developed Podzols (see Ball (1966) for discussion of this sub-group)) to the 'typical' highland association of Peat, Peaty Gley, and Peaty Podzol ranges from about 1,800 ft (550 m) in eastern Wales, through 1,100–1,200 ft (335–366 m) on Dartmoor and in Western Wales and the Southern Uplands of Scotland, *c.* 700 ft (213 m) in the Lake District, and 500 ft (152 m) in the Grampians, coming down to sea-level in northern Scotland and the Northern Isles.

A soil zone above that of the Peat/Peaty Gley/Peaty Podzol association, which, moving northwards, first

TABLE I Approximate altitudinal range of soil zones in some British hill areas

<table>
<tr><th rowspan="2">Soil Zone</th><th colspan="6">Hill area</th></tr>
<tr><th>Dartmoor
1</th><th>Wales
2</th><th>Lake District
3</th><th>Southern uplands
4</th><th>Southern Grampians
4</th><th>Orkney and Shetland hills
5</th></tr>
<tr><td>Rankers</td><td>—</td><td>>2,000 ft (northwest)</td><td>>2,000 ft</td><td>—</td><td>>2,500 ft</td><td>>900 ft</td></tr>
<tr><td>Peat</td><td>>1,500 ft</td><td>—</td><td>—</td><td>>2,000 ft</td><td rowspan="2">1,500–2,500 ft*</td><td rowspan="2">0–900 ft</td></tr>
<tr><td>Podzols</td><td>—</td><td>—</td><td>—</td><td>—</td></tr>
<tr><td>Peat/Peaty Podzol/ Peaty Gley</td><td>1,100–1,500 ft</td><td>1,200–2,000 ft (west); >1,800 ft (east)</td><td>700–2,000 ft</td><td>1,200–2,000 ft</td><td>500–1,500 ft</td><td>—</td></tr>
<tr><td>Brown Podzolic Soil</td><td><1,100 ft</td><td>0–1,200 ft (west); 1,200–1,800 ft (east)</td><td><700 ft</td><td><1,200 ft</td><td><500 ft</td><td>—</td></tr>
</table>

(1) Clayden and Manley (1964)
(2) Ball (1959 and 1967)
(3) Hall (1965); Hall and Folland (1970)
(4) Romans (1970)
(5) Ball and Goodier (1974)

*In Scotland, the altitude at which hill peat becomes dominant starts at sea-level in the north and west, and rises to about 2,000 ft in the Cairngorms (Pearsall, 1950; McVean and Ratcliffe, 1962; Birse, 1971).

becomes conspicuous in North Wales, is present in the Lake District, and becomes more widespread in central and northern Scotland, is one of generally thin soil cover with Rankers and Raw Mineral Soils as the dominant groups. By slowing the rate of plant growth and increasing the natural erosion of soil material, the climatic influences of lower temperature and higher wind exposure counteract the simple picture of increased rainfall always producing increased leaching and podzolization and greater peat accumulation. This zone commences at about 2,000 ft (610 m) in Wales and the Lake District, and at about 2,500 ft (660 m) in the Grampians, but begins at only about 900 ft (275 m) in Orkney and Shetland, where ground above this height has active frost- and wind-induced ground patterning. Kubiena (1970), in comparing the Cairngorms and the Austrian Alps, puts a ranker zone on the Cairngorms at *c.* 3,000 ft (915 m) as equivalent to the soils at *c.* 9,000 ft (2745 m) in the Alps.

Major processes in Highland Zone soils

The major processes that have affected the development of soils in the Highland Zone of Britain are interrelated but may be considered separately as podzolization, gleying, and peat formation. Podzolization has been discussed by Romans (1970), who describes it as a temperature-controlled weathering and leaching process in which organic constituents, derived from a peaty humus surface horizon, attack the mineral fabric of the topmost mineral horizon and form soluble complexes with iron and aluminium present in oxides and hydrous oxides derived from mineral weathering. The soluble complexes are leached down the profile and their iron and aluminium is progressively deposited in Bh or Bs horizons, when microbial and fungal activities destroy the organic part of the complex.

Bloomfield (1970) reviews in the same report his important laboratory studies of iron transport, emphasizing the role in mobilizing iron of leaf leachates containing organic compounds of the type called polyphenols, rather than of peat-derived compounds. Iron is complexed with the polyphenols in the ferrous form and the reaction products are redeposited by sorption on residual ferric oxide. Deciduous and coniferous species give leaf extracts which can mobilize and transport iron, deciduous species often having higher activity in this respect. This is the reverse of field correlations, which suggest that conifers normally have a stronger podzolizing effect. Bloomfield ascribes this apparent contradiction to the influence of soil fauna, especially earthworms, which survive better in the deciduous ecosystem, in counteracting leaching. The extent to which Bloomfield's studies explain podzolization in field soils is not yet certain, but there is support, reviewed by Davies (1970), for an important role in element mobilization and transport for polyphenols in leachates reaching the soil as drip from a leaf canopy.

Podzolization can be thought of as a two-stage process: (1) release; and (2) transport of iron and aluminium. Brown earth pedogenesis involves relatively slow low-intensity weathering and release of 'fresh' (Bascomb, 1968) pedogenic iron and aluminium hydrous oxides in low levels, the greater proportion of which then remain *in situ* to accumulate in an 'aged' form. From this situation, when acidity increases, possibly accompanied by changes in supported plant species or leaf composition, then as a result of slower biological destruction and incorporation of organic matter in the surface soil, a stage is reached, whether gradually or at some abrupt change of weathering character is not known, when polyphenols and/or other organic compounds develop a stronger attack on soil minerals. The iron and aluminium mobilized as organo-mineral complexes by this attack may be re-deposited more or less *in situ* if the organic part of the complexes is rapidly destroyed. Such a situation gives Brown Podzolic Soils (see Ball, 1966), which when treated in the laboratory with alternative fairly mild extractants (Ball and Beaumont, 1972) are found to have generally higher 'fresh' iron and aluminium, with a greater proportion in the 'fresh' rather than the 'aged' forms, compared with Brown Earths on the same parent material. Significant transport of aluminium, which is more soluble than iron at a given pH, is shown in analysis of modal Brown Podzolic Soils, but there is only slight transport of iron and the visually distinct eluvial Ea and illuvial Bs horizons of the well developed podzol have not developed.

Pedogenetic equilibrium then seems to be delicately poised (as was noted also by Pigott, quoted in Pennington (1969, p 110)). The nutrient and organic matter cycles and the soil-faunal characteristics established under deciduous woodland and probably also under grassland as a woodland successor can apparently sustain this profile type over a very long period. If the biological regime, through vegetation and/or soil faunal changes, becomes further impoverished, then because polyphenols and other organic compounds remain stable longer, translocation of the mobile complexed iron downwards through the profile is possible before these compounds are destroyed, and in this case well developed Peaty Podzols occur. There is a complex unresolved interaction between general soil chemistry, water, fauna in the soil and plants on it, and the physico-chemical and organo-chemical properties of the iron and aluminium compounds involved which makes a simple picture of how deposition takes place not yet fully convincing. It is known that changes of ground cover can produce distinct eluvial and illuvial horizons of shallow depth quite quickly from a Brown Podzolic Soil, but that these changes are generally ineffective in this regard on a Brown Earth, presumably because of their low proportions of 'fresh' easily mobilized iron.

It is possible that greater understanding of the action of different chemical extractants on different categories of soil iron and aluminium will provide more sensitive definition of the stage of podzolization reached in soils, including those largely sterilized from subsequent pedogenesis by burial in archaeological sites or beneath erosion deposits, than can be provided by soil morphology.

Gleying is the process of reduction of iron oxides and hydroxides from a ferric to a ferrous state in a soil, due to anerobic conditions caused by waterlogging of soil pores. Mobilization of iron and its maintenance in a ferrous form requires a combination of organic matter, to give complexing agents similar to those involved in podzolization, and permanent or long-term waterlogging to ensure that the ferrous iron is not, or is only locally during seasonal aeration, reoxidized to the ferric form. Characteristic grey colours result in gleys from ferrous iron compounds, and these colours may be mottled with yellow, brown, or red if seasonal oxidation occurs preferentially, for example along root channels.

Podzolization and gleying both play a role in the Peaty Podzols (otherwise termed Peaty Gley Podzols) of highland Britain. In a simplified model, initial leaching increases acidity and allows acid *mor* humus to accumulate at the surface; more severe subsequent leaching develops to give mobilization and transport of iron and aluminium with organic matter. The deposition of transported material in a thin poorly permeable pan layer creates waterlogging in the overlying E horizon. This encourages the growth of peat which, acting as a generally moist sponge, further increases the degree and duration of gleying of the E horizon. A slightly different order of events is proposed by Taylor and Smith (1972), who suggest that the change in a wet climate from initial friable *mor* humus to greasy more waterlogged peat occurs at an earlier stage of pedogenesis. This surface wet peaty horizon again encourages gleying beneath it, followed by mobilization and transport of iron to be deposited below in a pan layer. It is probably a 'chicken or egg' situation as to whether peat or pan came 'first' in most peaty gley podzols.

Where waterlogging is total throughout the profile, owing either to physiographic location or to the soils being of heavy texture, causing slow percolation of drainage water, the entire mineral profile can be gleyed beneath a peaty O horizon to form Peaty Gleys. By accentuating physical breakdown of rock particles, waterlogging brings about a reduction of large pore spaces because of closer packing of the fine material, and this decreases permeability, which further intensifies the gley situation.

Peat requires little comment here. Although peaty humus is a term used to describe the humified O horizons of acid soils on quite dry sites, peat is strictly the material formed through the accumulation under anaerobic conditions of slightly humified but recognizable plant remains. It forms in basin sites of high watertable under a wide climatic range and more widely over a range of relief in areas of high rainfall and humidity and relatively low temperatures. This 'blanket-bog' or its sub-category of 'hill peat' is what we are concerned with in the British uplands. The history of peat development is important to considerations of soil development in the Highland Zone and has, for example, been discussed for Scotland by Durno and Romans (1969), for mid-Wales by Moore (1972; 1973), and for Ireland by Mitchell (1972).

Influences of man on 'natural' trends of soil development in the Highland Zone

Post-glacial British vegetation history, related soil development trends, and major features of human settlement are summarised in Table II, drawn largely from Pennington (1969). There is general agreement that the basic picture is sound, but some reservations should be borne in mind. Among these are the problems in inferring abrupt climatic change as a cause of spread or decline of key species (Smith, 1972); the fact that many of the changes in the pollen record used as period boundaries are not synchronous from place to place (Smith and Pilcher, 1972); and the fact that the succession of forest types identified from lowland sites is often not clearly seen in the pollen record at upland sites (Durno, 1973).

Archaeological and pedological interests meet in attempts to define man's environment at different periods and to use archaeological data to interpret the course of soil development. A fundamental problem

TABLE II Late Glacial and Post-Glacial periods and their characteristics in Britain (summarized largely from Pennington, 1969)

	Climatic Period (Pollen Zone)	*Time*	*Climatic Tendencies*	*Vegetation Features*	*Soil Features*	*Human Settlement Features*
Recent	(VIII–modern)			Upper oak limit *c.* 1,500 ft		Arable farming extends to suitable upland (e.g. around Tregaron, Wales, in 1180 AD)
		450 AD				
	Sub-Atlantic (VIII)		Cool, wet oceanic	General relative birch in-increase, with beech and hornbeam in south	Peat growth continues to create the 'typical' highland peaty soil association. Peat growth accelerated in uplands	Celtic monastic movement extends farming. Increased forest clearance due to Celtic pastoral farming with arable in south Iron Age ——450 bc
		500 bc				
	Sub-Boreal (VIIb)		Warm, dry, continental	Pine continues in north; decline of elms with increase of ash; spread of birch and heather	Increased deforestation speeds onset of podzolization under heath on lighter northern soils. Progressive soil leaching aided by forest clearance	Bronze Age ——1700 bc Upland settlement in Lake District, Wales, Dartmoor
Post-Glacial		3000 bc				
	Atlantic (VIIa)		Warm, wet, oceanic ('Climatic Optimum')	Mixed oak forest of the climatic climax; alder and lime with oak and elm; limited birch in north and west; forests to *c.* 2,500 ft	Persistence of soils derived in equilibrium with natural environment. Peat growth commences in Pennines above 1,200 ft	Neolithic farming begins ——3500 bc
		5500 bc				——Mesolithic *c.* 5600 bc
	Boreal (VI) (V)		Relatively warm, dry	Elm-oak-hazel-birch-pine	Soil development proceeds to mature profiles in equilibrium with climate and natural vegetation, the latter as forest often protecting acid soils from strong podzolization	
		7600 bc				
	Pre-Boreal (IV)		Sub-arctic	Pine, birch, and/or juniper forest; relative decline in grasses and herbs	Rapid humus accumulation and onset of profile development on stable sites	
		8500 bc				
	Zone III ('Younger *Dryas*')		Sub-arctic with local glaciation and major periglacial conditions	Treeless tundra-heath with dwarf birch, arctic willow and juniper	Frost-affected raw mineral soil	
		8800 bc				
Late Glacial	Zone II (Allerod Interstadial)		Cool, temperate	Birch, poplar, pine and willow	More stable, humose soil	Upper Palaeolithic
		10000 bc				
	Zone I ('Older *Dryas*')		Sub-arctic with local glacial and widespread periglacial conditions	Treeless tundra with dwarf birch and arctic willow	Frost-affected raw mineral soil	
		12300 bc				
Glacial			Cold, arctic			Palaeolithic—

to which I offer no conclusive answer is how far present observed differences between sites were a cause of their selection or rejection by early man, and how far they are differentiated now as a result of this selection. On balance I believe there were real original differences guiding choice and there was certainly a pedological-ecological basis for many land-use decisions in early and mediaeval history, for example, marginal to the Highland Zone in North and South Wales (Grimes, 1945; Jones, 1963, 1966; Crampton and Webley, 1960).

Bidwell and Hole (1965) grouped man's influences on soils as either 'beneficial' or 'detrimental' to his continuing use. Beneficial effects include the addition of materials that improve the soil moisture regime and increase soil nutrient status as a counterbalance to leaching, as well as the reduction of erosion hazards. Detrimental effects include the removal of nutrients by crops or stock at a faster rate than they are replaced by the natural nutrient cycle, leading to greater acidity and leaching; and an increase in erosion through forest clearance and the creation of bare ground in susceptible locations.

Man's interventions in the Highland Zone are mostly considered to be detrimental, but one beneficial possibility should be mentioned. Man-made soils ('Plaggen' soils) are created by the addition of turf, peat, and seaweed to sandy soils and of shell-sand to peats. Conry (1971) describes such soils in Ireland and contends that, though most were formed in the late 18th and early 19th centuries, the addition of sea-sand to peat had been carried out in pre-Christian times. I have traced no record of such soils associated with coastal settlements in Britain (other than the relatively recent lazy-beds of the western seaboard).

Of the two main detrimental effects on soils of man's activities in the highland soil, erosion can obviously be critical locally. McVean and Lockie (1969), for example, illustrate severe recent erosion due to overgrazing and burning, giving gullying and the exposure of rock scree over whole slopes. Such erosion could well have occurred from earliest times, both naturally in man's absence and accelerated by man, but so far as I am aware it is not yet known whether any specific erosion periods affecting highland areas generally, as distinct from locally, occur in association with particular phases of human settlement. If it were possible to date the buried mature soils and the immature Rankers above them, formed in covering material eroded from upslope, which were previously mentioned as occurring in a number of scattered Scottish localities, this would be useful, but the material available is not really suitable for carbon dating. It seems probable anyway that periods more recent than those of interest to you here are generally involved (e.g. Ragg, 1973). Occasionally erosion can even have a 'beneficial' effect. On Snowdon, soils formed on rapidly weatherable volcanic ash are Brown Earths on unstable colluvial slopes, whereas this same parent material on a stable site carries more acid, less fertile Peaty Podzols.

The second main detrimental effect of man which I come to finally is, of course, the most widely discussed mutual interest of pedologists and archaeologists in the Highland Zone. How far did man create new pedogenetic trends which would not have developed under undisturbed woodland cover or how far did he simply accelerate a trend that already was developing? I cover this aspect briefly because it leads into Dr R. T. Smith's subject, and because Professor Dimbleby, who has carried out (e.g. 1962, 1965) and stimulated so much of the research in this field may, I hope, contribute in discussion.

Dimbleby included upland heaths and moorlands in Yorkshire in his heathland development study (1962). In the former, on the Tabular Hills, near Scarborough (*c.* 600–750 ft OD (183–228 m)), Bronze Age barrows covered soils without a podzolic Ea horizon (probably comparable with Brown Podzolic Soils) and also quite well developed iron podzols, from which Dimbleby inferred that podzolization was progressing rapidly in the area at the time of barrow construction. Bronze Age barrows on moorland sites in the Cleveland Hills near Guisborough (1,200–1,400 ft (366–427 m)) covered Peaty Podzols and Peaty Gleys. Because pollen data showed woodland to have formerly occupied these latter sites, and it was considered that woodland could not have survived on the soil types beneath the barrows, a woodland clearance was inferred as having triggered the podzolization and gleying. On balance it was proposed that disturbance of the ecological equilibrium by man had a predominant effect on soil development (Dimbleby, 1962, 45). Peat accumulation on the North Yorkshire Moors not far east of Dimbleby's sites was subsequently shown by Simmons (1969) to have begun in late Boreal/early Atlantic times, which would suggest a general climatically controlled peat–gley–podzol tendency on higher areas prior to man's major Bronze Age intervention.

Simmons (1962; 1964) again, in his study of Dartmoor, has demonstrated that forest cover had become weakened before the Bronze Age in the area now occupied by Brown Podzolic and Peaty Podzol soil zones. Settlement then would have brought considerable woodland clearance, but by the Iron Age most settlement was on lower ground, and peat by then covered most of the moor above 1,600 ft (488 m). Climatic deterioration affecting land which had been cleared but abandoned controlled the expansion of Peaty Podzols in the higher sectors.

In Wales, Smith and Taylor (1969; see also Taylor, 1973), working in north Cardiganshire, considered that woodland decline above about 1,000 ft (305 m) OD was a natural change and that Bronze Age man cleared secondary woodland rather than a primary climax forest, following the spread of ericaceous species and development of peaty O horizons commencing at about the Atlantic–Sub-Boreal transition. Moore (1972b), also working in mid-Wales, considers that there is a strong argument for climatic deterioration as a major factor in upland forest disappearance.

For Scotland, Durno (1973) has recently reviewed the evidence for vegetation history and has suggested that Brown Earth and Brown Podzolic Soils (combined as 'Brown Forest Soils' in the Scottish classification) and Podzols were well developed by the Boreal period, and that the former extended to higher altitudes in the Atlantic with also a spread of gley soils, and that podzols increased at the expense of Brown Forest Soils after the Sub-Boreal/Sub-Atlantic transition as a result of a cooler climate and 'natural' forest recession. Durno and Romans (1969) in their consideration of peat development in Scotland and Northern England discern a spread from initiation in the Boreal period to a relatively uniform upland peat-forming climate for all highland northern Britain by the start of the Sub-Atlantic period.

I have not sufficient grasp of the scattered evidence to be convinced totally of the correct interpretation, but it seems to me on balance that the highland trends in soil formation due to climate, geology, and relief have been clearly running in the directions of leaching, acidity, podzolization, gleying, and peat formation throughout Post-glacial time. For the British highlands generally, man has only intervened to hasten or slow the rate of these trends, rather than being in a position to alter the whole trend from one pedogenetic system to another. Locally there seems no doubt that, where a fringe site was subjected to human intervention at a particular episode and where fortunate chance adds enough evidence together, the nature of this intervention and the change of rate of the processes can be followed.

REFERENCES

Avery, B. W. (1973). Soil classification in the Soil Survey of England and Wales. *J. Soil Sci.*, 24, 324–338.

Ball, D. F. (1959). Soil profiles and patterns in Wales. *Nature Wales*, 5, 765–774.

Ball, D. F. (1966). Brown podzolic soils and their status in Britain. *J. Soil Sci.*, 17, 148–158.

Ball, D. F. (1967). Soils of Wales: The distribution of major soil groups. *Trans VIIIth Int. Congress of Soil Science, Bucharest*, 1964, V. 69–79.

Ball, D. F. (in press). Site and soils. *In* Chapman, S. B. (ed.). *Methods in Plant Ecology*. Oxford: Blackwells.

Ball, D. F. and Beaumont, P. (1972). Vertical distribution of extractable iron and aluminium in soil profiles from a Brown Earth–Peaty Podzol association. *J. Soil Sci.*, 23, 298–308.

Ball, D. F. and Goodier, R. (1974). Ronas Hill: A preliminary account of its patterned ground features resulting from the action of frost and wind. *In* Goodier, R. (ed.). *The Natural Environment of Shetland*. Edinburgh: Nature Conservancy Council, 89–106.

Ball, D. F., Mew, G. and Macphee, W. S. (1969). Soils of Snowdon. *Fld Stud.*, 3, 69–107.

Bascomb, C. L. (1968). Distribution of pyrophosphate-extractable iron and organic carbon in soils of various groups. *J. Soil Sci.*, *19*, 251–268.

Bidwell, O. W. and Hole, F. D. (1965). Man as a factor of soil formation. *Soil Sci.*, 99, 65–72.

Birse, E. L. (1971). *Assessment of Climatic Conditions in Scotland 3. The Bioclimatic Sub-Regions*. Aberdeen: Macaulay Institute.

Bloomfield, C. (1970). The mechanism of podzolisation. *Welsh Soils Discussion Group Rept.*, 11, 112–123.

Bunting, B. T. (1965). *The Geography of Soil*. London: Hutchinson.

Burges, A. (1951). The ecology of the Cairngorms. 3. The *Empetrum-Vaccinium* zone. *J. Ecol.*, 39, 271–284.

Clayden, B. and Manley, D. J. R. (1964). The soils of the Dartmoor granite. *Dartmoor Essays, 1964*. Devonshire Assn. for Adv. Lit. and Art; 117–140.

Conry, H. J. (1971). Irish plaggen soils—their distribution, origin and properties. *J. Soil Sci.*, 22, 401–416.

Crampton, C. B. and Webley, D. (1960). The correlation of prehistoric settlement and soils in the Vale of Glamorgan. *Bull. Board Celtic Stud.*, 18, 387–396.

Davies, R. I. (1970). The podzol process. *Welsh Soils Discussion Group Rept.*, 11, 133–142.

Dimbleby, G. W. (1962). *The Development of British Heathlands and their Soils*. Oxford For. Mem. 23. Oxford: Clarendon Press.

Dimbleby, G. W. (1965). Post-Glacial changes in soil profiles. *Proc. Roy. Soc.*, B, 161, 355–362.

Duchaufour, I. (1956). *Pedologie, Applications Forestières et Agricoles*. Nancy: Ec. Nat. Eaux For.

Durno, S. E. (1973). Vegetation chronology. *In* Tivy, J. (ed.). *The Organic Resources of Scotland, Their Nature and Evaluation*. Edinburgh: Oliver and Boyd; 24–37.

Durno, S. E. and Romans, J. C. C. (1969). Evidence for variations in the altitudinal zonation of climate in Scotland and northern England since the Boreal period. *Scot. Geogr. Mag.*, 85, 31–33.

Fitzpatrick, E. A. (1971). *Pedology: A Systematic Approach to Soil Science*. Edinburgh: Oliver and Boyd.

Grimes, W. F. (1945). Early man and the soils of Anglesey. *Antiquity*, 19, 169–174.

Hall, B. R. (1965). The soil associations of Furness. *Proc. North of England Soils Discussion Group*, 3, 3–10.

Hall, B. R. and Folland, C. J. (1970). *Soils of Lancashire*. Bull. 5, Harpenden: Soil Survey of England and Wales.

Jenny, H. (1941). *Factors of Soil Formation*. New York: McGraw-Hill.

Jones, G. R. J. (1963). Early settlement in Arfon: The setting of Tre'r Ceiri. *Trans. Caernarvonshire Hist. Soc.*, 24, 1–20.

Jones, G. R. J. (1966). Rural settlement in Anglesey. *In* Eyre, S. R. and Jones, G. R. J. (eds.). *Geography as Human Ecology*. London: Edward Arnold; 199–230.

Jowsey, P. C. (1973). Peatlands. *In* Tivy, J. (ed.). *The Organic Resources of Scotland: Their Nature and Evaluation*. Edinburgh: Oliver and Boyd; 109–121.

Kubiena, W. L. (1953). *Soils of Europe*. London: Murby.

Kubiena, W. L. (1970). *Micromorphological Features of Soil Geography*. New Jersey: Rutgers Univ. Press.

McVean, D. N. and Lockie, J. D. (1969). *Ecology and Land Use in Upland Scotland*. Edinburgh University Press.

McVean, D. N. and Ratcliffe, D. A. (1962). *Plant Communities of the Scottish Highlands*. Nature Conservancy Monographs 1. London: H.M.S.O.

Metcalfe, G. (1950). The ecology of the Cairngorms. 2. The mountain *Callunetum*. *J. Ecol.*, 38, 46–74.

Mitchell, G. F. (1972). Soil deterioration associated with prehistoric agriculture in Ireland. *Trans 24th Int. Geol Congress, Symp. 1*, 59–68.

Moore, P. D. (1972a). Initiation of peat formation and the development of peat deposits in Mid-Wales. *Proc. 4th Int. Peat Congress I-IV*, Helsinki, 89–100.

Moore, P. D. (1972b). The influence of post-Weichselian climatic fluctuations upon forest composition and development in Mid-Wales. *In* Taylor, J. A. (ed.). *Research Papers in Forest Meteorology: An Aberystwyth Symposium*. Aberystwyth: Cambrian News; 20–30.

Moore, P. D. (1973). The influence of Prehistoric cultures upon the initiation and spread of blanket bog in upland Wales. *Nature, Lond.*, 241, 350–353.

Pearsall, W. H. (1950). *Mountains and Moorlands* Collins.

Pennington, W. (1969). *The History of British Vegetation*. London: English Universities Press.

Ragg, J. M. (1973). Factors in soil formation. *In* Tivy, J. (ed.). *The Organic Resources of Scotland, Their Nature and Evaluation*. Edinburgh: Oliver and Boyd; 38–50.

Romans, J. C. C. (1970). Podzolisation in a zonal and altitudinal context in Scotland. *Welsh Soils Discussion Group Rept. 11*, 88–101.

Simmons, I. G. (1962). An outline of the vegetation history of Dartmoor. *Rep. Trans. Devon Ass. Advan. Sci.*, 94, 555–474.
Simmons, I. G. (1964). Pollen diagrams from Dartmoor. *New Phytol.*, 63, 165–180.
Simmons, I. G. (1969). Pollen diagrams from the North York Moors. *New Phytol.*, 68, 807–827.
Smith, A. G. and Pilcher, J. R. (1973). Radiocarbon dates and vegetational history of the British Isles. *New Phytol.*, 72, 903–914.
Smith, R. T. (1972). A reconsideration of the role of climate in the development of post-Weichselian forest types. *In* Taylor, J. A. (ed.). *Research Papers in Forest Meteorology: an Aberystwyth Symposium.* Aberystwyth: Cambrian News; 1–19.
Smith, R. T. and Taylor, J. A. (1969). The post-glacial development of vegetation and soils in northern Cardiganshire. *Trans. Inst. Brit. Geogr.*, 48, 75–96.
Taylor, J. A. (1973). Chronometers and chronicles, a study of palaeo-environments in west central Wales. *In* Board, C., *et al.*, (eds.). *Progress in Geography Vol. 5.* London: Edward Arnold; 250–334.
Taylor, J. A. and Smith, R. T. (1972). Climatic peat—a misnomer? *Proc. 4th Int. Peat Congress I-IV.* Helsinki; 471–484.

Early agriculture and soil degradation

R. T. Smith

Synopsis

This paper discusses concepts of soil degradation and considers that in practice the link between former agriculture and present soil morphology is a difficult one to forge. Within such a variable medium as soil, fields provide the most reliable templates but unless they are examined on a systematic basis the investigator may fail to read essential clues to former management which underpin and make intelligible the pattern of soil morphology and variability. Several case studies are introduced to illustrate different types of degradation as well as problems of method. While these support the thesis that man has been a major agent in degradation, it is clear that arable activities themselves, while significant in this respect, may be overshadowed in their long-term influence by the more insidious demands of traditional pastoralism.

INTRODUCTION

A short title often has too narrow or too general a connotation. It has not been my intention simply to seek examples of man's destructive impact, which the title tends to imply, but rather to examine the assumption that agriculture has necessarily been detrimental to soil resources and to gain insight into the ways in which degradation processes operate. For this reason, whether agriculture was early or late seems hardly to matter, and I have not therefore restricted myself simply to sites of prehistoric significance.

Soil degradation or degeneration implies that man, assisted by natural agencies, has brought about a measurable loss of soil quality. It signifies changes in the nature of soil from its partial removal to processes modifying soil horizons such as podzolization and plough pan formation. It may therefore have different manifestations in different soils. Because natural processes may be principally involved in these changes, controversy has existed over whether they would occur anyway over great lengths of time or are of a type which would never have occurred without man's interference (Dimbleby, 1962, 1965; Duchaufour, 1970). What we have in mind is a variety of processes either initiated or accelerated by man, which have led to a more rapid evolution of soils and perhaps landscapes as well. Degradation can therefore be viewed as a special case of soil evolution treated in relation to the changing value of soil to successive generations, rather than in more academic and essentially geological terms. Before considering the degradation issue it is necessary to establish former agriculture as a fact.

SOME PROBLEMS OF METHOD

A major difficulty in soil interpretation, as already implied, is that of establishing cause and effect. In the field this may entail eliminating possible natural origins for a variety of topographic and pedological features before building up an understanding of the type and extent of changes attributable to man. The context of former agriculture is, of course, provided by fields, without which one will only stumble upon the evidence by accident. There are certainly many geometric layouts suggestive of fields, and while those associated with plough terraces were obviously cultivated, it is unwise to assume that all enclosed areas served this function. Very small enclosures may have been sheep folds, while the more extensive areas enclosed in antiquity probably had territorial rather than agronomic significance.

Soil evidence of former cultivation may take the form of plough or spade markings (Fowler and Thomas, 1962; Fowler and Evans, 1967; Thomas, 1969) or material remains such as charcoal and potsherds which may also be associated with a layer of small and fragmented stones (Cornwall, 1958). However, the legacy of agriculture at each site is a function of soil type as well as its subsequent history, and one cannot therefore predict what will constitute soil profile evidence of former cultivation—frequently it does not exist in any identifiable form. For this reason, as with any controlled experiment, one is obliged to compare

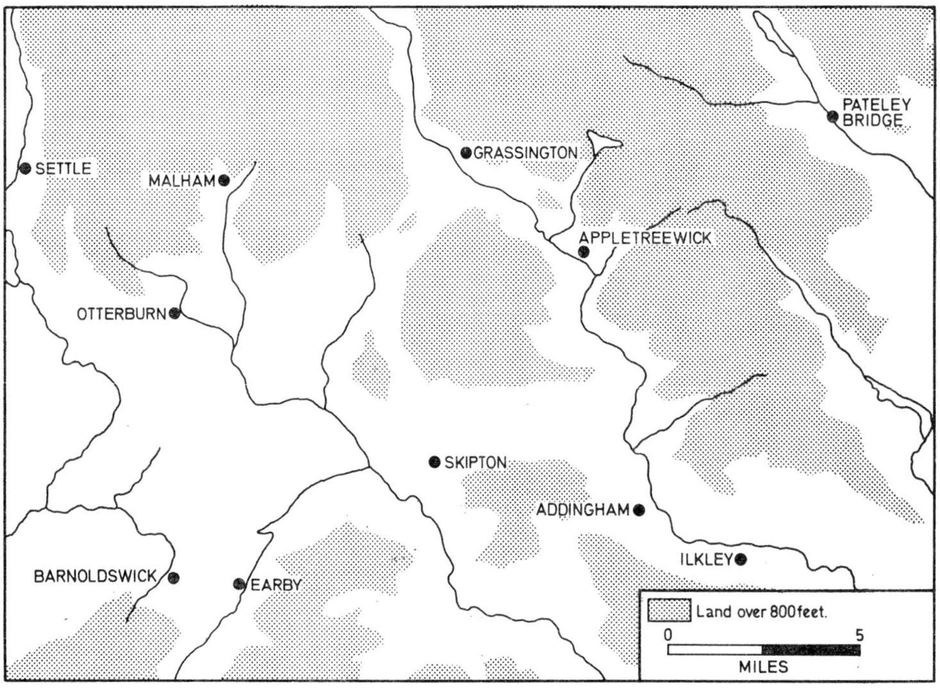

Fig. 1 General location map for west Yorkshire sites

the condition of the presumed agricultural soil with soils beyond the field boundaries.

Sampling within fields should be conducted so that soil characteristics are amenable to explanation of a consistent kind, otherwise one will simply gain scattered evidence of the effects of cultivation without gaining insight into the agricultural methods of the time. This is the kind of information most likely to explain why soil degradation arose and emphasizes the need for a multi-disciplinary approach.

Even when cultivation has been demonstrated, it may not be possible to distinguish between soil profile features acquired at the time of former cultivation and features attributable to subsequent deflected pedogenesis. Hence the precise role of cultivation, as opposed to the passage of time, cannot be known with certainty. It is this same principle which renders problematical the interpretation of some buried soils. Again, if one considers the hillside as a land unit prone to slow soil movement under a humid climate, it is clear that any estimate of 'cultural erosion' will contain an element of exaggeration, particularly in cases where arable use ceased many centuries ago. A further example of the problem of process rates is provided by thin soils on the Pennine limestone. Apparent soil loss from fields in these situations must be equated with the rate of solution of the underlying rock before one can account properly for the denudation.

The question of dating is certainly not the least of the problems encountered, since fields have vague origins: indeed, in the case of 'Celtic fields', it is often unclear as to whether the name refers to field type or to its antiquity (Bowen, 1961). The marks of an early agricultural phase may have been overprinted or erased by later agriculturalists, just as reoccupation of earlier structures may account for the predominance of finds attributable to later archaeological periods (e.g. Roman and post-Roman in West Yorkshire—Miss M. Faull, private communication). Field type alone should not therefore be relied upon for dating except when accompanied by other archaeological evidence.

Many contributions in the field of palynology have helped indicate the scale of former cultivation in our uplands, the principal cultigens, and the main agricultural episodes in conjunction with radiocarbon dating. But pollen analysis often presents too generalized a picture of changes for optimum integration with archaeology, and, in relation to early field systems, this is why Dr Judith Turner's attempts to identify directional components of pollen rain (Turner, 1970) seem such a promising development provided that suitable sites are available. Aside, however, from the work of Professor Dimbleby using buried soils in North Yorkshire (1962) and that of Dr Winifred Pennington, notably in the Lake District (1964, 1970) where the technique was linked to chemical analyses of lake sediments, research has not specifically attempted to show the pedological consequences of land use activities, let alone those arising from cultivation. This problem, in any case, is one which pollen analysis on its own is ill-equipped to solve.

EARLY AGRICULTURE IN CRAVEN

A study of lynchet fields

Most widespread in lowland Craven are the remains of lynchet fields, mainly on lower slopes. Frequently narrow and strip-like, they reflect constraints of topography or underlying structure, but some are surprisingly squarish or rectangular, as at Otterburn (see Figs. 1 and 2). In this first example, the field has a double riser to the east and a single riser downwards to the west, signifying a westward movement of soil by ploughing (Curwen, 1939; Wood, 1961). Slopes increase to around 15° towards the top of the field and there is a pronounced terrace or bench at the slope foot (Fig. 3), which is restricted to this lynchet. The field has a sheltered southerly aspect with gentler gradients at top and bottom (with plough teams in mind), and intensive arable use from medieval times is therefore assumed, especially since it is so near the village.

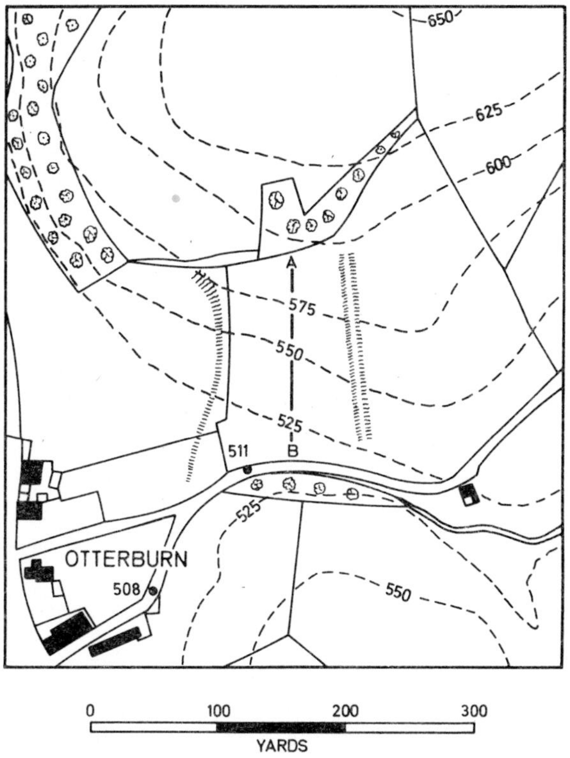

Fig. 2 Plan of Otterburn lynchet field

The slope foot area was surveyed in detail with numerous borings, and a pit was dug at point B which revealed 40 in of sandy loams overlying a clay-rich soil layer. As will be seen from Fig. 4, this latter matches very closely the texture of three soil samples taken higher up the field from 4-8 in depth, of which the lower panel in Fig. 4 shows the average. Charcoal fragments were found throughout the soil to 40 in, but none below this level, suggesting that much of the material had in fact been derived by hill wash and doubtless also by traction, since the bench must have served as a headland.

Although it would be inadvisable to attribute all of this accretion to the lynchet builders on account of the lack of dating evidence, it is nevertheless possible to estimate the amount of soil that has moved off the higher parts of the field as a consequence of man's initial and continued disturbance of the hill slope. Allowing for errors of estimation necessitated by reducing the bench section to a simple geometrical form, it can be put conservatively that around 30,000 ft^3 of soil have moved. Spread evenly over the 'denuded' part of the field, this corresponds to a layer 4 in thick. These figures do not account for losses which the bench feature may have sustained nor do they account for the disappearance of considerable quantities of clay which, at a guess, have been lost to the stream at the slope foot.

Figure 5 illustrates a complex of strip lynchets which run up-and-down the hillslope at the west end of Appletreewick, opposite Low Hall farm. The lines represent lynchet risers progressing upwards from west to east, as at Otterburn. The risers are, however, not purely or even mainly composed of displaced plough soil, but boulders and stone cleared from the strips. This would have resulted from downwastage of the soil mantle on the slope by hillwash and lateral displacement by ploughing, and would certainly account for why the risers are so well preserved. Figure 6 shows the structure of one lynchet edge and illustrates the survival of key elements such as burial of an earlier soil and its truncation on the negative lynchet below. Figure 7 illustrates the general drift of soil to the positive side of the lynchet, from which we can visualize ploughing commencing and being concluded at the foot of the riser to the next higher lynchet. The survival of plough soil is to be seen about 12 in below the surface on the positive side of the lynchets in the vicinity of point A, as a distinct layer comprising larger numbers of small pieces of limestone and also included charcoal fragments. It is

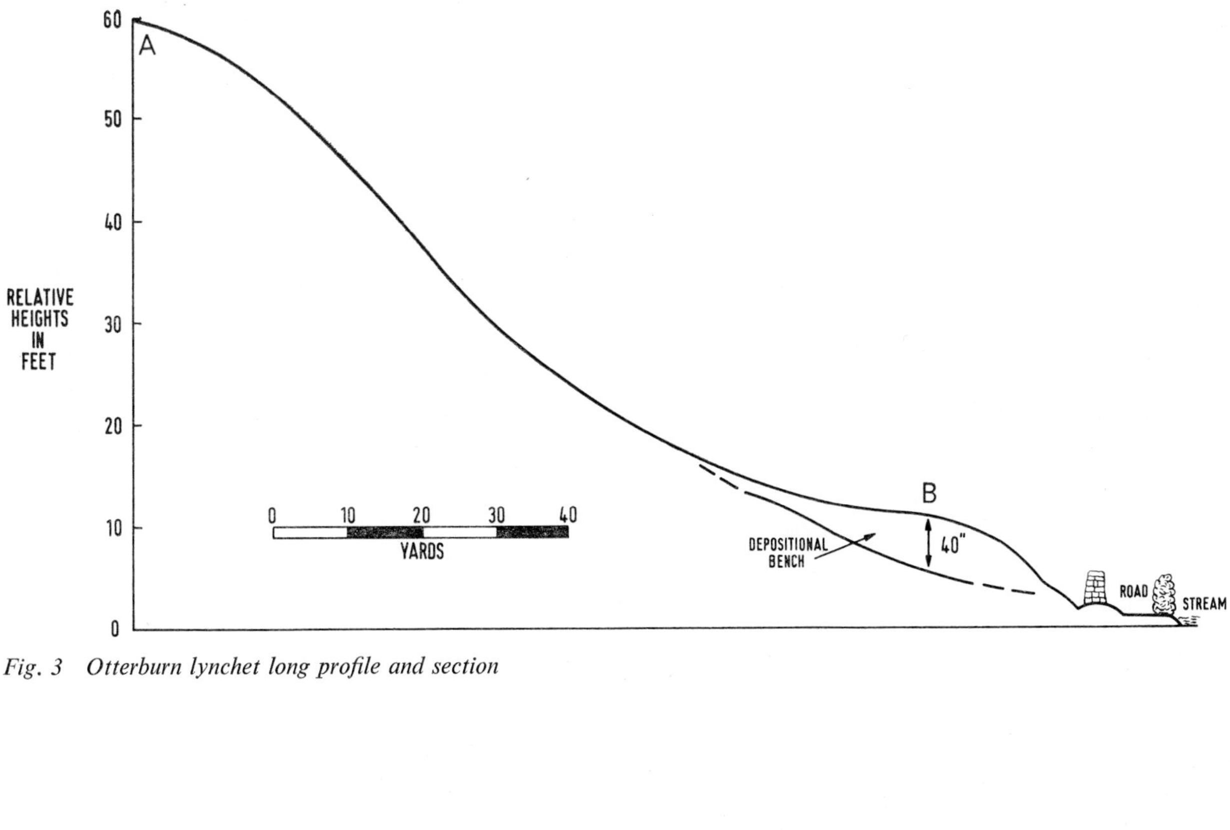

Fig. 3 Otterburn lynchet long profile and section

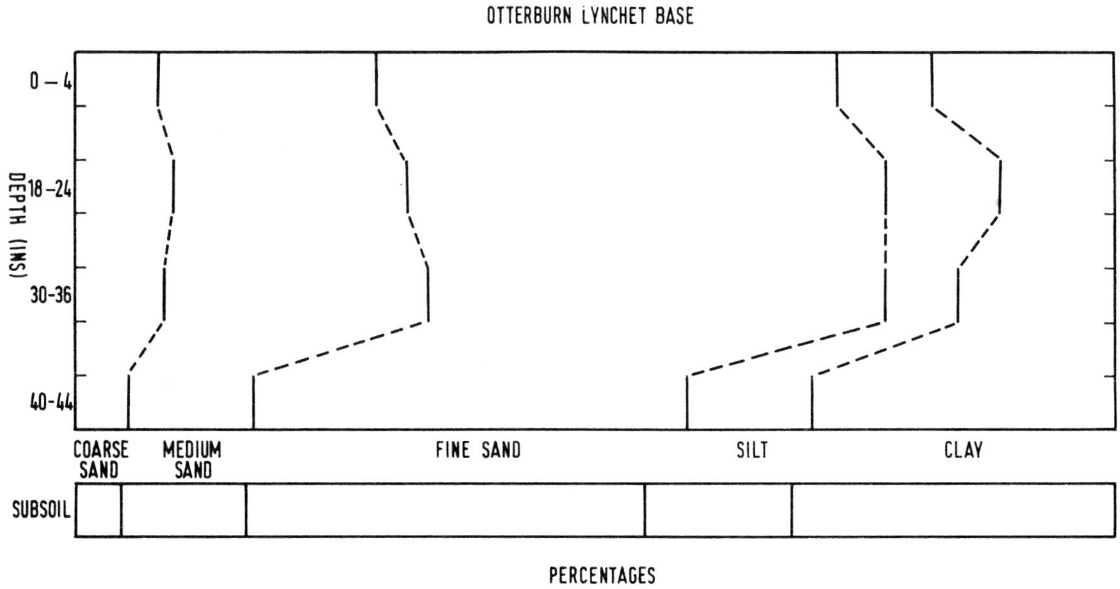

Fig. 4 Mechanical analysis data for point B *on Fig. 2*

assumed that, since these objects are all too large for earthworms to move or ingest, they will tend to sink in the soil in the course of time, a process which has unquestionably led to the apparent pile of stones on the lynchet edge being surmounted by 6–8 in of turf and organic-rich loam.

In view of the steepness of the slopes, which average around 15° and attain 22° in places, one assumes there must have been a particular attraction to these soils. Indeed, they are sandy loams which overlie reef knoll limestone, rich in phosphate (available P about 36 ppm) and, while tending now towards dryness under pasture, are south-facing and moderately sheltered. Circumstances would then have eased the toil of ploughing, but stoniness seems likely to have been a worsening feature of cultivation as time went on. There

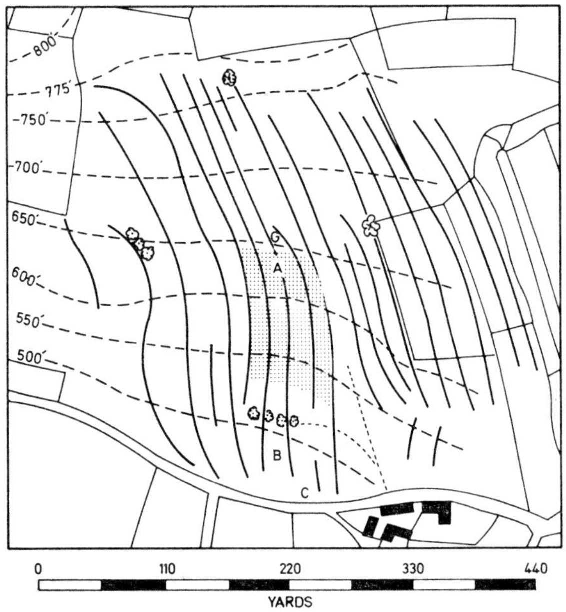

Fig. 5 Plan of lynchet hill-slope at Appletreewick

are suggestions from Figure 5 and from the less well developed lynchets in the west that subdivision of originally wider strips took place and that, as seen at point G on Fig. 5, this subdivision may have been influenced by the emergence of rocky ledges as soil was lost from the slopes. Later on, it may have been decided to use the lower slopes more intensively. What is particularly interesting is the fact that lower risers also have a stone core, illustrating that in time the slope foot area has accumulated substantial quantities of soil (Fig. 8). Soil thicknesses were at one time, therefore, apparently more uniform than at present. A major pit was excavated at point B and mechanical analyses (Fig. 9) show the sedimentary nature of the materials below about 20 in. Survival of this evidence is surprising in view of earthworms (Atkinson, 1957), yet the disturbance wrought in the subsoil is minimal, probably because of the re-use of old worm channels. Certainly most of their food would be restricted to the top soil layers, and deeper penetration would only be encouraged by cold or drought. At 15 in depth a more stony layer may have represented the last of possibly several phases of cultivation. Rock was encountered at about 52 in depth, but a pre-agricultural 'buried' soil could not be identified with certainty at this point.

At point C, pottery examined by Dr Jean le Patourel and dated between the 12th and 14th centuries was obtained from about 18 in below the surface, which may, of course, partially represent the effects of earthworm submergence previously mentioned.

On these slopes the rapid infiltration characteristics of the soil and the existence of minor breaks of slope have undoubtedly prevented soil erosion occurring on a much more massive scale.

Early use of Malham Moor

Archaeologists do, I believe, thrive on controversy and the following problem, the history of the limestone pavements above Malham village, probably represents one of the greatest intellectual (if not actual) death traps in the subject.

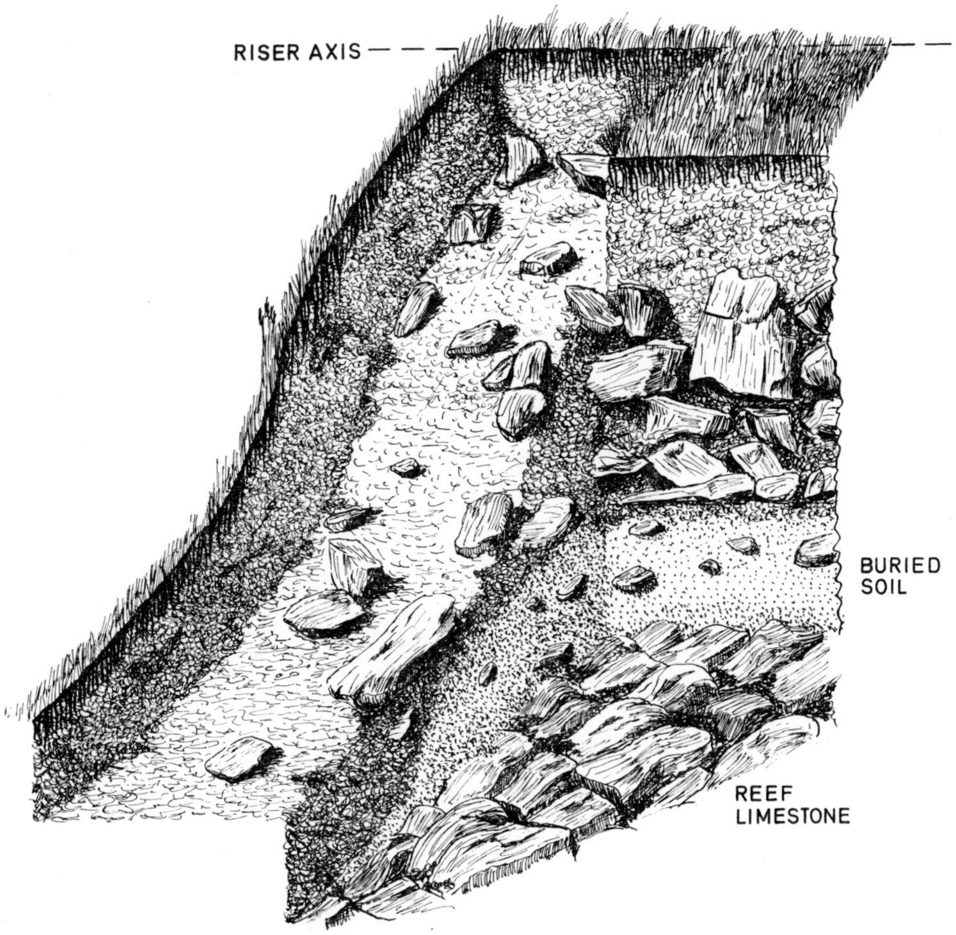

Fig. 6 Excavated lynchet riser at point A

The vegetational history of this area has been studied by M. E. and C. D. Pigott (1959), while Dr Arthur Raistrick (1929, 1939, 1962, 1971) and, more recently, Mr Alan King (1970) have studied the early settlement and land use. Figure 10 shows an attempt to allocate the principal sites to various periods but, while based on limited excavation, the remains are frequently so poorly preserved that much of the story must yet remain in the melting pot.

Between Torlery Edge and abutting on to Broad Scars is an area containing large ancient 'enclosures' and smaller walled areas either tumbled on the limestone pavement, where they are frequently difficult to trace, or partially sunk in basin areas between upstanding dry limestone areas. One such area of early stone 'lineaments' is marked on Fig. 10. From a ridge axis in the east, somewhat sinuous and discontinuous stone lines run out on to Broad Scars, terminating in an earthen grassy bank surmounted by stone. It seems that there were once at least two or three field strips within this area, which is now approximately 50% bare limestone. The lack of straight field edges is very reminiscent of the field complex at Grassington (Raistrick and Chapman, 1929), but a matter of great importance here is whether the field boundaries were to keep animals in and prevent them from straying on to dangerous areas of pavement, or were intended to keep animals off! Whether the fields were substantially barren in the first place seems highly unlikely in either context.

A number of early walls on Malham Lings utilize low rock outcrops, as if to save effort, while farmsteads and hut foundations shelter under, or even partially utilize, exposed limestone surface so that by the Roman period, at a very conservative guess, there was

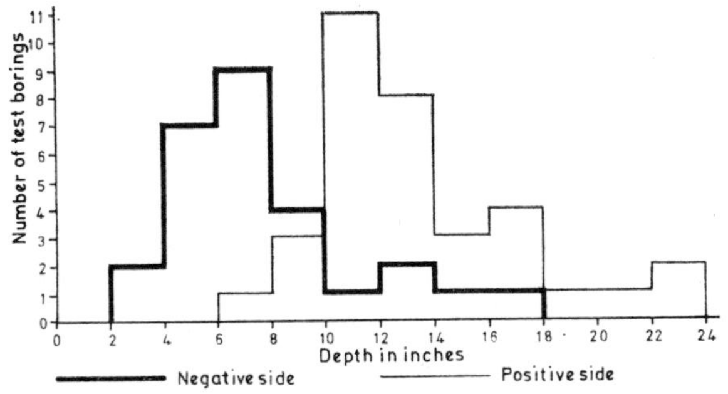

Fig. 7 Depth of lynchet soils within stippled area on Fig. 5

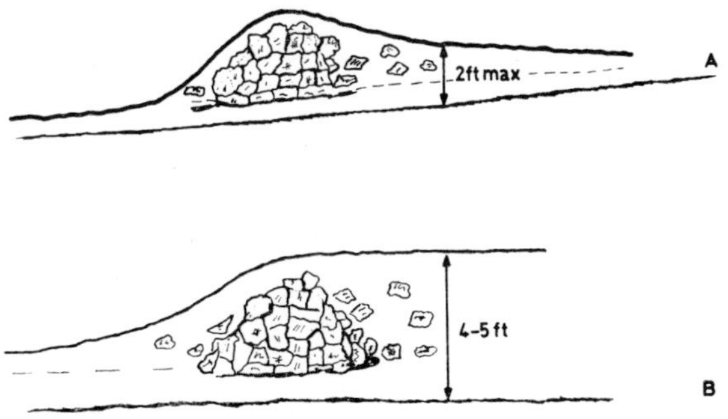

Fig. 8 Variations in lynchet riser form at Appletreewick

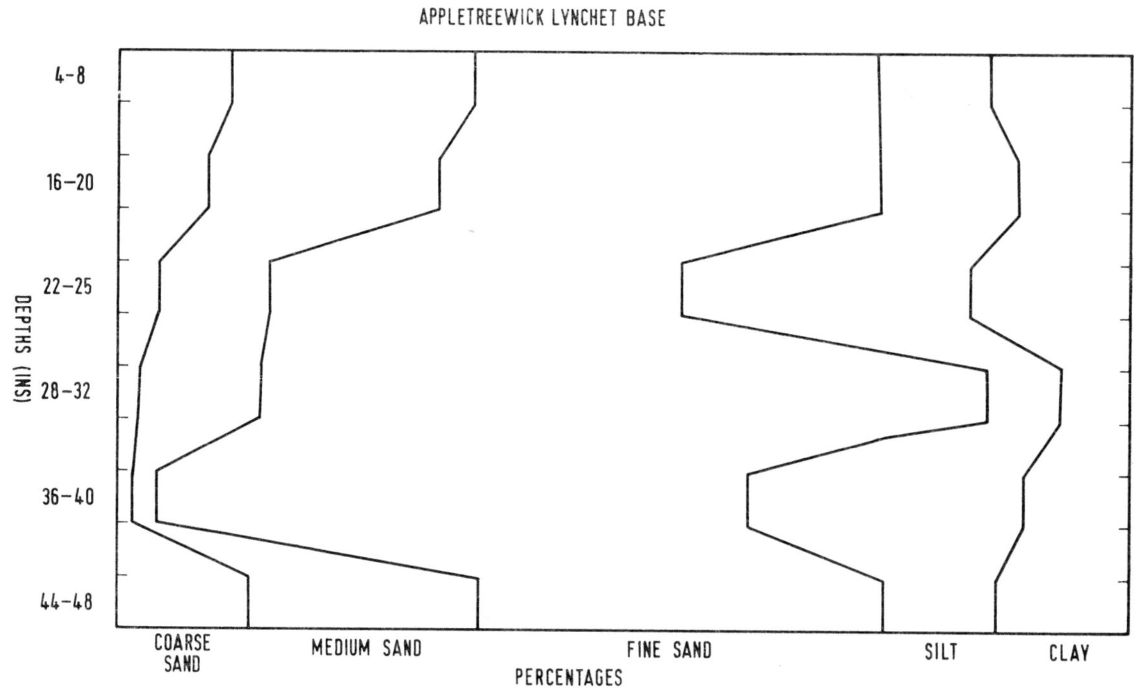

Fig. 9 Mechanical analysis data for point B *on Fig. 5*

considerable limestone already exposed. There is no doubt that the existence of much hummocky turf at the present time is due to lowering by solution. Estimates noted in Corbel (1959), Sweeting (1964), Pigott (1965), and Clayton (1966), which make rather different assumptions, propose a solution of limestone of around 3–7 cm in 1000 years. The concentration of this attack along joints and consideration of relative solubility of different limestone types could, however, explain the more rapid sinking of certain areas and the consequent emergence of limestone benches, as is observed (see Fig. 11).

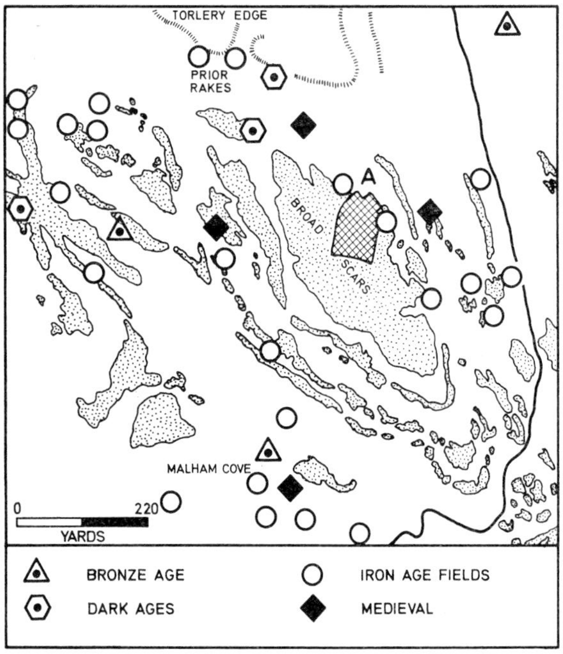

Fig. 10 Distribution of archaeological sites on Malham Moor (after Raistrick, 1962)

As regards the probability of former cultivation, if we pessimistically say that, at present, cereals will not ripen above 500 ft, and we take literally Professor Lamb's (1966) statement that annual temperatures in the Bronze Age might have been 2°C warmer than now (Manley, 1957), we see that with a standard lapse-rate of 0·6°C for every 300 ft of elevation, ripening would have been possible to well over the height of this area at 1200 ft, on the basis of macro-climate. We do not know the extent to which trees may have originally offered shelter.

The soils are light silt loams and would have been easy to cultivate with a simple ard or perhaps even less sophisticated means within original woodland openings. The mechanical composition of one soil tested was 6% coarse sand, 21% fine sand, 43% silt, and 30% clay, corroborative data being found in Bullock (1971). This material appears to have a largely loessic aeolian origin (Pigott, 1962). Using the Chepil and Woodruff (1963) formula

$$X = a \frac{I}{(RK)b}$$

erodibility x is a function of one critical soil factor I, which is the percentage of the soil over 0·84 mm in particle size. On this theoretical basis alone, where the local soil only scores 4%, the soil within the problematical fields appears most vulnerable to blowing unless the residue-roughness factor *(RK)* as denominator was kept particularly favourable.

A further point to note is that shallow soils on limestone are not necessarily very good pasture soils because of a depth limitation on moisture reserves. They would not, however, limit cereal growth, so that there may have been some conscious preference operating in the past.

A final possibility is that the Norse word *lings* was applied to an area which had been allowed to degenerate to ling or which originally had a thicker

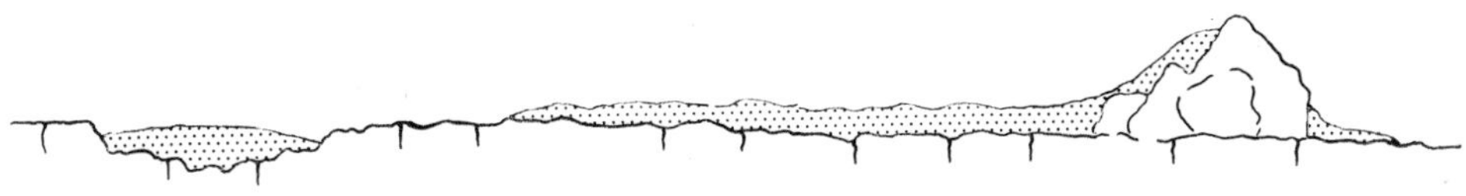

Fig. 11 *Sketch section at the edge of an ancient field on Malham Lings*

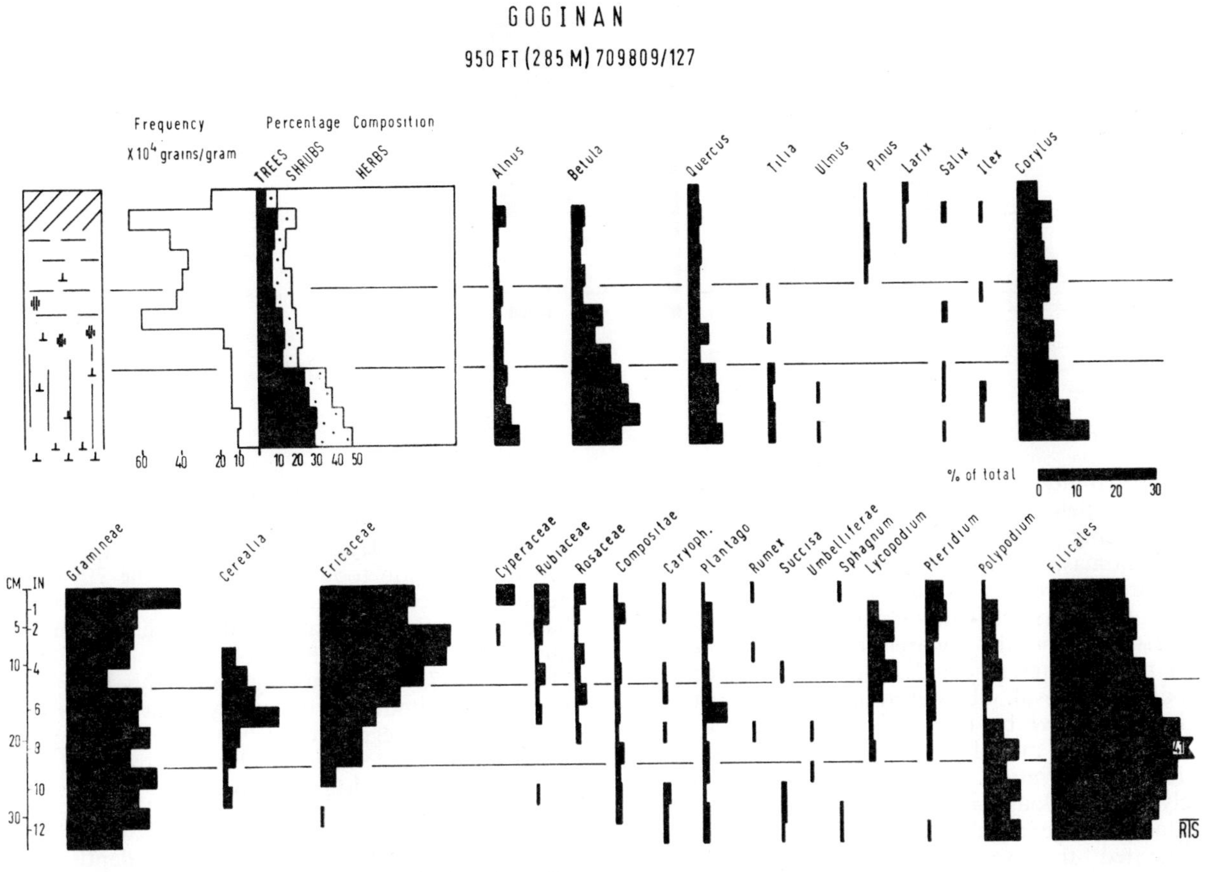

Fig. 12 *Goginan pollen diagram and stylized soil profile*

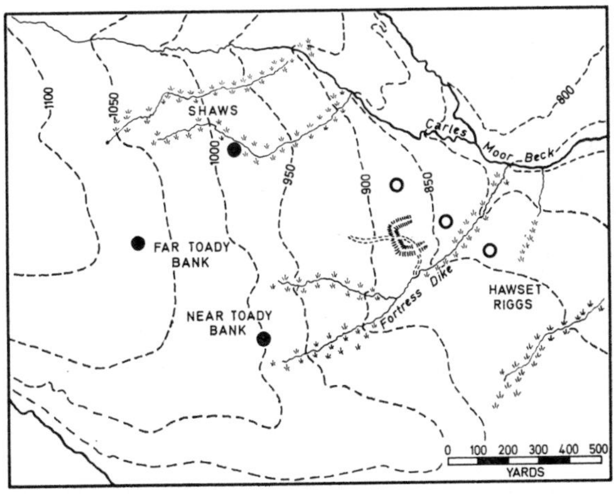

Fig. 13 *Location of Fortress Dike earthwork and selected sites*

and therefore more acidic surface soil. Since there is now a total absence of the plant up on the limestone surface, it is possible that subsequent clearance by burning was followed by severe soil losses and a large increase of calcareous habitat.

This illustrates classically how field work can generate hypotheses. A start will soon be made on the analysis of pollen from grykes and a deep peat section in Gordale Beck, which it is hoped will begin to favour one or other of these ideas.

CULTIVATION OF ACID SOILS

The first example concerns a hillslope above the village of Goginan in Cardiganshire (Smith, 1970). The soil is Denbigh series (Ball, 1963, 1966; Rudeforth, 1970), a silty clay loam developed on Silurian shales. The profile has been analysed as below:

	Coarse sand (%)	Fine sand (%)	Silt (%)	Clay (%)
0–3 in surface	21	9	42	28
6–8 in 'pan' ..	11	4	54	31
14–16 in sub-soil ..	38	9	32	21

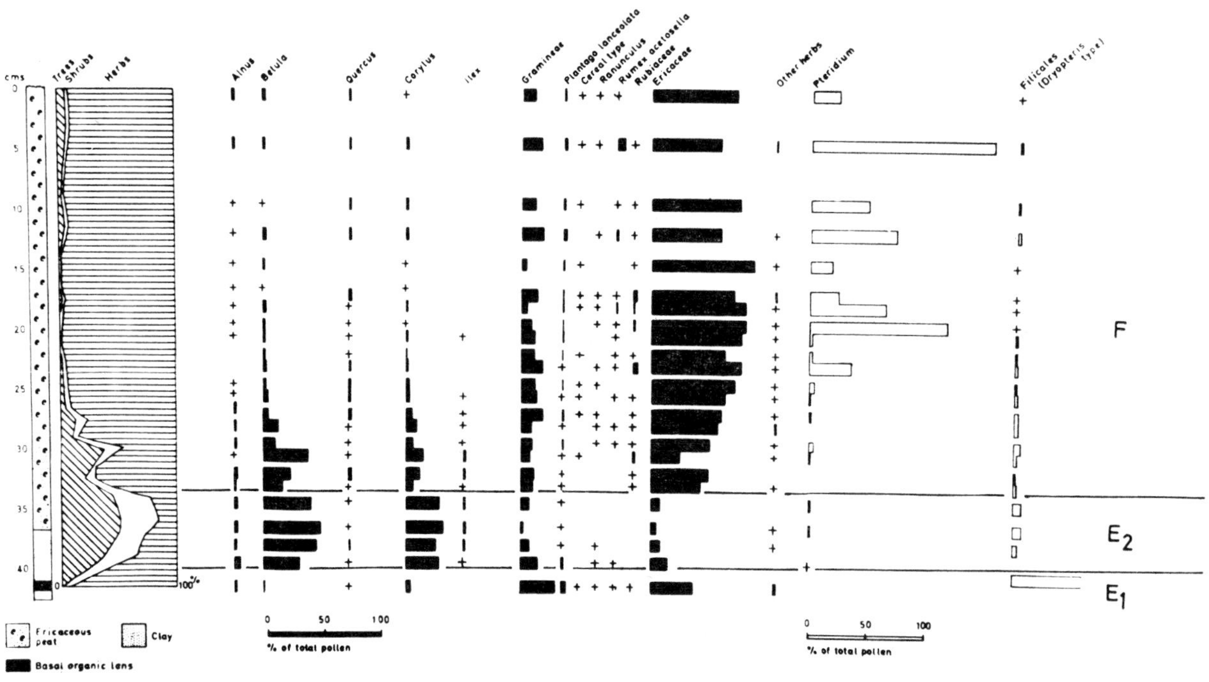

Fig. 14 Pollen diagram from the ditch at Fortress Dike

The probability is that this site, which lies within distinctive field boundaries of stone and turf, was most recently ploughed at the time of the Napoleonic wars (Thomas, 1963). The pollen data (Fig. 12) show that former cereal cultivation is separated from the present by a phase of abandonment and rise of *Calluna vulgaris* (ling), but this apparent rise of *Calluna* on the total pollen diagram could be due to 19th century woodland removal. The dating must be admitted as highly speculative, but the consistent nature of a gleyed or mottled area in mid-profile is considered indicative of former cultivation. In this fine-textured soil it is likely that a plough pan, once formed, could have created drainage impedance, which would in turn have accelerated the weathering in its vicinity, thus producing more finer-grade material.

At Fortress Dike, near Pateley Bridge, an earthwork of Romano-British affinity (Fig. 13) has been investigated (Tinsley and Smith, 1974). It appears that cereal cultivation took place here in the 7th century ad as indicated by a radiocarbon date for peat at the base of a section excavated in the ditch between inner and outer mounds (Fig. 14). The pollen record (Tinsley, 1972) illustrates that after this brief period there was a withdrawal of activity in the area as shown by woodland regeneration, but probably by later medieval times the area had been cleared and set on its course towards heather moorland.

Soil buried beneath the inner mound was a podzol with an eluvial horizon of about 4 in depth. It was while investigating the present depths of eluvial

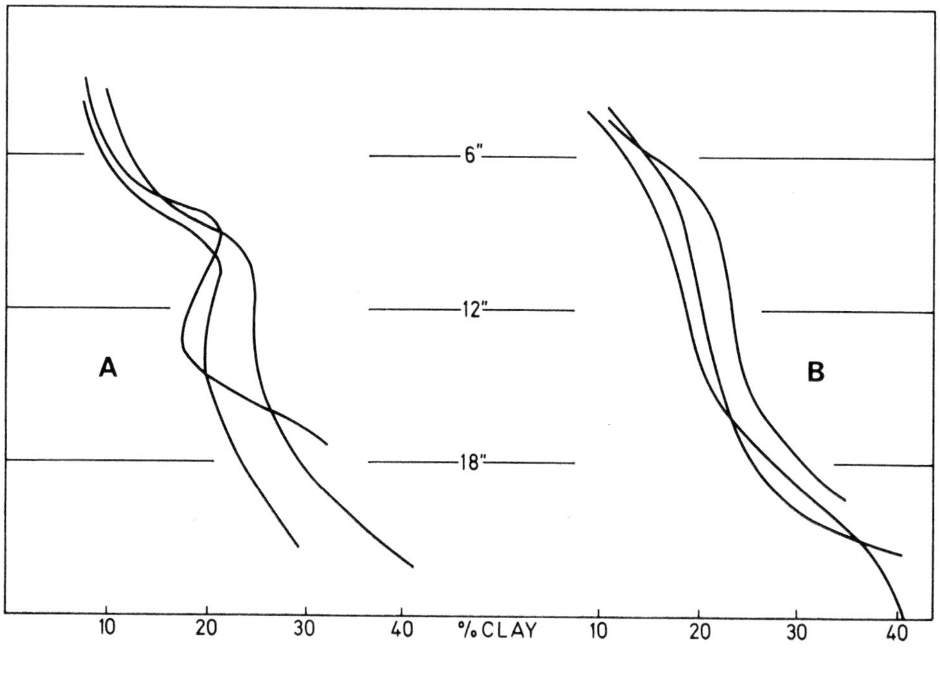

Fig. 15 Mechanical analysis data for six profiles near Fortress Dike earthwork

horizons (normally about 12 in) that I became aware that in the vicinity of the earthwork there was a more rapid build up of clay within the top 12 in of the soil. A number of pits were dug and, while almost a quarter of these were too shallow, owing to stoniness, to exhibit any normal horizonation, the sites on Fig. 13 were finally selected for mechanical analysis (Fig. 15). The results were rather more dramatic than had been my initial impression, particularly in view of the superficial peat which now overlies the surface at all sites. The curves A represent sites (open circles) around the earthwork, while the series B represent remaining moorland sites. The A curves, one assumes, illustrate the effect of former cultivation on one-time shallower, less highly differentiated podzols. They point to an accelerated movement of clay superimposed on a natural, longer-term pedological gradient, represented one assumes, by series B. It is possible that minor changes in parent materials account for these differences but it is doubtful whether even this can argue against such good agreement. That surface drainage impedance derived from this process seems possible, which may lend support to views expressed elsewhere on pedogenic peat formation (Taylor and Smith 1972).

DISCUSSION

We shall distinguish initially between degradation involving soil loss, and alteration *in situ*.

It has seemed to me that soil loss from slopes, assuming that one could define and interpret the deposited materials, provides the best opportunity for demonstrating a cause–effect linkage. The Otterburn study is an elementary extrapolation from simple measurements. Its failing lies not so much in the estimation of total gains and losses as in being unable to define the time span involved. It is, however, a simple, fairly short length of convexo-concave slope, suitable for illustrating the effects of slopewash. The lynchet slope at Appletreewick was not amenable to the same simple 'balance sheet' approach, principally because the area contributing to the slope foot deposits could not be precisely defined. The circumstances at Appletreewick did, however, allow one to see how the early farmers adjusted their field system to increasing stoniness. The scale of soil movement was assessed and insight was provided into natural factors preventing degradation of a more serious kind from occurring. Both these studies illustrate that, where accumulation takes place with the accompaniment of earthworms, particular care is needed in identifying the original ground surface.

The enigmatic situation on Malham Lings is the more absorbing because a solution on the basis of the very limited physical remains seems almost unattainable. One is faced with soil lowering by solution of underlying limestone and the possibility of surface wind erosion, both of which present an open-ended system to the investigator, in contrast to the more closed attributes of the previous examples. This particular locality above Malham Cove probably represented a well drained and relatively open terrain above densely wooded lowlands in prehistoric times, and may therefore have constituted the best land originally available for cultivation, or indeed any farming based on fields. However, the survival of walls is incidental to the broad expanse of limestone pavement. One wonders therefore whether it is simply the rate of solution which makes it appear today that man was, in the remote past, instrumental in causing local denudation. Otherwise, the possibility must remain that soil loss by deflation was promoted by progressive reduction in tree cover, which may have persisted in the deep grykes towards the edge of the limestone pavement, a view which takes note of the Pigotts' work at Malham Tarn Moss (Pigott and Pigott, 1959). Certainly the limited survival of ancient walls proves only that certain structures may have continued to have significance up to the time when this area was abandoned for habitation.

At Goginan and Fortress Dike, the degradation involves internal or *in situ* alteration of the soil. Given the pollen analytical evidence, there seems every probability that the key features arise from former ploughing rather than variations in parent material or siting. The striking fact about both is the degree of development of the plough-induced features, given the probability of very limited agricultural use. This warns against using such features as indicators of the duration of cultivation and illustrates how permanent may become the marks of former cultivation, when exploited by subsequent weathering in soils with low earthworm activity.

Following the cessation of cultivation at these and other upland sites (Smith and Taylor, 1969; Smith, 1970), reduced pressure on the land was eventually reflected in the development of heath vegetation. In fact, it is a feature of the majority of pollen records involving upland cultivation that the episodes are of limited duration and, while evidence of woodland regeneration can be seen particularly during earlier prehistory (Simmons, 1971), it is rare in the post-Roman period (Tubbs and Dimbleby, 1965; Tinsley and Smith, 1974). This must indicate the general retreat of parent woodland as much as the likelihood of soil deterioration of the kind implied by Dr Ball. In fact, linkage of former agriculture, or simply human activity, with *in situ* soil degradation tends to be as circumstantial as was the evidence cited for man-induced degradation above Malham Cove. Indeed, that cessation of agriculture was ever reliable evidence of soil impoverishment or of shifting cultivation seems doubtful, yet with limited information to the contrary, such as would be provided by population changes, it nevertheless remains as a reasonable assumption.

Recent research in hill land improvement (e.g. Eadie, 1970; Floate, 1970) paradoxically throws light on the chemical degradation of soils, the process of podzolization having been discussed by Dr Ball. There are various approaches to sward and soil improvement, but few doubt that, in order to maintain an optimum condition, the duration and intensity of grazing should be regulated. There must be an efficient utilization of, and an effective contribution to, the nutrient cycle and this applies as much to grazing systems as it does to agricultural production. When soil is cultivated there are greater nutrient demands and the nutrient cycle itself is speeded up as mineralization of organic matter is stimulated. Under upland conditions it would be almost impossible to say whether greater degradation had arisen from loss of nutrients in crops or from ineffective uptake and enhanced leaching in the arable soil.

Carrying the argument a stage further, it is perfectly legitimate to postulate that the blame for degradation lies as much, if not more, with the subsequent often protracted periods of 'abandonment' as with the specific act of cultivation. This conception of the principal degradation process in our upland soils illustrates just how separated cause and effect may become in the evolution of landscape (Smith, 1972). While discussing degradation, it is easy to overlook some of the beneficial side-effects of former agriculture. It is when considering these, however, that one becomes aware of the essentially subjective element in the definition of degradation features. This problem is illustrated at Appletreewick, where, because of soil loss from the lynchets, the shallow phosphorus- and calcium-rich stony soils sustain the growth of a more productive sward than is to be seen on neighbouring previously uncultivated land, which has experienced acidification. A similar increase in lime status seems likely to have characterized parts of Malham Moor if certain hypotheses are realistic. At Goginan it appears that former cultivation of the hillside and hilltop area has led to a reversal of soil conditions in a marginally peaty habitat, so that a brown earth with a mole population exists alongside peaty gleys and podzolized soils.

Vita-Finzi's work (1969) in the Mediterranean region has indicated amounts of erosion from slopes occurring within historical times and argues that valley siltation had some beneficial effects. It is possible to argue that contour lynchets also increased the amount of available cultivable land, though by modern standards their areal extent and accessibility are limiting. Up-and-down lynchets seem likely to have led to the build-up of deeper soils on the lower, gentler, moister and more accessible slopes.

Provoking and controversial though examples of this sort tend to be, they constitute but local and perhaps only temporary reversals within the much broader context of degradation.

CONCLUSION

It is evident that in pursuance of agriculture man caused manipulation and erosion of soils which under no other circumstances would have occurred, while in addition on-going processes were catalysed, both on sloping terrain and hill land. Man has thus tended to create high-energy environments where low-energy, more stable, and self-perpetuating systems once existed. In the effort to find such a common denominator and since the beneficial effects of man's agricultural activities have often been accidental, one may well feel inclined to agree with Hyams (1952) that, so far as soil is concerned, man's behaviour has been largely parasitic, an argument which carries no small weight at the present time.

ACKNOWLEDGEMENTS

I should like to thank my colleagues, Mr (now Professor) G. R. J. Jones and Dr S. R. Eyre, and also Mr I. P. Jones and Miss M. Faull, for discussion or assistance at various stages of this work.

Thanks are also due to Mrs B. S. Crosby for carrying out the mechanical analyses for the Appletreewick and Otterburn sites and to Mr G. Bryant and Mr T. Hadwin for the diagrams. Mr Mason of Low Hall, Appletreewick, and Mr Haggas of Grove Farm, Otterburn, are particularly to be thanked for allowing various excavations to be carried out.

REFERENCES

Atkinson, R. J. C. (1957). Worms and weathering. *Antiquity,* 31, 219–233.

Ball, D. F. (1963). *The soils and land use of the district around Bangor and Beaumaris.* Memoir, Soil Survey of England and Wales. Harpenden.

Ball, D. F. (1966). Brown podzolic soils and their status in Britain. *J. Soil Sci.,* 17, 148–158

Bowen, H. C. (1961). *Ancient fields.* London: British Assoc. Adv. Sci.

Bullock, P. (1971). The soils of the Malham Tarn Area. *Fld. Stud.,* 3, 381–408.

Chepil, W. S. and Woodruff, N. P. (1963). The physics of wind erosion and its control. *Adv. Agron.,* 15, 211–302.

Clayton, K. M. (1966). The origin of the landforms of the Malham area. *Fld. Stud.,* 2, 359–384.

Corbel, J. (1959). Erosion en terrain calcaire—vitesse d'erosion et morphologie. *Annls. Geogr.,* 68, 97–120.

Cornwall, I. W. (1958). *Soils for the archaeologist.* Phoenix.

Curwen, E. C. (1939). The plough and the origin of strip lynchets. *Antiquity,* 13, 45–52.

Dimbleby, G. W. (1962). *The development of British heathlands and their soils.* Oxford Forestry Memoir No. 23, Clarendon Press.

Dimbleby, G. W. (1965). Post glacial changes in soil profiles. *Proc. Roy. Soc.,* B, 161, 355–362.

Duchaufour, P. (1970). *Precis de pedologie.* Paris: Masson.

Eadie, J. (1970). Sheep production and pastoral resources. *In* Watson, A. (ed.). *Animal populations in relation to their food resources.* British Ecol. Soc. Symp., 10: Blackwell, 7–24.

Floate, M. J. S. (1970). Decomposition of organic materials from hill soils and pastures. *Soil Biol. Biochem.,* 2, 173.

Fowler, P. J. and Thomas, A. C. (1962). Arable fields of the pre-Norman period at Gwithian. *Cornish Archaeol.,* 1, 61–84.

Fowler, P. J. and Evans, J. G. (1967). Plough-marks, lynchets and early fields. *Antiquity,* 41, 189–301.

Hyams, E. (1952). *Soil and civilization.* Thames and Hudson.

King, A. (1970). *Early Pennine settlement.* Dalesman Publ. Co.

Lamb, H. H., *et al.* (1966). Atmospheric circulation and the main climatic variables between 8000 and 0 BC. *In* Sawyer, J. S. (ed.). *World Climate from 8000 to 0 B.C.* Roy. Met. Soc., 174–217.

Manley, G. (1957). The climate at Malham Tarn. *Ann. Rep. Field Studies Council, 1955–1956.*

Pennington, W. (1964). Pollen analyses from the deposits of six upland tarns in the Lake District. *Phil. Trans. Roy. Soc.,* B, 248, 205–244.

Pennington, W. (1970). Vegetational history in north west England. *In* Walker, D. and West, R. G. (eds.). *Studies in the vegetational history of the British Isles.* Cambridge.

Pigott, C. D. (1962). Soil formation and development on the Carboniferous Limestone of Derbyshire. *J. Ecol.,* 50, 145–155.

Pigott, C. D. (1965). The structure of limestone surfaces in Derbyshire. *Geogr. J.,* 131, 41–44.

Pigott, M. E. and Pigott, C. D. (1959). Stratigraphy and pollen analysis of Malham Tarn and Tarn Moss. *Fld. Stud.,* 1, 84–101.

Raistrick, A. (1929). The Bronze Age in West Yorkshire. *Yorkshire Archaeol. J.,* 29, 354–365.

Raistrick, A. (1939). Iron Age settlements in West Yorkshire. *Yorkshire Archaeol. J.,* 34, 115–150.

Raistrick, A. (1971). *Malham and Malham Moor.* Dalesman Publ. Co.

Raistrick, A. and Chapman, S. E. (1929). The lynchet groups of upper Wharfedale. *Antiquity,* 3, 165–181.
Raistrick, A. and Holmes, P. F. (1962). Archaeology of Malham Moor. *Fld. Stud.,* 1, 73–100.
Rudeforth, C. C. (1970). *The Soils of North Cardiganshire.* Memoir, Soil Survey of England and Wales. Harpenden.
Simmons, I. G. (ed.). (1971). *The Yorkshire Dales.* National Park Guide No. 9, H.M.S.O.
Smith, R. T. (1970). *Studies in the post-glacial soil and vegetation history of the Aberystwyth area.* Unpubl. Ph.D. Thesis, University of Wales.
Smith, R. T. (1972). A reconsideration of the role of climate in the development of post-Weichselian forest types. *In* Taylor, J. A. (ed.). *Research papers in forest meteorology.* Aberystwyth.
Smith, R. T. and Taylor, J. A. (1969). The post-glacial development of vegetation and soils in northern Cardiganshire. *Trans. Inst. Brit. Geogr.,* 48, 75–96.
Sweeting, M. M. (1964). Some factors in the absolute denudation of limestone terrains. *Erdkunde,* 18, 92–95.
Taylor, J. A. and Smith, R. T. (1972). Climatic peat—a misnomer? *Proc. 4th Int. Peat Congress. I-IV* Helsinki; 471–484.
Tinsley, H. M. (1973). *A palynological study of changing woodland limits on the Nidderdale moors.* Unpubl. Ph.D. Thesis, University of Leeds.
Tinsley, H. M. and Smith, R. T. (1974). Ecological investigations at a Romano-British earthwork in the Yorkshire Pennines. *Yorkshire Archaeol. J.,* 46, 23–33.
Thomas, A. C. (1969). Bronze Age spade marks at Gwithian, Cornwall. *In* Gailey, A. and Fenton, A. (eds.). *The Spade in Northern and Atlantic Europe.* Belfast.
Thomas, D. (1963). *Agriculture in Wales during the Napoleonic wars.* Univ. Wales Press.
Tubbs, C. R. and Dimbleby, G. W. (1965). Early agriculture in the New Forest. *Advan. Sci.,* 88–97.
Turner, J. (1970). Post-Neolithic disturbance of British vegetation. *In* Walker, D. and West, R. G. (eds). *Studies in the vegetational history of the British Isles.* Cambridge: University Press.
Vita-Finzi, C. (1969). *The Mediterranean valleys.* Cambridge.
Wood, P. D. (1961) Strip lynchets reconsidered. *Geogr. J.,* 127, 449–459.

Soils and archaeology in Scotland

J. C. C. Romans and L. Robertson

Synopsis

Nine soil profiles, either buried or otherwise preserved in an archaeological context which span the period from Early Neolithic to Iron Age–Roman times, are described. Attention is drawn to micromorphological features present in certain Neolithic soils which may be associated with short-term 'slash and burn' cultivation and to their absence at another site where a more prolonged period of agricultural activity is probable. The nine soil profiles are thereafter linked chronologically to illustrate the progressive evolution of freely drained lowland soils on the drier eastern side of Scotland from brown forest soils to podzols over the last 5000 years. Some regional variations are noted.

During the past 24 years, the soils exposed by excavation at a number of archaeological sites in northern Scotland have been examined. This conference provides an opportunity to review the accumulated evidence as it pertains to the progressive evolution of the soil profile. Chronologically the earliest records are from Neolithic sites dating back to around 5,000 years ago, with secondary features of Beaker Age. These are linked to a later group spanning the Iron Age to Roman period from *c.* 400 BC to 300 AD, by records from a single Bronze Age site.

Three Neolithic sites on the eastern side of Scotland include a barrow at Daladies near Edzell in Angus, built on a fluvioglacial gravel terrace about 40 m OD, excavated by Professor S. Piggott; a burial mound, near Boghead Farm at Fochabers in Morayshire, placed on a small stream side terrace cut into morainic sand and gravel at about 60 m, excavated by Miss A. S. Henshall; and a substantial stone circle at Raigmore, Inverness, set on the sandy raised beach at about 18 m, excavated by Mr D. D. A. Simpson. The fossil soil profiles buried below the mounds at Edzell (Romans *et al.,* 1973) and Fochabers are very similar. Both were acid brown forest soils with oak charcoal present in the A horizons, together with very minor amounts of oriented clay which had been deposited in pores within the upper 10 cm of the profile subsequent to the introduction of the oak charcoal. These are features which would be consistent with 'slash and burn' cultivation in a deciduous forest in which oak was an important constituent. At Edzell the barrow site and contiguous ground were until recently under cultivation, but the profile exposed in nearby gravel pit sections is a podzol (with thin iron pan present locally). At the Fochabers site the present-day soil is a humus podzol which is continuously developed over the upper surface of the Neolithic burial mound, and over a peripheral Beaker burial. The same profile is extensively exposed in nearby forest road sections. The stone circle at Raigmore has been dated to about 1600 BC with the underlying settlement at about 3000 BC (Anon, 1973). When the largest stones in the SW quadrant at Raigmore were removed, the soil profile exposed resembled the buried soil at Fochabers, but charcoal was scarce. Microscopic examination indicated that no oriented clay and only one piece of oak charcoal was present in thin sections prepared from the buried soil, though some additional charcoal from a disturbed 'occupation site' uncovered below one of the stones may be derived from Scots pine.

On the Isle of Arran a podzol profile was found below a substantial mound of accumulated debris in the forecourt area at Monamore Chambered Cairn near Lamlash (Mackie, 1963–64). The profile was developed on a fine sandy loam till derived from sandstone and felsite and located on a hillside terrace at about 125 m OD. Carbon-14 datings from this site suggest that the podzol profile was contemporaneous with the brown forest soil at Daladies.

The Bronze Age site was at Almond Bank near Perth. Ten cist graves that were exposed during the opening up of a new gravel pit were excavated and recorded by Mrs M. E. C. Stewart. No buried soil was seen, but one of the samples examined was packing material taken from between the headstone of cist X and the side of the grave. This sample has been examined microscopically and appears to be mixed-up material from the surface layers of a Bronze Age soil. The genetic characteristics of the Almond Bank soil closely resemble those of an intergrade between an acid brown soil and a podzol, and this is confirmed by comparison with soils of the Ettrick Association previously examined from profile sites in Midlothian.

The present day vegetation on the most closely comparable Midlothian site is *Calluna vulgaris* with *Nardus stricta* and *Molinia caerulea*. Pollen in the Bronze Age soil was very scarce. The species represented included members of the Gramineae and Ericaceae with some ferns and traces of birch, hazel, alder, sedges, mosses, and herbs. The total pollen count is too low to be regarded as significant, but the assemblage is not at variance with a probable vegetation deduced from examination of soil thin sections. Charcoal recovered from the graves included oak, probably hazel, and other unidentified species, so that, whilst the microscopic evidence suggests cleared land kept open by human influence and perhaps by grazing, there was certainly nearby deciduous woodland which included oak trees of moderate size (annual ring width of oak charcoal was *c.* 3 mm).

Iron Age and Roman sites have provided evidence that podzolic soils by that time were widespread. At Dalnaglar in north-east Perthshire (Stewart, 1961-62) the soil uncovered below the wall of a circular enclosure at an altitude of about 325 m, though not entirely undisturbed, appeared to have the B horizon characteristics of a podzol or brown podzolic soil. At Kilphedir at an altitude of about 130 m in the Strath of Kildonan, Sutherland, it was evident that the indurated B_3 horizon of a podzol, with a thin iron pan developed on its upper surface, had formed the floor of an excavated hut circle (Fairhurst, 1970-71), and that there had been further development of thin iron pan in overlying occupation debris, so dating the transition from podzol to peaty podzol with thin iron pan at this site.

The Roman marching camp at Kirkbuddo in Angus lies about 8 km south-south-east of Forfar at about 145 m OD, and was probably constructed between AD 140 and 211. The buried soil below the earth bank surrounding the camp was found to be a podzol (Romans, 1962), and the morphological indications were that this type of profile had been developing for at least hundreds, and possibly over a thousand, years before the camp was built. Examination of soil thin sections, which were subsequently prepared, suggested that an acid brown soil had been present prior to the onset of podzolization, and that the acid brown soil was genetically somewhat similar to that identified at Almond Bank. The indications of podzolization at Kirkbuddo were confirmed in a forest road cutting across the line of a Roman road in Parkneuk Wood about 7 km east-south-east of Crieff in Perthshire, at an altitude of *c.* 55 m.A bleached podzolic A_2g horizon overlying imperfectly drained subsoil was present beneath the foundation of the Roman road.

From these scattered observations, an incomplete outline pattern is beginning to emerge, suggesting that in north-east Scotland about 5,000 years ago brown forest soils under a mixed deciduous forest (within which oak was an important constituent) had developed on free-draining moraines, fluvioglacial outwash sands and gravels around the margins of the main mass of the Grampian Mountains, and had extended along the fluvioglacial terraces of the main through valley systems and on to sandy high raised beaches. These soils proved attractive to an immigrant population with agricultural experience, whose activities are reflected both in direct site evidence of slash and burn procedures, and in a general correlation between flat sandy soils, which 5,000 years ago might have been rated as Class I arable land (Bibby *et al.*, 1964) and the distribution of stone circles (particularly along the Moray coastal plain and along the higher sandy terraces of the Rivers Spey and Avon).

On the higher hillslopes at altitudes between 450 and 600 m, the presence of contemporaneous podzolic soils is confirmed by the survival of bleached A_2 and ochreous B horizons below the lower surface of the blanket peat. A vegetation dominated by pine and heather with juniper was most probable. The concentration of pine forests around and particularly to the north of the Cairngorm Mountains has been demonstrated in regional pollen studies by Durno (1967) and confirmed by radiocarbon dating of pine stumps by Pears (1972). On lower slopes of valley sides, brown podzolic soils under birch woodland were most probably present (Romans, 1970).

In the Western Highlands much less direct evidence is available, but the buried soil at Monamore does at least show that podzolization had already extended to low level sites at the time of Neolithic settlement, and must reflect the high rainfall on the western seaboard rather than human influence on soil and vegetation.

Turning again to north-east Scotland, it is clear that, on the low-lying, free-draining, light-textured parent materials a transition from brown forest soil to podzol took place somewhat later in time than the peripheral Beaker burial in the mound at Fochabers, and later than the building of the Raigmore stone circle. At Fochabers there is no evidence for more than a single interlude of forest clearance exploiting a small terrace within an area of moundy morainic topography. At Raigmore there is a broad stretch of level sandy raised beach. The comparative scarcity of charcoal and the complete absence of oriented clay from the surface layers of the 'fossil' soil taken with direct site evidence of human occupation suggest that the local forest had been cleared and regeneration prevented for some time before the circle itself was built. As an occupation time span of at least 1,500 years is indicated by the archaeological evidence, it is quite remarkable that these low-base status sandy soils did not podzolize more quickly. This invites speculation that agricultural management practices in the more intensively settled areas during the Neolithic–Beaker period may have been more advanced than has previously been appreciated. At Almond Bank in Perthshire there were indications of cleared ground and of a Bronze Age soil intermediate between an acid brown soil and a podzol, with deciduous woodland not far away. At Daladies near Edzell there was no site evidence to date the change from brown forest soil to podzol, but considering that even today freely drained soils in Angus and Kincardineshire tend to have more strongly developed podzolic horizons (particularly the indurated B_3 horizon) than is usual in the Perth–Dunkeld area, it may be reasonably supposed that the change took place earlier at Daladies than at Almond Bank.

The morphology of the humus podzol developed at Fochabers includes a deep-down tonguing of the bleached A_2 and underlying dark-brown humus-iron B horizons at intervals along the exposed sections. This is a feature particularly reminiscent of the humus podzols found in remnant areas of the Old Caledonian Pine Forest around the Cairngorm Mountains and is not unlike the 'egg-cup podzols' found below the isolated stumps of large Kauri pine trees in New Zealand (Luke, 1968). If this analogy is accepted, it would imply that formation of the humus podzol in the Moray coastal region was associated with colonization of the now leached soils by a pioneer generation of Scots pine trees after long cultivation had exhausted the fertility. At Fochabers some of the tongues have been modified by a rise in the ground-water table which has redeposited B horizon material as concretionary iron around the tips of the deeper tongues. If this rise in the ground-water level (also noted at Daladies and at Almond Bank) can be equated with increased rainfall during the Sub-Atlantic period (post-2,500 years ago), it would confirm that podzolization of the light sandy soils was well advanced before the onset of wetter Sub-Atlantic climatic conditions and must have begun during the Bronze Age.

On the heavier soils developed on glacial tills derived from sediments and lavas of Old Red Sandstone age, which are predominant in Strathmore from Perth to the east coast, the transition from brown forest soil to podzol must generally have been later. The evidence from Kirkbuddo on this point is inconclusive, but a discontinuous marl bed of Sub-Atlantic age present in the upper layers of the peat at nearby Restenneth Moss may represent calcium carborate leached from the B and C horizons of brown forest soils in the surrounding catchment area. Most of the red tills of Strathmore were originally slightly calcareous, and carbonate can still be detected locally 6–8 ft below ground surface.

ACKNOWLEDGEMENT

The authors wish to thank Dr S. E. Durno of the Department of Pedology, Macaulay Institute for Soil Research, for access to unpublished pollen analyses.

REFERENCES

Bibby, J. S. and Mackney, D. (1969). *Land Use Capability Classification.* Tech. Monogr. Soil Surv. Gr. Br. No. 1.

Durno, S. E. (1967). *Scottish Woodland History since Boreal Time.* Unpubl. Ph.D. Thesis, University of Aberdeen.

Fairhurst, H. and Taylor, D. B. (1970–71). A Hut Circle Settlement at Kilphedir, Sutherland. *Proc. Soc. Antiq. Scot.,* 103, 65–99.

Luke, J. (ed.). (1968). Soils of New Zealand. *Soil Bur. Bull. N.Z.,* 26(1), 64.

Mackie, E. W. (1963–64). New excavations on the Monamore Neolithic chambered cairn, Lamlash, Isle of Arran, in 1961. *Proc. Soc. Antiq. Scot.,* 97, 1–34.

Pears, N. V. (1972). Interpretation problems in the study of tree-line fluctuations. *Forest Meteorology,* 31–45.

Press and Journal (Aberdeen) (15th August 1973). No. 37005.

Romans, J. C. C. (1962). The origin of the indurated B_3 horizon of podzolic soils in North-east Scotland. *J. Soil Sci.,* 13, 141–147.

Romans, J. C. C. (1970). Podzolisation in a zonal and altitudinal context in Scotland. *Welsh Soils Discuss Grp.,* 11, 88–101.

Romans, J. C. C., Durno, S. E. and Robertson, L. (1973). A fossil brown forest soil from Angus. *J. Soil Sci.,* 24, 125–128.

Stewart, M. E. C. (1961–62). The excavation of two circular enclosures at Dalnaglar, Perthshire. *Proc. Soc. Antiq. Scot.,* 95. 134–158.

The ecology and behaviour of deer in relation to their impact on the environment of prehistoric Britain

R. E. Chaplin

Synopsis

There are features of the social structure, biology, and behaviour of the red, fallow, and reindeer in contrast to that of roe and elk that may have predisposed them to management by early man. These are described and discussed. A number of the management techniques available to prehistoric man could have affected the spectrum of plant species and the cycle of woodland regeneration. The existence of such a management system has not been demonstrated, but the more sophisticated techniques of palaeozoological and palaeobotanical analysis now available should enable such activities to be recognized.

Our knowledge of the biology and ecology of our largest terrestrial mammals is of very recent date and is still extremely incomplete. Much of the literature on deer and other game species is derived from hunters' tales and owes little to critical observation or analysis. There are a number of reservations that must be made about applying the data from modern species to those in the past. Over the last five to ten millennia, the pressures on our species have been highly selective. Our residual gene pool has survived against selective human pressure for a reduction and modification of the natural habitat parallel with climatic and related variations.

In many parts of Europe, by the 18th and 19th centuries AD, deer had been exterminated over large areas and subsequently deer from elsewhere were introduced to restock the land for hunting purposes. Also, additional blood lines have been introduced to existing herds to 'improve' upon Nature's own selection (Whitehead, 1964, 1972).

Many populations survive in very artificial environments. A good example of these are the roe deer in many parts of Germany. Here a large number of roe deer are managed under Government supervision with the backing of a long hunting tradition. Thus in the high forests deer are given artificial feed in the winter, when natural forage is insufficient and they are not molested when they leave the forests to feed on farm crops as the farmer is well compensated for any damage done. This, combined with the regulation of the age and sex structure of the population to a male : female ratio of 1 : 1, gives rise to what many would consider a highly artificial age and sex structure, population level, and behavioural activity.

Alien plants and animals also complicate the situation. Our forests are now very different from what they were. The mosaic of deciduous and coniferous species has to a large extent been replaced by that of coniferous monoculture. Some deer are very adaptable and all (but notably the roe) have made great use of the early stages of the new softwood forests. But as the canopy forms and occludes the ground cover and with it the key food plants, the local populations are reduced.

The alien species of deer recently introduced to this country do not at this moment concern us. It could be a very different situation in 20 years' time. On the prehistoric scale we must, however, consider as alien the fallow deer, apparently introduced to this country in Roman times. The fallow deer has adapted itself well to the habitat and problems of the agricultural and technological landscape. When red and roe dwindled and bear and wolf became extinct, the fallow maintained numerous residual populations. It is now ubiquitous in England and Scotland, less so in Wales (Whitehead, 1964). Because of the long period of interaction of red, roe, and fallow deer, it is almost impossible to consider the original red/roe relationship in Britain and much of Western Europe without the effect of this interaction.

Finally, we should not forget that now most of the less endearing members of the fauna—the bear, boar, wild cattle, wolf, etc.—have long been extinct in the British Isles and man has been the sole large predator. I would not, however, wish to imply that it was impossible or foolhardy to attempt a reasoned assessment of the biology and ecology of the early populations as long as this is done and read with an awareness of the problems. In fact, the more I learn about the biology and behaviour of these animals, the more certain I am that the overall pattern of the key parameters of population biology can in many cases be validly extrapolated backwards.

In the present Post-glacial phase, four species of deer—reindeer (*Rangifer tarandus*), elk (*Alces alces*), red (*Cervus elaphus*), and roe (*Capreolus capreolus*)—were naturally present in Britain. Two of these (the elk and the reindeer) were transient, being a part of a faunal complex not associated with the climax vegetation of most of Britain. The red and the roe are typically widespread in mixed woodland associations. The real upland zones, by virtue of their natural vegetation, would be the areas in which the two faunas would interdigitate and interact.

Today the reindeer has a circumpolar distribution within the tundra-forest margin zone. In Canada and much of Russia it is wild, but in Northern Scandinavia it has for centuries been semi-domesticated (Whitehead, 1972). The Canadian and Russian data may therefore be the most suitable basis for prehistoric models. Both woodland and tundra forms of the reindeer are recognizable in the flesh, but less so from their bones. The woodland form is probably a secondary adaptation of the species and is to be expected on purely biological grounds. Reindeer are ground feeders and browsers and depend particularly on lichens and other ground plants for the bulk of their food at certain seasons, but available shrubs and trees will not be spared.

The reindeer is a sociable animal forming large herds. The abundance, herd behaviour, and regular seasonal migration of the reindeer make them an ideal quarry for early hunters and predisposes them for incipient domestication. Migration has evolved because of the seasonal nature of the habitat. When considering the movement of the reindeer, that which in the Tundra may mean a 600-mile walk may, as in the Cairngorms, be achieved by a 2000 ft climb. Ecologically, uplands are a condensation of biotic events normally found over vast horizontal distances. Recent investigations of the reindeer in the wild (Henshaw, 1969) have revealed complex behavioural patterns associated with a differential antler cycle between males, females, and juveniles. In feeding situations, dominance is associated with antlers. Males cast their antlers in December and do not begin the regrowth until Spring, as do juveniles. This and related behaviour patterns are strikingly different from those of other deer and emphasize the long period over which this complex physiological and behavioural system has evolved as an adaptation to tundra conditions. It incidentally places the reindeer clearly into this Tundra/forest fringe habitat.

The elk (*Alces alces*) is the largest of the cervidae, with an adult European male weighing perhaps 500 kg. The distribution of the elk is circumpolar but in the New World it is called a moose. The favoured habitat is extensive areas of woodland and scrub, and it is particularly numerous in parts of Canada, Russia, and Europe where the birch-pine associations are found through the broad band of lakes and moraine deposits. It is intolerant under present pressures of an open landscape. It was formerly numerous throughout the northern forests but is now less so, and has disappeared from the southern edges of its former distribution (Whitehead, 1972).

Elk feed on a broad spectrum of deciduous shrubs and herbs and also on aquatic plants, for which they will dive up to 20 ft below the surface. In winter the main foods are the bark and twigs of both deciduous and coniferous species. It is able to feed on trees up to about 7 m high by leaning on them.

The species is not highly sociable and is essentially solitary or family-unit-oriented. It is sedentary, occupying a broad feeding range to cover winter and summer needs. Surprisingly for such a large animal, it normally calves first at 2 years of age and twins are usual. Population growth in the right habitat can be explosive.

The red deer (*Cervus elaphus*) is also circumpolar in distribution, being found throughout the deciduous woodland and equivalent plant associations across Europe, Asia, and North America (where it is known as the wapiti). In Europe the most northerly populations are found in Southern Norway, Sweden, Finland, and the British Isles. Southwards it extends through North Africa and the Middle East (Whitehead, 1972). There is a considerable variation in size and general characteristics of populations over this range. The largest are those of the forests of central and eastern Europe, which contrast with those in harsher environments such as the present Scottish Highlands.

The red deer is very adaptable. The change in the British red deer in Post-glacial times from large to smaller forms is well attested archaeologically, and this is associated with the change from a woodland to a hill habitat brought about by human activity. In the highland areas there is a movement of the herds between summer and winter ranges which is a response to the climate and food supply (Darling, 1937). The performance of hill red deer, by which I mean growth rates, density, recruitment, and fecundity, are all much lower than those of the lowland forests. A female in the hills will calve for the first time at 3–4 years rather than at 2. There are years when they will be barren and the calf success rates run at only about 33% of all females (Mitchell, 1969). In lowland woodland, annual breeding and an 80–90% recruitment are more normal.

All races of red deer have a strong social structure, forming small herds of females and young males and separate groups of mature males for most of the year. Both herds occupy a discrete seasonal range in response to climate and food supply.

The roe deer has the widest latitudinal distribution of the European deer, being found in forest habitats from Northern Sweden and Finland southwards to the Mediterranean. Its range is continuous across Russia into China and Korea, with two main sub-species recognized beyond the Urals (Whitehead, 1972). It is the smallest of the European deer, standing 64–74 cm at the shoulder and weighing about 35 kg.

Roe flourish only in woodland cover or areas free of disturbance and have their greatest density in the earlier stages of forest growth or regeneration. They are essentially solitary animals and do not form large social groups (Prior, 1968). Bucks are polygamous but do not form rutting herds as do red deer and reindeer. Roe deer populations are capable of rapid growth, as females give birth for the first time at 2 years of age, and 1–2 young is normal. In a sample drawn from 27 populations in England and Scotland, 63% of the animals had two or more foetuses (Chaplin, in lit.).

The fallow deer (*Dama dama*) is almost certainly a Roman introduction, but I will mention it briefly here as it aids a later discussion. It has been very successful in adapting to human pressures. It is a social species with generally distinct adult male, female, and juvenile groups and sub-groups occupying a limited geographical range (Chaplin and White, 1970).

For the greater part of their range, red and roe deer are found in the mixed woodlands of Europe. Their numbers and density are set by the winter capacity of their range, social behaviour, and disease and predation.

All the deer that I have mentioned will be attracted to woodland glades and early stages of woodland growth. They are all grazers and browsers, and mature woodland where the ground cover is shaded out is unattractive.

In grown coniferous forests in upland Britain, roe deer management aims at one deer to about 80 acres (32 ha) to reduce tree damage. In contrast, if one overlooks tree damage, an open forest area may support one roe to every 2 acres or less. Deer are opportunists and will take what is there.

Individual roe and elk can be tamed but they are not known to have been domesticated on any scale until recently (Yazan and Knorre, 1964). By contrast red, fallow, and reindeer have all been domesticated in various ways. In particular, free-ranging populations have for centuries been manipulated and managed (Whitehead, 1950). The latter have survived man's onslaught far better than did the roe and elk until they received specific protection. The other large grazers of the forest—bison, aurochs, and pig—were not very successful either, but it may be misleading to link them in this context.

The only constant feature that marks out red, reindeer, and fallow deer from the others is their herd behaviour and discrete but extensive territorial range. The more fecund elk and roe with their non-herd social grouping and more specific ecological needs have not done so well in this Post-glacial.

Although in certain situations elk and roe may congregate on a common feed lot, they behave as individuals. By contrast fallow deer and reindeer are found in and act in social units. Within their range the herd has a significant degree of stability and predictability.

The carrying capacity of deer range can be increased by manipulating the vegetation, the simplest technique for which is fire. The growth following a forest fire is very attractive to all wild grazers. I doubt if the grazing population will entirely prevent regeneration, but it will slow it down and regeneration could be selective (see, for example, Stitcher and Shaw (1966) for a study of the utilization of herbs and browse by whitetail deer and its consequences).

Herd productivity may also be increased by the selective culling of male animals. In polygamous species of deer the males are fertile as yearlings, and a ratio of about 4 breeding males of graded age to 30 females are all that are necessary to ensure optimum productivity in the female.

Age is a key factor in wildlife management, and the size and complexity of the antlers of male deer are a general indication of age. It is therefore not difficult to manage these species on a sustained yield basis. The range of red and fallow deer is related to range quality but is quite small in comparison with the obligatory migration of Tundra reindeer. The exploitation of the woodland species could be carried out by sedentary peoples, that of reindeer only by seasonal hunters or nomads.

It is interesting that the earliest domesticated animal in Europe is the wolf, itself a social species predatory upon the deer herds. It is possible that the rational exploitation of social species by early man was a precursor or even an accompaniment of the early domestication phase in northern Europe (Chaplin, 1966). A substantial proof of this hypothesis as a valid generalization has, however, been lacking. In a recent study of the fauna of peri-Neolithic sites, Jarman (1972) may have gone some way towards supplying this. In nearly all prehistory the large ungulates dominate the mammal food spectrum, but the frequency of the pairs red deer/pig and cattle/roe deer found by Jarman are interesting, and a most detailed study is called for to see how significant this is.

A full explanation of this exploitation can, however, only come from the most rigorous analysis of the relevant parameters (Chaplin, 1971) in very large collections of bones for sites in critical locations and supported by ample zoological, botanical, and cultural studies. It is also necessary to ask the palaeobotanists if they can find any evidence of the use of fire as a deliberate technique of woodland manipulation rather than by accidental or natural fires (?). Hypotheses are useful but they do need to be tested occasionally!

To summarize, I would suggest that there are features of the social structure, biology, and behaviour of the red, fallow, and reindeer in contrast to that of roe and elk that could predispose them to management by early man. A number of the techniques available could have affected the spectrum of plant species and the cycle of woodland regeneration. The existence of such a management system has not been demonstrated but could be investigated by the more sophisticated techniques of palaeozoological and palaeobotanical analysis now available.

ACKNOWLEDGEMENTS

Much of the data from which this paper has been drawn were collected during a continuing long-term study of the biology of native and alien deer in Britain.

I am grateful to the Natural Environment Research Council, the Royal Society, the Passmore Edwards Museum, the Department of Anatomy, University of Cambridge, their Graces the Duke and Duchess of Bedford, and the Forestry Commission for financial and practical support in this study.

REFERENCES

Chaplin, R. E. (1966). The use of non-morphological criteria in the study of animal domestication from bones found on archaeological sites. *In* Ucko and Dimbleby (eds.). *The Domestication and Exploitation of Plants and Animals.* London: Duckworth.

Chaplin, R. E. and White, R. W. G. (1970). The Sexual Cycle and Associated Behaviour Patterns in the Fallow Deer. *Deer,* 2, 561–565.

Chaplin, R. E. (1971). *The study of Animal Bones from Archaeological Sites.* London: Seminar Press.

Darling, F. F. (1937). *A Herd of Red Deer.* Oxford: Oxford University Press.

Henshaw, J. (1969). Antlers—The Bones of Contention. *Nature, Lond.,* 224, 1036–1037.

Jarman, M. R. (1972). European Deer Economies and the Advent of the Neolithic. *In* Higgs, E. S. (ed.). *Papers in Economic Prehistory.* Cambridge: University Press.

Mitchell, B. (1969). The Potential Output of meat as estimated from the Vital Statistics of Natural and Park Populations of Red Deer. *In* Bannerman, M. M. and Blaxter, K. L. (eds.). *TheHusbanding of Red Deer.* Aberdeen: The Highlands and Islands Development Board and the Rowett Research Institute.

Prior, R. P. (1968). *The Roe Deer of Cranborne Chase.* London: Oxford University Press.

Stitcher, W. M. and Shaw, S. P. (1966). Use of Woody browse by Whitetail deer in heavily forested areas of North Eastern United States. *Transactions of the Thirty-First North American Wildlife and Natural Resources Conference.* Washington: The Wildlife Management Institute.

Whitehead, G. K. (1960). *Deer and their Management in the Deer Parks of Great Britain and Ireland.* London: Country Life.

Whitehead, G. K. (1964). *The Deer of Great Britain and Ireland.* London: Routledge and Kegan Paul.

Whitehead, G. K. (1972). *Deer of the World.* London: Constable.

Yazan, Y. and Knorre Y. (1964). Domesticating Elk in a Russian National Park. *Oryx, 7,* 301–304.

The intimate relationship: an hypothesis concerning pre-Neolithic land use

Pam Evans

Synopsis

By exercising some of the dietary parameters acknowledged by modern cattle breeders and considering the composition of floral nutrients in high forest, it is possible to suggest that the settlement pattern of Mesolithic man in Britain, as on the Continent, can be construed in terms of the preferential habitat of Bos primigenius *for secondary and often open areas, and the rise of Atlantic communities is thus viewed as a direct result of land loss on a traditional economy.*

"Since livestock depend for their existence on plant food . . . (an) intimate relationship must always have existed between the composition of flocks and herds and the character of the vegetation prevailing in and around the area of settlement" (Clark, 1952). To the modern stockman who has at his disposal a variety of breeds of every domestic species selectively bred to utilize an infinite number of economic habitats and economic emphases, this assessment of the prehistoric situation is almost shocking, implying as it does that the selection of settlement sites depends upon their suitability to stock, as opposed to the modern habit of selecting stock varieties most suited to the pre-existing environment. Clark's statement originally applied to fully developed mixed-farming communities but, as with so many of his *memorabilia,* redirection by no means impairs its veracity, and the further back in time it is applied as a principle the greater its significance becomes.

It is a commonplace of late Pleistocene archaeology that the settlement pattern of man is determined by the feeding habits of the main faunal element in the economy, and that where the species concerned is migratory, that pattern will exhibit seasonal rotation; and of Neolithic archaeology that settlement is orientated upon the availability and exploitation of a number of resources, of which beast are but one. The shift in emphasis between the animal-imposed and the human-selected habitat will vary in direct relationship to the diversity and importance of the number of elements in the economy. In these islands the long millennia between the reindeer and the rick present a dynamic sequence of climatic, geographical, botanical, and cultural development within which the principles governing settlement selection are not open to analysis, since the interrelations of the factors mentioned are imperfectly understood and their prevalence in space and time far from clear. Opinion is divided between those who see the encroaching forest as an active agent displacing man and driving him to the extremes of impoverishment suggested by current interpretation of the Atlantic littorine sites, and those who see man as an active agent clearing and modifying the forest cover, thus attributing the onus of site selection to human kind. In very broad terms any such analysis is *ipso facto* invalid, since the land loss incurred in these islands removes from even hypothetical availability an area which on the east coast alone is as large as all England. This fact coupled with the onset of insularity implies variations and permutations of the stresses felt by communities, both human and animal, in chronological contemporaneity on the Continent.

The significance of herd-association in the 'Mesolithic' economy has lately attracted much attention; Jarman (1972) has examined the role of deer in this context, and the elucidation of Eastern European economies by Tringham (1971) has emphasized the number of sites that demonstrate preferential hunting of one species, and the possibility of spontaneous domestication of a few, which occur in this area. Bender and Phillips (1972) present a similar situation in pre-Neolithic France. The species preferred include the horse, the elk of the Kunda, the pigs of Azov, the aurochs of Bolsaya Akkarza, and the deer of Star Carr. Isolated examples of possible domestication, such as those from Brittany, from Rocadour and Chateauneuf-les-Martigues, from the whole eclectic structure of Ertebølle economics, or from Soroki II, demonstrate that a very close association between man and a preferred species occurs recurrently across all the borders of absolute or botanical 'time'; human cultures; geographical regions, and animal species. To assume, therefore, that this neither could nor did occur in these islands is to rely upon negative evidence.

There is, in the material culture of the British Isles, an extremely conservative element which remains manifest as late as *c.* 6850 bc at Mother Grundy's Parlour in the Pennines, and comparably late at Caldey Island off the South Wales coast; Lacaille (1954) and Coles (1971) emphasize the strength of these traditions in Scotland. At the same time, it is polite to notice that McBurney (1959), in speaking of the Late Glacial cave industries of South Wales and of the Creswellian and Magdalenian elements therein, finds "strong confirmation in the industrial tradition of that period of a number of traits that have been attributed on purely typological grounds to the Mesolithic", and the recent discovery in Lancashire of the shattered and shattering Late Glacial elk felled by typologically Post-glacial implements (Hallam *et al.,* 1973) coupled with the incidence of microlithic technology at Hengistbury Head (Mace, 1959) of possible Allerød date and the 'snapped flake fragment' from Kent's Cavern (Campbell and Sampson, 1971) all indicate that the transition from 'Palaeolithic' to 'Mesolithic' was as devious and individual in the British groups as it was on the Continent. Nor is evidence for herd association altogether lacking here; for the Pleistocene inhabitants of Tornewton Cave (Sutcliffe and Zeuner, 1957) the Reindeer Stratum provides not only an illustration of the selective exploitation of this animal's non-edible resources, shed antler, but also of the preferential use of bovid rib bones, and it is nice to recall that at the Soroki II site referred to above, the exploitation of *Bos* took place in a material lithic context markedly macrolithic and in an area where lingering Palaeolithic influence was strong. It is likely that herd association is a habit of formidable antiquity, and its consummate development in late Pleistocene contexts may be as much the result of appreciation of this fact by scholars and of the multiplicity and diversity of remains as to an idiosyncratic economic adaptation in any real sense; but that it existed is beyond dispute. What is in dispute is the extent to which traditions stemming from economically viable habits may have persisted in any given locality at any time, and this archaeology is unable to assess, but it would be unrealistic to insist that the co-existence and confluence both demonstrable in the lithic industries did not occur in the relationships formed between man and the herds.

Finds from Star Carr (Clark, 1971) and the calculations based upon them demonstrate that, whilst nearly ten times as many red deer as *Bos* were taken, the clean carcass weight was only two-and-a-half times as great. In view of the lack of skeletal evidence for the species or ratios of species hunted by the Highland Zone groups, this figure is of some significance, for it suggests that for every four red deer only one *Bos* kill need be assumed, and that the chances of demonstrating association with *Bos* are only a quarter of those of demonstrating deer-association. Whilst it remains true that as a rule Maglemosian groups and their descendants do not display a specific association, the reverse is to be inferred from both the late Upper Palaeolithic groups and from the continental evidence referring to the so-called 'Tardenois' and associated microlithic communities with which the Highland Zone is more directly related, especially near the coasts. Thus we are presented with comparable situations both in topographic and in material culture terms to those which elsewhere gave rise to herd association on the Continent. It is relevant to note in this context that *Bos* association is a European, rather than a Near Eastern, phenomenon, and that a case has even been made out for *Bos* domestication (as opposed to herding) in several parts of Europe independently (Bökönyi, 1969). Indeed, the earliest records for domestic cattle are from Greek and not Near Eastern Early Neolithic sites (Higgs and Jarman, 1972), and it may be that cattle herding was a European contribution to the complex of mixed farming economics, both suited to that complex already familiar with the practice amongst other species, and suited to its reception by non-agricultural European communities through long familiarity with *Bos* species.

Bos primigenius has been described variously in the literature as an inhabitant of forest, closed woodland, open woodland, and parkland environments, and all these ascriptions are of value in demonstrating both how adaptable the beast was, and how the preferred habitat—whichever it may have been—could be dispensed with when necessary, a fact less true of the red deer and scarcely at all of the roe. What is not demonstrable is whether the aurochs's success in a wooded environment is the result of preference or of adaptation, and this is of importance in assessing the likely movements of herds when alternatives are presented. In early periods, the picture is confused by the possibility of competition by more restricted species, *Bison,* and by the fact that both reindeer and elk have woodland subspecies. Records of *Bos primigenius* are still too few, and more intimately, too restricted in the numbers represented per site, for any meaningful analysis of the number of habitats to be made, and in any case only a very small number of the available habitats—mires, bogs, subterranean or other chance burial conditions—return finds *in situ*. Elsewhere, on man's occupation sites, the exact habitat of hunted beast cannot be located and is usually inferred as wooded owing to an overall concept of continuous tree cover. Any inquiry, therefore, into the habits of beast starts from the *a priori* assumption that the preferred habitat is unknown. In Ireland the existence of *Bos primigenius* is as yet unproven and, in view of this and of the very distinct sequence of occupation and development, discussion of Irish sites must be deferred.

The early evidence from Tor Newton suggests two interpretations: either the reindeer in question was of the woodland type, or the *Bos* concerned was of possible migratory habit—a trend represented in several *Bos* species. Climatic evidence would seem to favour the latter, and it may be suggested that a pattern of seasonal movement, perceptible here in the Late Glacial, was one which was retained by the succeeding species under increasingly hostile floral conditions. The deer associations of Europe noted by Jarman (1972) ought not to be subject to this possibility, dealing as they do with red deer; and together with this species the constant numerical supremacy of the pig is emphasized. However, as *Bos* takes a secondary place in this quantitative survey, so does the roe deer, and this little animal is an inhabitant of scrubland by preference who "tends to shun . . . the more heavily stocked areas of mature timber where undergrowth is sparse" (Forestry Commission, 1970). It may be that the constancy of the red deer/pig and roe deer/*Bos* complex observed by Jarman reflects some degree of differential distribution in the forest, either seasonally exploited by human groups or aligned upon herd association with one of the species. Smith (1970) contends that the Atlantic forest was no less than a mosaic of communities, some of which must have been secondary, and it is into this niche that it is suggested that the *Bos*/roe deer fauna be placed, rather than that the ambivalent placing of *Bos* in a high forest situation, simply extended from the preferential habitat of the red deer, should be unquestioningly accepted.

Between the time of the occupation at Star Carr and that at Portland, the area of maritime plain and lowland grazing available to the aurochs and roe deer of the former site was submerged. On the west coast, and generally over the Highland Zone, land loss, whilst less in quantity, assumes even greater qualitative significance owing to the lack of extensive areas of inland plain, into and across which adaptation from coastal to inland habitats would be facilitated. Topographically, only the Severn Basin, the Cardigan and Mersey/North Wales flats, the Solway Firth, and Morecambe Bay compare with the expanses of the east coast, for elsewhere the transition from near sea-level to highland is abrupt and at best only locally modified by firths and river mouths. There is no doubt that the foremost sufferers from this reduction were the herds of herbivores that fed upon these areas, and only secondarily the herds of man who in turn fed upon the herbivores. Man's omnivorous feeding habit facilitates his transition from one environment to another, whereas the stringent demands endured by the herbivores (and the horse is a noteworthy native example) impose both a greater time span and greater stress during the adaptive period. Higham and Message (1969) have already suggested that *Bos primigenius,* beast, be considered as an open country species and the very unsuitability of the animal's size and shape to high forest noted by Grigson (1969), who denies any reduction in size throughout the Holocene in Britain, supports this. However, Degerbøl (1963), Jarman (1969), and Herre (1969) all discuss an overall reduction in stature which they attribute variously to domestication, interference and subjection to a common biological rule, arguments which are not yet resolved. The two *Bos primigenius* recovered at Morton, eastern Scotland (Coles, 1971) include both 'normal' and the smallest aurochs yet recorded, and from this the assumption must be drawn that it was not local feeding grounds which were responsible for what reduction there may or may not be; but it is possible that the restriction of feeding grounds necessitating adaptation from one habitat to another gave rise to an undue number of runt individuals per herd during the period of maximum stress, and it is therefore of interest to note that the mid-fifth millennium date for the Morton midden (Site B) refers to the Main Post-glacial shoreline at this site. Naturally the presence of this runt aurochs also raises the bedevilled question of the presence of two breeds of aurochs in Britain, summarized in the report cited, and the evidence will not sustain argument as to whether the easy-kill, the over-kill, the cull, the congenital inefficiency of the individual, or a pheno-morphological response to genetic or botanical developments—all possible interpretations—was responsible for its presence.

Since both *Bos primigenius* and his environment are extinct, it would seem that the best way to approach his habit is through his stomach, and to offer some of the known dietary parameters of modern cattle as indications. It is well known that pasture grass contains more protein than cattle are internally equipped to use, and that to feed cattle on grass alone is wasteful of land. The tardy arrival of aurochs in the fauna, replacing bison at the period when tree cover begins to formulate, may be due to this fact and, if so, strengthens the case for direct application of modern dietary parameters to the aurochs. Of tree leaves, however, it may not be so well known that those grown in shade yield a higher protein content than those grown in open sunlight (Pirie, 1968), so that forest edge or scrubland leaves would thus be poorest in this feeding constituent. However, lignin, the woody tissue which grows in the cell wall, depresses digestibility in cattle. Lignin increases in quantity with the age of the plant, replacing in part and supplementing the cellulose of the cell wall, and thickening it. Cellulose is highly digestible and converts into carbohydrate. It may be that in the preferred diet the higher protein content of shade-grown leaves is sacrificed, if indeed it is needed at all, to the higher proportion of cellulose unmitigated by quantities of lignin, which would tend to be the overall condition of leaves browsed in mature forest where the age of the plants would be greater in general than those grown in the marginal areas. Moreover, in the areas of young and secondary growth the starch content would again be increased on average over the shaded forest, since starch is a direct response to the photosynthesis generated by sunlight, and somewhat reduced under a full canopy. It is also in the scrub and open areas that a high proportion of seeds will be available, which cannot be taken under the canopy where the herbaceous layer is unable to develop. Seed fat—linseed is an extreme example—yields two-and-a-quarter times as much energy as carbohydrates, of which starch is the highest gross energy-yielding item, and nearly twice as much protein and is a necessary part of the diet (Tyler, 1964). Decorticated groundnut cake, linseed block, and fish meal today supply this need and are a normal supplement to the 'green' feed. Even amongst the trees the seeds exhibit their value, for as well as supplying the much needed fats, seeds are the richest part of the plant in protein. Russel (1947) quotes the protein content of elm parts as: seeds 44%, fruit 27·8%, leaf 18·1%, seed wings 4·7%. These figures have been tested by Dr Pirie at Rothamstead Experimental Station and early results on other plant species agree with this order (N. Pirie, personal communication). Thus the postulated protein sacrifice may be made up by this fact alone.

Both *Bos primigenius* and the subsequent domesticates, *Bos taurus* and *Bos longifrons,* belong to the 'beef' rather than the 'dairy' strain, and as such would not require the fat-rich diet that milch cows now need. Milk production would be restricted only to that period after calving down before the calves were weaned, and extra fat would thus be sought by a normally constructed herd for a limited season and not all the year round. This increases the overall capacity of the herd to thrive on fodder which today may seem inadequate or marginal. This viability is enhanced by the fact that recent beef-raising practices in France and Ireland have demonstrated that the entire male beast exhibits an overall increase in utility of fodder over the castrate. Thus the 150–200 lb superiority of the 22-month steer over the bullock represents an enhanced live weight gain per pound of fodder (Taylor, 1974). Turning these figures upside down, it could be suggested that the steer could survive on a maintenance ration lower than that required by the castrate, and thus in a 'wild' herd the amount of land available for maintenance is in excess of its modern counterparts. Happily, one of the breeds concerned in these experiments is the Charolais, much used in comparative tables by prehistorians. In Ireland, the movements of steers are severely restricted by law, so that no knowledge has been gained about their behaviour, whether they are given to vagrancy in numbers or as individuals as has been suggested (cf. Jewell, 1963), but it has been shown that when yarded or pastured together they accord amicably with each other.

One of the most widely recognised requirements of beast is salt, and this applies to red deer as well, who will go to some hazard to obtain it. Of the sodium chloride of which salt is compounded, it is the sodium which is the vital mineral. This, together with calcium and potassium, forms the basic (in the chemical sense) mineral intake of cattle and must be balanced against the production of the sulphuric, phosphoric, and carbonic acids produced by the animal. Quantitatively, calcium and phosphorus are the most important of these; indeed, beast deprived of the former will go to bizarre lengths, evening turning carrion upon their own kind, to obtain it. It is unlikely, however, that even in the Highland Zone a sufficient shortage of calcium to effect such behaviour would ever arise, and finds of *Bos* are too scattered to make their distribution over limestone and chalk areas worth analysing for this. Moreover, being free-ranging animals, 'wild' cattle would not be restricted to areas where the mineral was in short supply. The need for sodium, however, is open to investigation. Mackereth (1966) indicates that after the opening up of the forest, sodium, amongst other minerals, became lost by erosion and/or other factors in measurable quantities. Pirie (1968) supplements this by declaring that manuring of trees with materials which include additional sodium will replace the slow loss of development in trees which has resulted from just the processes which Mackereth suggests, both suggestions which imply that the climax forest was richer in this mineral than modern stands; the hypothesis can be taken to include scrub and secondary growth, since it is dependent on soil factors. That examples of soil degradation did occur before the 'Neolithic' has been shown by Dimbleby (1965) at Iping Common, and by Crampton and Webley (1966) in the Highland Zone at Mynydd Troed, and suggestions have been put forward that the Atlantic climate in itself may have generated a like process in western areas, but this effect is assumed to be local and sporadic and not of general import. The significance of sodium as a determining factor in beast's use of land lies in the assignation of the creature as either an open-country or a woodland species. Placed in the latter group the supply of sodium would no doubt suffice in its availability, as it presumably did for the other ruminants, the deer. Whether Atlantic and Boreal deer exhibited the same desire to augment the supply by coming to coastal sites cannot yet be demonstrated on skeletal evidence. But if cattle are placed in that other niche and regarded as an open-country species, it can be seen that the sodium supply, as a direct result of the closure of the canopy, would become overloaded by the preference for an open habitat most obviously available in coastal areas where the sodium intake is high. What is important here is the matter of balance and not that of quantity. The simplest way of redressing this balance would be an increased amount of phosphorus production, provoked by grazing on phosphorus-rich land. The simplest way of achieving this would be by symbiosis with that redoubtable fire-raiser, Mesolithic man. The recent publications of palaeobotanists have stressed the evidence for intense burning of tracts of upland and inland heights, and a number of these are associated with the presence of microlithic groups. Not only on the heights, but as far into the forest as Ascott-under-Wychwood, Oxfordshire, and beneath the earthworks at Woodhenge (J. G. Evans, personal communication) is the effect of burning displayed. Whether or no this was deliberate fire-raising, perpetrated as part of an economic policy, and strongly suggesting herd-association with *Bos primigenius*, cannot yet be decided; Smith (1970) has presented all the arguments for and against its deliberate inception. It is even suggested that the Boreal hazel maximum may be the result of firing by human communities on certain sites, and the High Furlong elk (Hallam *et al.*, 1973) already mentioned demonstrates that a Late Glacial faunal element and a fully Post-glacial material culture were combined as immediately as the first encroachment of tree cover over the British Isles. It may be that the burnt Allerød soils of south-east England (e.g. Evans, 1966) could be relevant in this context. However this may be, conditions resulting from this epidemic of pyromania were admirably suited to fulfilling the chemical requirements of *Bos,* as that species became increasingly dependent on the open habitat, becoming progressively restricted to coastal tracts.

There is thus a possibility of the reverse of the normally accepted tenet whereby cattle and deer are lured by the presence of salt, and that, far from 'Mesolithic' hunters stalking the glades of Oxfordshire with pan salt from Pembrokeshire to put upon the tail of the aurochs, the tail, flying before an excess of this commodity, was more gratified by the supply of its balancing agent, phosphorus. Salt has long been a traditional supplement in cattle feed, either as a 'lick' of rock salt or as a constituent in dry foodstuff, but it is interesting to observe that stockmen in Orkney, where salinity is unusually high owing to winds and the small size of the islands' circuits of maritime pasture, do not in fact give any additional salt to their herds, which are perhaps the finest in all the British Isles.

As the Post-glacial tree cover increased in density, so did the land loss on the south and east coasts increase in area through the rising sea, and it would be unrealistic not to expect this to be reflected in the distribution of the fauna. There is as yet insufficient evidence to show this in the finds of *Bos,* but account must be taken of the ubiquity of littorine human communities on the west coast. Rather than a reflection of groups of haggard little men glancing furtively over their shoulders at the inexorable march of the trees, it may equally be regarded as being due to the attraction of coastal plains such as Cardigan Bay and the Solway Firth, where the magnificent aurochs grazed for most of the winter months. What seasonal indications there are do suggest rotational lean-month occupation, even as far north as Morton, and it may be well to regard these stations not as the pitiful hole-ups of a limpet-bashing minority but as stations receding before the rising sea, orientated specifically upon the presence of such splendid animals as the Borth Beast. Such portentous eructations in the flora as are exhibited in the pollen diagrams both from the cliff section at Aberaeron (Taylor, 1973) and in zone C 18 at Bowness Common (Walker, 1966) suggest that considerable activity may have occurred in these localities at least in the late Atlantic, prior to which the west coast furnished areas of floral communities (cf. especially Walker, 1966) directly comparable with those which in the 17th century AD fattened the best beef in Britain by the thousand head (Trow-Smith, 1959). As far north as the Argyll coast, the incidence of horse finds suggests that pockets of open maritime environment were still in existence in Atlantic times and frequented by littoral communities such as those from the Albyn Distillery and associated sites (Lacaille, 1954). In one case *Bos* is associated with horse, and in later periods, of course, the two occur within a generalized 'botanical' contemporaneity in the wind-swept and salt-laden levels of Caithness and Orkney.

The growing interest of late Maglemosian derived cultures in the west coast (Wainwright, 1960) and their late Atlantic appearance and connections with the Severn Basin (Wainwright, 1963; Grimes, 1951) on both north and south shores may not be disconnected with the association of *Bos primigenius* with these maritime pastures. Finds from Margam (Swansea Bay), Borth, and other stations on the Welsh coast demonstrate the presence of beast on the western seaboard, which is also the area in which the Late Glacial traditions were most clearly seen to linger. It is of singular interest that at Westward Ho! on the west coast of Devon (Churchill and Wymer, 1965), a mid-fifth millennium sea-level midden, although lacking aurochs and containing a fauna indicative of mud flats and forest rather than maritime grassland, yielded pollen analytical evidence not only for the sedge and saltmarsh facies which must once have existed but also for considerable quantities of ivy (*Hedera* sp.). Ivy is also uncommonly rampant at the site of Oakhanger, Hampshire (Dimbleby, 1960), and here the phenomenal quantities have given rise to some speculations, amongst which deliberate harvesting is not omitted. It is true that in both cases a non-anthropogenic cause for the rise can be effectively postulated; it is also true that ivy will make good creels and casies. It may not be so well known that ivy is an effective agent when fed to lactating cows, in drying them off through the effects on the milk, which is distasteful to the calf (Forsyth, 1954). The mass movements of herds is not facilitated by the presence of sucking calves. It is of equal interest in this context that both the date obtained by radiocarbon for Westward Ho! and the lithic industry represented there are very similar to those from Stump Cross, Grassington, Yorkshire. The tenuous material culture threads and many others across the cultural and topographical boundaries that interconnect these sites are too complex and delicate to be discussed here, but the implications that lie behind such apparently minor elements in any aspect of a site, whether it be the plantain and weeds of White Gill and Morton, the microlithic similarities of Oakhanger, Stump Cross and Iping, or the existence on high ground above the South Wales littorine stations of the Solva, Pencoes, Bruton, and Nab Head axes all point to a possibility of cross-cultural dependence or manipulation of some common economic parameter.

In France, the 'Tardenois' stations of Brittany have provided ample proof of the existence of *Bos*-associated communities on the west coast and, however strenuously van Zeist (1964) may argue against the theory of disturbances in the highland Breton bogs being anthropogenic, similar disturbances in Britain at Loch of Park, Scotland (Vasari, 1968), or Bloak Moss (Turner,1965), at Aberaeron (Taylor,1973) or Bowness Common (Walker, 1966) must be regarded in the light of the principle that non-agricultural groups may be limited in their choice of settlement to the habitats available to the animals which they exploited. When reason is seen to regard beast as an open-country species it is rewarding to review the settlement patterns exhibited in the Highland Zone in Mozley's evocative terms: "I found myself faced with unfamiliar combinations in a flora and fauna which I knew", and to suggest that the intimate relationship between the herds and the area of settlement was not degraded into a game of hide-and-seek in the forest, but was the result of a traditional balance established in high antiquity which survived all the pressures exerted by the Holocene sequence, to be finally transformed and readjusted by immigrant populations and economies with multi-faceted exploitation as a *sine qua non* of their existence.

REFERENCES

Bender, B. and Phillips, P. (1972). The early farmers of France. *Antiquity,* 46, 254–389.

Bökönyi, S. (1969). Archaeological problems and methods of recognising animal domestication. *In* Ucko, P. J. and Dimbleby, G. W. (eds.). *The Domestication and Exploitation of Plants and Animals.* London: Duckworth; 219–230.

Campbell, J. and Sampson, L. G. (1971). *A New Analysis of Kent's Cavern, Devonshire, England.* University of Oregon, Anthropological Papers, No. 3.

Churchill, D. H. and Wymer, J. J. (1965). The kitchen midden site at Westward Ho!, Devon, England: ecology, age and relation to changes in land and sea level. *Proc. Prehist. Soc.,* 31, 74–83.

Clark, J. G. D. (1952). *Prehistoric Europe: The Economic Basis.* London: Methuen.

Clark, J. G. D. (1971). *Excavations at Star Carr.* Cambridge: University Press.

Coles, J. M. (1971). The early settlement of Scotland: excavations at Morton, Fife. *Proc. Prehist. Soc.,* 37, 284–366.

Crampton, C. B. and Webley, D. (1966). A section through the Mynydd Troed Long Barrow, Brecknock. *Bull. Board Celtic Stud.,* 22, 71–77.

Degerbøl, M. (1963). Prehistoric cattle in Denmark and adjacent areas. *Occ. Pap. Roy. Anthropol. Inst.,* No. 18, 69–79.

Dimbleby, G. W. (1960). *In* Rankine, W. F. and Dimbleby, G. W. Further excavations at a Mesolithic site at Oakhanger, Selbourne, Hants. *Proc. Prehist. Soc.,* 26, 246–262.

Dimbleby, G. W. (1965). *In* Keef, P. A. M., Wymer, J. J., and Dimbleby, G. W. A Mesolithic site on Iping Common, Sussex, England. *ibid.,* 31, 85–92.

Evans, J. G. (1966). Late-glacial and Post-glacial subaerial deposits at Pitstone, Buckinghamshire. *Proc. Geol. Ass.,* 77, 347–364.

Forestry Commission Leaflet No. 45 (1970). *The Roe Deer.* London. H.M.S.O.

Forsyth, A. A. (1968). *British Poisonous Plants.* Bulletin 161, Ministry of Agriculture, Fisheries and Food, London: H.M.S.O.

Grigson, C. (1969). The uses and limitations of differences in absolute size in the distinction between the bones of aurochs *(Bos primigenius)* and domestic cattle *(Bos taurus). In* Ucko, P. J. and Dimbleby, G. W. (eds.). *The Domestication and Exploitation of Plants and Animals.* London: Duckworth; 266–277.

Grimes, W. F. (1951). *The Prehistory of Wales.* Cardiff: National Museum of Wales.

Hallam, J. S., Edwards, B. J. N., Barnes, B., and Stuart, H. J. (1973). A Late Glacial elk with associated barbed points from High Furlong, Lancashire. *Proc. Prehist. Soc.,* 39, 100–128.

Herre, W. (1969). The science and history of domestic animals. *In* Brothwell, D. and Higgs, E. (eds.). *Science in Archaeology.* London: Thames and Hudson; 257–272.

Higgs, E. S. and Jarman, M. R. (1972). The origins of animal and plant husbandry. *In* Higgs, E. S. (ed). *Papers in Economic Prehistory.* Cambridge: University Press; 3–14.

Higham, C. F. W. and Message, M. A. (1969). An assessment of a prehistoric technique of bovine husbandry. *In* Brothwell, D. and Higgs, E. (eds.). *Science in Archaeology*. London: Thames and Hudson; 315–330.
Jarman. M. R. (1969). The prehistory of Upper Pleistocene and Recent cattle. Part I. *Proc. Prehist. Soc.*, 35, 236–266.
Jarman, M. R. (1972). European deer economics and the advent of the Neolithic. *In* Higgs, E. S. (ed.). *Papers in Economic Prehistory*. Cambridge: University Press; 129–145.
Jewell, P. (1963). Cattle from British archaeological sites. *Occ. Pap. Roy. Anthropol. Inst.*, No. 18, 80–101.
Lacaille, A. D. (1954). *The Stone Age in Scotland.* London.
Mace, A. (1959). The excavation of a late Upper Palaeolithic open-site on Hengistbury Head, Christchurch, Hants. *Proc. Prehist. Soc.*, 35, 233–259.
Mackereth, F. J. H. (1966). Some chemical observations on Post-glacial lake sediments. *Phil. Trans. Roy. Soc.*, B, 250, 165–213.
McBurney, C. (1959). First season's fieldwork on British Upper Palaeolithic cave deposits. *Proc. Prehist. Soc.*, 25, 260–269.
Mozley, A. (1959). *Ecological Processes.* London: H. K. Lewis.
Murray, J. (1968). Some aspects of ovicaprid and pig breeding in Neolithic Europe. *In* Coles, J. M. and Simpson, D. D. A. (eds.). *Studies in Ancient Europe*. Leicester: University Press; 71–82.
Payne, S. (1972). On the interpretation of bone samples from archaeological sites. *In* Higgs, E. S. (ed.). *Papers in Economic Prehistory*. Cambridge: University Press; 65–82.
Pirie, N. (1968). Food from the forest. *New Sci.*, 420–422.
Russel, F. C. (1947). The chemical composition and digestibility of fodder shrubs and trees. *Imperial Agricultural Bureau Publications*, No. 10. Aberystwyth.
Smith, A. G. (1970). The influence of Mesolithic and Neolithic man on British vegetation: a discussion. *In* Walker, D. and West, R. G. (eds.); *Studies in the Vegetational History of the British Isles.* Cambridge: University Press: 81–96.
Sutcliffe, A. J. and Zeuner, F. E. (1957–1958). Excavations in the Torbryan Caves, Devonshire. I. Tornewton Cave. *Trans. Devon Archaeological Exploration Society*, 5, 127–145.
Taylor, E. (1974). Chief Supervisor, The Royal Dublin Society. Personal Communication.
Taylor, J. A. (1973). *Chronometers and Chronicles: A Study of the Palaeo-environments of West Central Wales.* Progress in Geography Vol. 5. International Reviews of Current Research; 248–334.
Tringham, R. (1971). *Hunters, Fishers and Farmers of Eastern Europe,* 6000–3000 B.C. London: Hutchinson.
Trow-Smith, R. (1959). *A History of British Livestock Husbandry, 1700–1900.* London: Routledge and Kegan Paul.
Turner, J. (1965). A contribution to the history of forest clearance. *Proc. Roy. Soc.*, B, 161, 343–355.
Tyler, C. (1964). *Animal Nutrition.* London: Chapman and Hall.
Vasari, Y. and Vasari, A. (1968). Late and Post Glacial macrophytic vegetation in the lochs of northern Scotland. *Acta Bot. Fenn.*, 80.
Wainwright, G. J. (1960). Three microlithic industries from south-west England and their affinities. *Proc. Prehist. Soc.*, 26, 193–202.
Wainwright, G. J. (1963). A re-interpretation of the microlithic industries of Wales. *ibid.*, 29, 99–133.
Walker, D. (1966). The Late Quaternary history of the Cumberland lowland. *Phil. Trans. Roy. Soc.*, B, 251, 1–210.
van Zeist, W. (1964). A palaeobotanical study of some bogs in western Brittany (Finistere), France. *Palaeohistoria,* 10, 157–181.

Ungulate populations, economic patterns, and the Mesolithic landscape

P. Mellars

Synopsis

The carrying capacity of prehistoric environments for ungulate populations must be reconstructed on the basis of present-day observations in analogous ecological situations. Observations in North America and Europe suggest that the optimum carrying capacity of deciduous and mixed deciduous–coniferous forests for ungulate species may be in the region of 1,000–2,500 kg/km². The carrying capacity of pure coniferous forests seems to be much lower than these values, possibly in the region of 200–500 kg/km². Removal of tree cover — for example by burning — produces dramatic increases in the carrying capacity of all forested environments, and may increase the local biomass of ungulate populations by a factor of × 10. This kind of increase in the density of animal populations could have far-reaching implications for the behaviour and organization of contemporaneous hunter–gatherer communities.

Information regarding the distribution and abundance of the food supplies available to prehistoric groups is of critical importance to the prehistorian from several points of view. At the most basic level the total quantity of food available in any environment imposes a clear limit on the maximum size of the human population the environment will support. Again, ethnographic studies have shown that variations in the density of food resources at different points in space exert a strong influence on the sizes of human residential groupings, and on the frequency with which the group is obliged to move from one settlement location to another (Birdsell, 1968; Lee, 1969). Thirdly, it is evident that the local abundance of food supplies has a direct bearing on the amount of time and energy that must be devoted to harvesting the resources, and on the degree of selectivity that can be exercised in the harvesting process (Lee, 1968; 1969).

The archaeological record, of course, provides a notoriously distorted picture of the food supplies actually consumed by prehistoric groups, and several writers have recently suggested that the apparent preoccupation of Palaeolithic and Mesolithic communities with hunting activities might well be illusory (e.g. Lee, 1968, 43; Mellars, 1975). Certainly there are grounds for thinking that Mesolithic populations occupying the heavily forested landscape of early Post-glacial Europe obtained a major portion of their total subsistence requirements from sources other than meat. At the same time, however, evidence recovered from sites such as Star Carr and Thatcham in England and many sites on the continent leaves no doubt that the exploitation of several species of native ungulates (red deer, roe deer, aurochs, boar, and 'elk') made an important contribution to the food supply of at least some Mesolithic communities (cf. Jarman, 1972), and reasons will be given later for thinking that these resources may have played an appreciably more important role in the long-term survival strategies of the human groups than a purely quantitative assessment of the dietary situation might suggest. If this suspicion is correct, the overall abundance of ungulate populations in different environments might emerge as one of the crucial variables controlling several aspects of human behaviour and organization, including the maximum level at which the human populations themselves could be maintained.

It is perhaps unnecessary to point out that attempts to reconstruct the distribution and density of prehistoric animal populations on the basis of present-day observations encounter difficulties from several points of view. The most obvious difficulty stems from the fact that almost all the environments at present occupied by ungulate populations have been modified to some extent by human interference—logging operations, forest fires, agricultural activities, and so on. As will be shown later, most of these processes have the effect of substantially increasing the food resources available to herbivorous species and thereby increasing the overall 'carrying capacity' of the environment (Leopold, 1950; Longhurst, 1961; Taber, 1963). One of the major problems encountered in assembling the data summarized in Tables I–III has therefore been to select situations in which the effects of human disturbance, if not entirely absent, are at least kept to a minimum. A second difficulty hinges on the problem of showing that the present-day populations are truly in balance with the food resources of the environment. Under natural conditions it is assumed that a more or less healthy balance between animal populations and environmental resources would be maintained on the one hand by the food supplies themselves, and on the other hand by the activities of natural predators such as wolves and bears (Longhurst, 1961, 311; Leopold, 1950, 575–8). Under present conditions the elimination of most of these natural predators (with the exception of man) has allowed ungulate populations in many areas to rise far above the long-term carrying capacity of the environment, leading to serious over-utilization of the available food supplies. Fortunately, the effects of this over-exploitation are fairly easy to detect in most cases, so that this source of uncertainty can be controlled to a considerable extent (Hosley, 1956, 232; Cowan, 1956, 558). Lastly, and perhaps most important, it is necessary to take into account the total number of species present in any environment. Ecological principles dictate that a wide range of species will in general be capable of achieving a more efficient utilization of the food resources available in

TABLE I Population density and biomass of ungulates in some deciduous and mixed deciduous-coniferous forest situations in Europe and North America

Area	*Forest Type*	*Species*	*Density (per km²)*	*Biomass (kg/km²)*	*Source*
Arkansas: Ozark highlands	Oak, pine, hickory	White-tailed deer	6·2–8·3	465–620	Segelquist and Green (1968); Segelquist, *et al.* (1969)
Minnesota	Pine, aspen, birch	White-tailed deer	6·2–8·5	465–635	Kohn and Mooty (1971)
New York: Adirondacks	Beech, maple, birch	White-tailed deer	5·5–8·3	410–620	Tierson *et al.* (1966)
Pennsylvania Allegheny forest	Beech, birch, maple	White-tailed deer	5·8–9·2	435–690	McCain (1939)
Missouri	Oak, hickory	Wapiti	10·8	2,376	Murphy (1963)
USSR: National Parks	Mixed deciduous/ coniferous forest	Moose, Red deer, Roe deer, Boar	? ? ? ?	4,000	Bannikov (1967)
USSR: unprotected forests	Mixed deciduous/ coniferous forest	?	?	90–1,000	Bannikov (1967)
Germany: Anhalt region	?Mixed deciduous/ coniferous forest	Red deer Roe deer Fallow deer Boar	2·25 16·9 9·0 5·6	1,520	Leopold (1936)
Germany: Brandenburg region	?Mixed deciduous/ coniferous forest	Red deer Roe deer Fallow deer Boar	6·2 31·0 3·1 7·2	2,090	Leopold (1936)

In calculating biomass values, average weights of different species have been taken as follows: white-tailed deer 75 kg, wapiti 220 kg, red deer 100 kg, roe deer 25 kg, fallow deer 50 kg, boar 75 kg—cf. Bourlière (1963), Mystkowska (1966), Siuda *et al.* (1969), Van Den Brink (1967), Murphy (1963).

any habitat—and therefore producing a higher biomass—than can be achieved by a single species. In practice, the importance of this factor is largely dependent on the particular species of animal involved. Thus species such as the Eurasian red deer and the closely related American wapiti, which are able to utilize a wide range of both herbaceous and browse vegetation, are capable of existing at substantially higher biomass densities in most environments than are animals like the white-tailed deer or the moose, which depend almost exclusively on browse forage for their year-round subsistence requirements (Longhurst, 1961, 311–6; Flerov, 1952, 137–8). Viewed in these terms, it is apparent that the comparatively wide range of ungulate species that has been documented for the Post-glacial forests of Europe would have offered appreciably more attractive hunting conditions than those afforded by the much more limited numbers of species characteristic of most present-day forest situations.

Ungulate populations in deciduous and mixed deciduous–coniferous forests

Table I summarizes information on the present-day ungulate populations in a number of deciduous and mixed deciduous-coniferous forest situations in Europe and North America. An examination of these statistics reveals a considerable range of variation in the total biomass densities recorded in these areas, ranging from around 400–600 kg/km² in several American forests to as high as 4,000 kg/km² in mixed deciduous-conifer forests of the USSR. For reasons outlined above, however, the question of how far these figures can be taken as an accurate reflection of the *potential carrying capacity* of the environments in question for ungulate populations requires closer examination.

The lowest biomass levels recorded in Table I are based on populations of the white-tailed deer (*Odocoileus virginianus*) in the eastern and central portions of the USA. All the data relate to areas heavily dominated by mature or semi-mature 'closed-canopy' forests, in which the vegetation types range from almost pure deciduous forest (predominantly beech, birch, and maple) in New York State and Pennsylvania to a mixture of predominantly oak and pine in the Ozarks Plateau region of Arkansas (McCain, 1939; Tierson *et al.*, 1966; Segelquist and Green, 1968; Kohn and Mooty, 1971). In each case the figures are based on detailed census studies and refer to the year-round populations of deer in clearly defined areas. The most striking feature that emerges from these observations is the marked uniformity in the overall densities of the deer populations, which can be seen to embrace a considerable variety of vegetation types. At the same time, the consistency of the observations strengthens the view that the density of 6–8 deer per square kilometre is close to the long-term carrying capacity of these environments for this particular species. It should perhaps be added that in the case of three of the studies cited (McCain, 1939; Tierson *et al.*, 1966; Segelquist and Green, 1968) the publications make it clear that the areas examined were characterized by continuous tree cover, with no areas of open vegetation resulting from recent forestry operations, fires, or agricultural activity. Hence the deer densities can apparently be taken as a true reflection of those which are capable of existing under essentially 'natural' vegetational conditions.

The main point to be emphasized in connection with these observations is that all the population density and biomass statistics relate to a single species of ungulate. Moreover, as already pointed out, the white-tailed deer is known to have rather specialized feeding habits and to subsist (at least during the critical winter season) almost exclusively on browse forage provided by shrubs and immature trees (Hosley, 1956, 189–206; Longhurst, 1961, 311). Equally significant is the relatively small size of the animal, which allows it to browse to a maximum height of around 5 ft. Larger animals such as the wapiti and moose, on the other hand, are capable of reaching food at much higher levels, in some cases up to 8–10 ft above the ground (Cliff, 1939: 561). Making allowance for these factors, it would not seem unreasonable to suggest that exploitation of the same environments by a wider range of both browsing and grazing ungulates would result in biomass densities at least twice as high as those recorded for the white-tailed deer alone. Hence the potential carrying capacity of these American forests for a broad range of ungulate species might well be in the region of 1,000–1,500 kg/km^2.

Considerable support for this conclusion is provided by studies of a 'captive' herd of wapiti *(Cervus canadensis)* occupying a 2,373-acre (960-ha) enclosure in Missouri (Murphy, 1963). The entire herd was restricted to this enclosure over a period of eight years and obtained the whole of its year-round food requirements from within this area. Approximately 90% of the land within the enclosure was covered by dense closed-canopy forest in which oak and hickory formed the dominant species. The remaining 10% had been cleared of trees and supported open grassland. Extermination of the entire wapiti herd in 1959 revealed a total of 103 animals (10·8 per km^2), yielding a biomass of approximately 2,376 kg/km^2.

Two features suggest that this biomass may be somewhat above the true carrying capacity for the major vegetation type involved (i.e. oak–hickory forest). On the one hand there were signs that the herd was over-using the available forage supplies, which would eventually have led to a depletion of these resources on a long-term basis. On the other hand it is clear that the small area of open grassland was contributing appreciably more food per unit area than that available in the forested parts of the enclosure (Murphy, 1963, 411). In addition it may be recalled that, although the recorded biomass refers to only a single species of ungulate, the species in question is known to be a highly efficient utilizer of both browse and herbaceous forage (Longhurst, 1961, 315–6; Cliff, 1939, 561–2). Hence the biomass of 2,376 kg/km^2 may well be significantly higher than the total carrying capacity of oak–hickory forest for ungulate populations in general. Nevertheless, the data provide a strong indication that the potential carrying capacity of these American deciduous forests for ungulate species is in excess of 1,000 kg/km^2 and might well reach 2,000 kg/km^2 under favourable conditions.

Biomass densities appreciably higher than these figures have been reported for ungulate populations occupying some of the National Park game refuges in the mixed deciduous–coniferous forest zone of the USSR (Bannikov, 1967). Average biomass levels for these areas, based on a total of four ungulate species (red deer, roe deer, wild boar, moose) have been estimated by Bannikov (1967, 259) at 4,000 kg/km^2. These figures are believed by Bannikov to provide a more accurate reflection of the true carrying capacity of Russian forests than the much lower densities recorded from unprotected areas outside the National Parks, where several of the major species (notably red and roe deer) have only recently been introduced and are currently increasing in numbers. However, Bannikov points out that the ungulate herds in the National Parks are maintained at artificially high levels by protection from natural (as well as human) predators, and that the present densities undoubtedly reflect varying degrees of overpopulation (Bannikov, 1967, 257). How far these populations may also be maintained by logging and other forms of forest clearance is unfortunately not made explicit in Bannikov's paper, but one gains the impression that this is not regarded as a major factor in the areas considered. In any event, it is clear that the exceptionally high biomass levels recorded in the Russian National Parks must be regarded as maximum figures, and the true carrying capacity of the forests under completely natural conditions is likely to be appreciably lower than the figures quoted. Making allowance for this adjustment, the true level of the ungulate carrying capacity of the Russian forests may not be far removed from that of the American forests—say in the region of 1,500–2,500 kg/km^2.

It remains to comment on the population densities quoted by Leopold (1936, 465) for several ungulate species in German forests. Unfortunately, Leopold gives very little information on the vegetational conditions under which these populations were living, and it would seem that at least some of the species were dependent to some extent on artificial feeding. Nevertheless it is worth observing that the biomass figures that emerge from Leopold's data are well in line with those provided by the more fully documented studies discussed above.

Ungulate populations in coniferous forests

All specialists in wildlife management seem agreed that areas of pure coniferous forest offer extremely poor prospects for most forms of animal life (e.g. Leopold, 1936, 460–1; Cowan, 1956, 552; Webb, 1960, 149–50; Taber, 1963, 207). Two principal factors appear to contribute to this situation. On the one hand the exceptionally dense canopies formed by many coniferous species have the effect of 'shading out' most forms of shrub and immature tree growth in the understorey. At the same time the accumulation of thick layers of pine needles and other forms of litter on the forest floor exerts a strongly inhibiting influence on the development of any kind of herbaceous vegetation (Webb, 1960, 149). Under these conditions the food resources available to herbivorous species are inevitably in very short supply.

TABLE II Population density and biomass of ungulates in American and European coniferous forests

Area	*Forest type*	*Species*	*Density (per km²)*	*Biomass (kg/km²)*	*Source*
Vancouver Island British Columbia	Douglas fir	Black-tailed deer	0·77	77	Cowan (1956, 552)
Oregon: coastal region	Douglas fir, hemlock, spruce	Black-tailed deer	0·77	77	Cowan (1956, 606)
Washington: coastal region	Douglas fir, hemlock	Black-tailed deer	0·81	81	Cowan, (1956, 551, 606)
New Jersey: Lebanon forest	Pine	White-tailed deer	2·16	162	Cumming (1969)
Germany ('maximum desirable density')	Spruce	Red deer	0·8–1·6	80–160	Webb (1960); Elssmann (1969)

Average weights of different species have been taken as black-tailed deer 100 kg, white-tailed deer 75 kg, red deer 100 kg—cf. Bourlière (1963) and Mystkowska (1966)

Quantitative data on the abundance of ungulate populations in coniferous forests is limited but appears to bear out the generalization that the overall population density and biomass levels that can be maintained in these environments are consistently lower than those encountered in either pure deciduous or mixed deciduous–coniferous situations (Table II). Observations in three separate areas of mature Douglas Fir forest in the north-western coastal areas of the USA and Canada have revealed year-round population densities of black-tailed deer in the region of 1–2 per square mile, yielding biomass levels of around 40–80 kg/km² (Cowan, 1956, 551–2, 606; Longhurst, 1961, 313). A somewhat higher figure of 162 kg/km² has been reported for populations of white-tailed deer inhabiting areas of predominantly pine woodland in the Lebanon State Forest region of New Jersey (Cumming, 1969, 259). Ungulate densities in the coniferous forested areas of Europe are less well documented, and in many cases it is clear that unnaturally high populations are maintained by artificial feeding of the animals during the winter. However, several authorities have emphasized the extremely low carrying capacity of the intensively managed spruce forests of Germany (e.g. Leopold, 1936, 460–1; Webb, 1960, 149). Thus the maximum population densities of red deer these forests are capable of maintaining on a long-term basis are usually estimated in the region one animal per square kilometre (circa 100 kg/km²); higher densities result in over-utilization of the available forage resources and consequent damage to forest regeneration (Webb, 1960, 152; Elssmann, 1969). All these figures are, of course, based on populations of a single species of ungulate, and utilization of the same environments by a wider range of species would no doubt allow somewhat higher biomass densities. Even allowing for this correction, however (say by increasing the observed biomass values by a factor of x2), the total carrying capacities of these coniferous forest environments would appear to fall far below that of the forests composed largely or entirely of deciduous species.

Seasonal variations in biomass and population density

All the discussions so far have focused on the overall densities of ungulate populations in varying environments on a year-round basis. In practice, of course, the distributions of most ungulate species tend to vary significantly at different seasons of the year, giving rise to substantial variations in population density at different periods and in different portions of the annual range. The mechanisms underlying these seasonal movements are evidently complex, and it is clear that the resulting patterns of distribution depend on a wide variety of local as well as regional factors—topography, climate, food resources, tree cover, prevalence of insects, and so on. Among populations occupying the more northerly latitudes, however, it would seem that the periods of maximum concentration almost invariably coincide with the winter season, when the effects of low temperatures, heavy snowfall, and reduced food supplies combine to restrict the animals to the most favourable portions of the annual range (cf Severinghaus and Cheatum, 1956, 138–42). This pattern reaches its most extreme form in the 'yarding' behaviour exhibited by several species of both American and Eurasian deer. Studies of three separate American species (white-tailed deer, mule deer, wapiti) have shown that the total area occupied during the winter season frequently amounts to only 10–15% of that utilized during the summer months, and in periods of exceptionally severe weather the yarding areas may fall to only half of this amount (Table III). Comparable data for European deer populations are more difficult to obtain, but the existence of broadly similar patterns of movement is suggested by Ingebrigsten's (1924) study of red deer migrations in Norway, and by the current investigations of red deer populations on the island of Rhum in the Inner Hebrides (Lowe, 1966).

The effects of forest fires on ungulate populations

In recent years the traditional picture of Mesolithic Europe as a landscape dominated by continuous closed-canopy forest has come increasingly under attack. Evidence is accumulating to show that in many areas the usual patterns of vegetational development during the Boreal and Atlantic periods were interrupted by factors which led to a temporary recession of tree growth and a simultaneous expansion of herbaceous and (in many cases) shrub vegetation. The frequent occurrence of charcoal in association with these deforestation horizons strongly suggests that fire was the primary agent responsible for the forest destruction (Dimbleby, 1961; Smith, 1970; Simmons, 1969). Without entering into the question of how far these fires may or may not have been started deliberately by the Mesolithic groups themselves, it is worth asking what effects the fires might have had on the contemporary animal populations.

The impact of forest fires on the food supplies of herbivorous species has been summarized by Cowan (1956, 604) in the following terms:

> "The burned area immediately develops a covering of new plant growth. Grass, fireweed and many species of annuals usually dominate, while the roots of a variety of shrubs and small trees usually survive the fire and send up an abundance of succulent sprouts. The sprouting species are supplemented quickly by others, such as the dogwoods, cascara, elders and red alder that usually come in by seed. Usually within five years, more or less, there is an abundance of shrubs and trees producing highly palatable food of excellent nutritive quality, and the reaction of the deer population is frequently spectacular."

A number of studies carried out in North America have shown the remarkable impact which forest fires can have on the population levels of several species of ungulates. Detailed observations on an area of dense Chaparral shrubland in northern California which was burned accidentally in 1948 showed an increase in the resident black-tailed deer populations from around 4–8 per square kilometre to as high as 40 per square kilometre (Taber and Dasmann, 1957, 235; Taber, 1961, 226–8). In other words, the population density on the burned area increased by a factor of at least x5. A similar rate of increase has been recorded for populations of moose occupying burned-over areas of the Kenai plateau in southern Alaska (Spencer and Hakala, 1964). Even greater population increases have been reported for areas of coniferous forest. Thus a series of fires which destroyed areas of mature Douglas Fir forest on Vancouver Island, British Columbia, were followed by increases in the local black-tailed deer populations from less than one to more than ten per square kilometre (Cowan, 1956, 552). Similarly, a combination of burning and logging operations in an area of pine forest in New Jersey appears to have increased the population density of white-tailed deer from around 2·1 to 14·5 per square kilometre (Cumming, 1969, 259).

These and other studies have shown that forest fires tend to increase not only the *quantity* but also the nutritive *quality* of the food supplies available to herbivorous populations (Einarsen, 1946; DeWitt and Derby, 1955; Lay, 1957; Leege and Hickey, 1971). This in turn can have a marked effect on both the weight and reproductive rates of the animals. Thus studies of black-tailed deer populations in Tillamook County, Oregon, showed that animals feeding on areas of recently burned forest were between 30% and 50% heavier than those inhabiting adjacent areas of

TABLE III Relative sizes of summer and winter ranges occupied by North American deer

Species	*Area*	*Percentage of annual range occupied during winter*	*Source*
White-tailed deer	Michigan	7–10	Severinghaus and Cheatum (1956, 138)
White-tailed deer	Wisconsin	10	Severinghaus and Cheatum (1956, 138)
White-tailed deer	New York	12–13	Severinghaus and Cheatum (1956, 138)
White-tailed deer	Pennsylvania	10–11	Severinghaus and Cheatum (1956, 139); Hosley (1956, 214)
Black-tailed deer	California	12	Leopold, *et al.*, (1951)
Mule deer	Utah	5·8	Rasmussen (1939)
Wapiti	Idaho	10	Leege (1968, 237)
Wapiti	'National Forests'	13–18	Trippensee (1948, 344)

unburned forest (Cowan, 1956, 606). Clear increases in the reproductive rates of animals occupying burned-over areas have been recorded in both the Californian black-tailed deer studies (Taber and Dasmann, 1957, 236; Taber, 1961, 226–7) and the Alaskan moose investigation (Spencer and Hakala, 1964, 22–4) referred to above. Similar correlations between the effects of burning and the weight and reproductive rates of deer populations have been observed among the experimental red deer herds on the island of Rhum (Lowe, 1971, 444–6).

It should perhaps be noted that the benefits to herbivore populations from forest fires are in most cases fairly short-lived. In the California Chaparral studies, the maximum deer densities were observed in the year immediately following the fire; densities decreased progressively in each successive year and within five years had fallen almost to pre-fire levels (Taber and Dasmann, 1957, 235; Taber, 1961, 226–8). In other contexts the maximum populations may not occur until five or six years after the fire, or in some cases after an interval of ten years. The exact timing of the vegetational changes and the attendant fluctuations in animal populations clearly depend on a number of variables, including the character of the original vegetation, the intensity of the fire, the size of the area burnt, etc. (Cowan, 1956, 610; Spencer and Hakala, 1964, 23–5). In almost all situations, however, the beneficial effects of forest fires seem to disappear within 10–25 years (Cowan, 1956, 610; Spencer and Chatelain, 1953, 546; Spencer and Hakala, 1964, 30). By this time almost all the shrub vegetation and regenerating tree growth has grown out of reach of the animals and the closing in of the tree canopy shades out most forms of herbaceous vegetation on the forest floor. It follows from this that any policies of deliberate forest-burning on the part of hunter–gatherer communities would need to be repeated at frequent intervals to maintain any long-term benefits for the animal populations.

Cultural implications

The true role of hunting in the Mesolithic economy remains to be established. If this question is viewed in purely quantitative terms, several considerations suggest that the exploitation of animal populations may have contributed appreciably less to the year-round subsistence requirements of Mesolithic communities than the collection of vegetable foods (Mellars, 1975). At the same time, however, it would almost certainly be a mistake to minimize the importance of hunting in the basic ecological balance maintained between the human groups and food resources in general. According to the well known 'law of the minimum', the critical factor which determines the maximum level of any biological population is not so much the *overall* abundance of food resources on a long-term basis but rather the quantities of these resources available *during the periods of maximum scarcity* (Boughey, 1968, 2). In the case of human populations occupying the northern latitudes of the world, these periods of scarcity usually occur during the winter season when almost all varieties of vegetable foods are in extremely short supply (Dimbleby, 1967, 29–38). To some extent, of course, this seasonal shortage of plant foods could have been counteracted by building up reserves of such easily stored commodities as hazel nuts and perhaps acorns, which could be harvested during the autumn and preserved in a reasonably fresh and edible condition throughout the winter months (Mellars, 1975). However, this economic strategy suffers from one serious drawback, the highly unpredictable nature of mast yields from one year to another, which periodically results in seasons of almost complete crop failure (Dimbleby, 1967, 37). In these circumstances it is fairly easy to envisage how the presence of relatively large and stable populations of ungulates might have had a crucial bearing on the ability of certain Mesolithic groups to survive throughout the winter season. It is true, of course, that the hunting of large animals can also be a highly unpredictable activity, and that a single hunter may often go for several days or even weeks without making a kill (Lee, 1968, 40; Woodburn, 1968a, 53). In practice, however, the effects of these short-term fluctuations in hunting success can be largely overcome by social and residential structures which allow for the pooling of food supplies between a relatively large number of individual hunters (Woodburn, 1968b, 106). In the presence of these safeguards it is probable that the systematic exploitation of ungulate populations by Mesolithic groups would allow populations to be maintained at a far higher level than those that could be supported by the harvesting of vegetable foods alone.

Seasonal variations in the distribution and density of ungulate populations are likely to have influenced the behaviour of Mesolithic communities in several important respects. The obvious relationships between the distribution of food resources and the settlement patterns of hunter–gatherer groups have been discussed by several authors (Birdsell, 1968; Higgs *et al.*, 1967; Clark, 1972). Thus Clark (1972, 26–8) points out that the maximum size of the human group that can be supported in any settlement is directly related to the quantity of food which can be obtained within a particular area of movement—in Vita-Finzi and Higgs's (1970) terms, the 'catchment area' of the site in question. According to this model, areas with rich and concentrated food resources will tend to support larger settlements than areas where the food supplies are more scattered. The same point has been made by Birdsell (1968, 235–6) on the basis of cross-cultural ethnographic observations:

> "Where large food resources are concentrated either regionally or seasonally, local groups take on a very different nature. They will be larger in size, different manifestations of territoriality can be expected, and their principles of descent, marriage and recruitment can be expected to show wide variety."

The same factor of food concentration, of course, impinges equally and in a similar way on the maximum length of time throughout which any settlement can be occupied. Viewing this relationship from the standpoint of 'input-output economics', Lee (1969, 81) writes:

> "The Bushmen typically occupy a camp for a period of weeks or months and eat their way out of it. For instance, at a camp in the nut forests . . . the members will exhaust the nuts within a one-mile radius during the first week of occupation, within a two-mile radius the second week, and within a three-mile radius the third week. As time goes on, the members of the group must travel farther to reach the nuts, and the round-trip distance in miles is a measurement of the 'cost' of obtaining this desirable food."

Hence the density of local food resources can be seen as one of the major factors controlling both the size and temporal duration of hunter–gatherer settlements.

The impact of seasonal concentrations of ungulate populations on the economic and social patterns of hunter–gatherers can be argued in other ways. A heavy concentration of animals in any area must inevitably increase the frequency of hunter-encounter with the animal prey, and thereby increase both the efficiency (in terms of the expenditure of time and energy) and the overall productivity (in terms of food produced) of the hunting process. In fact, controlled studies have shown that the rate of hunting success in any area tends to vary in direct proportion to the local density of animal populations (Holsworth, 1973). Situations characterized by high densities of animals must therefore represent highly productive situations from an economic point of view.

Reference to the subject of hunting productivity raises the question of cooperative hunting procedures, involving the use of some form of 'drive'. Examples of the use of such drives could be quoted from a wide variety of cultural contexts (ranging from the North American Indians of the Great Plains area to the 18th century occupants of the Island of Rhum in the Inner Hebrides (Watson, 1925, 89)) and there is no doubt that these methods are capable of producing much higher yields of food on a *per capita* basis than those provided by the activities of single hunters. Use of such cooperative hunting strategies would of course provide a strong incentive to the formation of relatively large and stable social groupings capable of providing and coordinating the manpower necessary to operate the drives. Whether or not such methods were in fact employed in the Mesolithic is, of course, very difficult to determine from the archaeological record, and it might well be that the productivity levels attained by individual hunting practices under conditions of high animal concentrations would obviate the need for more highly organized procedures. Nevertheless, it is worth recalling that even in the absence of cooperative hunting methods a heavy dependence on the products of hunting at one season of the year would confer a strong adaptive advantage on the formation of large residential units. As already noted, such groupings would permit the pooling of food resources between a large number of individual hunters and thereby help to minimize the short-term uncertainties and fluctuations in supply inherent in this type of subsistence activity. Within the context of the heavy concentrations of animals envisaged here, this kind of social integration might also be necessary to prevent conflicts arising from the uncoordinated activities of too many individual hunters within a small and heavily populated area.

Many of the foregoing remarks would apply equally to the effects of various forms of forest clearance on the ecological relationships between human and animal populations. Thus the heavy concentrations of animals that seem invariably to characterize areas of recently cleared or burned-over forest would provide hunting conditions at least as favourable as those resulting from seasonal concentrations of the herds, and it is reasonable to assume that the human groups would focus their attention on these areas. At the same time, these conditions might have encouraged the formation of both larger and more permanent residential groupings than those located in areas of undisturbed forest. Quite apart from these purely local concentrations, however, it is important to emphasize the *overall* increases in ungulate populations that have been observed to result from forest clearance activities (Leopold, 1950; Longhurst, 1961). Coupled with the evidence for parallel increases in the weight and reproductive rates of the animals, this clearly adds up to a substantial increase in the total food resources available to the human communities. It is perhaps interesting to speculate on what effects this kind of overall increase in food supplies (if maintained by repeated episodes of forest destruction) might have on the long-term population levels of Mesolithic groups. Lastly, and perhaps most significant, it is worth recalling the magnetic attraction which areas of recently cleared forest can be seen to exert on herbivorous populations. Several writers have commented on the tendency for deer and other animals to be drawn towards these areas from extensive tracts of surrounding forest, attracted by the abundant and highly nutritious growth of new vegetation (Taber and Dasmann, 1957, 236; Taber, 1961, 226, 231; Spencer and Chatelain, 1953, 546; Spencer and Hakala, 1964, 30). It is apparent that this pattern of behaviour would have provided the human groups with an effective means not only of *predicting* the distributions of the animal populations with a high level of accuracy, but also of *controlling* these distributions to some extent.

In short, I am suggesting that some deliberate policy of forest destruction on the part of Mesolithic communities (or for that matter any other hunter–gatherer groups) would have provided a means of influencing animal populations in three significant ways: (a) by increasing the total numbers of the animals; (b) by increasing the weight, general health, and reproductive rate of the animals; and (c) by controlling the distribution of the herds at different seasons of the year and in different portions of the annual range. How far this pattern of man-animal relationships can be described as a simple form of 'domestication' would seem to reduce largely to a question of the definition of terms.

REFERENCES

Bannikov, A. G. (1967). Some remarks concerning determination of biomass of wild ungulates in natural geographical zones of the U.S.S.R. *In* Petrusewicz, K. (ed.). *Secondary Productivity of Terrestrial Ecosystems.* Warsaw and Cracow; 255–267.

Birdsell, J. B. (1968). Some predictions for the Pleistocene based on equilibrium systems among recent hunter-gatherers. *In* Lee, R. B. and DeVore, I. (eds.). *Man the Hunter.* Chicago: Aldine; 229–240.

Boughey, A. S. (1968). *Ecology of Populations.* London: MacMillan.

Bourlière, F. (1963). Observations on the ecology of some large African mammals. *In* Howell, F. C. and Bourlière, F. (eds.). *African Ecology and Human Evolution.* Chicago: Aldine; 43–54.

Clark, J. G. D. (1972). Star Carr: a case study in bio-archaeology. *Addison-Wesley Modular Publications,* 10, 1–42.

Cliff, E. P. (1939). Relationship between elk and mule deer in the Blue Mountains of Oregon. *Trans. N. Am. Wildl. Conf.,* 4, 560–569.

Cowan, I. McT. (1956). Life and times of the coast black-tailed deer. *In* Taylor, W. P. (ed.). *The Deer of North America.* Harrisburg: Stackpole; 523–617.

Cumming, J. A. (1969). Prescribed burning on recreation areas in New Jersey: history, objectives, influence and techniques. *Proc. Annual Tall Timbers Fire Ecology Conference,* 9, 251–269.

DeWitt, J. B. and Derby, J. V. (1955). Changes in the nutritive value of browse plants following forest fires. *J. Wildl. Mgmt.,* 19, 65–70.

Dimbleby, G. W. (1961). The ancient forest of Blackamore. *Antiquity,* 35, 123–128.

Dimbleby, G. W. (1967). *Plants and Archaeology.* London: Baker.

Einarsen, A. S. (1946). Crude protein determination as an applied management technique. *Trans. N. Am. Wildl. Conf.,* 11, 309–312.

Elssmann, H. (1969). Moglichkeiten zur Qualitiatsverbesserung beim Rotwild; dargestellt am Beispiel des Fichtelsbirges. *Z. Jagdwiss.,* 15, 41–62.

Flerov, K. K. (1952). *Fauna of the U.S.S.R.: Musk deer and deer.* Moscow: Academy of Sciences. (English translation by the Israel programme for Scientific translations, Jerusalem, 1960).

Higgs, E. S., Vita-Finzi, C., Harris, D. K., and Fagg, A. E. (1967). The climate, environment and industries of Stone-age Greece. *Proc. Prehist. Soc.,* 33, 1–29.

Holsworth, W. N. (1973). Hunting efficiency and white-tailed deer density. *J. Wildl. Mgmt.,* 37, 336–342.

Hosley, N. W. (1956). Management of the white-tailed deer in its environment. *In* Taylor, W. P. (ed.). *The Deer of North America.* Harrisburg: Stackpole; 187–259.

Ingebrigsten, O. (1924). *Hjortens utbredelse i Norge.* Bergen: Naturvidenskabelige Rekke Nr. 6.

Jarman, M. R. (1972). European deer economies and the advent of the Neolithic. *In* Higgs, E. S. (ed.). *Papers in Economic Prehistory*. Cambridge: University Press; 125–147.

Kohn, B. E. and Mooty, J. J. (1971). Summer habitat of white-tailed deer in north-central Minnesota. *J. Wildl. Mgmt.*, 35, 476–487.

Lay, D. W. (1957). Browse quality and the effects of burning in southern pine forests. *J. For.*, 55, 342–347.

Lee, R. B. (1968). What hunters do for a living, or how to make out on scarce resources. *In* Lee, R. B. and DeVore, I. (eds.). *Man the Hunter*. Chicago: Aldine; 30–48.

Lee, R. B. (1969). !Kung Bushman subsistence: an input-output analysis, *In* Damas, D. (ed.). *Ecological Essays*. Ottawa: National Museums of Canada (Bulletin No. 230); 73–94.

Leege, T. A. (1968). Prescribed burning for elk in northern Idaho. *Proc. Annual Tall Timbers Fire Ecology Conference,* 8, 235–253.

Leege, T. A. and Hickey, W. O. (1971). Sprouting of northern Idaho shrubs after prescribed burning. *J. Wildl. Mgmt.*, 35, 508–515.

Leopold, A. S. (1936). Deer and dauerwald in Germany. *J. For.*, 34, 366–375, 460–466.

Leopold, A. S. (1950). Deer in relation to plant succession. *Trans. N. Am. Wildl. Conf.*, 15, 571–578.

Leopold, A. S., Riney, T., McCain, R., and Tevis, L. (1951). The Jawbone deer herd. *California Fish and Game,* Game Bulletin No. 4.

Longhurst, W. M. (1961). Big-game and rodent relationships to forests and grasslands in North America. *La Terre et la Vie,* 1961, 305–326.

Lowe, V. P. W. (1966). Observations on the dispersal of red deer on Rhum. *In* Jewell, P. A. and Loizos, C. (eds.). *Play, Exploration and Territory in Mammals*. London: Zoological Society; 211–228.

Lowe, V. P. W. (1971). Some effects of a change in estate management on a deer population. *In* Duffey, E. and Watt, A. S. (eds.). *The Scientific Management of Animal and Plant Communities*. Oxford, London, Edinburgh: Blackwell; 437–456.

McCain, R. (1939). The development and use of game drives for determining white-tail deer populations on Allegheny National Forest. *Trans. N. Am. Wildl. Conf.*, 4, 221–230.

Mellars, P. A. (1975). Settlement patterns and industrial variability in the British Mesolithic. *In* Longworth, I. H. and Sieveking, G. (eds.). *Problems in Social and Economic Archaeology*. Cambridge University Press (in press).

Murphy, D. A. (1963). A captive elk herd in Missouri. *J. Wildl. Mgmt.*, 27, 411–414.

Mystkowska, E. T. (1966). Morphological variability of the skull and body weight of the red deer. *Acta Theriologica,* 11, 129–194.

Rasmussen, D. I. (1939). Mule deer range and population studies in Utah. *Trans. N. Am. Wildl. Conf.*, 4, 236–243.

Segelquist, C. A. and Green, W. E. (1968). Deer food yields in four Ozark forest types. *J. Wildl. Mgmt.*, 32, 330–337.

Segelquist, C. A., Ward, F. D. and Leonard, R. G. (1969). Habitat-deer relations in two Ozark enclosures. *ibid.*, 33, 511–520.

Severinghaus, C. W. and Cheatum, E. L. (1956). Life and times of the white-tailed deer. *In* Taylor, W. P. (ed.). *The Deer of North America*. Harrisburg: Stackpole; 57–186.

Simmons, I. G. (1969). Evidence for vegetation changes associated with Mesolithic man in Britain. *In* Ucko, P. J. and Dimbleby, G. W. (eds.). *The Domestication and Exploitation of Plants and Animals*. London: Duckworth; 113–119.

Siuda, A., Zurowski, W., and Siuda, H. (1969). The food of the roe deer. *Acta theriol.*, 14, 247–262.

Smith, A. G. (1970). The influence of Mesolithic and Neolithic man on British vegetation: a discussion. *In* Walker, D. and West, R. G. (eds.). *Studies in the Vegetational History of the British Isles*. Cambridge University Press; 81–96.

Spencer, D. L. and Chatelain, E. F. (1953). Progress in the management of the moose of south central Alaska. *Trans. N. Am. Wildl. Conf.*, 18, 539–552.

Spencer, D. L. and Hakala, J. B. (1964). Moose and fire on the Kenai. *Proc. Annual Tall Timbers Fire Ecology Conference,* 3, 11–33.

Taber, R. D. (1961). The black-tailed deer: a review of ecology and management. *La Terre et la Vie,* 1961, 221–245.

Taber, R. D. (1963). Land use and native cervid populations in America north of Mexico. *Trans. International Union of Game Biologists,* 6, 201–225.

Taber, R. D. and Dasmann, R. F. (1957). The dynamics of three natural populations of the deer *Odocoileus hemionius columbianus*. *Ecology,* 38, 233–246.

Tierson, W. C., Patric, E. F., and Behrend, D. F. (1966). Influence of white-tailed deer on the logged northern hardwood forest. *J. For.*, 64, 801–885.

Trippensee, R. E. (1948). *Wildlife Management—Upland Game and General Principles*. New York, Toronto, London: McGraw Hill.

Van Den Brink, F. H. (1967). *A Field Guide to the Mammals of Britain and Europe*. London: Collins.

Vita-Finzi, C. and Higgs, E. S. (1970). Prehistoric economy in the Mount Carmel area of Palestine: site cachment analysis. *Proc. Prehist. Soc.*, 36, 1–37.

Watson, W. J. (1925). Deer and boar in Gaelic literature. *In* Ross, J. (ed.). *The Book of the Red Deer*. London: Simpkin, Marshall, Hamilton, Kent; 75–100.

Webb, W. L. (1960). Forest wildlife management in Germany. *J. Wildl. Mgmt.*, 24, 147–161.

Woodburn, J. (1968a). An introduction to Hadza ecology. *In* Lee, R. B. and DeVore, I. (eds.). *Man the Hunter*. Chicago: Aldine; 49–55.

Woodburn, J. (1968b). Stability and flexibility in Hazda residential groupings. *In* Lee, R. B. and DeVore, I. (eds.). *Ibid.*, 103–110.

The ecological setting of Mesolithic man in the Highland Zone

I. G. Simmons

Synopsis

The environmental relations of the microlith-using Sauveterrean folk who were present on the uplands between c. 8500 and 5000 bp, are considered. Their hunting economy is thought to have been migratory in nature, with camps of different sizes at various seasons. Their use of the mid-Flandrian forests was dominated by their cull of large mammals, especially red deer, and the zone of open plant communities above the forest would have been of particular importance, since the carrying capacity of open scrub for deer is higher than that of mature forest. Using fire as the primary tool, Mesolithic populations probably manipulated the woodland edge habitat to produce more browse for ungulates and more Corylus *nuts for direct consumption. The possibility of herding of red deer is also discussed. It is concluded that although these people exerted an influence on the ecology of the uplands, their effects were small compared with later prehistoric time.*

Purpose of paper

I wish to approach the contribution of Mesolithic man to the landscape of the Highland Zone from an ecological viewpoint. Not all the ecosystems of the relevant period will have been interactive with man, but some biotic and abiotic materials will have been appraised as resources, and conscious alteration of the environments will have occurred; other parts of man's surroundings may have been altered unconsciously.

It is therefore certain that ecological changes will have accompanied man's occupance of the Highland Zone. What is less easy to describe is the scale of such changes and hence the effects on landscape. A small-scale change in ecology, such as a moss made more abundant by an increased frequency of burning, can scarcely be said to contribute to landscape changes, yet it is different only in degree from large-scale clearance of forest by pastoral domesticates which took place in much later times. The arbitrariness of the division between ecological change leading to landscape change and ecological change not leading to landscape change is not pursued further here (I mention it to suggest that the two should not necessarily be equated); furthermore, any effects of man are imposed upon the 'normal' processes of ecological succession and adjustment.

Mesolithic man in the Highland Zone: culture type and time span

When the upland fringes are considered, early Mesolithic people of the Maglemosian culture must be included, the Star Carr folk being an obvious example (Clark, 1954). If they moved on a seasonal basis, then did they penetrate the uplands at all? There seems to be virtually no evidence for Maglemosian-type implements at upland sites during the Flandrian I chronozone (i.e. before 7500 bp). As indirect evidence we have Jones's (1971; forthcoming) find, the skeleton of a *Bos primigenius,* embedded in mire deposits at Kildale Hall (North Yorkshire) at 968 m OD. The bones were associated with a layer of charcoal and have a date of 10350 ± 200 bp, placing the episode firmly within the Maglemosian epoch; is this possibly a remnant of the summer activities of people of the Star Carr (9388 ± 209 bp) type? This is possibly the most likely explanation (the other being the year-round presence of such people well inland who may have contributed the implements found near Seamer Carrs in lowland Cleveland) but it may be a rather conventional wisdom. In Ireland the comparable Larnian people have been dated from 7680–5290 bp, bringing them up to contact with Neolithic people and overlapping with the later Mesolithic remains from western England (Mitchell, 1970, 1971).

The Mesolithic presence on the uplands themselves appears to be signified mainly by microlithic remains of the Sauveterrian type, associated with the spreads of charcoal, which are usually interpreted as hearths, and occasional traces of rudimentary settlement forms. Exceptions to the general pattern show industries which include virtually Palaeolithic material, as at Sheldon in Derbyshire (Radley, 1965), or which include implements with a Maglemosian cast to them (Radley and Marshall, 1965). Where associated organic materials have been dated, the upland sites usually fall between 8500 bp and the opening of the Neolithic, i.e. they are 'late' Mesolithic in age; additional confirmation is given by the number of undated sites from uplands where the relative chronology given by pollen analysis also suggests the later reaches of Mesolithic time (Radley, 1969). The phenomena at North Gill (North York Moors), which I attributed to human activity (Simmons, 1969a, 1969b), have now been dated at 6366 ± 69 bp, which adds to the cluster of 'late' upland sites. A further phenomenon of many upland sites, shared by some lowland sites (e.g. in Ireland at Newferry, Smith and Collins, 1971), is the continuance of Mesolithic culture into 'Neolithic' time, evidenced by the mingling of artefactual types. Hence an 'ending' of the Mesolithic period may be impossible to trace: given an altitudinal separation of Mesolithic and Neolithic folk, the economy of the former may have persisted into the Bronze Age; without such a compartition, a gradual mergence would seem inevitable.

The economy of Mesolithic folk has always been assumed to be of the food-collecting rather than food-producing type and to have had an emphasis on hunting and gathering (Clark, 1968). On the positive side, there is the evidence from Star Carr, paralleled by many other European sites, of many animal bones, showing concentrations of particular species, which presumably did not accidentally drop dead at that individual spot, especially the fish. Also, the microliths at the upland sites have been assumed to be dominated by material suitable for arrowheads. Gathering is shown almost exclusively by the occurrence of the nuts of hazel *(Corylus avellana)* at many Mesolithic sites.

Negatively, there is nothing to suggest agriculture, except at those sites with distinct Neolithic artefactual affinities: no querns or cereal pollen, for example. This leaves one mode of subsistence unconsidered: that of herding (of red deer, for example), for which there appears to be neither positive nor negative evidence, since the occasional worn antler interpreted as symptomatic of tethering scarcely constitutes enough evidence for herding—the confinement of a single animal for ritual purposes might produce this effect. An economy based on the hunting of large mammals, and supplemented in season by fishing (the lack of fish at Star Carr is surprising) and gathering, seems to be in accord with all the evidence and all our assumptions.

One approach to the possibilities of reconstructing the settlement patterns of the hunters is through the typologies of settlements suggested for food-collecting peoples. Fitzhugh (1972), for example, erects a number of categories:

(a) A gathering site (i.e. meeting). Used one to two times per year at a particular time of year, by a large number of people.
(b) A base camp. A smaller site than (a), but which is a central focus during a portion of a particular season.
(c) An exploitation camp: intensive. Occupied by a single family over a variety of time periods in order to garner a variety of resources, and thus exhibiting a wide assemblage of tools and a lot of debris.
(d) An exploitation camp: light. Occupied briefly by a family; the small amount of debris and narrow range of tools suggest a narrow range of activities.
(e) A bivouac. Few structures and tools are found.

As far as the Maglemosians are concerned, at least part of the year seems to have been sedentary, and Clark (1972) postulates an occupation of some five months from the back end of the year through to April. This would certainly fit (b) above and could even be a gathering place, depending upon how 'large' is defined. If it means about 25 people, and if one purpose of the meeting was the sort of ritual in which the antler frontlets found at Star Carr might have been used, Star Carr might well be a gathering site.

By contrast, the microlith sites on the uplands seem much more ephemeral. They are mostly of the period prior to the *Ulmus* decline of *c.* 5000 bp and have generally been interpreted as being occupied for only short periods. They are mostly found at altitudes between 300 and 460 m, the lower figure of which might well represent an artificial level due to the presence of the moorland edge; and on both ridges and the flanks of hills, and often at spring-heads: on the east margin of Dartmoor, a considerable concentration of microliths was found at *c.* 245 m around spring-heads (Grieg and Rankine, 1956). The reduced industry of these sites is usually taken to be indicative of a specialized function which in terms of Fitzhugh's typology would be an exploitation camp

TABLE I Types of Mesolithic settlement in North Yorkshire

Locale	*Type of settlement*	*Numbers*	*Animal resources*	*Season*
Coast or Estuary	?Exploitation camp—light	Family group (?5)	Fish Shellfish Mammals	Winter—Early spring
Cuesta	Base camp or gathering site	Extended group (?25)	Mammals	Autumn, early summer
Upland	Exploitation camp—light	Family group	Mammals ?Fish	Summer

(light), presumably a camp from which the hunting of large mammals was carried out. If we accept that in our context the bivouac is not likely to leave any traces, then only (c), the intensive exploitation camp, is missing. There is no reason why a typology developed for Arctic North America should apply *in toto* to Mesolithic England, but it is worth noting the recent discovery of a large site for Mesolithic remains at Upleatham in North Yorkshire (NZ 636201/NZ 622199; at 170 m: Brown *et al.*, forthcoming). Here approximately equal numbers of microliths and scrapers were found (cf. the high microlith–scraper ratio on the high moors), and it has been interpreted as a site where food preparation took place, a view corroborated by the large number of hearth stones found. In terms of catchment area, its position within easy reach of the coast (both now and in earlier times when it was thought to be only a few kilometres east of its present positions), an estuary noted until recently for its wildfowl, and of the higher terrain inland, is clearly advantageous. Here, then, may be an example of an exploitation camp (intensive) or, more likely, the functional equivalent of Star Carr for the non-Maglemosian peoples, i.e. a base camp or gathering place. So in Cleveland it is perhaps not too fanciful to suggest that we can see emerging the outlines of the settlement pattern which would be similar to that shown in Table I.

There are any number of possible inaccuracies in this scheme (should a biannual visit to the large rivers to cull migratory fish be added?), but an annual round involving summer hunting on the upland, winter strand-looping, and passing through the intermediate site twice (with a pause for social/religious/group activities) does not seem totally unreasonable and has parallels among some groups of recent and near-recent food collectors.

Clues to the overall density of such people come mainly from parallels with modern situations, where a variety of density estimates can be found. For Star Carr-type people, Braidwood and Reid (1957) suggested 12·5 per 100 mile^2, and for a similar North American (Cree) culture in modern times, Cleland (1966) gives 0·9 per mile^2. Possibly 1 per mile^2 (0·35 per km^2) is a reasonable estimate, but the margins of error must be vast.

Habitats occupied in the Highland Zone during the Mesolithic

We may make a twofold division of habitat types: the first group are successional habitats of the Flandrian I chronozone, where in both uplands and lowlands an allogenic succession of biota took place

TABLE II Successional habitats of Flandrian I in the English uplands

Habitat / *Biota*	*Preforest* —— *leading to*	——→ *Forest*	*Wetlands*	*Coast*
Vegetation	*Empetrum* heath with tree and shrub thickets *(Pinus, Betula, Salix)*	*Betula–Pinus* followed by *Corylus, Ulmus, Quercus, Alnus, Tilia* to mixed-oak forest	Lakes with marginal veg., *Salix* carr. Streams with steady regime	Inland penetration of saltmarsh, mudflats, with rising sea level
Large Fauna	*Bos* *Alces* *Rangifer*	*Bos*, *Alces*, *Rangifer* } dimin. *Cervus elaphus*, *Capreolus cap.* } incr. *Sus scrofa*	Waterfowl *Esox* Salmonids	Seals Mollusca Crustacea

at a time of ameliorating climate—a series of forest types, for example, successively covered land but not synchronously within the entire British Isles. Within these changes, smaller scale succession, such as the filling-in of small lakes, was also continuing. Secondly, we note 'mature' habitats, which form the so-called 'climax' vegetation of Godwin's (1956) pollen assemblage Zone VIIa, or Atlantic period, i.e., chronozone Flandrian II, approximately 7500–5000 bp, covering later Mesolithic times. It was not homogenous, since there would have been minor successions within it; it was dominated by mixed oak forest, but coastal, aquatic, and 'above-the-forest' habitats also need consideration.

The successional habitats of Flandrian I in the uplands are shown in Table II. In the pre-forest period, the find of the *Bos* skeleton at Kildale Hall provides another example of a human habitat, and other bones found in the locality (reindeer, red deer, elk) show the luxuriant heath to have supported a large mammal fauna. The subsequent forests reveal the familiar pattern of transition towards the *Quercus*-dominated woodland of altithermal times, but we must remember that Mesolithic man was present during the immigration of the trees. Whether or not men influenced the course of the assembly of the 'climax' forest is open to the sort of discussion given by Smith (1970), with special emphasis on hazel and alder.

Eustatic rises in sea-level created different habitats quite far inland in the case of long estuaries such as those of the southern Lake District and the Tees. The littoral and off-shore fauna would presumably have

TABLE III Terrestrial habitats of Flandrian II in the English uplands

Habitat / *Biota*	*Forests*	*Hyper-forest*		*Aquatic*
Vegetation	*Quercus* dominant with stands or individuals of *Ulmus, Tilia, Alnus.* Successive phases of *Betula, Sorbus auc.* Perhaps some *Pinus*	Bog *Sphagnum* *Eriophorum* *Rynchospora* *Erica tetralix* Scrub *Betula/Corylus/Sorbus*	Grassland *D. flexuosa* *Nardus* *Ag. tenuis* *Fest. ovina* *Molinia*	Suite of plants of slow-flowing streams
Large fauna				
Herbivores	*Bos primigenius* *C. elaphus* *C. capreolus*	*C. elaphus* *C. capreolus*		*Castor*
Diversivores	*Sus scrofa* *Ursus*	*Sus scrofa*		
Carnivores*	*Canis lupus*	*Canis lupus*		*Esox* Salmonids

*Also present: Fox, badger, cat, marten, otter, lynx, *Mustela*

had a higher species diversity and biomass than today's, and thus spatially and biologically have presented a rich opportunity for subsistence gatherers and fishermen.

In late Mesolithic times, the climatic 'optimum' or altithermal period was passing, but temperatures and precipitation may well have exceeded those of the present, effects which would be most marked on the uplands. Table III gives some details of the terrestrial habitats of the time. The woodlands would be different from our present high forests in their more or less unbroken canopy, below which tall unbranched trees would stand amongst a relative lack of shrubs and ground flora. Being self-protective, the forest would be relatively homogenous, with not a great deal of species variation from sea-level to its altitudinal limit; thus the present differentiation between upland and lowland would have been less apparent. We would expect the soils beneath the forest to have been Brown Earths; particulate matter and nutrient loss to streams would be very low except where the root layer was broken.

The animal communities were probably comparable with large areas of deciduous forest today. From the point of view of prehistory, the abundance of the larger species is clearly of interest: present-day estimates tend to talk of individual species, whereas the whole suite is more interesting. The quantity of animal biomass for analogous environments has been investigated in some of the European IBP studies, and Petrusewicz (1967), for example, suggests the following biomass figures for the oak-dominated forests of central Europe:

Biomass (dry weight), kg/ha

Amphibians and reptiles	*Birds*	*Mammals*	*Total*
1·2	1·2	7·5	9·9

(A dry weight of 7·5 kg/ha ≏ 25 kg/ha live weight ≏ one large roe deer)

Other estimates are of the same order or rather lower (all values in kg/ha):

Oak–hornbeam forest in Czechoslovakia	Red deer, roe, hare, boar	Herbivs. + diversivs.	4·5
		Herbivs. only	1·5
		Total	10·1
		Ungulates	1·3
Mixed oak steppe in W. USSR	Herbiv. mamms. (inc. moose)+ birds	Mice and voles	0·9
		Squirrels and hares	0·1
		All else	2·2
Deciduous forests of W. USSR	Moose, red deer, roe deer, pig	Total	4·0

These statistics show us that, compared with the plant biomass of the forest ecosystem, the animal component is very small, and that cropping the herbivores and diversivores—then as now—allows access to only a small part of the energy flux and storage in the ecosystem.

The altitudinal limit of the forest is difficult to estimate and few authors of palaeo-ecological studies have committed themselves to firm estimates of the former tree-line. A number of studies of the North York Moors suggest that there was certainly closed canopy forest up to 245 m, and that above 335 m there may not have been; in between is a zone of uncertainty, which could also have been a zone of transition, which in this region would have been spatially very significant because of the low slope once above the lip of the valleys. For areas such as the Pennines and Dartmoor, the studied vagueness of most workers might collectively be interpreted to hint at a tree-line of *c.* 366 m. However, many local variations must have existed, for above this altitude we find tree-remains at the base of peat of 'Atlantic' times.

In areas of poor drainage above the limit of closed forest, blanket bog began to form during Flandrian II, mostly in response to the change of climate towards greater effectiveness of precipitation, which is held to have occurred around 7500 bp. Between the bogs and the forest, the pollen analytical evidence seems to suggest the presence of grasslands undergoing acidification, along with scrub or very open woodland with shade-intolerant trees and shrubs which are also tolerant of the more exacting environment outside the forest canopy. (Some species are suggested in Table III).

The importance of this zone to fauna would be the increased density of browse it would offer to the large mammal herbivores. Turcek (1969) estimates the average herbivore biomass of central European willow-poplar woodlands at 3·2 kg/ha, nearly twice some of the high forest estimates. In Scotland today, the highest densities of red deer are found near dense stands of small trees, and in close proximity to heather, water, and the wallow which accumulating blanket mire might provide (Batcheler, 1960).

The hyper-forest zone would therefore be a good source of browse for red and roe deer, especially in summer but probably also in winter, when the known ability of deer to traverse high altitudinal ranges would enable them to make use of the higher grounds during more clement spells in winter. The importance of the zone to diversivores is less certain, although Turcek (1969) remarks that dominance by diversivores characterizes unbalanced, disturbed, and seral communities in general.

Evidence of charcoal layers in blanket bogs from this period points to the possibility of the vegetation being subject to fire, and it is interesting to note that research from the USA suggests that burning improves both the quantity and quality of browse for ungulates (in this case the white-tailed deer). In Tennessee, a pine–deciduous forest sampled in 1968 (Dills, 1970), yielded (lb/acre) the following quantities of deer browse:

unburned	'68 burn	'67 burn	'66 burn
173	127	598	931

Thus, two seasons must pass before the quantity of browse from the burned areas exceeds that of the unburned, but the eventual difference is considerable. In summer (but not apparently in January), the protein content is higher from the burned areas also. In more general terms, burning seems to reduce the height of the existing browse, bringing more of it within reach of smaller ungulates; it allows the addition of more browse plants by facilitating the germination of seeds, and it increases the palatability of the vegetation.

The formation of peat beneath carpets of *Eriophorum* spp and *Sphagnum* spp represents not only a storage of energy (tapped by human peat-burning groups), but a storehouse of water also, combining with the forest to hold run-off and make streams less liable to variations in flow than at present. When growing quickly, *Sphagnum* bog can envelop forest quite quickly (i.e. in the order of 10–30 years), and so rapid lateral spread of bog at the expense of woodland, especially the hyper-forest scrub, was doubtless occurring during Flandrian II.

The streams would be low in silt and dissolved nutrients and not prone to 'flashy' regimes. The latter tendency would be reinforced by the presence of beaver *(Castor europea)* whose activities would mean slower runoff and deeper pools, and hence less scour. These factors would, according to Cornwall (1968), improve the conditions for migratory fish such as trout and salmon; presumably pike would also benefit from being able to find plenty of weedy pools without a strong current in which to lay their eggs.

The subsistence resources of man

Because the complete suite of large mammals is nowhere present in Europe (*Bos primigenius* has disappeared entirely, the wolf and moose are lacking from much of their natural range), and because the remaining forests of Europe are probably not very similar to the Flandrian II stage forests of highland Britain, the relative numbers of animals per unit area are difficult to ascertain, especially for the largest beasts such as *Bos,* at *c.* 1000 kg liveweight. An estimate for the Białowieza forest in eastern Poland, which includes *Bison bonasus,* gives a ratio of 14 red deer : 11 roe deer : two bison per 1000 ha, but no pigs are included (Borowski *et al.,* 1967). Most writers, especially Clark in the single context of Star Carr, and Jarman (1972) in the wider European context, agree that red deer were the most important food source of Mesolithic man. That red deer and pig are found at more than 80% of all the sites cannot be regarded as insignificant (and that they do not compete for food is also important), neither can the fact that roe deer and wild cattle appear at *c.* 50% of the sites listed. Elk seems to be confined to the Baltic area in the later Mesolithic periods, and so perhaps it can be disregarded as far as the later microlithic cultures of the uplands are concerned.

Many small animals were doubtless taken, but the evidence is minimal. Land mammals such as squirrels and small rodents may well have been eaten, as would birds (especially water fowl) and fish, where we may note that their absence, taken by Clark to mean that Star Carr was unoccupied in the summer, is paralleled at an Archaic period site at Raddatz, Wisconsin (Cleland, 1966), where numerous remains of water-fowl were found but no fish. Beaver would have been sought for their pelts but are also edible.

Plants must also have been eaten, but very little evidence exists. However, their value for nutrition, to say nothing of their usefulness in social, medicinal, and magical purposes, as well as for construction and bedding, which presumably count as subsistence activities, is obvious. The outstanding exception to the lack of evidence is the nut of *Corylus avellana.* This item turns up repeatedly in excavations at Mesolithic sites (Dimbleby, 1967), and pollen analysis suggests that it was quite plentiful during Flandrian II. However, it was probably less frequent and certainly less productive in the mature forest itself than at the forest edges, especially at the altitudinal limit. The evidence for its presence at that limit is a little stronger than for some lower altitudes, since the chance of the presence of a large proportion of the nearly identical *Myrica gale* pollen is likely to be less. Further, biotic influences like grazing and burning would be conducive to the flowering and nut production (as well as browse production) of hazel, since both these are likely to cause stump-sprouting.

Manipulation of habitats and herds

If Mesolithic peoples wanted to improve (a) the game populations and (b) their chances of killing them in the sort of forest described above, then there is the need for (a) to improve the quantity of browse and for (b) to reduce at least some of it to improve the chances of sighting game and of being able to follow it. However, there was probably not a great deal of undershrub in these forests in any case.

For the purpose of (a), however, the best place would be at the upper edge of the forest, where it gave way to open land, especially near water where animals regularly came to drink. The obvious tool is fire, and the species encouraged would be birch (apparently not a preferred browse for deer), alder, hazel, ash, and possibly *Rhamnus* and *Frangula,* all pioneer species. The flourishing of hazel would have the side effect of producing more nuts. This sort of phase is, I think, recorded at North Gill in the North York Moors, now dated at 6366 $\pm$ 69 bp. At the altitudinal limit of forest, of course, even sporadic manipulation by fire could result in deforestation, which would allow leaching of the soils, and I suggested in 1969 that one consequence could be the formation of blanket bog. It is interesting to note that Moore (1972, 1973) has implicated Neolithic man in the formation of blanket bog on the uplands of Wales. If burning techniques were successful at higher altitudes, no doubt they would have been tried at lower levels also, probably sporadically.

Another way of improving the game populations would have been by herding, as suggested by Jarman (1972), probably of male red deer. If so, then a seasonal migration becomes quite likely because of the concentration of the animals and hence their ability to eat out the food of a local area quite quickly. So again, areas with the most browse would become attractive, and so would also the manipulation of such areas to provide more browse or at least a steady supply of it. Dimbleby's interpretation of very high *Hedera* pollen frequencies at some Mesolithic sites as resulting from the gathering of ivy for fodder confirms this idea. To go higher in the summer might also be advantageous in order to escape some of the insects that might have worried the animals, though I suggested previously that there would be less differentiation between highland and lowland than at present. Altogether, herding might just have been a more powerful spur to habitat manipulation than hunting.

The evidence for habitat alterations associated with Mesolithic man has been very well summarized by Smith (1970) and by Dimbleby (1962), to which could be added the cumulative detail of more evidence of the same type that has been brought forward since their publication. Their findings may perhaps be summarized as:

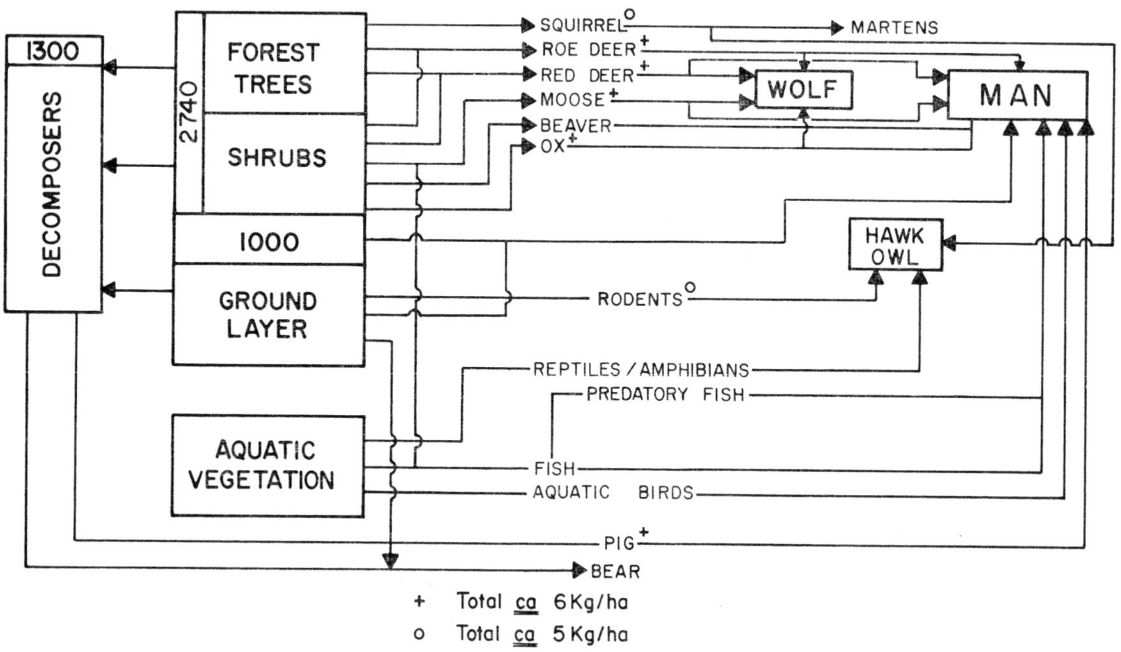

Fig. 1 Food levels of altithermal forests. Figures for vegetation in kg/ha

(a) Expansions of *Corylus* and *Alnus* could have been helped by human (i.e. Mesolithic) activity, and

(b) Small clearances occurred in which *Plantago lanceolata* grew; some of these are uncertain in their dating because of outdated assumptions of the synchroneity of the boundary between Godwin's Zones VI and VII. That the small clearances might have had considerable ecological effects is suggested by the evidence of an inwash stripe in a peat-filled slack in North Yorkshire, which on pollen analytical grounds would be Mesolithic in age (Jones, 1971, forthcoming). Obviously, enough forest was removed to allow soil erosion in this one place at least.

My reading of this body of evidence (and there seems to have been no accumulation of evidence of any different character than that summarized by Smith and by Dimbleby) is that it suggests sporadic clearance of forests at the lower altitudes but more purposeful alteration of the vegetation at the forest margins, which could have led to more or less permanent vegetational change. This does not conflict with any of the more hypothetical models described above, nor does it provide any way of differentiating or confirming them. There is clearly scope for problem-oriented research here.

Ecology into landscape

Figure 1 sets out a reconstruction of the food levels of the altithermal forests and shows man's position in it. No surprises emerge, except that man is at the top of a rapidly narrowing energy pyramid. The main feedback loop from man to the environment was probably fire, and there are enough contemporary examples of its power to alter the ecology of marginal areas to allow us to imagine that it could have been a strong force for habitat alteration in the uplands. To assess the contribution of Mesolithic man to the landscape depends perhaps on how good an observer you are. There must have been lots of small changes in the forests, but mostly these would have been associated with clearances which were both small and temporary. If there were larger-scale changes, they were near the altitudinal limits of the forests, and the initiation of blanket bog would have been the most considerable of these.

Thus, I would suggest that Mesolithic men did exert an effect on the ecology of, and contribute to the development of the landscape of, Highland Britain, but that their numbers and their economy rendered these effects very small when compared with the changes wrought in Bronze Age and Iron Age times.

ACKNOWLEDGEMENTS

I should like to thank all the people who took the trouble to read and comment on an earlier (and much longer) version of this paper, especially Brian Roberts, Alan Smith, and Judy Turner. Geoffrey Dimbleby and Don Spratt also read the draft and allowed me the use of unpublished material.

REFERENCES

Batcheler, C. L. (1960). A study of the relations between roe, red and fallow deer, with special reference to Drummond Hill Forest, Scotland. *J. Anim. Ecol.*, 29, 375–384.

Borowski, S., Krasinski, A., and Mitkowski, L. (1967). Food and role of the European Bison in forest ecosystems. *Acta theriol.*, 12, 367–376.

Braidwood, R. J. and Reed, C. A. (1957). The achievement and early consequences of food production: a consideration of the archaeological and natural-historical evidence. *Cold Harbor Spring Symposia on Quantitative Biology*, 22: *Population Studies: Animal Ecology and Demography*, 19–31.

Brown, D. R., Goddard, R. E., and Spratt, D. A. (forthcoming). Mesolithic settlement sites at Upleatham, N. R. *Yorkshire Archaeol. J.*

Clark, J. G. D. (1954). *Excavations at Star Carr*. Cambridge: University Press.

Clark, J. G. D. (1968). The economic impact of the change from late-glacial to post-glacial conditions in Northern Europe. *Proc. VIIIth Int. Cong. Anthro. and Ethnol. Sci.*, Tokyo and Kyoto, Vol. III, 241–244.

Clark, J. G. D. (1972). *Star Carr: a case study in Bioarchaeology*. Cambridge, Mass: Addison-Wesley Modular Publications in Anthropology, No. 10.

Cleland, C. E. (1966). *The Prehistoric Animal Ecology and Ethnozoology of the Upper Great Lakes Region*. Anthrop. Papers of the Museum of Anthropology, University of Michigan, No. 29; Ann Arbor; University of Michigan.

Cornwall, I. W. (1968). *Prehistoric Animals and their Hunters*, London: Faber and Faber.

Dills, G. G. (1970). Effect of prescribed burning on deer browse. *J. Wildl. Mgmt.*, 34, 540–545.

Dimbleby, G. W. (1962). *The Development of British Heathlands and their Soils*. Oxford For. Mem. 23.

Dimbleby, G. W. (1967). *Plants and Archaeology*. London: John Baker.

Fitzhugh, W. W. (1972). *Environmental Archaeology and Cultural Systems in Hamilton Inlet, Labrador*. Smithsonian Contributions to Archaeology, No. 16.

Godwin, H. (1956). *History of the British Flora*. Cambridge: University Press.

Grieg, O. and Rankine, W. F. (1956). A stone age settlement system near East Week, Dartmoor: mesolithic and post-mesolithic industries, *Proc. Devon Archaeol. Soc.*, 5, 8–25.

Jarman, M. R. (1972). European deer economies and the advent of the Neolithic. *In* E. S. Higgs, (ed.). *Papers in Economic Prehistory*. Cambridge: University Press; 125–145.

Jones, R. L. (1971). *A contribution to the late Quaternary ecological history of Cleveland, north-east Yorkshire*. Ph.D. Thesis, University of Durham.

Jones, R. L. (forthcoming). The activities of mesolithic man: further palaeo-botanical evidence from north-east Yorkshire. *In* Davidson, D. A. and Shackley, M. L. (eds.). *Sediments in Archaeology*. London: Duckworth.

Mitchell, G. F. (1970). Some chronological implications of the Irish mesolithic. *Ulster J. Archaeol.*, 33, 3–14.

Mitchell, G. F. (1972). The Larnian culture: a minimal view. *Proc. Prehist. Soc.*, 37, 274–283.

Moore, P. D. (1973). The initiation of peat formation and the development of peat deposits in mid-Wales. *Proc. 4th Int. Peat Cong.* Helsinki; 89–100.

Moore, P. D. (1972). The influence of prehistoric cultures upon the initiation and spread of blanket bog in upland Wales. *Nature, Lond.*, 241, 350–353.

Petrusewicz, K. (1967). (ed.). *Secondary Productivity of Terrestrial Ecosystems*. Warsaw and Cracow: Panstwowe Wydawnictwo Nauk, 2 Vols.

Radley, J. (1968). A mesolithic structure at Sheldon. *Derbyshire Archaeol. J.*, 80, 26–36.

Radley, J. (1969). The Mesolithic period in north-east Yorkshire. *Yorkshire Archaeol. J.*, 42, 314–327.

Radley, J. and Marshall, G. (1965). Maglemosian sites in the Pennines. *Ibid.*, 41, 394–402.

Simmons, I. G. (1969a). Pollen diagrams from the North York Moors. *New Phytol.*, 68, 807–827.

Simmons, I. G. (1969b). Evidence for vegetation changes associated with mesolithic man in Britain. *In* Ucko, P. J. and Dimbleby, G. W. (eds.). *The Domestication and Exploitation of Plants and Animals*. London: Duckworth; 111–119.

Smith, A. G. (1970). The influence of mesolithic and neolithic man on British vegetation: a discussion. *In* Walker, D and West, R. G. (eds.). *Studies in the vegetational History of the British Isles*. Cambridge: University Press; 81–96.

Smith, A. G. and Collins, A. E. P. (1971). The stratigraphy, palynology and archaeology of diatomite deposits at Newferry, Co. Antrim, Northern Ireland. *Ulster J. Archaeol.*, 34, 3–25.

Turcek, F. J. (1969). Large mammal secondary production in European broad leaved and mixed forests. Some results and methods of recent research. *Biologia, Bratisl.*, 24, 173–181.

Neolithic and Bronze Age landscape changes in northern Ireland

A. G. Smith

Synopsis

Pollen analytical and radiocarbon studies show a minor impact of man on the generally forested landscape as early as c. *3600 bc (conventional radiocarbon years), with weed species and possible food plants coincident with the earliest known Neolithic. Forest clearance at the elm decline, just before 3000 bc, affected forest cover in various ways but still within a generally forested landscape. Elm barking by cattle is discussed as a contributory factor. The clearances, possibly with changing emphasis on pastoral and arable agriculture, lasted several centuries, but general forest recovery took place around 2600–2700 bc. During Beaker and Early Bronze Age times, major changes took place in the upland landscape, with woodland giving way to rough pasture, heath, and blanket bog. Woodland tended to persist, however, on slopes with broken ground. Major deforestation was also carried out in the lowlands during the Bronze Age, but a contrast is drawn between subsequent landscape history in particular lowland and upland localities.*

INTRODUCTION

Over the last few years a number of workers in the Palaeoecology Laboratory, Queen's University, Belfast, have made pollen analytic and radiocarbon studies of a wide variety of sites, both upland and lowland. This work is still largely unpublished, however, and the time is not ripe for a detailed review of the large number of radiocarbon-dated pollen diagrams now available. This paper sets out only to summarize some of the published results and to point to some of the broader conclusions from the new work. One of the first conclusions to be drawn, once it was possible to estimate the duration of events, was that the *Landnam* phases, coming regularly at the elm decline of the Atlantic—Sub-boreal transition, were more prolonged episodes than had been suspected (Pilcher *et al.*, 1971). It was Iversen's opinion that, on ecological grounds, the classical Danish *Landnam* phases lasted probably no more than 50 years (Iversen, 1956; personal communication, 1970). The Irish *Landnam* phases have proved to have lasted several centuries. I shall return to the elm decline shortly: first let us consider the late Atlantic period.

THE EARLIEST NEOLITHIC PERIOD

Detailed studies of the Atlantic—Sub-boreal transition have revealed some possible signs of human interference with the forest vegetation well before the beginning of the elm-decline clearance phase. Such evidence first came to light in a study of occupations, of essentially Mesolithic character, of the diatomite deposits of the River Bann at Newferry, Co. Antrim (Smith and Collins, 1971). It can be seen in Fig. 1 that, associated with occupation layers below an ash spread dated to about 3300 bc, there is a marked rise of the curve for grasses and the first appearance of plantain pollen. Because of the unusual riverain situation of this site, it was impossible to rule out the possibility that these changes could have been brought about by quite local alterations of the condition of the diatomite flats. Accordingly, a detailed pollen diagram was constructed by Dr A. Crowder, from a nearby raised bog at Ballyscullion. A part of this diagram, from below the elm decline, is given in Fig. 2. In this, there are a number of features more certainly indicative of human interference. At 347 cm, below a level dated to 3,580 ± 60 bc (UB-116), the grass-pollen values increase and a number of pollen types appear which may belong to weed species or, possibly, even to food plants. These include *Plantago lanceolata* (ribwort plantain), *Urtica* (nettle), *Chenopodiaceae* (goosefoot), *Polygonum* cf. *bistorta* (cf. bistort), and *Pteridium* (bracken). Pollen of the woodland herbs *Endymion* (bluebell) and *Allium* (garlic) is also present. There is a reduction in the pine and, later (344·5 cm), oak values which suggests that these were perhaps affected by clearance to a greater extent than other species. Nevertheless, these changes are, perhaps, not so marked as to preclude a relatively unspecific opening of the forest cover. Even this, however, would presumably have had little visual impact on the total landscape. The continued abundance of tree pollen shows either that the countryside continued to be generally densely forested, or that the clearance was some distance from the site investigated. From the accumulation rate of approximately 0·65 mm per year, considering the persistence of *Plantago* pollen over some 55 mm, this clearance phase appears to have lasted almost a century. It cannot therefore be interpreted as a single phase of slash-and-burn agriculture, and is perhaps a reflection of the continued activity of a relatively settled community. That such a community may have been Neolithic rather than Mesolithic is suggested by the scatter of radiocarbon dates for Neolithic levels at the site at Ballynagilly, Co. Tyrone (excavated by A. ApSimon) as early as 3800–3500 bc (Smith, Pearson, and Pilcher, 1970a, 1970b, 1973a). The pre elm-decline clearance at Ballyscullion begins above a level dated to 3865 ± 90 bc (UB-296) and below a level dated to 3580 ± 60 bc (UB-116) at about 3700 bc. These dates are plotted in Fig. 3, which illustrates the clear temporal correlation between the earliest Neolithic occupation at Ballynagilly and the pre-elm decline clearance in the lowlands around Lough Beg, at Ballyscullion. This early clearance was carried out, then, at a time when Neolithic populations had arrived in the country, but it is impossible to be certain that it does not reflect some form of land use, possibly even a new form of land use, by a Mesolithic population (cf. Smith, 1970, p. 89).

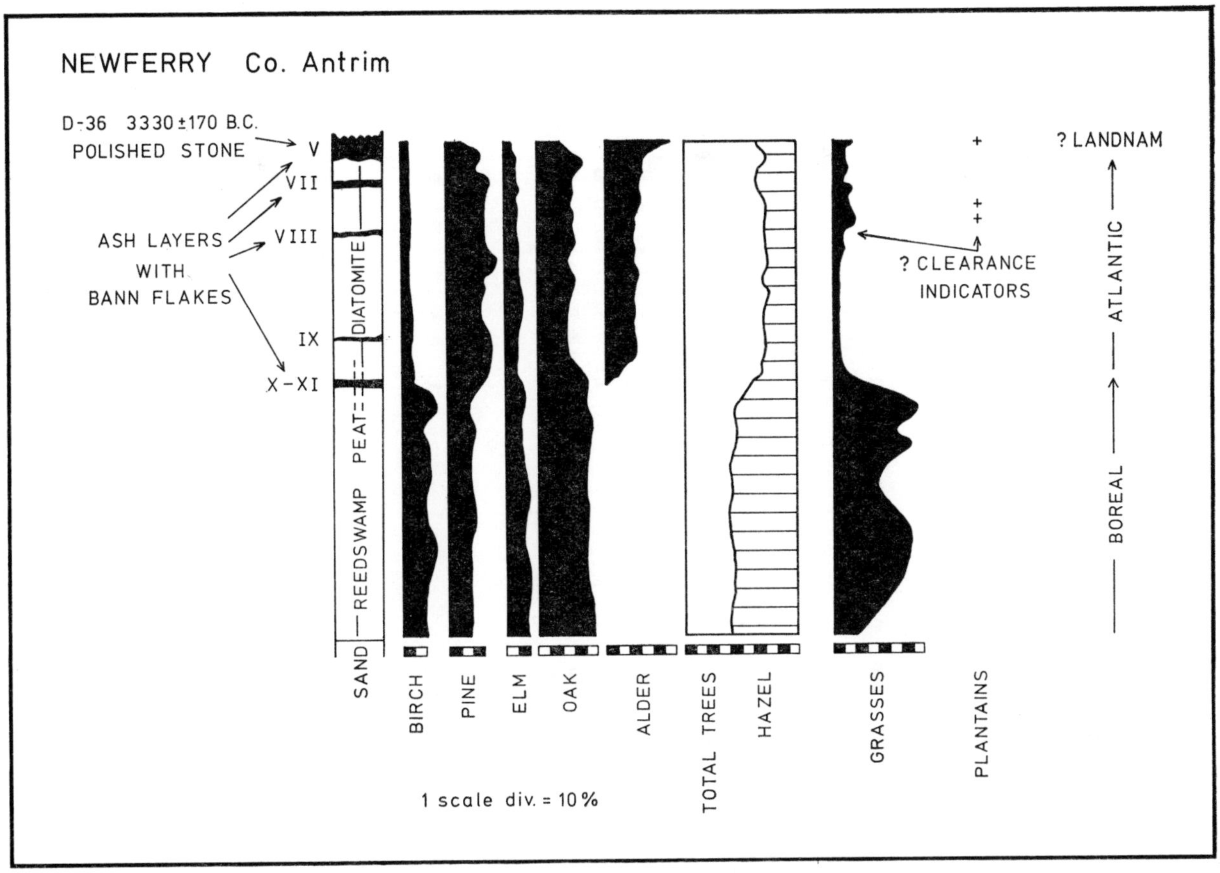

Fig. 1 Generalized pollen diagram for Newferry, Co. Antrim based on Smith and Collins (1971, Fig. 9)

THE ELM DECLINE

The prolonged nature of the clearance phases coming at the elm decline is illustrated in Fig. 4 (re-drawn from Pilcher *et al.,* 1971) which sets out the durations of three stages: A—clearance and farming, B—farming, and C—regeneration, derived from deposition-rate curves. The three sites examined show differences in the rate of clearance, but pollen of cereal type is present in the first stage at two of the sites. This stage, which lasted between 100 and 400 years, has only sporadic occurrence of plantain pollen; it seems likely, then, that the emphasis was on arable agriculture. Because of the low fertility of forest soils under primitive techniques, new ground may continually have been opened. Again we can hardly think of single episodes of slash-and-burn. It is entirely plausible, however, that we are seeing the combined effects of a whole series of such small clearances. In the next stage (B) cereal pollen is absent and plantain pollen relatively abundant; emphasis appears to have shifted to pastoral agriculture, and perhaps we can envisage more extensive areas clear of forest cover, possibly areas of former arable land kept open by grazing. Taking the broad view, however, the non-tree pollen values are still so low as to suggest a generally forested landscape. Regeneration of this forest cover appears to have been relatively rapid, taking perhaps 50–100 years.

It will clearly be of interest to try to correlate this general regeneration with strictly archaeological evidence for economic or cultural change. The general regeneration appears to have been taking place in the later part of the Neolithic period, around 2600–2700 bc. The broad picture in Neolithic times remains, in the words of G. F. Mitchell (1956), of the countryside becoming a mosaic, with areas of virgin forest, tillage patches, rough pastures, and areas of secondary forest in various stages of regeneration.

However, whether Neolithic man deliberately sought out areas where elm was growing as having soils most suitable for agriculture is still a debatable point. Some of the Neolithic clearances (for example, Beaghmore and Ballynagilly: Pilcher *et al.,* 1971) appear to have involved pine as much as elm. In any event, as has been pointed out previously (Smith, 1970), it is rather difficult from relative pollen diagrams to determine whether or not certain species were affected.

There have been many attempts to explain the elm decline, but I should like now to put forward some new observations which appear relevant. I am much indebted to Mr L. Coles, Chairman of the Cardiff Branch of the National Farmers Union, for pointing out to me, and demonstrating on his farm at Leckwith, that cattle will nowadays bark elms to such an extent that quite large trees may be killed. According to Mr Coles, this happens most frequently as winter approaches when, of course, herbage is becoming short. Mr Coles states that wych elm *(Ulmus glabra)* appears to be more often barked than English elm *(Ulmus procera)*. The elm bark is, apparently, torn off in long strips and eaten by the cattle with some relish. The collecting of elm bark, as well as other parts of the tree, for use as cattle fodder is mentioned by Nordhagen (1954), but, so far as I am aware, the barking of elms by the cattle themselves has not hitherto been noted. Mr Coles states that he has never

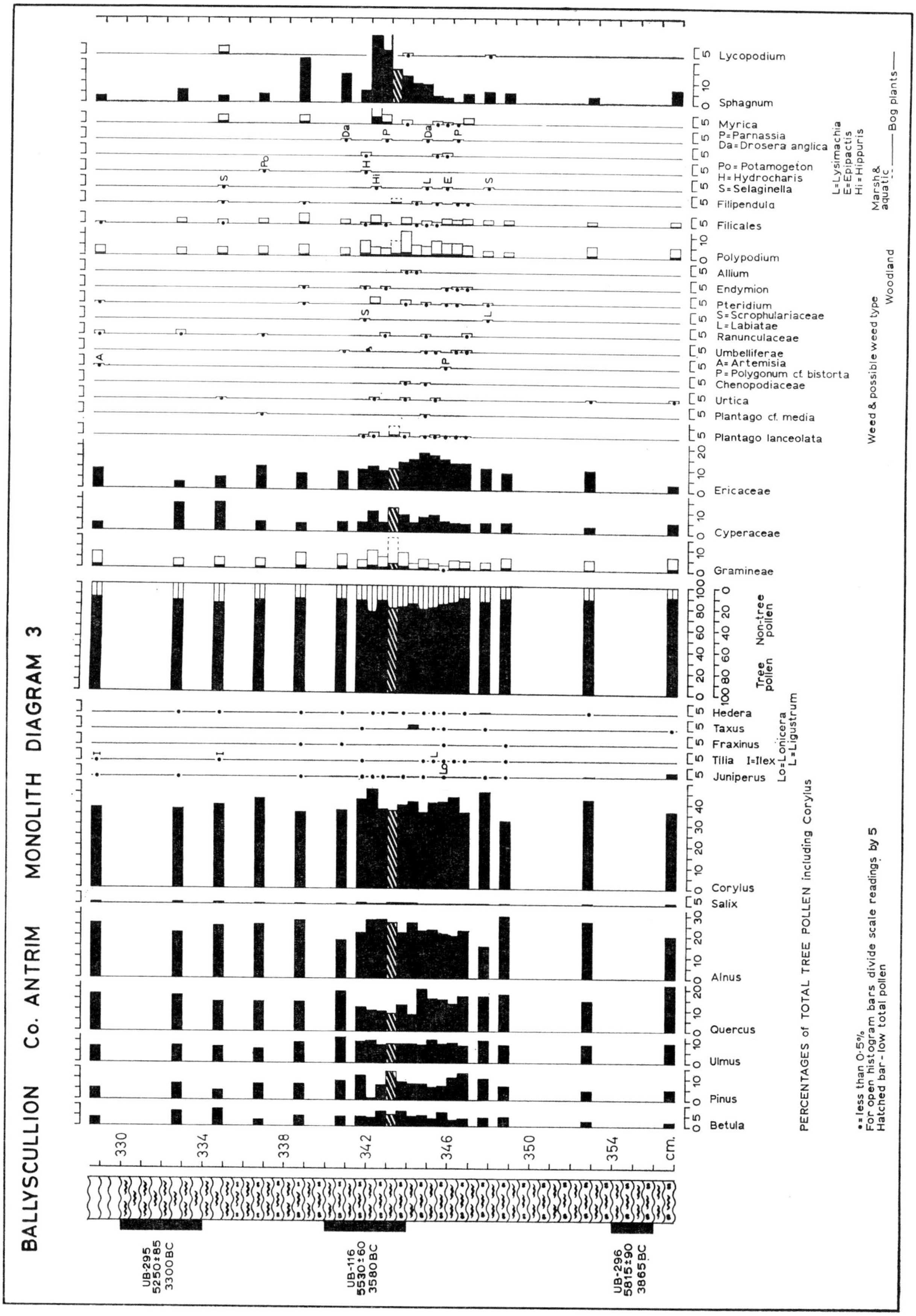
BALLYSCULLION Co. ANTRIM MONOLITH DIAGRAM 3
UB-295 5250±85 3300BC
UB-116 5530±60 3580BC
UB-296 5815±90 3865BC
330 334 338 342 346 350 354 cm.
Betula
Pinus
Ulmus
Quercus
Alnus
Salix
Corylus
Juniperus
Tilia I=Ilex
Fraxinus
Taxus
Hedera
Lo=Lonicera L=Ligustrum
Tree pollen
Non-tree pollen
Gramineae
Cyperaceae
Ericaceae
Plantago lanceolata
Plantago cf. media
Urtica
Chenopodiaceae
A=Artemisia P=Polygonum cf. bistorta
Umbelliferae
Ranunculaceae
S=Scrophulariaceae L=Labiatae
Pteridium
Endymion
Allium
Weed & possible weed type
Woodland
Polypodium
Filicales
Filipendula
S=Selaginella
H=Hydrocharis
Po=Potamogeton
Da=Drosera anglica
P=Parnassia
Myrica
L=Lysimachia E=Epipactis Hi=Hippuris
Marsh & aquatic
Bog plants
Sphagnum
Lycopodium
PERCENTAGES of TOTAL TREE POLLEN including Corylus
•=less than 0·5%
For open histogram bars divide scale readings by 5
Hatched bar - low total pollen

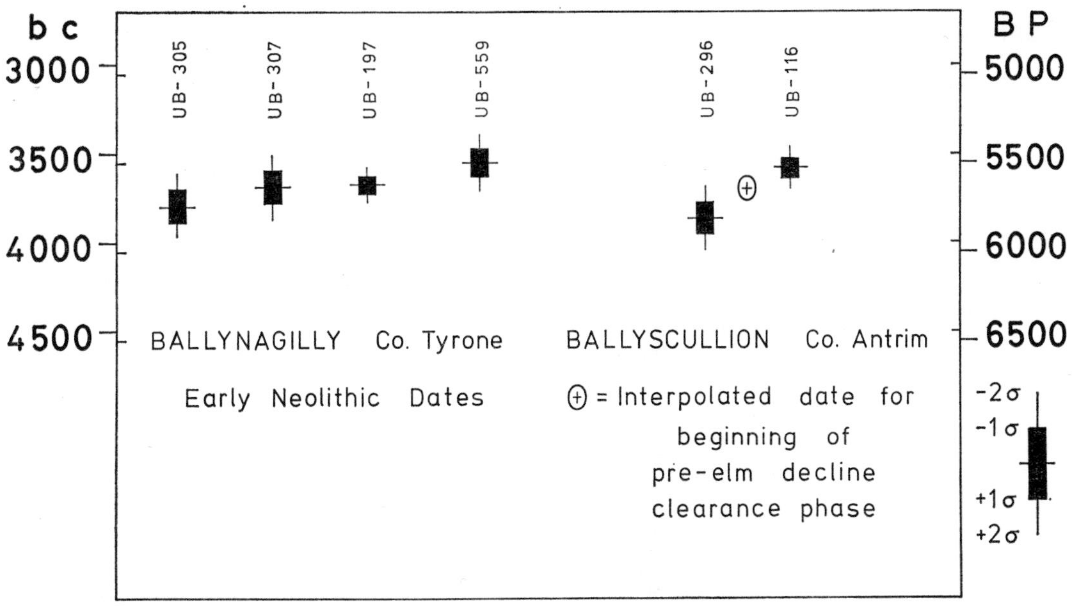

Fig. 3 Plot of the earliest Neolithic radiocarbon dates at Ballynagilly, Co. Tyrone, compared with those bracketing the pre elm-decline clearance phase at Ballyscullion, Co. Antrim (see Fig. 2)

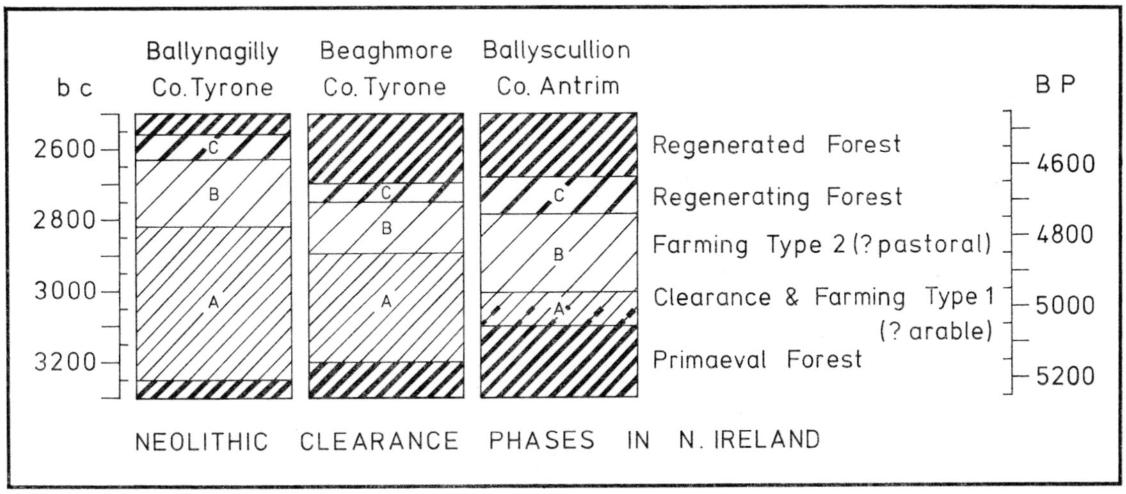

Fig. 4 Diagram (after Pilcher et al., *1971, Fig. 2) showing durations of the phases within the elm-decline clearance phases at three sites in the north-east of Ireland. The boundaries of the stages are dated from deposition rate graphs and must not be taken as fixed points. Within the limits of the methods the beginnings of the clearance phases could have been contemporaneous*

seen other species stripped of their bark by cattle. Whether this is due simply to the ease with which elm bark peels or whether cattle can in some way detect elms is perhaps immaterial.

The important feature is that the barking appears to be a selective process. Trees up to about 40 cm in diameter can be killed. Among the trees shown to me, however, many had survived. This was particularly the case where they were close grown or multi-stemmed, preventing access by the cattle. While some trees had been killed outright, and others only damaged, one was observed in which the main trunk had been killed and had snapped off, but regeneration was beginning from bark remaining on the stool. In the conditions of a natural forest there would be fewer multiple-stemmed trees so that access would be less restricted, and constant winter barking by cattle could presumably reduce the elm population substantially. It would possibly also reduce the pollen production of trees only damaged.

Another point of interest mentioned by Mr Coles is that in the Leckwith area cattle will survive the winter in good condition in young woodland (regenerating after clear-felling), provided that they have a large enough area to range over, without supplementary feeding of any kind. A good proportion of their diet under these conditions appears to consist of leaves of ivy *(Hedera helix)* (cf. Troels-Smith, 1960). Thus, the

---

Fig. 2 (facing page) Pollen diagram calculated on the basis of total tree pollen (including Corylus*) from the raised bog at Ballyscullion, Co. Antrim; analysis by Dr A. Crowder. Features described in the text between the radiocarbon samples UB-296 and UB-116 suggest opening of the forest cover by man in the late-Atlantic period*

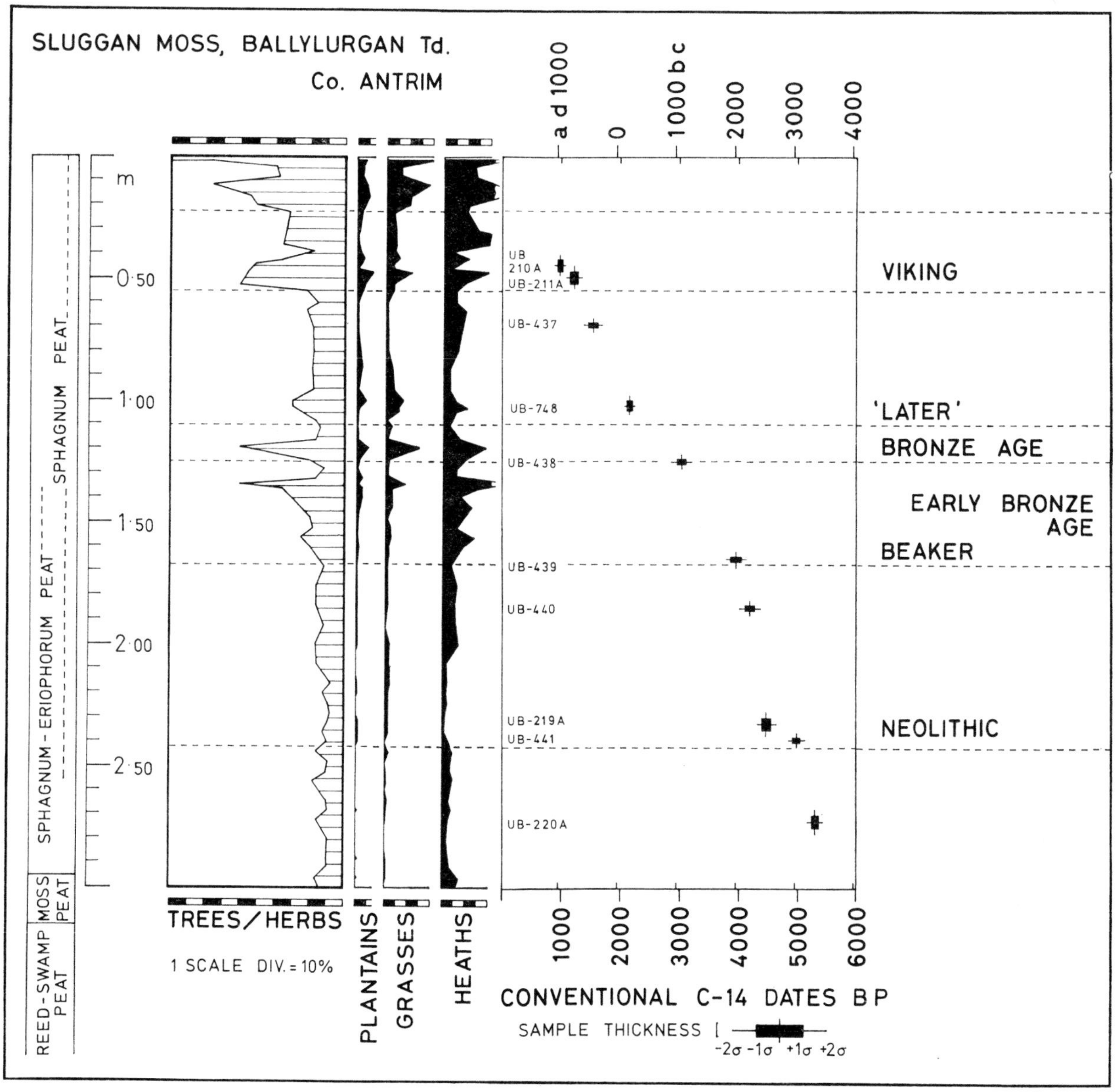

Fig. 5 Selected curves from a pollen diagram from a lowland raised bog at Sluggan, Ballylurgan Td., Co. Antrim; analysis by I. C. Goddard. The pollen sum is total tree pollen. The dashed lines show levels at which there are indications of forest clearance. The age of the clearances indicated by the radiocarbon dates is noted in terms of archaeological periods, the names of which refer essentially to the beginning of the clearance phases. The first large-scale clearances were apparently in the Bronze Age, after which substantial recovery of the forest cover is indicated by the rise of the tree pollen curve. The next episode of relatively open conditions did not come until Viking times, but even thereafter there was considerable regeneration and the area clearly remained well wooded until quite recent times

overwintering of cattle may have been much less of a problem for Neolithic man, under relatively forested conditions, than it has been in the more recent past under more intensive systems of land use.

Winter barking of elms by freely ranging cattle thus may well have been a contributory factor, if not the only one, to the Atlantic–Sub-boreal 'elm decline' in some areas. The very slow decline of the elm curve at Ballyscullion, for instance, lasting through the hundred years or so of stage A of the clearance phase, with little evidence of open pasture, might well be attributable to such a process (cf. Pilcher *et al.,* 1971). Can we, then, envisage the herding of cattle throughout the forests alongside a more intensive and localized land use for crop growing in the first stage of the Irish *Landnam* phases? On a wider scale, the constant, relentless, and wide-ranging nature of such barking would do much to explain the relative synchroneity of the elm decline. This synchroneity has been further illustrated in the review of radiocarbon-dated pollen diagrams by Smith and Pilcher (1973) though, because of the limitations of the methods, a possible diachroneity of the order of centuries must remain.

The Bronze Age

We have seen that in late Neolithic times there was almost complete recovery of the forest cover. The constitution of the forests may in some cases have changed (Pilcher *et al.,* 1971), but there can be little doubt that the landscape continued to be densely

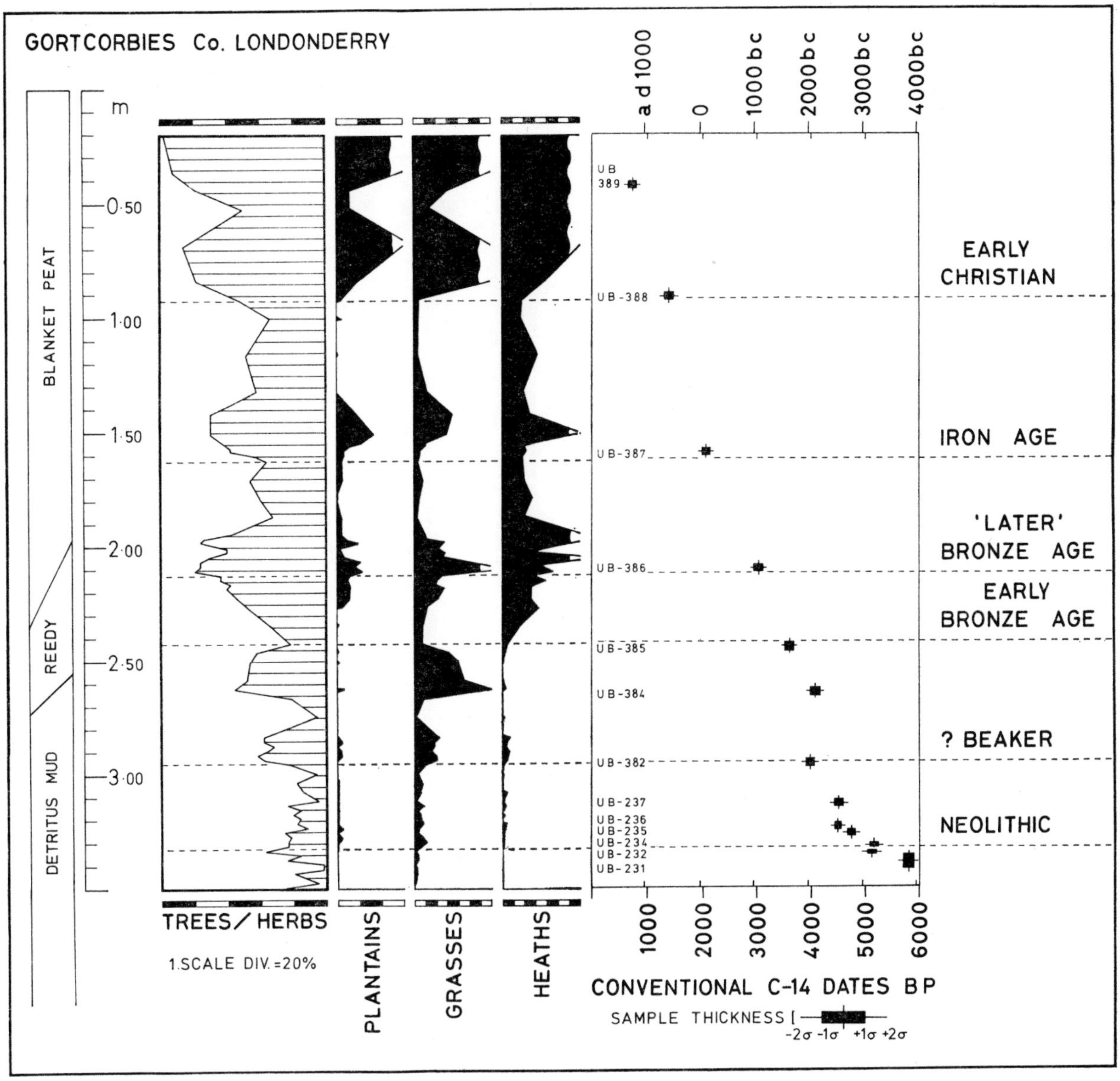

Fig. 6 *Selected curves from a pollen diagram from an upland valley bog in Gortcorbies Td., Co. Londonderry; analyses by I. C. Goddard. The pollen sum is total tree pollen. The dashed lines show levels at which there are indications of forest clearance. The age of the clearances indicated by the radiocarbon dates is noted in terms of archaeological periods, the names of which refer essentially to the beginning of the clearance phases. In each case the recovery of the tree-pollen curve shows that some regeneration took place, but on an ever-diminishing scale after the Early Bronze Age*

tree-covered. In the Bronze Age, however, much more dramatic clearance was carried out and, perhaps in the uplands in particular, the forests never subsequently regained their former dominance. This may be illustrated by reference to two pollen diagrams prepared by I. C. Goddard of which extracts are given in this paper. The first (Fig. 5) is from Sluggan Bog, Co. Antrim, a lowland site much circumscribed by rivers and mires. The decline of tree pollen and increased values for plantains just above 1·70 m indicate gradually increasing woodland clearance which, from the radiocarbon dates, must have been carried out in Beaker and Early Bronze Age times. There ensued a period of regeneration, as demonstrated by the recovery of the tree-pollen curve. Then, in the Later Bronze Age, there followed two further episodes of clearance, the first more rigorous than the second, from which it was separated by a period of regeneration. Thereafter, the tree-pollen values continue at a level of about 80%. The area appears, then, to have remained relatively well wooded for some considerable time. We see no substantial change in the tree-pollen curve until *c.* 0·50 cm depth, where substantial clearance is indicated. The radiocarbon dates show that the open conditions thus created were in existence in Viking times, even though it is difficult to be certain that the clearance began as a response to the Viking pressures. The sustained recovery of the woodlands after the Bronze Age attacks stands in strong contrast to the story at the other site to be discussed, Gortcorbies, Co. Londonderry.

The Gortcorbies site is on the lower margin of the present blanket bog at an altitude of *c.* 250 m. The area was apparently occupied in Neolithic times (May,

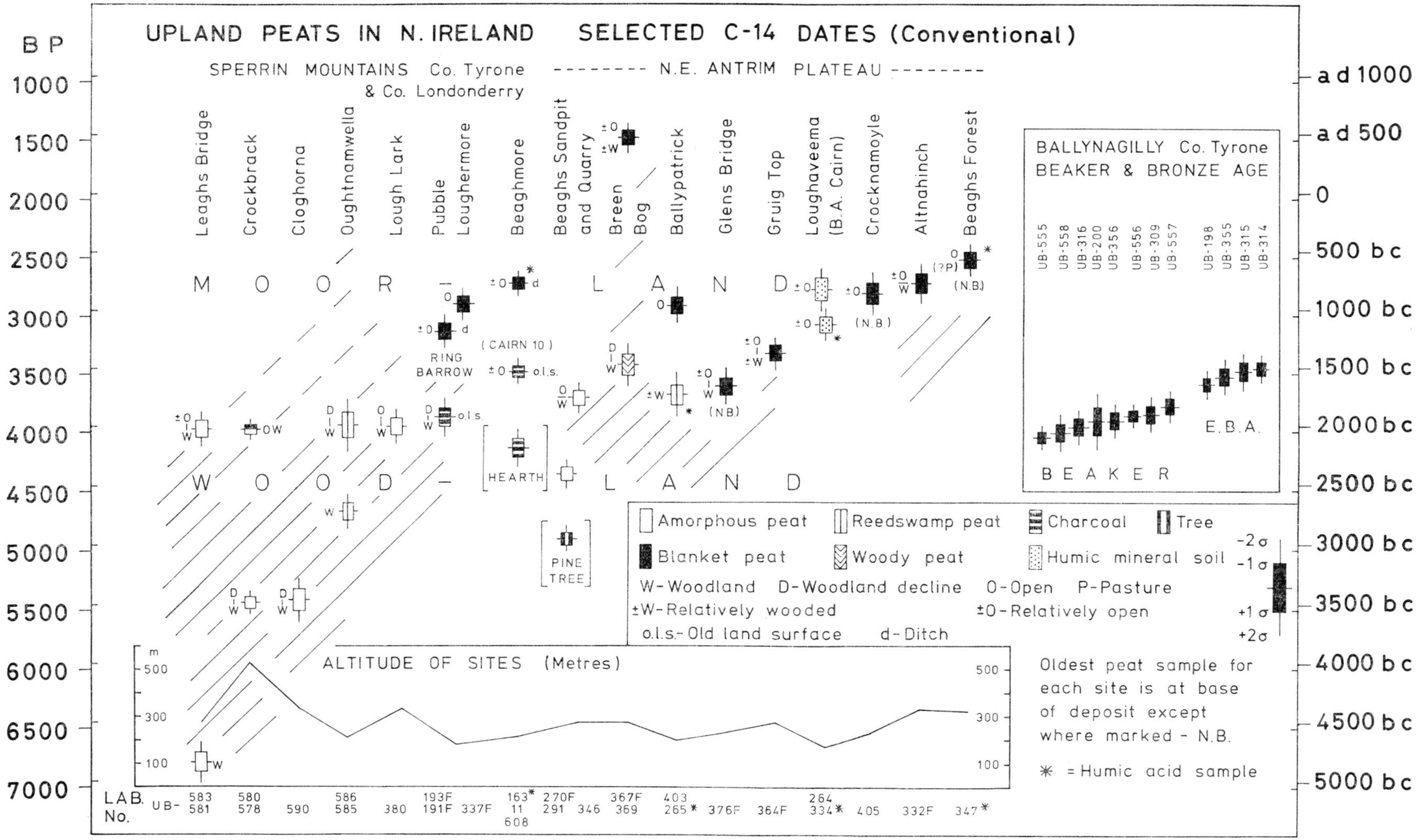

Fig. 7 *Radiocarbon dates from basal levels of upland peats in N.E. Ireland. The dates were obtained in the Belfast laboratory and may be traced from their laboratory numbers in the published date lists (see references). The information is assembled from the work of several members of the Palaeoecology Laboratory, Queen's University, Belfast, particularly that of Dr A. Goddard. The hatched indication of woodland cover must be regarded only as approximate. Radiocarbon dates are included, for purposes of comparison, for Beaker and Early Bronze Age samples from A. ApSimon's excavations at Ballynagilly, Co. Tyrone*

1950) and has produced Beaker and Early Bronze Age finds (May, 1948, 1950). It will be seen in the outline diagram (Fig. 6) that, after a Neolithic occupation phase, major clearance is indicated by a fall of the tree pollen curve just above 3·00 m. At this level there are temporary peaks of the plantain and grass curves. The radiocarbon dates show this period to be one of rapid deposition, the two determinations UB-382 and UB-384 being indistinguishable (Smith, Pearson, and Pilcher, 1971b, 457–9). Both determinations are close to 2,000 bc but are separated by some 0·3 m of deposit. They both thus date the deposit to Beaker times, but make it impossible to be certain of the exact relationship of this culture to the pollen diagram. The attribution of the clearance just above 3·00 m shown in the diagram must therefore be regarded as only tentative.

The marked minimum of the tree-pollen curve in the Gortcorbies diagram centred on 2·50 m, with an abundance of grass pollen alone, must be due to the local growth of reedswamp species and is presumably unconnected with human activity. It will be noted, however, that, before this local development, the recovery of the tree-pollen curve indicates a return to a dense forest cover. In the regeneration phases that follow the ensuing clearances, the tree-pollen values never again return to such high levels. We must envisage, then, a general decline of forest cover from a point just above 2·50 m onwards, beginning around 1600 bc. The opening of the forest cover shown by the falling tree-pollen curve at this point appears to a large extent to be due to the increase of heaths. This may be connected with the local initiation of heath and blanket bog above the site. The deposits there, however, have not yet been investigated. The rises of the plantain and grass pollen curves at *c.* 2·25 m are a clear indication of human influence. This apparently became much intensified in the Later Bronze Age around 1000 bc, as witnessed by the rapid decline of the tree-pollen curve and other features at 2·10 m. Indeed, the tree pollen values fall to almost 20%, a value which can be produced by the few remaining hedgerow trees in present-day farmland. During the Later Bronze Age, then, we must envisage the area as substantially cleared of woodland. From the rise of the tree-pollen curve above 2·00 m, however, it is clear that a considerable part of the area so cleared eventually became re-afforested. A repetition of the pattern in the pollen diagram shows that a further large-scale clearance, followed again by substantial but even less complete regeneration, took place in the Iron Age (1·60 m and above). It may be noted parenthetically here that charcoal from above two supposedly Neolithic hearths at the site has been dated to 130 ± 95 bc (UB-434E) and 20 ± 95 bc (UB-435E) and that a single sherd of Iron Age pottery was found at the nearby stone circle site (Smith, Pearson, and Pilcher, 1971b; May, 1948). These facts suggest that the locality itself was occupied in the Iron Age.

The Later Iron Age regeneration was followed by yet another massive clearance, with tree-pollen values so low as to suggest very open landscape. This penultimate major attack on the woodlands is shown by the radiocarbon dates to have been in Early Christian times. Yet another partial regeneration then took place before the final decline to the present treeless condition, which began in the period of Norman influence.

The pollen diagram from Sluggan Bog previously described may not be typical of lowland, though rather similar results were obtained by Mitchell at Littleton Bog, Co. Tipperary (Mitchell, 1965). The Gortcorbies pollen diagram is, however, paralleled in many respects by the pollen diagram from Beaghmore, Co. Tyrone (Diagram I, Pilcher, 1969), in particular by the general woodland decline and increase of heaths after 2000 bc. The same features can be observed in a pollen diagram from Ballynagilly, Co. Tyrone (Pilcher and Smith, unpublished). The episodes of clearance and regeneration at Gortcorbies appear, however, to be rather more marked than elsewhere. From the archaeological evidence, prehistoric man actually occupied the area of the site itself, and the area is clearly one that has been under heavy but intermittent pressure for a very long period. By comparison with the lowlands, the upland soils would have been both more easily worked and more readily degraded. In the case of Gortcorbies, however, the soil–vegetation complex appears to have been enormously resilient and to have withstood many periods of prolonged exploitation. The more vigorous, and frequent, utilization of the upland (as compared with the type of lowland utilization exemplified by Sluggan) was perhaps to some extent facilitated by ease of access once the dense forest cover had been broken in the Bronze Age. Perhaps by then, also, the higher altitudes were losing their forest cover as they were elsewhere. Indeed, it is the changing soil and vegetational conditions in the Bronze Age of the more elevated hills which present the most radical and striking landscape change in the uplands since the establishment of forest cover in the early Post-glacial. I refer, of course, to the initiation of upland peat and blanket bog.

From the radiocarbon dating associated with pollen analytical and stratigraphic studies, particularly those of Dr A. Goddard in N.E. Antrim and Miss A. McKenna in the Sperrin Mountains, it is now possible to sketch out a preliminary picture of the age and origin of the upland peats. The evidence from the pre-peat soils and the basal layers of the upland peats is that the blanket bog soils began to accumulate in places previously occupied by both woodland, often apparently secondary, and open ground which may well have been rough grazing. This supposed pasture, presumably, itself replaced woodland but only in a few instances are there deposits suitable for investigation of the earlier history (e.g. at Beaghmore, Co. Tyrone—Pilcher, 1959). As a preliminary to the detailed treatment, which must await full publication, particularly of Dr Goddard's work, an attempt has been made in Fig. 7 to set out the broader results which have already been published in *Radiocarbon*. The radiocarbon dates of the lower peat deposits are plotted, together with an indication of the nature of the vegetational cover; whether open or wooded, and periods of woodland decline. An attempt has been made by diagonal hatching to give an impression of the extent and duration of woodland cover, though this purely visual device does not pretend to strict accuracy. For comparison, the radiocarbon dates are also plotted for Beaker and Early Bronze Age locations at Ballynagilly, Co. Tyrone (ApSimon, 1969; Smith, Pearson, and Pilcher, 1970a, 1971a, 1973a). Except where noted, the oldest sample for each site is from the base of the peat or the humic mineral soil beneath. Some of the determinations (marked with an asterisk) are based on humic acid; these should be treated with some caution since such dates tend to be too young (Smith, Pearson, and Pilcher, 1971a, 121).

Looking at the broad spread of dates, it will be noticed that some of the Sperrin Mountain peats are older than those of the Antrim plateau. One of the sites investigated is, however, rather different in character. The Leaghs Bridge site, where the peat began to form before 4500 bc, is towards the lower altitudinal limit of the blanket peat on the margin of a valley deposit. Even earlier peat initiation is known from valley sites in Co. Antrim. The Crockbrack and Cloghorna sites are, however, more comparable with the majority of the County Antrim sites and the peat formation does here appear to have begun at an earlier date, around 3500 bc. At first sight this does not appear necessarily to be connected with rainfall differences, since, according to Cruickshank (1970), both areas apparently receive an annual rainfall of more than 1,250 mm. Cruickshank points to a general correlation of the lower limit of blanket peat growth with this isohyet, with some exceptions due mainly to topography and, perhaps to a smaller extent, to parent material. It may be, however, that the Sperrin Mountains, rising to higher altitudes, were wetter in the past, under *generally* drier conditions, than the Antrim plateau. Crockbrack (*c.* 530 m) is the highest site investigated, and Cloghorna, while no higher than the highest Co. Antrim sites, lies in a col between steep hills from which there would be considerable run-off. The pollen evidence at the two sites suggests a decline, but not a complete disappearance, of the woodland (with few signs of human interference) at the level of the radiocarbon samples. The peats themselves are relatively amorphous (with pine roots at Cloghorna) and are not typical blanket peats. They appear to have accumulated under relatively wooded conditions. The transition to a more typical blanket peat is dated at Crockbrack to *c.* 2000 bc. It is at this time that the pollen evidence at the Sperrin Mountain sites shows that tree cover was becoming much reduced with quite open conditions becoming established at two of the sites. By comparison with the Ballynagilly radiocarbon dates, this opening of the forest cover clearly took place in Beaker times.

The earliest date for peat initiation on the Antrim Plateau (aside from valley bog sites) is *c.* 2400 bc (UB-346, Beaghs Sandpit). Here again the peat was of an amorphous character. The reduction of woodland cover, or establishment of open conditions, and the more general initiation of peat growth was slightly later than in the Sperrin Mountain sites, taking place around 1300–1700 bc, a period within which the Early Bronze Age dates from Ballynagilly fall (cf. Beaghs Sandpit and Quarry, Breen Bog, Ballypatrick, Glens Bridge). Even so, woodland persisted at one site (Breen Bog) and there is at least one other site (Altnahinch) at which this transition did not take place until after 1000 bc. The pollen evidence from the other sites (Loughaveema, Crocknamoyle, Beaghs Forest) having dates for blanket peat or humic mineral soil within the period 500–1000 bc is that the conditions were by then quite open.

It is clear from this work that, while there were exceptions, it was predominantly in Beaker and Early Bronze Age times that the growth of blanket peat began. Thus, the findings at Goodland, Co. Antrim, are confirmed though, at that site soil deterioration appears, perhaps, to have begun in the Neolithic period (Case *et al.*, 1969). Even where peat had already started to accumulate before the Bronze Age there was still, then, a marked decline of woodland cover. By the Later Bronze Age many of the sites were in an open condition. Large areas of the uplands must by that time have been supporting heath or blanket bog vegetation. On the other hand, some areas continued to support woodland, and we should not think of an upland landscape so devoid of woodland as at present. Persistence of woodland is evident at Breen Bog in Antrim, and particularly at the Tyrone sites, Cloghorna and Oughtnamwella. These latter sites are in an area with steep broken slopes, where the peat cover has not become continuous. It seems likely that it was mainly on these steeper slopes that some woodland was able to persist. At the Breen site the woodland did not disappear until Early Christian times and, at Oughtnamwella, hazel scrub persisted until well after 100 bc (UB-588, Smith, Pearson, and Pilcher, 1973b).

The two archaeological sites investigated in Co. Tyrone, Beaghmore (Pilcher, 1969) and The Pubble, Loughermore (Smith, Goddard, I. C. and A., *et al.*, in prep.) have peat initiation beginning rather late. In both cases there is a long history of land use before the peat began to accumulate. The use of the pre-peat soils at Beaghmore for pasture is suggested, *inter alia*, by high percentages of plantain pollen (Pilcher, 1969, Diagram 3, Diagram 4, o.l.s.). At The Pubble there is evidence of several phases of woodland clearance and regeneration, and again of utilization for pasture, before the blanket peat began to accumulate. (This history is much disguised by the conventions of Fig. 7.)

DISCUSSION

The relationship between human activity and the initiation of upland peat is clearly a complex subject. The analysis of the changing soil and vegetational conditions that must be made for individual sites must await publication of the separate investigations. The pioneer investigations of this problem by Proudfoot, Dimbleby, and Mitchell at Goodland, Co. Antrim (summarized by Case *et al.*, 1969) point the way to such analysis. In contrast to that site, however, in many areas the peats have formed without soil podzolization. While, as Mitchell (1972) points out, much blanket peat has formed over soils that have been used for agriculture, there are cases with little direct evidence of human intervention, and the processes leading to the accumulation of peat may well have varied from area to area. The coincidence of the radiocarbon dates for the decline of high-level woodland and the initiation of blanket peat growth with the dates for the first metal-using cultures shown in Fig. 7 is, of course, very striking. But, equally, we must remember the strong correlation pointed out by Cruickshank (1970) between the lower altitudinal limit of blanket peat today with the 1,250 mm isohyet.

The question of climatic change must, of course, enter into any discussion of the origin of upland peats. It will be of much interest in this connection to see whether the preliminary indications that the main boundary horizon of the lowland bogs (RS C of Jessen, 1949), in so far as it proves synchronous, falls in the period around 2500–2000 bc will be sustained by further work. The first indication of such an age came at Fallahogy, Co. Londonderry (Smith and Willis, 1958). We now see that, while there is no sharp stratigraphic change, the *Sphagnum–Eriophorum* peat at Sluggan Bog (Fig. 5) was giving way to a much purer and generally less humified *Sphagnum* peat around this time. We may also point to the scatter of radiocarbon dates centred on 2000 bc for the final pine decline (Smith and Pilcher, 1973) which marks Jessen's pollen Zone VII–VIII boundary, the opening of the Sub-atlantic period. With respect to the climatic conditions of this period it is worth quoting Jessen's conclusions directly: "The rapid formation of ombrogenous peat in the Irish raised bogs in Zone VIII can only be explained by assuming that the atmosphere had a greater content of moisture than in Sub-boreal time. In Sub-atlantic time the climate became more oceanic than it had been earlier . . . The less favourable effects of the Sub-atlantic climate on the growth of trees, and the accelerated extension of blanket bogs as a consequence of the increase of rainfall, played a great part in the disappearance of the woods but it is difficult to compare the effect of these two factors with that due to farming, cattle rearing and other encroachments . . . In Ireland most of the areas from which the woods disappeared were probably turned into fields and pastures while other parts became covered by bogs" (Jessen, 1949).

We are now moving into a climate of opinion which is beginning to see connections between farming, soil exhaustion, and peat formation, and between the removal of trees and peat initiation (Goddard, 1971). The processes envisaged by Jessen must not, however, necessarily be discarded. Indeed, the preliminary indications of a broadly coeval change of lowland bog stratigraphy and initiation of peat at many upland sites, around 2000 bc, does much to keep his arguments alive, even though they oppose his conclusion that the opening of the Sub-atlantic period was at approximately 500 bc. These considerations perhaps support the first of two alternative explanations of the origin of blanket peat put forward by Mitchell (1972) that there may have been a shift towards wetter climatic conditions, leading towards the inevitable formation of blanket peat where the 1,250 mm isohyet was crossed, and that the activities of early man may have only accelerated this process. The alternative, that man's interference with the environment, and the consequential soil deterioration, *without the intervention of climatic deterioration,* was the primary cause of blanket peat formation, appears to me a less tenable explanation. The very resilience of the soil–vegetation complex at a site such as Gortcorbies, at the lower limit of the blanket peat, for instance, speaks against it. The important question, if we accept a climatic deterioration in the later Post-glacial, is to what extent the formation of blanket bog was inevitable. Even without the intervention of man, we would probably still have seen on the Antrim Plateau at a later date the sort of peat initiation under relatively wooded conditions that took place around 3500 bc and before in the Sperrin Mountains. Whether under some topographical and soil conditions woodland unaffected by clearance or grazing could have so reduced the soil water content by transpiration and maintenance of free drainage as to prevent the initial waterlogging that must precede peat initiation is more imponderable. Clearly, much remains to be learned about the processes involved in this major landscape change of the Highland Zone.

ACKNOWLEDGEMENTS

Parts of the work described here have been supported financially, or by the loan of equipment, by the following: Department of Scientific and Industrial Research (latterly Natural Environment Research Council), The Wenner-Gren Foundation, and The Royal Society. I wish to express my sincere thanks to these bodies. I should also like to thank my former colleagues, research assistants, and students in Belfast, in particular Mr G. W. Pearson (radiocarbon dating), Dr J. R. Pilcher, Dr A. Crowder, Mr I. C. Goddard, Dr A. Goddard, Mr A. ApSimon, Dr P. Q. Dresser, and Miss A. McKenna for their co-operation and enthusiasm. I am indebted to Mrs E. Brown for preparing Figs. 3–7.

REFERENCES

ApSimon, A. M. (1969). An early Neolithic house in Co. Tyrone. *J. Roy. Soc. Antiq. Ireland,* 99, 165–168.

Case, H. J. *et al.* (1969). Land use in Goodland Townland, Co. Antrim from Neolithic times until today. *Ibid.,* 99, 39–53.

Cruickshank, J. G. (1970). Soils and pedogenesis in the north of Ireland. *In* Stephens, N. and Glasscock, R. E. (eds.). *Irish Geographical Studies.* The Queen's University of Belfast; 89–104.

Goddard, A. (1971). *Studies of the vegetational changes associated with initiation of blanket peat accumulation in North-East Ireland.* Unpub. Ph.D. thesis. The Queen's University of Belfast.

Iversen, T. (1956). Forest clearance in the Stone Age. *Scient. Am.,* 194, 36–41.

Jessen, K. (1949). Studies in Late Quaternary deposits and flora-history of Ireland. *Proc. Roy. Ir. Acad.,* 52B, 85–290.

May, A. McL. (1947). Burial mounds, circles and cairn, Gortcorbies, Co. Londonderry. *J. Roy. Soc. Antiq. Ireland,* 77, 5–22.

May, A. McL. (1950). Two Neolithic hearths, Gortcorbies, Co. Londonderry. *Ulster J. Archaeol.,* 13, 28–39.

Mitchell, G. F. (1956). Post-Boreal pollen diagrams from Irish raised bogs. *Proc. Roy. Ir. Acad.,* 57B, 185–251.

Mitchell, G. F. (1965). Littleton Bog, Tipperary: an Irish agricultural record. *J. Roy. Soc. Antiq. Ireland,* 95, 121–132.

Mitchell, G. F. (1972). Soil deterioration associated with prehistoric agriculture in Ireland. *Proc. 24th Int. Geol. Congr., Symp. 1,* 59–68.

Nordhagen, R. (1956). Ethnobotanical studies on bark-bread and the employment of wych-elm under natural husbandry. (In Danish, with English summary). *In* Studies in vegetational history in honour of Knud Jessen. *Danm. Geol. Unders.,* IIR, No. 80, 262–308.

Pilcher, J. R. (1969). Archaeology, palaeoecology and ^{14}C dating of the Beaghmore stone circle site. *Ulster J. Archaeol.,* 32, 73–91.

Pilcher, J. R. *et al.* (1971). Land clearance in the Irish Neolithic: new evidence and interpretation. *Science,* 172, 560–562.

Smith, A. G. (1970). The influence of Mesolithic and Neolithic man on British vegetation: a discussion. *In* Walker, D. and West, R. G. (eds.). *Studies in the Vegetational History of the British Isles.* Cambridge: University Press; 81–96.

Smith, A. G. and Collins, A. E. P. (1971). The stratigraphy, palynology and archaeology of diatomite deposits at Newferry, Co. Antrim, Northern Ireland. *Ulster J. Archaeol.,* 34, 3–25.

Smith, A. G., Pearson, G. W. and Pilcher, J. R. (1970a). Belfast Radiocarbon Dates I. *Radiocarbon,* 12, 285–290.

Smith, A. G., Pearson, G. W. and Pilcher, J. R. (1970b). Belfast Radiocarbon Dates II. *Ibid.,* 12, 291–297.

Smith, A. G., Pearson, G. W. and Pilcher, J. R (1971a). Belfast Radiocarbon Dates III. *Ibid.,* 13, 103–125.

Smith, A. G., Pearson, G. W. and Pilcher, J. R. (1971b). Belfast Radiocarbon Dates IV. *Ibid.*, 13, 450–467.

Smith, A. G., Pearson, G. W. and Pilcher, J. R. (1973a). Belfast Radiocarbon Dates V. *Ibid.*, 15, 212–228.

Smith, A. G., Pearson, G. W. and Pilcher, R. J. (1973b). Belfast Radiocarbon Dates VI. *Ibid.*, 15, 599–610.

Smith, A. G. and Pilcher, J. R. (1973). Radiocarbon dates and vegetational history of the British Isles. *New Phytol.*, 72, 903–914.

Smith A. G. and Willis. E. H. (1962). Radiocarbon dating of the Fallahogy Landnam phase. *Ulster J. Archaeol.*, 24–25, 16–24.

Troels Smith, J. (1960). Ivy, mistletoe and elm: climatic indicators—fodder plants. *Danm. Geol. Unders.*, IVR, 4, No. 4, 1–32.

The effect of Neolithic man on the environment in north-west England: the use of absolute pollen diagrams

Winifred Pennington (Mrs. T. G. Tutin)

Synopsis

Pollen evidence from ten sites within the region shows that, though at four sites (one upland and three on the coastal plain) there were minor and temporary vegetation changes before 5000 ¹⁴C-years ago, the effects of man on both upland and lowland landscapes increased dramatically in amplitude a few centuries before 5000 bp. Pollen counts in terms of numbers of grains deposited annually per unit area confirmed the results of percentage pollen analysis to indicate widespread destruction of upland forest around the axe-factory sites, and coastal clearances for cereal cultivation on a scale sufficient to bring about permanent changes in both vegetation and soils, at this time. Evidence from analysis of lake sediments indicates an increase in run-off and soil erosion from natural causes, combined with a rise in ground water level, at the same time as the change in land use which began c. *5100 ¹⁴C-years ago. The total effect was degenerative change in the upland soils from forest soils to peat, and the onset of instability of the lowland soils on slopes as a result of cultivation practices.*

INTRODUCTION

In that part of north-west England which stretches westwards from the Langdale axe-factory sites to the Neolithic settlement sites at Ehenside Tarn and other places on the coastal plain of West Cumberland, there is an abundance of sites at which accumulating organic deposits have preserved in temporal succession the pollen record of Neolithic vegetation changes. Comparison of data from such a wide variety of kinds of site—sediments of both lowland and highland lakes, *mor* humus sections in the lowlands, and blanket peat profiles in the uplands—has made it possible to compare the regional changes that are common to all sites with the local vegetation histories which, differing from site to site, record the local environment. The elm decline at *c.* 5100 bp constitutes a regional change which has been shown to be synchronous, both across north-west Europe (Hibbert, Switsur, and West, 1971; Smith and Pilcher, 1973) and from site to site within north-west England (Pennington, 1970). The primary cause of the elm decline remains unproven, but the steep fall in the proportion of pollen contributed by elms (*Ulmus* spp.) can be used as a dated horizon in the correlation of pollen sequences from as yet undated profiles, making it possible to find out what was happening at the same time at this wide variety of sites. In this paper the pollen record of vegetation changes at this time from three particular areas of north-west England will be considered in detail: these areas are respectively the central Lake District uplands round the head of Great Langdale and the axe-factory sites (Bunch and Fell, 1949; Fell, 1964; Clough, 1973), the Lake District valleys, and the western coastal plain between the mountains and the Irish Sea, with its well-investigated site at Ehenside Tarn (Darbyshire, 1874; Piggott, 1954; Walker, 1966) and its wealth of lake- or peat-filled hollows round which scatters of Neolithic artefacts have been found and suggest the presence of as yet unknown settlement sites (Cherry, 1969; Pennington, 1970): Fig. 1.

Evidence from the composition of sediments in the large lakes of the Lake District, where the accumulating deposits record the environmental history of the catchments as well as changes in the lake ecosystems, has shown that the 2500 years before 5000 bp (constituting the Atlantic period) was a time of soil stability and hence of intense removal of bases from soils by leaching (Mackereth, 1965, 1966). It seems probable that within the Highland Zone as a whole, where base-poor bedrock prevails and the rainfall is high, a critical threshold for base-status of soils and for vegetation had been reached at the time of the elm decline (Pennington, 1965). In many lakes of the Lake District and other parts of the Highland Zone, a marked change in sediment composition, sometimes sufficiently intense to be accompanied by a visible stratigraphic change, accompanies the elm decline and indicates that the balance of soil maturation and soil erosion on the catchments changed greatly in early Neolithic time (Tutin, 1969; Pennington *et al.*, 1972, Fig. 18; Pennington, 1973, Fig. 7). Figure 2 shows how a close series of ¹⁴C dates in profiles from two Lake District lakes established that at this time redeposition of older organic material on top of

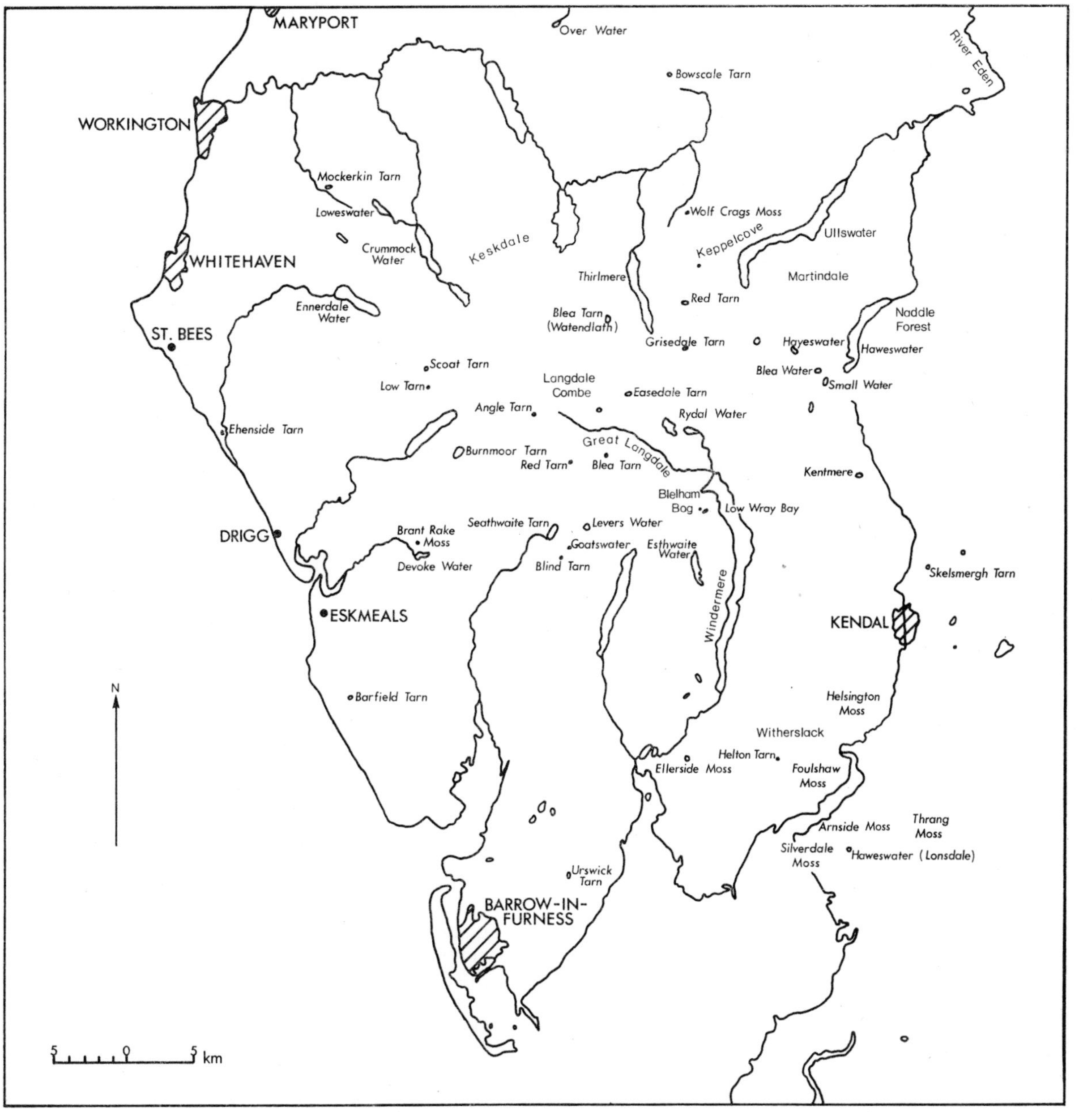

Fig. 1 Map of north-west England, showing sites mentioned in the text and others referred to in Pennington (1970), from which this is partially reproduced

younger occurred, indicative of intensified erosion of organic soils on the catchments. A still unanswered question is whether human settlement was the major cause of this ecological effect through disturbance of primary vegetation, or whether the first settlers to practise agriculture in the Highland Zone did so at a time of major environmental shift resulting from natural processes. If the latter is true, there is no doubt as to the profound effects of agriculture in accelerating these processes in the Highland Zone. In upland Britain the major environmental change during the Post-glacial period (the last 10,000 years) has undoubtedly been the decline in the capacity of the upland soils to support forest and the concomitant growth of peat. The biological productivity of the Highland Zone must have been enormously greater in Neolithic times than since 500 bc. The association between prehistoric land use and soil deterioration in the uplands has, of course, been demonstrated by pollen analysis for many years (e.g. Dimbleby, 1962; Pennington, 1965; Smith, 1970; Moore, 1973). If an attempt is made to explain all changes in pollen diagrams of the early Neolithic period in terms of the natural processes of soil impoverishment interpreted from pollen diagrams of previous interglacials (Andersen, 1969), it is difficult to account for the proven synchroneity of the elm decline. It is inconceivable that the process of natural soil degradation should have been synchronized to this extent when the variety of soil type and annual rainfall totals included in north-west Europe is recognised. The changes in composition of lake sediments just before 5000 bp indicate an increased precipitation/evaporation ratio which intensified run-off in hilly areas of the Highland Zone such as the Lake District, and led to accelerated peat formation in those areas of lower relief in north-west Scotland where blanket bog now descends almost to sea level

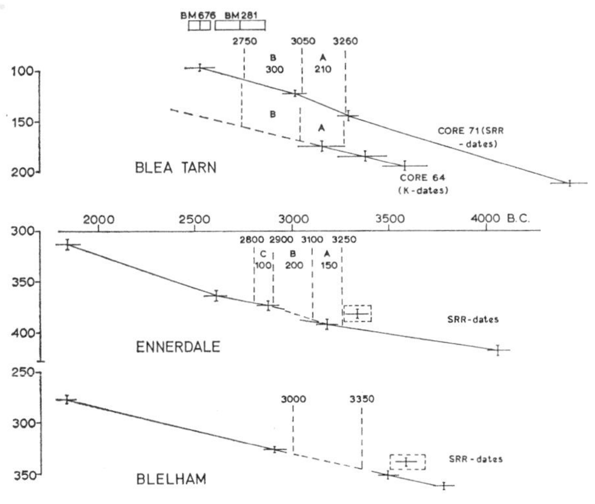

Fig. 2 *Depth/time-scales from the sediment profiles of three lakes. Stage A = period of declining elm* (Ulmus), *Stage B = period of continuous* Plantago lanceolata, *and Stage C = forest regeneration (cf. Pilcher* et al. *(1971)). The depth of each* ¹⁴*C-dated sample and the span of* ± *one standard deviation are shown*

(Pennington *et al.*, 1972). Accordingly, the evidence for Neolithic land use must be seen against a background of a natural process of deterioration of upland soils which, though it cannot be invoked as the primary cause of the synchronous vegetation changes at *c.* 5000 bp, had by this time produced in the Highland Zone a situation of ecological tension in which human activities led to the crossing of threshold values and so produced effects large in proportion to the numbers of men involved (cf. Smith, 1961; 1970).

ABSOLUTE POLLEN ANALYSIS

Absolute pollen analysis seeks to express the frequency of each type of pollen grain identified in terms of numbers rather than as percentages—numbers either per unit volume of fresh sediment (pollen concentration) or per unit area of accumulating surface per year (annual pollen deposition rates). The advantages of absolute over percentage pollen analysis have been discussed by Davis and Deevey (1964) and Davis (1967) and its limitations by the present author (Pennington, 1973), who was able to show that in a number of British lakes annual pollen deposition rates some 5000 years ago appear to have been controlled by the efficiency of the lake as a pollen trap rather than by the pollen production of the surrounding vegetation. Unless lake sites are carefully standardized, it is not possible to use annual pollen deposition rates as a quantitative measure of vegetation—of, for example, "the areal extent of Neolithic forest clearance in Europe" (Wright, 1971). Nevertheless, the assessment of actual numbers of grains, even in the form of pollen concentration and not annual deposition rates, has the advantage of providing independent curves for each pollen taxon, and so avoids the problem of interdependent percentages, where an absolute decrease in one major component leads inevitably to increases in others, quite independently of true changes in the others.

Conversion of pollen concentration values to annual deposition rates involves the use of a depth/time scale determined by ^{14}C dates. A satisfactory timescale of annual rates of sediment accumulation was obtained for Blea Tarn (Fig. 2) from the 1971 core, which was taken from a position chosen to avoid that part of the tarn where a stratigraphic change accompanies the elm decline (see Fig. 12 in Pennington, 1970). At other sites, in the valley lakes, redeposition of older material on top of younger was found at this horizon (Fig. 2 illustrates the timescales for Blelham Tarn and Ennerdale Water). This disturbance of the orderly annual deposition of pollen makes it impossible to calculate annual deposition rates for these sites for this period. An extreme example of stratigraphic disturbance at this time is found in Barfield Tarn on the Cumberland coastal plain, where a change from organic mud to pink clay indicates an acceleration of soil erosion of such amplitude as to bring into the tarn large quantities of the mineral soil, a red boulder-clay.

THE AREAS AND SITES INVESTIGATED

(a) Great Langdale and the central Lake District mountains

Within a radius of 2 km from the axe-factory sites on Pike of Stickle and the chipping floors on Mart Crag Moor and Thunacar Knott (Bunch and Fell, 1949; Clough, 1973) there are five sites from which pollen analysis has contributed to knowledge of environmental changes in early Neolithic times. In the sediments of two upland tarns (Blea Tarn, Langdale (187 m) and Angle Tarn, Bowfell (537 m)), the elm decline has been shown to be synchronous, to be accompanied by a stratigraphic change, indicative of increased run-off and soil erosion, and to be closely followed by an episode of sufficient disturbance of the forest (which extended up to at least the altitude of Angle Tarn) to allow the expansion of light-demanding herbs and grasses (Pennington, 1965; 1970; Tutin, 1969). In the sediments of the now filled-in lake in Langdale Combe, Walker (1965) found charcoal stratified into lake deposits shortly above the elm decline, and suggested the use of fire by man in the course of forest clearance. At Red Tarn Moss (Pennington, 1965) the elm decline was found recorded in forest humus (= *mor* (Iversen, 1964)) at the base of the blanket peat; this profile illustrates the transition from *mor* to peat, and its relationship to the disappearance of upland forest. Recently another peat profile has been analysed, that from which charcoal associated with a chipping floor on Thunacar Knott has been radiocarbon dated (Clough, 1973; Pennington, 1973a). At Quagrigg Moss on Scafell, the nearest peat section to the axe-factory workings on Scafell (altitude 518 m), a new peat profile has been analysed.

Blea Tarn, Langdale

Figure 14 in Pennington (1965) illustrates (i) the use of percentage pollen diagrams based on counts of 1000 grains and how this large sum (a) smooths out random variations from sample to sample and (b) includes in the counts herbaceous pollen types which may be present only as one grain in a thousand, and (ii) the stratigraphic change, with a permanent change in organic content of the sediment from the time of the elm decline, in the sediment profile of this small lake. Figure 12 in Pennington (1970) shows the three Copenhagen ^{14}C dates which established that the steep fall in percentage of elm pollen began about 5100 bp; this dating has been confirmed by the new series from SRR (Figs. 2 and 3). These diagrams show (a) the

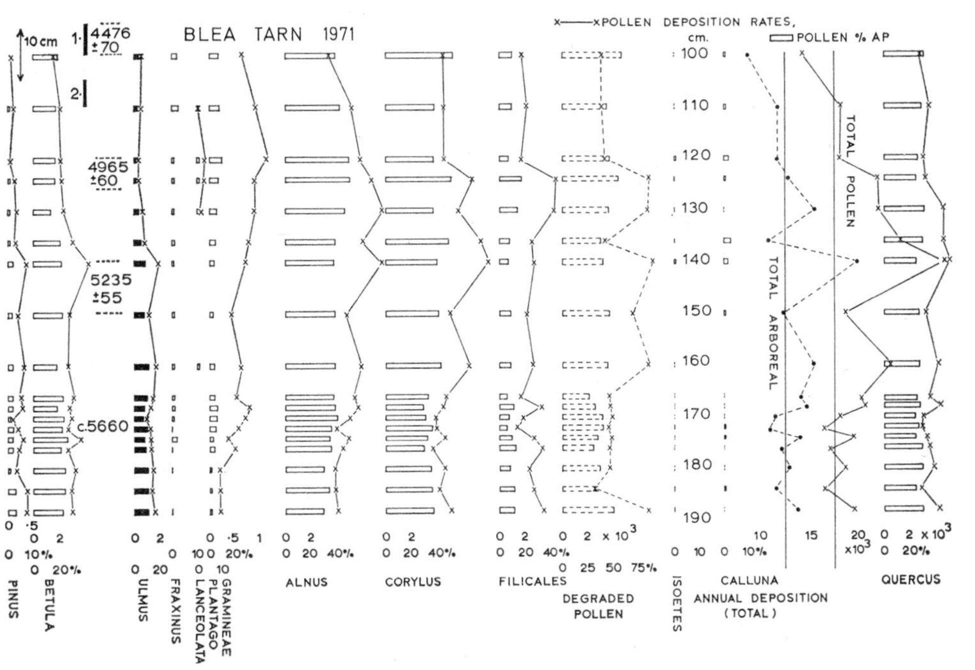

Fig. 3 Pollen diagram from part of a core taken from Blea Tarn, Langdale, Westmorland in 1971. ^{14}C dates are SRR-16, 17, and 18. Pollen values are given as percentages of total arboreal pollen (histogram blocks) and as annual pollen deposition rates (line graphs). 1 and 2 indicate the position on this timescale of the dated charcoal samples BM 281 and 676

reproducibility of percentage pollen analysis, and (b) the limitations of the percentage method, in the difficulty in deciding whether the percentage increase in alder pollen above the elm decline represents a real increase in alder or a decrease in other tree pollens, and whether fluctuations in *Corylus* in relation to the sum of other tree pollens represent changes in abundance of *Corylus* or of the other trees (cf. Smith (1970)).

Figure 2 shows that the new series of ^{14}C dates agrees so closely with the first series as to date the steep fall in percentage of elm pollen to within one standard deviation of the Copenhagen date. In Fig. 4 the pollen data are plotted both as percentages of the total arboreal pollen and as deposition rates of grains of each taxon (species, genus, or family identified) per square centimetre per year. (These counts have been published in another form, less completely but showing the 90% confidence limits of the counts, as Fig. 9 in Pennington (1973)).

The conclusions from the absolute diagram must be:

(i) *Quercus* (oak) remained stable, both in proportion of total pollen contributed and in deposition rates of pollen per year, throughout the period covered by this pollen diagram (*c.* 6200–4400 bp) within the area from which pollen was recruited to the Blea Tarn sediments.

(ii) *Betula* (birch) and *Pinus* show a fall in annual deposition rates (not shown in percentage counts) which exactly parallels that shown by *Ulmus* at the elm decline; as these three curves fall, there is a simultaneous rise in both percentage frequency and annual deposition rates of grasses, *Calluna* (heather), and *Plantago lanceolata* (ribwort plantain). A minor and short-lived version of this episode can be detected at *c.* 5700 bp.

From (i) and (ii) it can be deduced that the clearance shown by the rise of the herbaceous pollens took place in pine–birch woodland and not in oak woods, that the main clearance took place at the same time as the main elm decline (*c.* 5050 bp) and was maintained at least until 4400 bp, but that it was preceded by evidence for a minor and temporary episode *of the same kind* about 5700 bp.

(iii) From the maximum of the *Plantago lanceolata* curve at *c.* 5000 bp, there is a shift to lower totals of arboreal pollen deposited each year—that is, a permanent diminution in the amount of tree pollen reaching Blea Tarn each year. The two dates for charcoal from axe-factory chipping floors on the moorland of Thunacar Knott on the opposite side of Great Langdale, 4680 ± 135 bp (BM 281) and 4474 ± 52 bp (BM 676) (Clough, 1973) are shown in position on the timescale in Figs. 2 and 3, and clearly correspond with the pollen evidence for clearance in the upper woods of pine and birch at this time. The clearance episode of earlier date (*c.* 5700 bp) and similar type, suggests that the Neolithic effect on the primary vegetation was, though more intense, similar in kind to one of Mesolithic date for which no material evidence in artefacts remains.

From comparison of many pollen diagrams from the Lake District hills and valleys (Pennington (1970) and unpublished data), pine and birch can be supposed to have been more frequent at the upland sites, suggesting an upper fringe of birch–pine woods above the oak–elm–hazel forest. The close correlation between the pollen deposition rates of elm, birch, and pine in Fig. 3 must indicate that a selective disaster to the elm was taking place at the same time as the clearances in the upland birch–pine woods attributed to men, but since elm is the most base-demanding of the trees concerned it cannot be supposed that the elms were growing on the leached soils of the upland ridges among the birches and pines. The pollen evidence cannot tell us whether the elms, which from their ecological demands must have been growing among the oaks, were suffering from selective disease or from the effects of pollarding or ring-barking (Iversen, 1973) by men whose economy differed from that of the earlier peoples in that they possessed domestic animals fed on leaf fodder.

(iv) The absolute pollen diagram (Fig. 3) shows that another group of pollen taxa was deposited in greater numbers during the period approximately 5400–5000bp; these are *Alnus* (alder), *Corylus* (hazel), *Filicales* (ferns), and Degraded Pollen—the total of grains whose exines have been attacked by aerobic decay (in soils or aerated water) to a degree making recognition impossible. Though the numbers of grains are small by comparison, *Calluna* (heather) has the same distribution. All these taxa are likely to be recruited to lake sediments by inflowing streams; *Alnus* is universally common as a stream-side tree in the hill woodlands, *Calluna* pollen and fern spores have been shown to be carried to the sediments of a small upland lake mainly via the inflow streams (Peck, 1973), *Corylus* pollen and fern spores are common in the inorganic soils of the Lake District and *Calluna* in the organic soils (Pennington, 1964). This evidence indicates that during the period (*c.* 5400–5000 bp) run-off was increased and the relative importance of the stream-borne pollen component became greater. There are two possible explanations: either the human activity of late Mesolithic date had the effect of increasing run-off, possibly only in the higher parts of the Blea Tarn catchment, or there was a change in the amount or incidence of rainfall which increased run-off at this time. The absolute diagram shows clearly that the percentage rise in alder and hazel at this site (Fig. 3) represents a real increase in their deposition rates and is not the result of an absolute fall in oak pollen as might have been suspected. Since alder and hazel are both more base-demanding than *Quercus petraea* (sessile oak), it would be expected that they would decline rather than increase on the upland soils as Post-glacial leaching progressed (Pennington, 1973), so their increased pollen deposition rates at the elm decline are more readily to be understood as the effects of increased run-off (cf. the association with *Calluna* pollen, fern spores, and degraded pollen) than as indicative of a true increase in pollen production by these trees.

Angle Tarn, Bowfell

The pollen diagram from this high corrie tarn (Tutin, 1969), (Fig. 2), when shown to Dr Iversen in 1964, caused him to exclaim "A pine decline with the elm decline! How to explain that? Fire?" The Copenhagen ^{14}C date indicates a synchroneity within one standard deviation between the dates of the elm decline at Blea Tarn and at Angle Tarn, and a clearance episode shortly above the elm decline corresponding with that which at Blea Tarn has been correlated by ^{14}C dating with the period of the chipping floors on Thunacar Knott and Mart Crag Moor. Figure 2 (Tutin, 1969) shows how, *c.* 10 cm above the elm decline, the Angle Tarn profile records inwash of acid *mor* humus rich in pine pollen and fern spores, and how this is followed, from 190 cm onwards, by virtual disappearance of pine from the pollen recruited to the Angle Tarn sediments. This is now interpreted as the record of clearance of the upland pine and birch woods by fire—i.e. the same episode as is recorded at Blea Tarn but recorded at a higher site, within the zone affected by this high-level forest clearance. Figure 2 in Tutin (1969) gives the chemical analysis at the Angle Tarn site, which proved that this episode was accompanied by inwash of soils of the acid type to be expected in the uplands.

Peat profiles from these uplands: Red Tarn Moss and Thunacar Knott

These previously published radiocarbon-dated profiles which include the base of the local blanket peat and the vegetation changes spanning the transition from forest to peat bog have been re-analysed in greater detail since their importance was appreciated in terms of Iversen's (1964) classic statement: "The formation of *mor* is primarily a function of the high acidity which prevents the growth of those micro-organisms that attack pollen exines and other particularly resistant organic debris. Normally there is no deficiency in oxygen (Romell, 1922), but deep *mor* layers, as well as the humus-iron pan, may prevent the vertical drainage and thus reduce aeration, and, in moist climates, accelerate the growth of the *mor*, or even produce swamping. The blanket bogs of the British Isles are outstanding examples of this." These data from profiles from the mountains round the head of Great Langdale show that in that area man was involved in this change from *mor* to peat.

Red Tarn Moss

Mor, so highly humified that it consists of little other than alkali-soluble humus and pollen grains (cf. coprogenous *mor* of Iversen, 1964) accumulated above mineral soil. The pollen spectra from within the *mor* record an open vegetation with light forest (30 % of the total pollen is arboreal, 20 % *Calluna*) at the time of the elm decline. Just above the elm decline a clearance episode with fire, involving a great expansion of *Calluna,* is recorded. Simultaneously, pine pollen disappears and charcoal fragments become common within the *mor,* which also changes at this horizon from something like coprogenous *mor* to mycogenous *mor,* a soil change similar to that recorded by Iversen at Draved, South Jutland (1969) and there dated to *c.* 830 AD and attributed to a Viking clearance with fire. Within the accumulating *mor* at Red Tarn Moss is recorded *in situ* the clearance by fire of open pine–birch woods on acid soils and their replacement by *Calluna* heath, at the same time (in relation to the fixed horizon of the elm decline) as the fall in annual deposition rates of pine and birch in the sediments of Blea Tarn. This upland episode must have ended well before 2000 bc, for within this profile the presence of birch branches in the peat, *c.* 40 cm above the elm decline, shows that birch trees had recolonized the increasingly acid *mor* soil by the time of a radiocarbon date obtained on this wood—1940 ± 90 bc.

Thunacar Knott

This profile is that from the site of the first date for charcoal associated with the flakes of a chipping floor, though by the time the pollen samples were taken natural erosion had destroyed the peat face in existence when the charcoal samples were taken by Mr P. Johnson, and no macroscopic charcoal remained. The presence of microscopic pieces of charcoal in the basal samples is shown in Fig. 4. All samples in this profile post-date the elm decline, showing *(a)* that at about 5000 years ago the soil at this place was not peaty, but a well drained mineral soil, *(b)* accumulation of *mor* humus followed the chipping floor occupation which involved fire, and *(c)* that peat formation began some

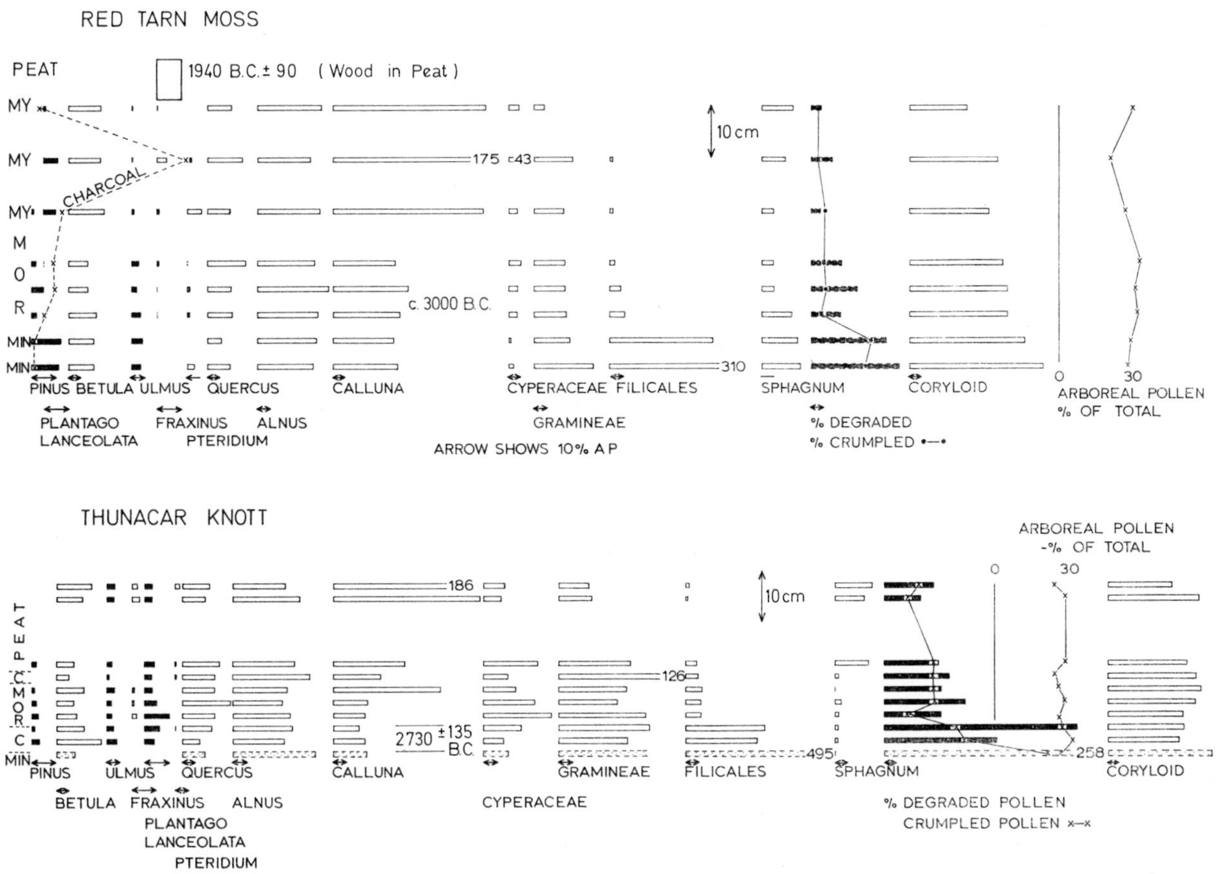

Fig. 4 Pollen diagrams from two peat profiles from the Langdale Fells, showing the sequence from basal mineral soil to mor *and so to peat. All pollen taxa are expressed as percentages of total arboreal pollen. The* ^{14}C *dates shown are NPL-122 at Red Tarn Moss and BM-281 at Thunacar Knott*

time later than the occupation. The end of the pine curve does, however, date the charcoal in this profile as belonging to the same vegetation episode—a general destruction of upland pine forest—as that at Red Tarn Moss, and both are therefore dated to the period spanned by the two radiocarbon dates (BM 281 and 676)—*c.* 2700–2400 bc. A long occupation of these uplands must be visualized.

The evidence from these four sites therefore all agrees to indicate that Neolithic man played an important part in destruction of the upland forest cover and that, after destruction of the forest, blanket peat began to form on top of forest *mor* soils (Red Tarn Moss) and mineral soils (Thunacar Knott) alike. This Lake District evidence agrees with that obtained by Moore (1973) from upland Wales. The Thunacar Knott profile

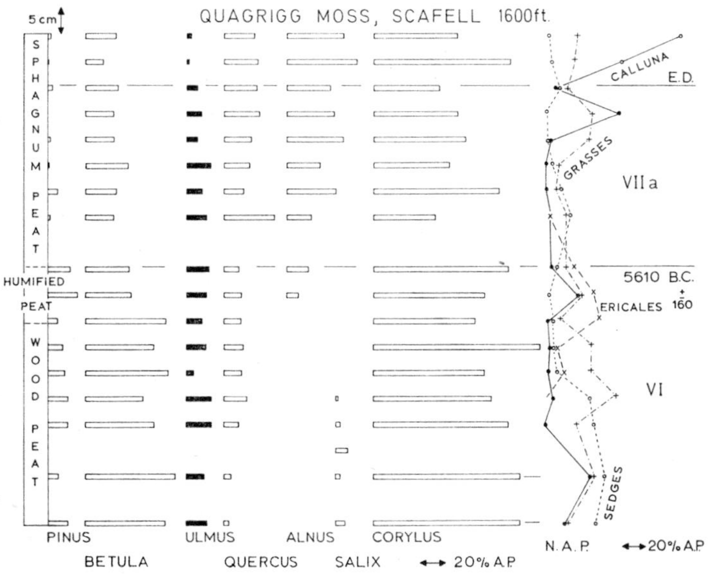

Fig. 5 Pollen diagram from Quagrigg Moss on Scafell, showing the change from wood peat to Sphagnum *peat and the expansion of* Calluna *at the elm decline. All pollen taxa are expressed as percentages of total arboreal pollen. The* ^{14}C *date is Y-2361 from Burnmoor Tarn nearby*

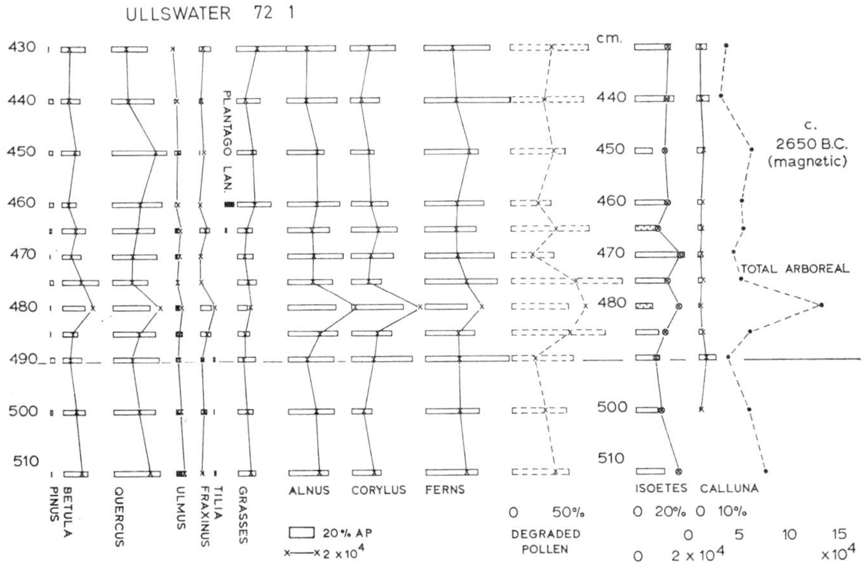

Fig. 6 *Pollen diagram from part of a core taken from Ullswater, Westmorland, in 1973, including the elm decline. The palaeomagnetic date (R. Thompson, pers. comm.) indicates the date of the end of the clearance episode. Pollen values are given as percentages of total arboreal pollen (histogram blocks) and as concentration per cubic centimetre (line graphs)*

firmly connects this Lake District environmental change with the presence of the axe-factory men, but men alone could not have brought about the complete change from forest to bog: their clearances must be viewed against a background of progressive soil acidification and paludification, and man must be seen as the factor which tipped the balance so that a natural threshold was crossed. The evidence for increased run-off during the period 5400–5000 bp provided by absolute pollen analysis at Blea Tarn (see above) supports a hypothesis that conditions were becoming wetter in the uplands (with a natural tendency towards extended peat formation) at this time.

Quagrigg Moss

This site, an extensive area of dissected peat on the southern shoulder of Scafell at about the same altitude as Red Tarn Moss and Thunacar Knott, was investigated as the nearest peat section to the axe-factory sites on Scafell, to find out whether the changes in the uplands recorded round the head of Great Langdale were also to be found near the other axe-factory sites. Exploration of Quagrigg Moss revealed that the *Sphagnum–Eriophorum* peat developed on the top of a wood peat, a common situation in the British uplands (Conway, 1954; Moore, 1973; Birks, 1972), and that peat formation must have begun in the deepest hollows of this upland saddle and progressively extended over wider areas until dissection began. The section analysed (Fig. 5) shows that at the time of the elm decline wood peat was forming, but at this level a change in peat composition must have occurred, because most of the post-elm decline peat has been destroyed by oxidation. The pollen diagram shows, however, a clear elm decline with no trace of human influence (i.e. total absence of any cultural pollens or expansion of grasses) but a marked and sudden increase in the proportion of *Calluna* to tree pollen. Some natural influence must therefore be supposed to have been affecting the upland peats in shallow basins at this time, leading to the changeover from woodland on peat to Callunetum.

This section therefore supports the hypothesis that naturally caused changes were leading towards an increase in the proportion of *Calluna* pollen and change from wood peat to blanket bog peat at this time.

(b) **The valley lakes of the Lake District**

Details of changes in pollen and sediment composition over the elm decline in the valley lakes will be described in another paper. Two examples only are considered here.

Ullswater

Figure 6 shows the pollen concentration diagram from part of a sediment core from Ullswater dated by palaeomagnetic measurements (Mackereth, 1971; Thompson, *pers. comm.*). It shows the elm decline and immediately above it a clearance episode with *Plantago lanceolata,* over by *c.* 2650 bc. There is a sustained rise in the proportion of grasses but no consistent change in the percentage or concentration of any tree except the elm. The elm decline is unusually gradual, indicative of a rapid rate of sediment accumulation. The unusually high frequencies of *Fraxinus* (ash) and *Plantago lanceolata* suggest that a different forest type and possibly rather pronounced vegetation disturbance may characterize the Carboniferous Limestone country which approaches the lower reach of Ullswater.

The sample from 480 cm shows a twofold increase in pollen concentration and a high proportion of degraded pollen, and is interpreted as the result of accelerated inwash of forest soils rich in both recognisable and degraded pollen.

Ennerdale Water

This large valley lake lies between the Lake District mountains and the coastal plain of West Cumberland; its outflow, the River Ehen, flows close by Ehenside Tarn. Figure 7 shows the pollen concentration diagram from the core of which the four ^{14}C dates spanning the elm decline are given in Fig. 2. The diagram shows evidence for *(a)* temporary decline in *Quercus* (oak) during the clearance episode which followed immediately after the elm decline, as shown by the curve for *Plantago lanceolata* and the expansion of grasses; *(b)* inwash of soil material rich in *Alnus* pollen, fern spores, and degraded pollen immediately above the elm decline—the percentage and absolute decrease in *Isoetes* spores within this sediment is interpreted as indicative of increased silting which this

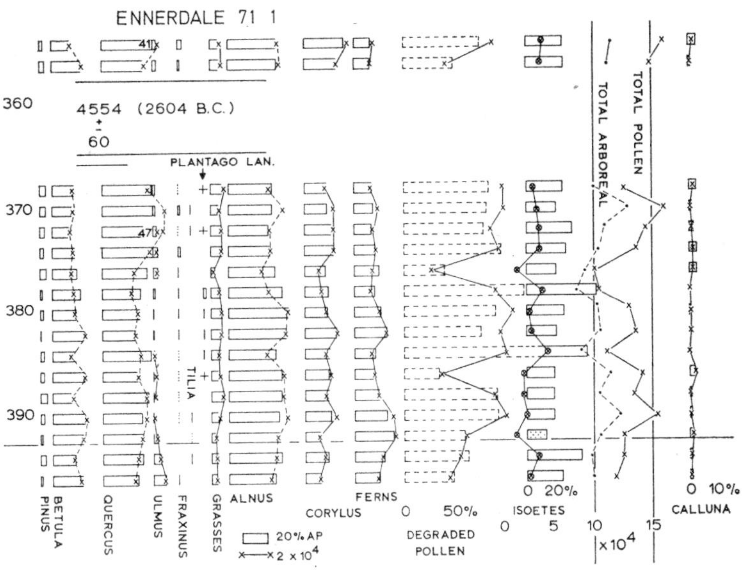

Fig. 7 *Similar diagram from part of a core taken from Ennerdale Water, Cumbria in 1971. The* ^{14}*C date is SRR-183; subsequently received* ^{14}*C dates are shown in Fig. 2, with the limits of the stages of the forest clearance*
Note the increase in values for Alnus, Corylus, *ferns, and degraded pollen immediately above the elm decline*

plant does not tolerate (cf. Pennington, 1965, 315)—and *(c)* a sustained decrease in the concentration of *Betula* (birch) pollen above the horizon of accelerated inwash.

The conclusions must be that in the sediments of this lake are recorded both the permanent decline in (upland) birch woods that began early in Neolithic time, and a temporary clearance of (valley-side and lowland) oak woods between the dates of *c.* 3200 and *c.* 2700 bc. Evidence from the coastal lowlands in the next section will support the view that in the sediments of this large lake the area from which pollen was recruited included both lowlands and uplands, so that changes in pollen values record both upland and lowland vegetation history.

(c) **The West Cumberland coastal plain**

Ehenside Tarn

Walker (1966) published pollen diagrams from the sediment profile of Ehenside Tarn in which he recognised a sequence of forest clearance episodes, beginning from before the time of the elm decline (Cumbrian Zone 16, Fig. 22 in Walker (1966)) but lacking any pronounced expansion of grasses or any record of cereal pollen until Cumbrian Zone 18, a horizon to which Walker assigned a tentative date of 2000 bc, by comparison of pollen zones with those in his radiocarbon-dated profile from Scaleby Moss near Carlisle.

Barfield Tarn

A very different vegetation history was recorded in the sediments of Barfield Tarn, *c.* 25 km south-east of Ehenside and also occupying a hollow in the boulder clay of the coastal plain. Figure 11 in Pennington (1970) shows the percentage pollen diagram, stratigraphy, and ^{14}C date. In this profile a striking stratigraphic change, from organic mud below to pink clay above, coincides with the steep fall in *Ulmus* percentages at the elm decline. There is a simultaneous expansion of the curves for grass, herb, and cereal

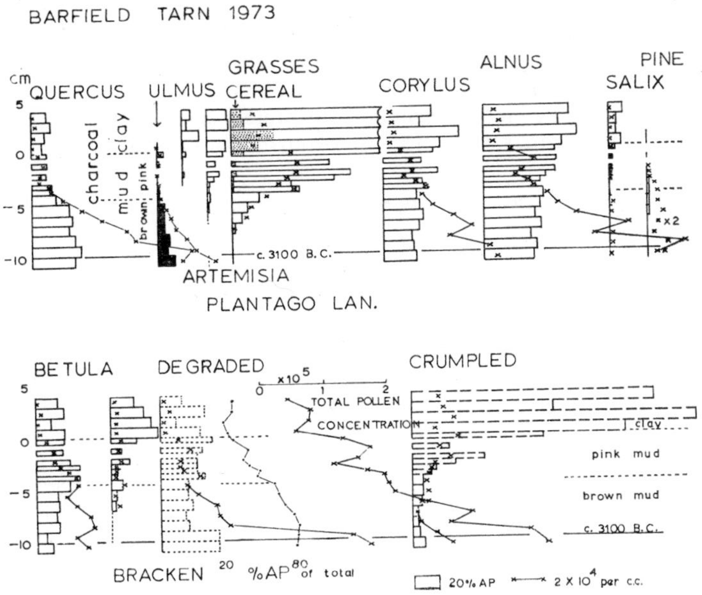

Fig. 8 *Pollen diagram from part of a core taken from Barfield Tarn, Cumberland, in 1973. Pollen values as in Fig. 6. The* ^{14}*C date is taken from a similar core obtained in 1965 (Pennington 1970, Fig. 11) by calculation of a timescale from K-1057 and other evidence*

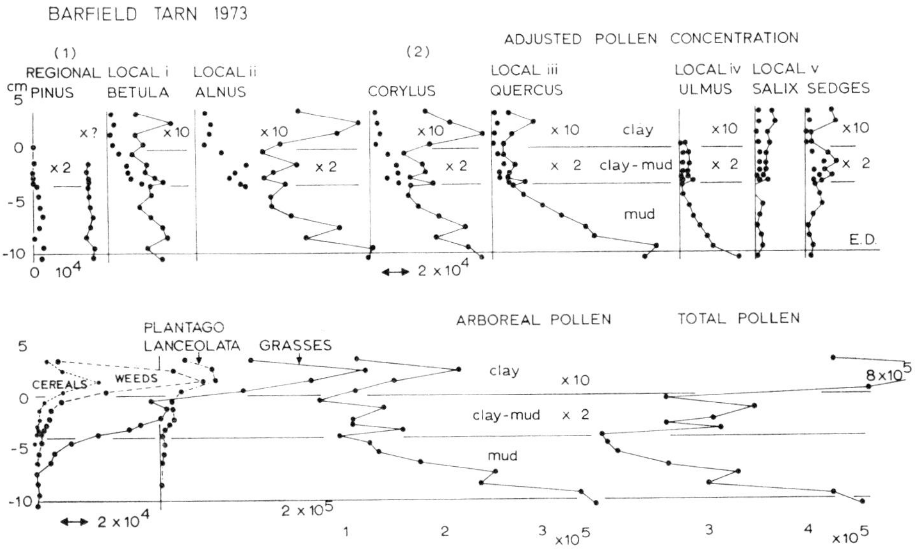

Fig. 9 *The same analyses as are given in Fig. 8, with alternative adjusted (right-hand) curves for pollen concentration to allow for an increased rate of sediment accumulation. X 2 and X 10 show the factors by which the concentration values were multiplied to produce these simulated deposition rates (see text)*
Cereals = grains of Gramineae more than 45 μ in diameter in fresh glycerine mounts. Weeds = Artemisia + Polygonum + *Compositae + Umbelliferae + Cruciferae + Chenopodiaceae*

pollen at the elm decline, and percentages of *Quercus* fall simultaneously and equally steeply with those of elm, indicating clearance of oak-elm woodland at the same time as disaster to the elms. There are pre-elm decline clearances of a very minor character, similar to those described by Walker at Ehenside, and here dated by the ^{14}C sample to *c.* 3700–3400 bc.

The sequence of pollen changes at Barfield Tarn was interpreted (Pennington, 1970) as indicative of a considerable clearance of oak or oak-elm woodland for pasture and cereal cultivation at the same time as the happening which produced the elm decline. This is similar to that found in many Irish pollen diagrams—e.g. at Fallahogy (Smith and Willis, 1961) where the elm decline is also a *Landnam* phase (Iversen, 1973, 87). The change in stratigraphy is interpreted as the consequence of greatly increased soil erosion, following cultivation for cereals of the boulder-clay slopes around the tarn.

Absolute pollen analysis of a replicate core (731) has confirmed that the percentage decline in oak as well as elm was an absolute decline, and that there was a real and simultaneous increase in the concentration of pollen of grasses, *Plantago lanceolata,* bracken (*Pteridium*-spores), cereals, and of herb taxa characteristic of the weed flora of arable land (e.g. *Artemisia*)—Fig. 8. Charcoal fragments were noted in all samples above the horizon of steepest fall in percentages of oak at −5 cm (Fig. 8), which suggests the use of fire by man in preparing the ground for cereal cultivation (Iversen, 1949).

In view of the decline in concentration of all taxa except grasses, herbs, and bracken as the brown organic mud passes into clay-mud and so into clay, the pollen concentration curves cannot be regarded as indicative of deposition rates, because of the probability of a change in accumulation rate. Some attempt has been made to estimate the change in rate of sediment accumulation resulting from soil erosion (^{14}C dating being impossible in clay) by consideration of taxa not involved in the local clearances. *Pinus* is regarded as non-local at these coastal sites (Walker, 1966) and therefore represents the regional component by definition constant at all sites. The upper part of Fig. 9 shows the concentrations of *(a)* regional *(Pinus)* and *(b)* local pollens. At −4 cm, the concentration of *Pinus* pollen is halved, indicating an approximate doubling of the rate of sediment accumulation. The right-hand values (the continuous curves) show the effect of doubling values for the local pollens to approach nearer to true deposition rates. *Betula* remains constant; this is interpreted as a constant annual contribution from marginal carr which remained undisturbed by man. *Alnus* and *Corylus* show a reduced decline, interpreted as indicative of a comparatively low involvement in clearance. *Quercus*

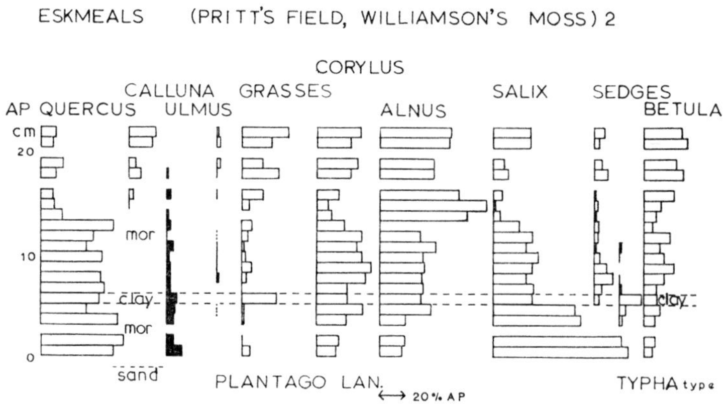

Fig. 10 *Pollen diagram from* mor *humus marginal to the wet hollow of Williamson's Moss, Eskmeals, illustrating (1) the clay band indicative of a raised water-level at the elm decline, with a change from local* Salix *fen carr to reedswamp (grasses (cf.* Phragmites*), sedges, and cf.* Typha latifolia*); (2) the post-elm decline clearance of* Quercus *(oak) with increase in grasses and* Calluna *(heather)—the site is interpreted as having been marginal to these two habitats. All taxa expressed as percentage of total arboreal pollen*

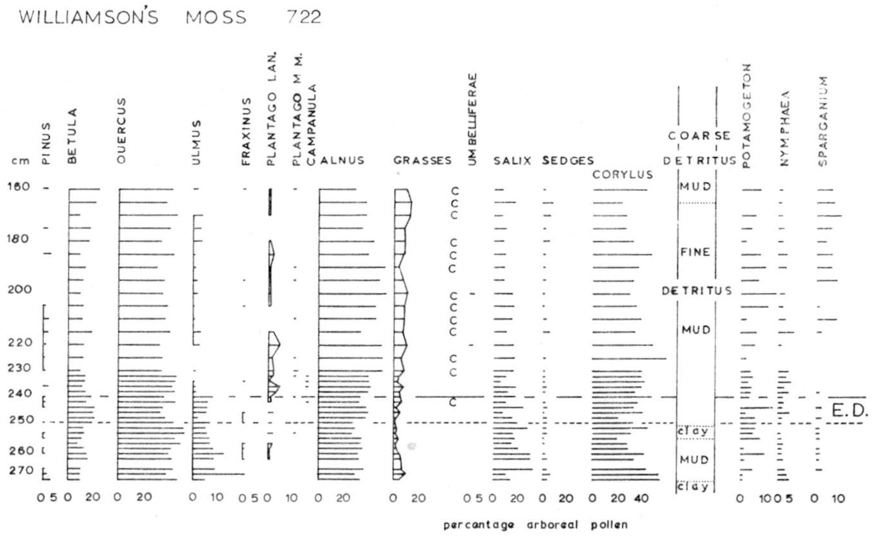

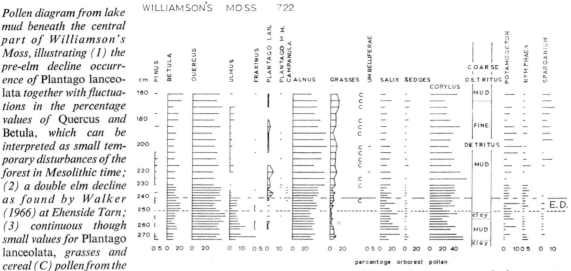

Fig. 11 *Pollen diagram from lake mud beneath the central part of Williamson's Moss, illustrating (1) the pre-elm decline occurrence of* Plantago lanceolata *together with fluctuations in the percentage values of* Quercus *and* Betula, *which can be interpreted as small temporary disturbances of the forest in Mesolithic time; (2) a double elm decline as found by Walker (1966) at Ehenside Tarn; (3) continuous though small values for* Plantago lanceolata, *grasses and cereal (C) pollen from the top of this double elm decline, indicating that local forest clearances failed to depress very much the percentage values for arboreal pollen reaching the middle of the existing lake—the interpretation is that both here and at Ehenside Tarn a belt of marginal carr and some oak and birch on drier margins remained. All pollen values are percentages of total arboreal pollen*

and *Ulmus* show an absolute decline even with the adjusted values, and it must be supposed that the absolutely increasing grasses and herbs were occupying land previously occupied by oaks and elms. *Salix* and sedges, the local damp-land pollens, show an absolute increase in agreement with the evidence from other sites for an increased precipitation/evaporation ratio and rising water-levels just above the elm decline.

Above 0 cm (the main stratigraphic change), no *Pinus* pollen was recorded, indicating still further dilution of the regional component by increased input of soil material. Multiplication by a factor of 10 is required to keep the *Betula* component constant. Figure 9 shows that such an adjustment would restore the annual input of *Alnus* and *Corylus* to its pre-elm decline level, but that *Ulmus* has disappeared and *Quercus* remains very sparse. Analysis was stopped at the + 4 cm level because of the overwhelming proportion of crumpled and so unrecognisable pollen (Fig. 8) interpreted as carried in with moving soil material.

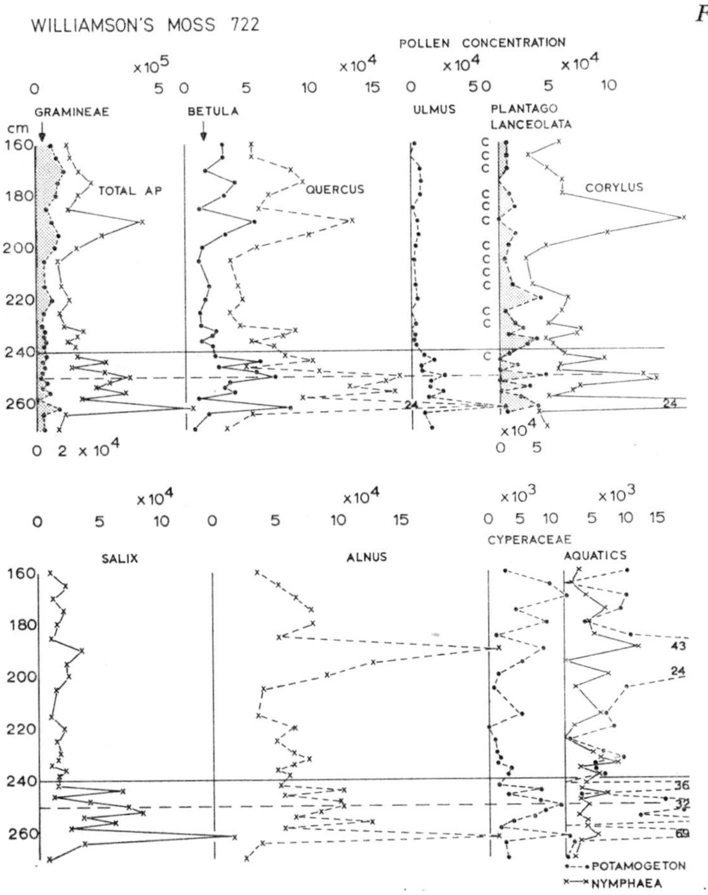

Fig. 12 *The pollen concentration diagram corresponding to Fig. 11. The variation in concentration shown by all taxa is related primarily to variations in total pollen concentration, which probably relate to changing deposition rates of sediment. The low concentrations of all pollens, including aquatics, between 205 and 230 cm are interpreted as indicative of increased input of material following clearance of oak woodland*

The lower part of Fig. 9 shows the absolute diagram for the clearance episode, based on these assumptions; it shows the curves for annual deposition of grasses and *Plantago lanceolata* rising *before* the curves for cereals and weeds. This suggests a different pattern of settlement from that found by Pilcher *et al.* (1971) in Irish Neolithic diagrams.

Williamson's Moss, Eskmeals (or Pritt's Field)

This coastal site, a peaty hollow on the raised beach containing the detritus muds deposited in a former pond, was investigated because of the local presence of Mesolithic and Neolithic artefacts (Cherry, 1969; Pennington, 1970). Figure 10 reproduces (from Fig. 13 in Pennington, 1970) a pollen diagram from the damp margin of the pond, where the deposit is *mor* humus stratified between sands. In this profile a band of clay at the elm decline indicates a rise in water level of the pond, with extension of the marginal reed belt, at this time. Seven centimetres above the elm decline a clearance of oak woodland is recorded with the precision that characterizes the pollen record from accumulating *mor* (Iversen, 1964; 1969). At a nearby position on the drier margin, a rough-out of a Cumbrian axe was recovered during draining operations, from *mor* humus containing pollen spectra similar to those found between 14 and 20 cm (Fig. 10). This associates the clearance of oak woods with users of Cumbrian axes.

The fine-detritus muds of the former pond in the lowest part of the hollow were then sampled by peat-borer; Figs. 11 and 12 show respectively the percentage and concentration pollen diagrams. Pollen spectra at the elm decline resemble those found by Walker at Ehenside (Walker, 1966) rather than those from the marginal *mor* (Fig. 10), emphasizing the importance of the site of accumulation in determining pollen spectra; this question will be discussed further in a separate publication.

The most interesting features of the pollen diagrams from the central part of Williamson's Moss are *(a)* indications of local Mesolithic activity, shown not only by the almost continuous presence of *Plantago lanceolata* but also by fluctuations in relative and absolute values for elm and oak on the one hand and birch on the other hand, which suggest temporary clearances and recolonization by birch, well below the elm decline; *(b)* indication in the pollen curves of reduction in willow carr followed by development of reedswamp, explicable in terms of a rise in water level, at the elm decline; and *(c)* an absolute decrease in all pollen including that of water plants (*Potamogeton* spp.) in the 25 cm section which immediately overlies the percentage and absolute fall in oak at 230 cm: this is interpreted as the result of dilution of the annual pollen increment by the accelerated entry of soil material during the local clearance of oak, soon after the elm decline. Further work at the site is planned, using a wide-diameter borer, for critical ^{14}C dating. Meanwhile, the results of pollen analysis have *(a)* confirmed the supposition of Cherry (1969) that the first and major occupation of the Williamson's Moss site took place between *c.* 3500 and 2700 bc, and *(b)* have distinguished between temporary clearances of Mesolithic type below the elm decline, and a major clearance of oak woodland accompanied by the cultivation of cereals (Fig. 11), beginning shortly above the elm decline.

CONCLUSIONS

Vegetation disturbance attributed to man before 3100 bc

In the sediments of Blea Tarn and Barfield Tarn there are radiocarbon-dated traces of small forest clearings from the period *c.* 3700–3100 bc; these lie beneath the elm decline in the profiles. Clearer pollen evidence for these disturbances of Mesolithic date has been found by Walker at Ehenside Tarn (Walker, 1966) and by the author at Williamson's Moss. There is therefore pollen evidence for the influence of Mesolithic man on forest composition both from the area of the axe-factory sites and from the coastal area of Neolithic settlement. In neither area has any trace of the use of fire in pre-elm decline time been found in the pollen profiles.

The elm decline—c. 3100 bc

At all sites investigated there are traces in litho-stratigraphy, sediment composition, and pollen analysis of the effects of increased run-off from the catchments and of a rise in water-level at the lowland pond (Williamson's Moss), coinciding almost exactly with the steep fall in elm pollen which can be used as a synchronous horizon. These effects, together with a general increase in *Calluna* pollen, can be interpreted as the results of an increased precipitation/evaporation ratio, with an increased tendency towards peat formation, in the Highland Zone at this time.

The steep fall in elm pollen at *c.* 3100 bc has been shown by absolute pollen analysis to have been a real decrease in elm, to a value between one-fifth and one-tenth of previous annual deposition rates. The presence of *Plantago lanceolata* at all sites investigated indicates the widespread dispersal in the Lake District of the pollen of this plant for the first time; this can most reasonably be attributed to the presence of man, but the pollen evidence cannot indicate whether the disaster to the elms resulted from the direct effects of a leaf-foddering culture.

The disturbance of percentage and absolute curves for other pollen taxa at the various sites can, however, be related to the pattern of early Neolithic occupation as revealed by artefacts. A clear distinction is found between: *(a)* upland sites round the Great Langdale axe-factories, where absolute falls in pollen deposition rates of pine and birch accompany the fall in elm, and record the clearance (including the use of fire) of light upland forest of distinct composition and *(b)* sites on the coastal plain, where absolute falls in pollen deposition rates of oak accompany or immediately follow the fall in elm, and coincide with the appearance of pollen of cultivated cereals, indicating clearance of oakwoods for agriculture, also including the use of fire. In the valley lakes, the lack of any clear picture of reduced annual deposition rates for oak pollen indicates that the oak woods of the lower hill slopes and the Lake District valleys were not being exploited by man at this date, but again the pollen evidence is inconclusive as to the presence or otherwise of a leaf-foddering culture exploiting the elms.

The length of time represented by the early Neolithic episode of disturbance

Figure 2 shows the span of time represented at the two sites where adequate ^{14}C dating was available. At Blea Tarn, period A of declining tree pollen (cf. Smith and Willis, 1961; Pilcher *et al.*, 1971) lasted *c.* 200 years, and period B, that of maximum deposition of pollen of grasses and *Plantago lanceolata*, about 300 years.

The two dates on charcoal represent the beginning of replacement of previous vegetation by bog; at this site there was no regeneration of the forest that had been attacked. In the Ennerdale profile, period C of forest regeneration lasted about 100 years, so that the episode of decreased deposition of oak pollen was over soon after 2800 bc on this time scale. At the coastal sites there is as yet no ^{14}C dating for the end of the episode, but this date for the end of the regional change in pollen deposition at Ennerdale agrees well with the terminal date of *c.* 2700 bc suggested by Cherry (1969) on typological evidence from Williamson's Moss.

The effect of Neolithic man on the environment

There is clear evidence from the sites discussed in this paper that in this region the effects of man on both upland and lowland landscapes increased dramatically in amplitude at the beginning of Neolithic time. Small temporary disturbances of pre-elm decline date were succeeded at the time of the elm decline by widespread destruction of upland forest and by coastal clearances for agriculture on a scale sufficient to bring about permanent change in both vegetation and soils. In the light of the evidence presented from lake sediments it seems probable that an increase in run-off and soil erosion from natural causes, combined with a rise in levels of ground water, operative at the same time as the new forms of land use which began *c.* 5100 bp, intensified both the degenerative changes in the upland soils from forest to peat bog and the tendency for lowland soils to move bodily down slopes as a result of cultivation practices. In this way began man's attack on the accumulated reserves of fertility present in the soils of the primary forest of the Highland Zone of northern England.

REFERENCES

Andersen, S. T. (1969). Interglacial vegetation and soil development. *Meddr. Dansk. Geol. Foren.*, 19, 90–102.

Birks, H. H. (1972). Studies in the vegetational history of Scotland II. Two pollen diagrams from the Galloway hills, Kirkcudbrightshire. *J. Ecol.*, 60, 183–217.

Bunch, B. and Fell, C. I. (1949). A stone-axe factory at Pike of Stickle, Great Langdale, Westmorland. *Proc. Prehist. Soc.*, 15, 39–55.

Cherry, J. (1969). Early Neolithic sites at Eskmeals. *Trans. Cumberland Westmorland Antiq. Archaeol. Soc.*, 69, 40–54.

Clough, T. H. McK. (1973). Excavations on a Langdale axe chipping site in 1969 and 1970. *Trans. Cumberland Westmorland Antiq. Archaeol. Soc.*, 73, 25–42.

Conway, V. M. (1954). Stratigraphy and pollen analysis of Southern Pennine blanket peats. *J. Ecol.*, 42, 117–147.

Darbyshire, R. D. (1874). Notes on discoveries in Ehenside Tarn, Cumberland. *Archaeologia*, 44, 273.

Davis, M. B. (1967). Pollen accumulation rates at Rogers Lake, Connecticut, during late-and post-glacial time. *Rev. Palaeobotan. Palynol.*, 2, 219–230.

Davis, M. B. and Deevey, E. S. (1964). Pollen accumulation rates: estimates from late-glacial sediment of Rogers Lake. *Science*, 145, 1293–1295.

Dimbleby, G. W. (1962). *The Development of British Heathlands and Their Soils.* Oxford Forestry Memoir No. 23.

Fell, C. I. (1964). The Cumbrian type of polished stone axe and its distribution in Britain. *Proc. Prehist. Soc.*, 30, 39–55.

Hibbert, F. A. Switsur, V. R., and West, R. G. (1971). Radiocarbon dating of Flandrian pollen zones at Red Moss, Lancashire. *Proc. Roy. Soc.*, B, 177, 161–176.

Iversen, J. (1949). The influence of prehistoric man on vegetation. *Geological Survey of Denmark*, IV, 3, 1–25.

Iversen, J. (1964). Retrogressive vegetational succession in the post-glacial. *J. Ecol.*, 52, 59–70.

Iversen, J. (1969). Retrogressive development of a forest ecosystem demonstrated by pollen diagrams from fossil mor. *Oikos*, 12, 35–49.

Iversen, J. (1973). The development of Denmark's Nature since the last Glacial. *Geological Survey of Denmark*, 7c, 1–125.

Mackereth, F. J. H. (1965). Chemical investigation of lake sediments and their interpretation. *Proc. Roy. Soc.*, B, 161, 295–309.

Mackereth, F. J. H. (1966). Some chemical observations on post-glacial lake sediments. *Phil. Trans. Roy. Soc.*, B, 250, 165–213.

Mackereth, F. J. H. (1971). On the variation in direction of the horizontal component of remanent magnetisation in lake sediments. *Earth Planet. Sci. Lett.*, 12, 332–338.

Moore, P. D. (1973). The influence of prehistoric cultures upon the initiation and spread of blanket bog in upland Wales. *Nature Lond.*, 241, 350–353.

Peck, R. M. (1973). Pollen budget studies in a small Yorkshire catchment. *In* Birks, H. J. B. and West, R. G. (eds.). *Quaternary Plant Ecology.* 14th Symposium of the British Ecological Society: Blackwell Scientific Publications; 43–60.

Pennington, W. (1964). Pollen analyses from the deposits of six upland tarns in the Lake District. *Phil. Trans. Roy. Soc.*, B, 248, 205–244.

Pennington, W. (1965). The interpretation of some post-glacial vegetation diversities at different Lake District sites. *Proc. Roy. Soc.*, B, 161, 310–323.

Pennington, W. (1970). Vegetation history in the north-west of England: a regional synthesis. *In* Walker, D. and West, R. G. (eds.). *Studies in the Vegetational History of the British Isles.* Cambridge: University Press; 41–79.

Pennington, W. (1973). Absolute pollen frequencies in the sediments of lakes of different morphometry. *In* Birks, H. J. B. and West R. G. (eds.). *Quaternary Plant Ecology.* 14th Symposium of the British Ecological Society: Blackwell Scientific Publications; 79–104.

Pennington, W. (1973a). Pollen analysis at the Langdale axe chipping site. *Trans. Cumberland Westmorland Antiq. Archaeol Soc.*, 73, 43–46.

Pennington, W., Haworth, E.Y., Bonny, A. P., and Lishman, J. P. (1972). Lake sediments in northern Scotland. *Phil. Trans. Roy. Soc.*. B, 264, 191–294.

Piggott, S. (1954). *The Neolithic cultures of the British Isles.* Cambridge: University Press.

Pilcher, J. R., Smith, A. G., Pearson, G. W., and Crowder, A. (1971). Land clearance in the Irish Neolithic: new evidence and interpretation. *Science*, 172, 560–562.

Smith, A. G. (1961). The Atlantic-Sub-Boreal transition. *Proc. Linn. Soc. Lond.*, 172, 38–49.

Smith, A. G. (1970). The influence of Mesolithic and Neolithic man on British vegetation: a discussion. *In* Walker, D. and West, R. G. (eds.). *Studies in the Vegetational History of the British Isles.* Cambridge: University Press; 81–96.

Smith, A. G., and Pilcher, J. R. (1973). Radiocarbon dates and the vegetational history of the British Isles. *New Phytol.*, 72, 903–914.

Smith, A. G. and Willis, E. H. (1961). Radiocarbon dating of the Fallahogy Landnam phase. *Ulster J. Archaeol.*, 24–25, 16–24.

Tutin, W. (née Pennington). (1969). The usefulness of pollen analysis in interpretation of stratigraphic horizons, both late-glacial and post-glacial. *Mitt. int. Verein. theor. angew. Limnol.*, 17, 154–164.

Walker, D. (1965). The post-glacial period in the Langdale Fells, English Lake District. *New Phytol.*, 64, 488–510.

Walker, D. (1966). The late Quaternary history of the Cumberland lowland. *Phil. Trans. Roy. Soc.*, B, 251, 1–210.

Wright, H. E. (1971). Late Quaternary vegetational history of North America. *In* Turekian, K. K. (ed.). *The Late Cenozoic Glacial Ages.* Yale; 425–464.

The evidence for land use by prehistoric farming communities: the use of three-dimensional pollen diagrams

Judith Turner

Synopsis

Several pollen diagrams covering the period from the Neolithic onwards have been prepared from various places on the same moss in Ayrshire. The evidence for forest clearance and land use differs significantly from one diagram to another, and these differences give an indication of the actual area of land cleared. A high peak in the grass and associated cultural indicator pollen types which occurred after ad 415 appears to have been caused by clearance of a particular tract of land to the northwest of the bog, whereas the Bronze Age series of smaller peaks, the landnam *of Iversen, appear to have been caused by successive migrations, through a much more extensive area, of people practising shifting agriculture.*

INTRODUCTION

In 1961 I began what I subsequently called a three-dimensional pollen diagram from lowland Ayrshire. Work continued throughout 1962 and 1963, and it soon became apparent that it was going to be a much longer project than originally envisaged. In 1967 I took it up again and, knowing it would be years before it was finished, wrote up the idea and the results, which were then available for the period ad 415 to the present day. The invitation to speak at this Conference has provided an incentive to continue the project, this time concentrating on the period from 3000 bc to ad 415, the period during which the diagram shows a series of *Landnam* episodes. The diagram is still not complete and doubtless will not be for some years to come, but it has during the last two months yielded some results which have a bearing on the theme of the Conference and about which I would like to talk today. Before doing so, however, I will say a little about the idea originally behind the diagram and also a little about the results obtained in 1967 (Turner, 1970).

As a research student I used to listen to Sir Harry Godwin speculating over coffee about the size of prehistoric populations and whether it would ever be possible to gain an idea of what they were and how they increased through studying prehistoric landscapes, for example, the proportion of the land that was being used for farming at any one time by the people living in the area. It seemed to me at that time that if pollen diagrams were ever to be really helpful in this connection it would be very useful indeed to know, whenever one had evidence for forest clearance on a diagram, the size of the area that was producing the characteristic decreases in tree pollen and increases in herbaceous pollen.

It also seemed to me at the time, a little naively perhaps, that the clearance of any one strip of land ought to show up on a pollen diagram from a deposit very close by and not on diagrams from further away and that, given enough diagrams scattered throughout the area, it ought theoretically to be possible to locate on the ground the actual area that had been cleared.

I chose the area north-east of Kilwinning in lowland Ayrshire principally because it had a number of raised bogs of various sizes with reasonably good farming land between, land which clearly had been forest-clad in early prehistoric times. Within this mosaic of bog and forest I hoped to be able to locate on the ground where the forest clearances had actually occurred.

Now all this was a long time ago, before people like Henrik Tauber had published their ideas on pollen transport, ideas which palynologists now use in interpreting their diagrams and which are highly relevant to a project such as this. I have used his model so extensively in interpreting the diagram that it is perhaps worthwhile at this stage to outline it briefly.

Tauber (1965, 1967) suggested that the pollen falling on to a bog or lake surface in the middle of a lowland forest would have done so in one of three ways. Some, derived from within a few hundred metres of the bog, would have been shed from the trees into the trunk space below and have drifted over the bog, settling to the ground under the force of gravity within a few hundred metres of the forest edge. Some, derived from distances of up to 10 km or more, would have travelled above the canopy of the forest in the local winds and again fallen on to the bog surface owing to gravity, but this time spreading fairly evenly all over it. Finally a certain amount, derived partly from both these sources and partly from even further away, would be washed out of the atmosphere when it rained.

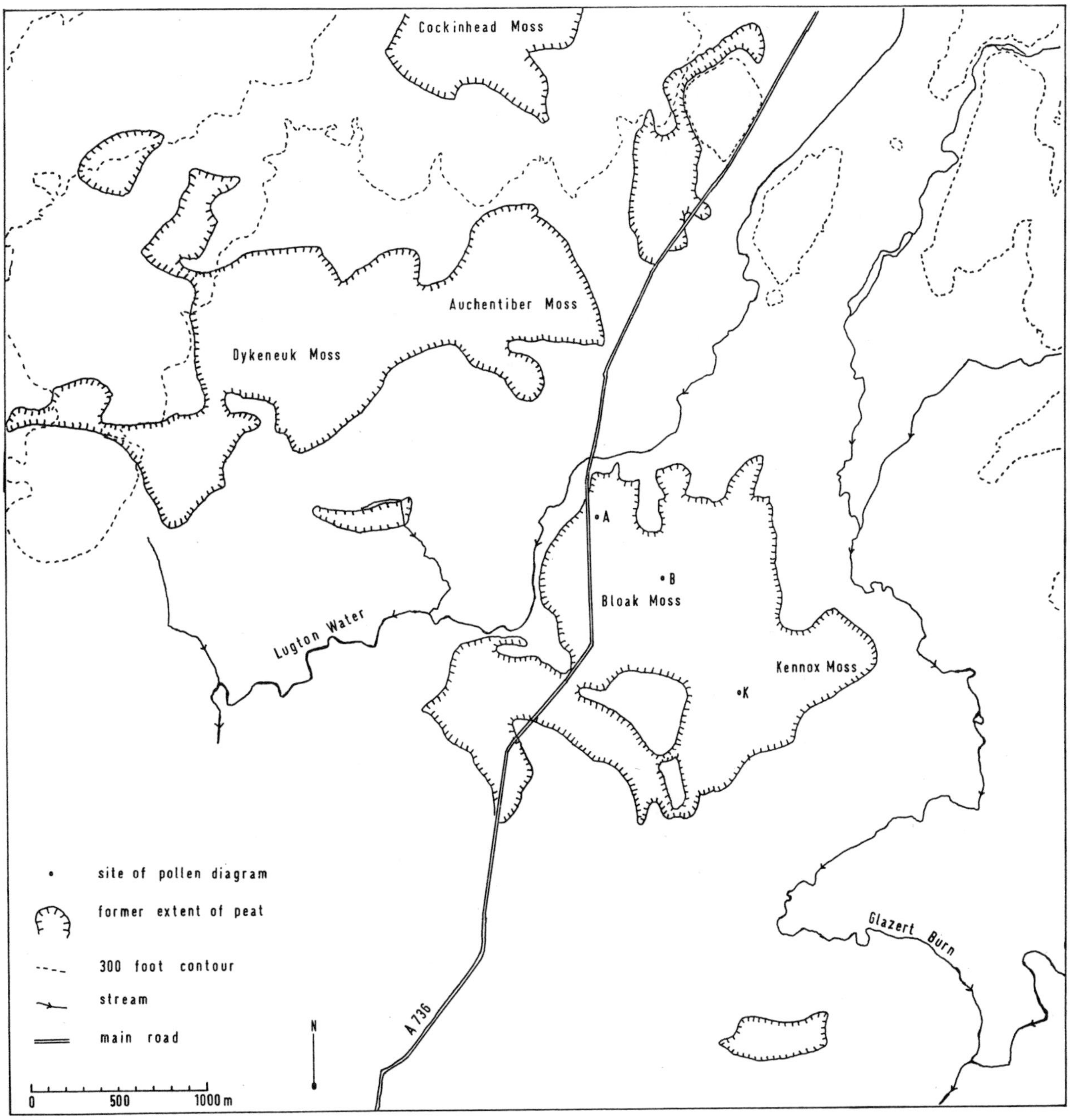

Fig. 1 Map of Bloak and Kennox mosses showing position of pollen diagrams and their relation to surrounding mosses

Tauber has provided fairly precise estimates for these three components in various situations, but for our purposes the most significant thing that arises from his work is the fact that a diagram from within a few hundred metres of the edge of a bog will contain a high proportion of pollen derived from within a few hundred metres of the forest edge. By contrast, a diagram from the middle of a large raised bog will contain a high proportion of pollen derived from much greater distances, from an area extending many kilometres from the bog.

THE POLLEN DIAGRAM

The bog from which the diagram comes and the surrounding area are shown in Fig. 1. Ordinary pollen diagrams were originally prepared from the sites marked *A* and *B* on Bloak Moss and from the site marked *K* on the south-eastern part of the moss known as Kennox Moss. These sites lie, more or less, on a straight line across the bog from south-east to north-west.

In terms of Tauber's model, Site *A*, which lies less than 100 m from the forest edge, would have been receiving a very high proportion of locally derived pollen, Site *B*, which lies near the centre of the moss complex, a very high proportion of regionally derived pollen; and Site *K*, which lies about 300 m from the forest edge, a mixture of both locally and regionally derived pollen.

All three diagrams have a number of features in common; features which are illustrated on the two diagrams from Sites *A* and *K* (Figs. 2–5).

The peat began forming in pollen Zone VIIa, shortly before the elm decline, except at Site *B*, where it began slightly later.

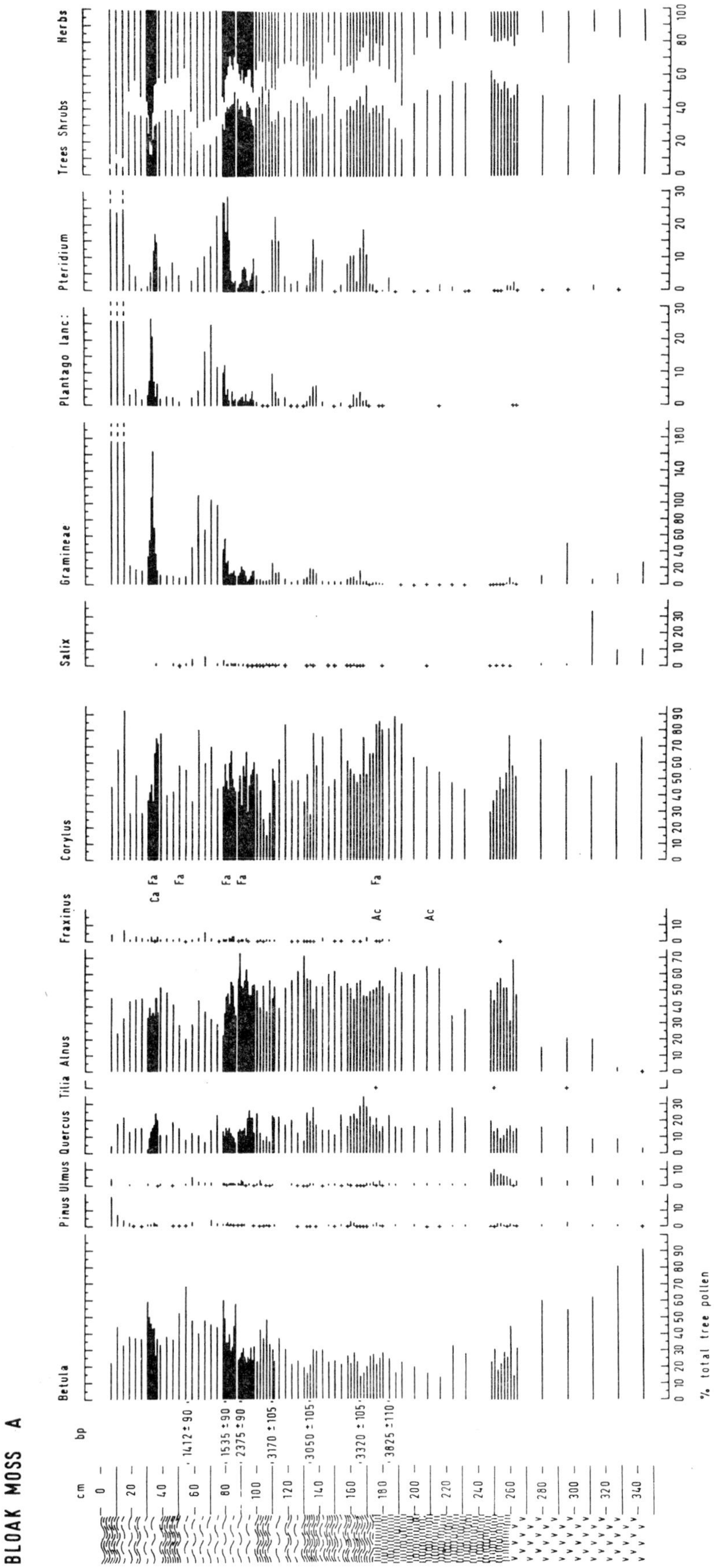

Fig. 2 **Pollen diagram from Bloak Moss, site A, with all pollen frequencies plotted as a percentage of total tree pollen**

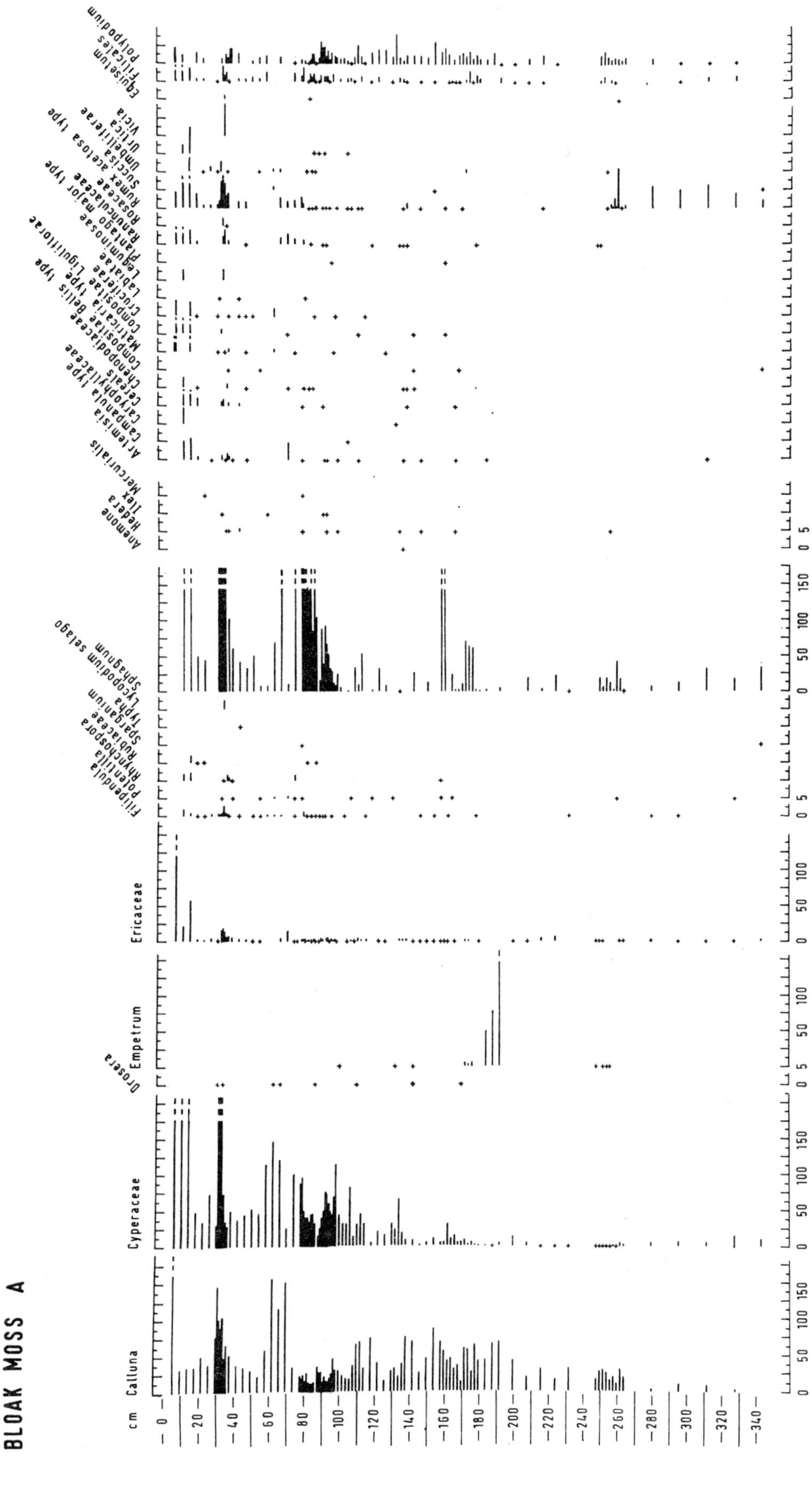

Fig. 3 **Pollen diagram from Bloak Moss, site A, with all pollen frequencies plotted as a percentage of total tree pollen**

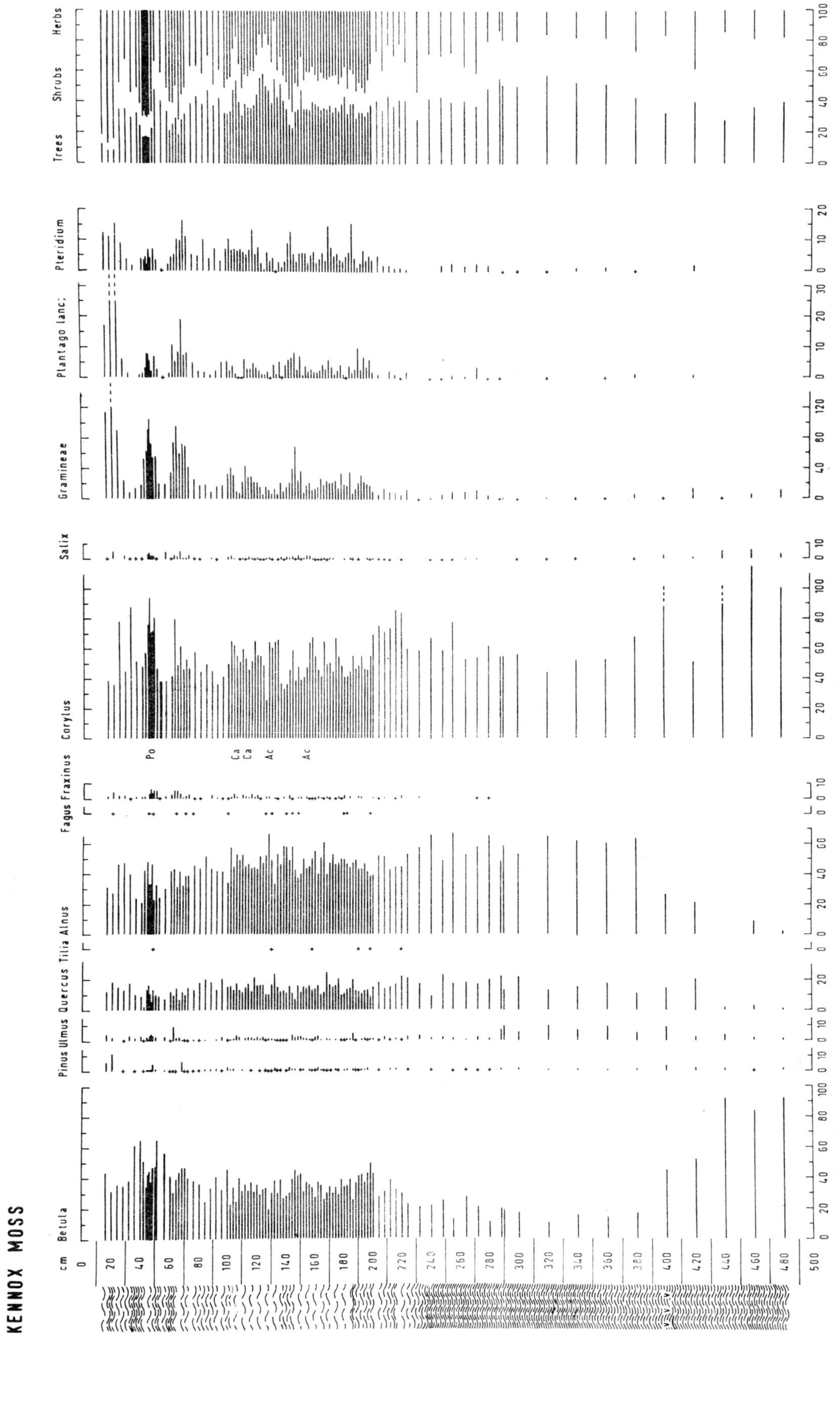

Fig. 4 Pollen diagram from Kennox Moss, site K, with all pollen frequencies plotted as a percentage of total tree pollen

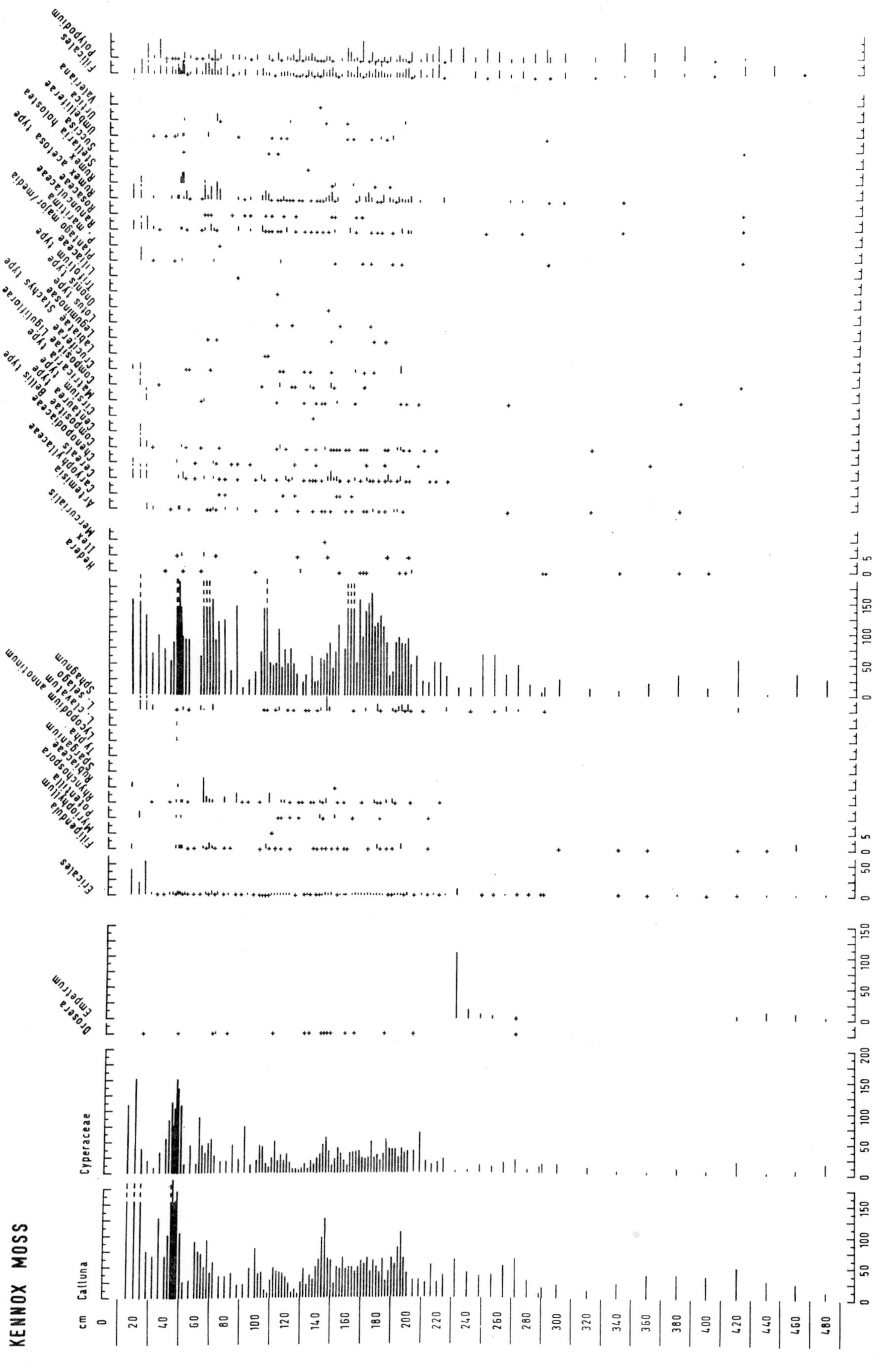

Fig. 5 **Pollen diagram from Kennox Moss, site K, with all pollen frequencies plotted as a percentage of total tree pollen**

The elm decline has not been dated but presumably it occurred at about 3000 bc. A short distance above the elm decline there is a period with high *Corylus* (hazel) frequencies, the *Fraxinus* (ash) curve begins, and there is a significant rise in the Gramineae (grass) frequency. Then follow a series of *Landnam*, characterized by increased Gramineae, *Plantago lanceolata* (plantain), and *Pteridium* (bracken) frequencies. These will be discussed later. The upper part of all three diagrams have two periods which must represent two episodes of substantial forest clearance before the final clearance, which occurs in the top few centimetres of the moss. According to the evidence of the radiocarbon dates, the first of these two major clearances took place between ad 415 and ad 580. The other clearance was too close to the top of the moss to be dated.

The upper part of the diagram

The upper part of diagrams *A*, *B*, and *K* had been completed in detail by 1967 and at that time I compared them, constructing the first part of the three-dimensional diagram.

The grass frequency, which I took as the best indicator of forest clearance, varies from one site to another at the level of the uppermost undated clearance. It reaches a peak of 184% T.T.P. (total tree pollen) at Site *A*, a peak of 138% T.T.P. at Site *B*, and a peak of only 105% T.T.P. at Site *K*. It is clear that during the upper undated clearance episode more grass pollen was falling on the north-west side of the moss near *A* and there was a gradient across the moss, with the least falling on the south-east at *K*. I interpreted this as meaning that a tract of land had been cleared to the north-west of Bloak Moss at that time, and that the clearance of that particular piece of land had caused the gradient in the grass-pollen frequency across the bog.

The grass frequency also varies at the level of the dated clearance below, but in a different way. It is much lower in the centre of the moss at Site *B* (mean frequency 30·7% T.T.P.) than at either Site *A* (mean frequency 75·6% T.T.P.) or Site *K* (mean frequency 75·1% T.T.P.), both of which lie much nearer the edge of the moss.

This result seemed best explained in terms of Tauber's model mentioned earlier. Site *B*, in the centre of the moss, would be receiving a larger regional pollen component than either *A* or *K*, both of which would be receiving a larger locally derived component. There must therefore have been more forest clearance in the vicinity of Bloak and Kennox Mosses than further away in the surrounding countryside.

The lower part of the diagram

In 1967, I was sufficiently encouraged by these results to decide that at some future date it would be well worth looking in much more detail at the earlier *Landnam* episodes to see whether or not they produced a uniform pollen rain over the bog surface or not. Would the third dimension to the pollen diagram add anything to what already could be seen on the diagram from Site *A*?

There was a problem with the lower part of the diagrams as they existed in 1967. Diagram *B* appeared to have seven rather than the four *Landnam* episodes that had been found at Site *A*, and the diagram from *K* resembled neither.

The obvious conclusion was that *Landnam* clearances were so small that they did not show on more than the diagram from very near them and that diagram *B*, giving the complex regional picture, could not be expected to correlate with either diagram *A* or *K*, both of which themselves should be different.

I was reluctant to accept this, partly because I did not think I had at that stage counted samples at sufficiently close intervals and partly because I believed I might even so be working too near the limits of resolution of pollen diagrams from raised bogs to be able to detect any significant pattern which there might have been in the pollen falling on to the moss during a *Landnam*.

The maximum resolution of the pollen diagram is the time interval represented by 0·5 cm of peat at Site *A* and 1 cm of peat at the other sites. At Site *A* the pollen samples were taken from blocks cut from a peat face, which had sliced easily into 0·5 cm pollen sample, whereas at the other sites, which had been sampled with a Hiller borer, it was only possible to slice the peat into 1 cm thick samples. The time taken for 1 cm of peat to form varied, as the radiocarbon evidence from Site *A* confirms; since raised bogs can even stop growing completely in places for a number of years, there is a very real possibility that one of the diagrams, although closely sampled, may have missed out, as it were, a particular *Landnam*. Clearly, however, I could not give up hope of finding a pattern in the distribution of pollen over the bog surface until I had counted that part of the diagram at 0·5 cm and 1 cm intervals where necessary.

What I have done to date is to count diagrams *A* and *K* in much more detail, and it is the result of this work—a comparison of the lower part of diagrams *A* and *K*—that I want to present now as new data.

A comparison of diagrams A and K between 3000 bc and ad 415

Figure 6 shows the grass and bracken frequencies at the two sites. The individual samples are plotted at their correct depth below the surface of the bog. Both sites have produced a series of peaks and troughs in the grass curve. The question is, how closely do they correspond? The period 3000 bc to ad 415 is a long time with nothing happening to the vegetation except a series of *Landnam* episodes; one *Landnam* looks much like another, so one obviously needs some other pollen frequency change or changes common to both diagrams (and preferably of regional significance) in order to help correlate the two diagrams. There are some, no one of which is entirely satisfactory, but which taken together give a reasonably consistent picture. They are as follows:

(a) the beginning of the *Fraxinus* curve at 184 cm on *A*, 232 cm on *K*
(b) very high *Corylus* values between 168 and 174 cm on *A*, 200 and 220 cm on *K*
(c) the beginning of the *Drosera* curve at 170 cm on *A*, 204 cm on *K*
(d) high values for *Polypodium* at 132 cm on *A*, 166 cm on *K*
(e) the highest Gramineae values at 110 cm on *A*, 146 cm on *K*
(f) a very low *Corylus* value at 106 cm on *A*, 126 cm on *K*.

Each of these levels is marked on Fig. 6 with a symbol.

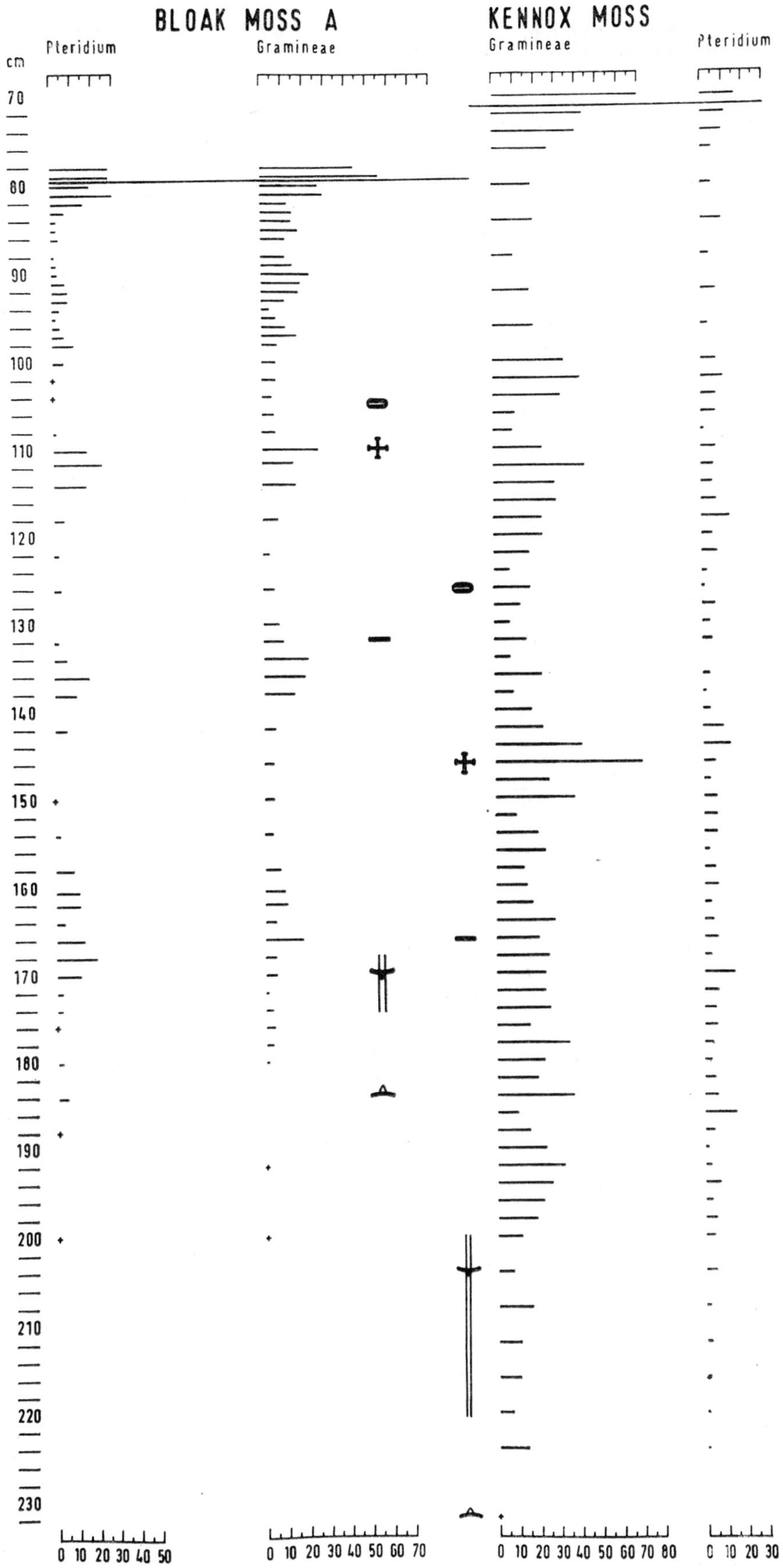

Fig. 6 *Grass and bracken frequencies from sites* A *and* K *plotted on a scale of depth below surface of the moss*

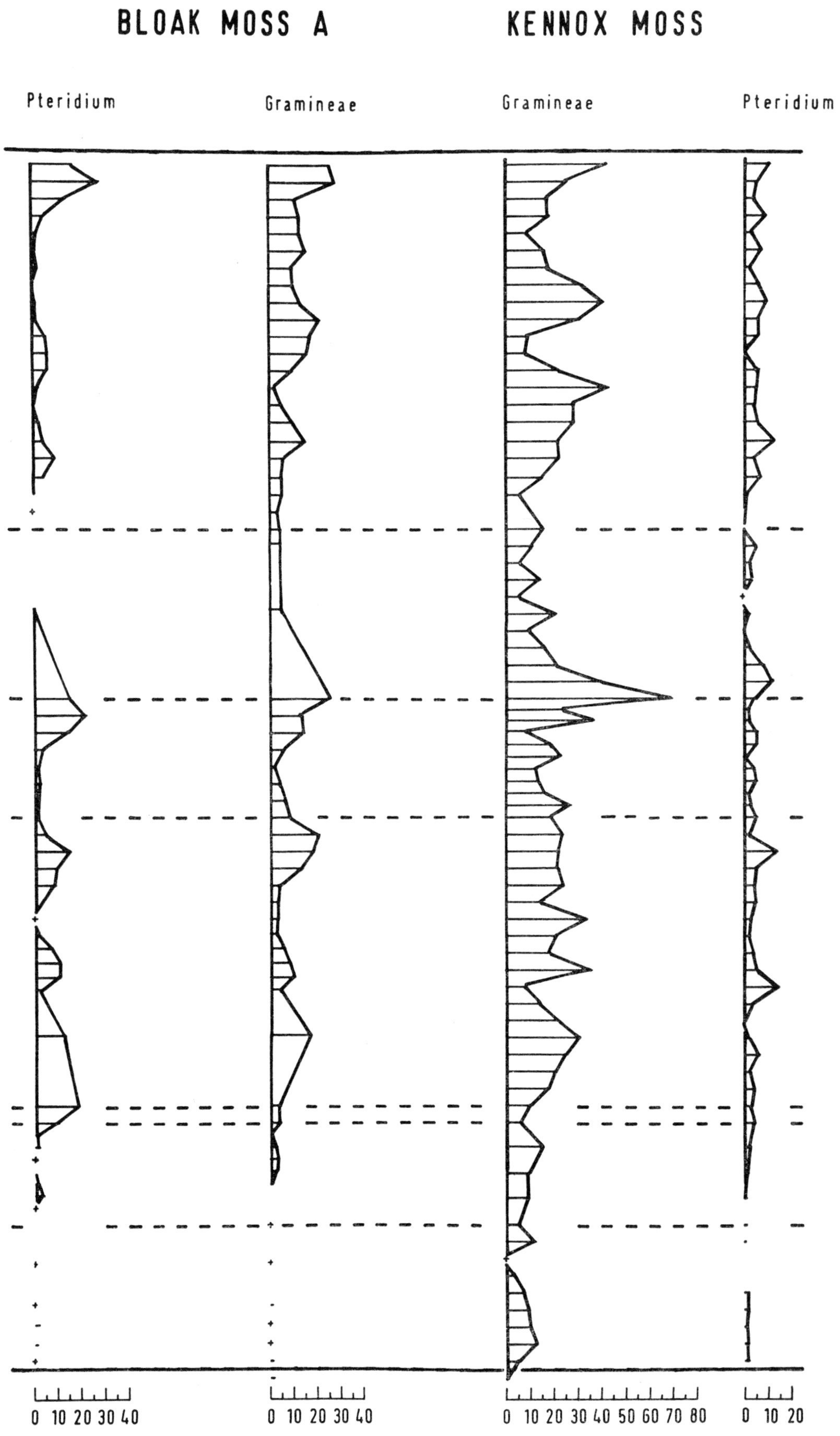

Fig. 7 *Grass and bracken frequencies from sites* A *and* K *plotted on an approximate time scale*

Figure 7 gives the grass and bracken frequencies replotted with the vertical scale adjusted in such a way that each of these correlation horizons is at the same level. This means that the vertical axis no longer measures the depth of the sample below the bog surface but instead approximates to a time scale.

How closely do the peaks and troughs in the grass curves correspond? Do they, like the grass curve in the upper part of the diagram, represent a single series of forest clearances in the region?

I believe that, within the limits of resolution of the diagrams, the match of peaks representing *Landnam,* although not by any means perfect, is quite good—too good for us to conclude that the Kennox pattern of clearance differs completely from that of Bloak Moss *A*. I am more struck by the similarity of the grass curves than with their differences.

I am not sure that my confidence that these two curves match quite well can be satisfactorily communicated by this objective presentation of data, for it arises partly from the way in which during the last four weeks the picture has grown clearer and clearer with each fresh batch of samples counted. Six weeks ago the two grass curves did not begin to correlate satisfactorily. A month ago, when I first listed the only possible features on which I could correlate this part of the diagrams independently of the *Landnam,* the number of *Landnam* episodes between each level did not correlate nearly as well as it does now. For example, there was only one *Landnam* instead of two on diagram *A* above the low *Corylus* horizon. Realising that if the independent correlation was correct there should be two, I filled in samples at 1-cm intervals from that very slow-growing peat and found the predicted extra *Landnam.* For the last month, as each fresh batch of samples counted has made the peaks and troughs of the grass curves resemble each other more closely, my confidence that they are both telling the same story has grown. It is as much for this reason, as for the objective data as they now stand, that I am more impressed with the similarities of the curves than with their differences.

There are, of course, differences, two of which require explanation. This first is that the grass values are consistently higher at Site *K* than at Site *A*. If one subtracted about 10% from each value at *K,* the curve would look much more like that from *A*. The second is that every grass peak at Site *A* is paralleled by a peak in the bracken spores, and these peaks consistently have their highest value just below the highest value in the grass peak. This is not the case with the Kennox diagram, on which the bracken curve has no such consistent relation with the grass curve.

CONCLUSIONS

The diagram from Site *A* is giving the most local picture, and I think it may well be recording the use by prehistoric man of a small piece of forest, up to a few hundred metres in diameter at the very most, very close to Site *A*. Exactly what he was doing is far from clear, but the initial rise in bracken spores indicates a lightening of the tree canopy, possibly due to some felling, and the subsequent peak in grass pollen indicates grassy glades in the area, perhaps grazed for a while by domesticated animals.

The diagram from Site *K* is giving a more strongly regional picture, and the fact that the grass curve is so similar to that from Site *A* must mean that what was happening right next to Site *A* was typical of what was happening in the region as a whole. This is an important conclusion, because it means that on about six occasions between 1875 bc and ad 415 prehistoric peoples moved into the region represented on this three-dimensional diagram and moved out again—or should I say they shifted into the region and shifted out again, the region being of the order of up to 10 km from the moss complex?

Several of these incursions into the region have been dated at Site *A*. The first, third, and fourth have inseparable dates—1270 ± 105, 1100 ± 105, and 1220 ± 105—and probably occurred in fairly quick succession between about 1400 and 1000 bc. The sixth took place around 425 bc. Perhaps I could finish by noting the interesting fact that the first four clearances, which follow each other so rapidly, occurred at a time when the peat was forming very quickly indeed at the edge of the bog, probably because the climate was much wetter then than either earlier or later. So it may be that there is a connection between climate and the pattern of land exploitation in this part of south-west Scotland. It would be interesting to see whether the upland part of Ayrshire to the east has a similar pattern of *Landnam* episodes during the Bronze Age or not, and whether the up to 10 km region I have been talking about into and out of which these peoples moved is any larger or not!

I have based these conclusions entirely upon what has emerged from the detailed diagrams from Sites *A* and *K*. The diagram from Site *B* with its six or perhaps seven *Landnam* may well correlate with the other two diagrams, but until I have found the correlation horizons, such as the low *Corylus* and the high *Polypodium* values, and correlated the *Landnam* peaks, peak by peak, with those from *A* and *K* I will not say more than that the initial results from diagram *B* are not inconsistent with these conclusions.

REFERENCES

Tauber, H. (1965). Differential pollen dispersion and the interpretation of pollen diagrams. *Danm. Geol. Unders.,* 89, 1–69.

Tauber, H. (1967). Investigations of the mode of pollen transfer in forested areas. *Rev. Palaeobotan. Palynol.,* 3, 277–286.

Turner, J. (1970). Post-neolithic disturbance of British vegetation. *In* Walker, D. and West, R. G. (eds.). *Studies in the Vegetational History of the British Isles.* Cambridge: University Press; 97–116.

Habitat change in coastal sand-dune areas: the molluscan evidence

Penelope J. Spencer

Synopsis

Land-snail analysis of coastal shell-sand deposits in North Cornwall and the Orkneys has demonstrated the former presence of woodland in these now open territories. In some instances deforestation took place prior to sand accumulation; in others the two processes were coeval. The areas studied were vital in the early settlement of Britain by farming communities and it is possible that deforestation was directly brought about by man. On the other hand, inundation of woodland by sand may have caused deforestation, and the subsequent open-country landscape and calcareous soils themselves have attracted agriculturists.

INTRODUCTION

Along the coasts of Britain and Ireland, particularly in the north and west, occur extensive tracts of calcareous sand, blown inland by onshore winds and containing large numbers of comminuted marine shells. The calcareous nature of the sand encourages the establishment of land-snail populations, the shells of which become incorporated into the sand deposits and preserved. These can be used to define the environmental changes that occurred during sand accumulation. Archaeological material buried by the sand can be related to the changes. The sands are all Post-glacial in age, and everywhere overlie a well defined buried soil horizon.

In this paper, the snail analyses of sand deposits from Cornwall and Orkney are described.

METHODS

Analysis and presentation of the results follow the methods described by Evans (1972). Results are shown as histograms of relative abundance (i.e. each species or group as a percentage of the total fauna) and in tabular form. In the histograms the snail species have been arranged ecologically, with shade-loving species on the left, intermediate species (those of catholic habitat preferences) in the centre, and open-country species on the right. A composite histogram on the far right shows the faunal changes of these three main groups.

THE SITES

Newquay (SW 800 625)

The sections examined are situated in the sand cliff on the west side of Towan Head, Newquay, Cornwall. The following two profile descriptions cover the main sequence:

Profile 1

Depth below surface (cm)	
0– 80	Topsoil and humified sand, noticeably rich in snail shells. The modern habitat is fixed dune pasture.
80–130	Blown sand, lightly humified. Poorer in shells than the horizons above and below.
130–140	Pronounced shell horizon.
140–180	Blown sand, poor in shells.
180	Band of *Mytilus* (edible mussel) fragments.
180–300	Blown sand with major shell horizons at 210, 240, and 260 cm.
300	Surface of buried soil.

Profile 2

0–125	Topsoil and calcareous blown sand. A compressed sequence of Profile 1.
125–150	Buried soil. Dark-brown calcareous loam; sandy at the surface, but becoming less so with depth.
150–200	Solifluction deposit or head. Angular rock fragments in a clayey matrix; non-calcareous.

Beneath the head are a non-calcareous coversand (probably an aeolian deposit of Last Glaciation age) and, at the base, a discontinuous Pleistocene beach gravel.

Twelve samples from the buried soil and overlying sands were analysed for land snails (Fig. 1; Tables I and II). The Pleistocene deposits below were devoid of shells.

In the buried soil, there is a strong shade-loving element, suggesting a vegetation cover of scrub or light woodland at the onset of sand deposition. In the overlying sands, open-country species predominate, and two xerophile species, not present in the buried soil, *Helicella itala* and *Cochlicella,* appear. The medieval introduction, *Helicella virgata,* comes in at the top of the sequence (80 cm in Profile 1). These changes indicate deforestation and the creation of open country, an environment in which phases of sand accumulation alternated with phases when stabilization of the dune surface took place and a vegetation cover of grassland obtained.

The creation of open-country conditions may have been brought about by the deposition of the sand. Open-country species of snail are, however, present from the very start of the sequence, suggesting that a degree of clearance may already have occurred prior to sand deposition. Marine shell middens and hearths are known from the sands (Kennard and Warren, 1903; Woodward, 1908) attesting to the presence of man in the vicinity. The age of these is unknown but, judging by the evidence from Gwithian (*see* below), deforestation may well have taken place in prehistoric times.

It is interesting, and not unique to this site, that shell sand is present *within* the buried soil at the base of the

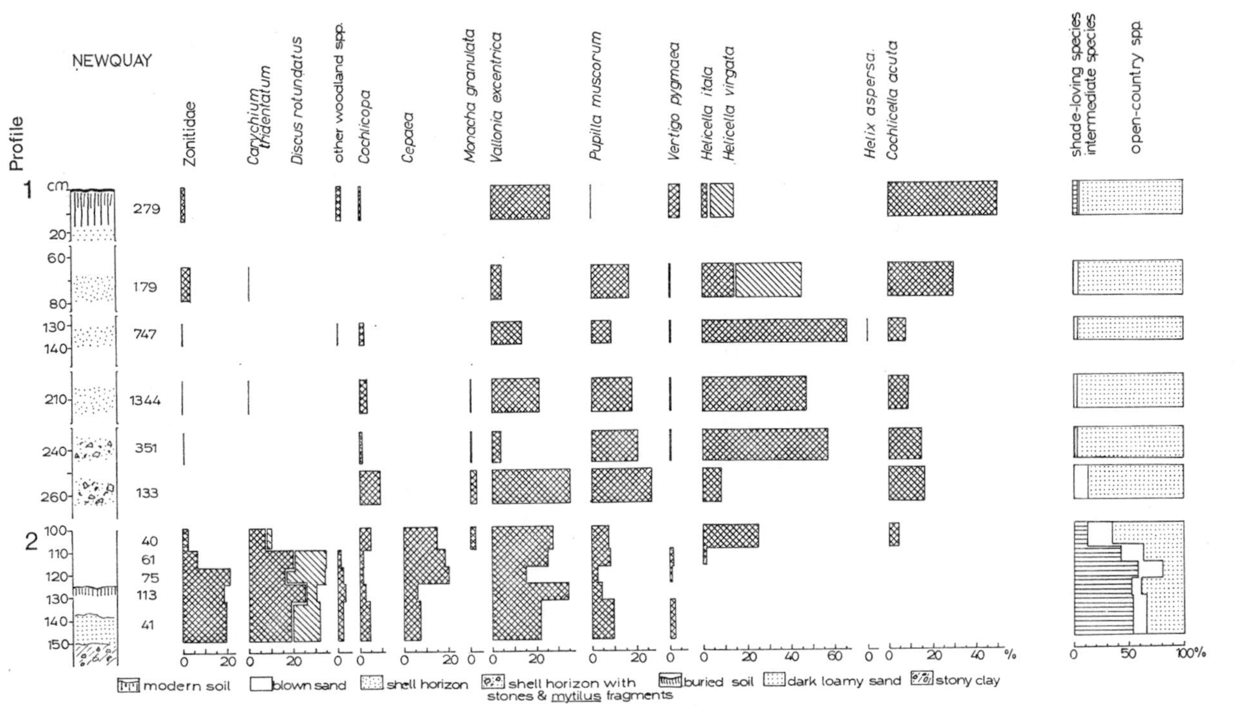

Fig. 1 Newquay: molluscan histogram

Post-glacial succession. This was probably incorporated by earthworm action during the initial period of deposition. If this is so, inundation must have been a gradual process to start with.

Perranporth (SW 759 556)

A steep cliff profile was examined at the edge of Penhale or Perran Sands, just north of Perranporth, Cornwall. The following profile is typical of the location:

Depth below surface (cm)	
0– 45	Modern turf and dune sand.
45– 50	Indurated sand.
50– 60	Dark humic blown sand.
60–100	Pale blown sand.
100–115	Buried soil. Buff-coloured with stone fragments.
115+	Head. A stony solifluction deposit.

TABLE I Towan Head, Newquay–Profile 2

cm weight (kg.)	140– 150 1·0	132·5 – 140 1·0	125– 132·5 1·0	117·5– 125 0·5	110– 117·5 0·5	100– 110 0·5
Carychium tridentatum (Risso)	3	5	29	12	12	3
Cochlicopa lubrica (Müller)	—	—	—	1	—	—
Cochlicopa lubricella (Porro)	—	2	3	—	—	—
Cochlicopa spp.	—	—	—	—	1	2
Vertigo pygmaea (Draparnaud)	1	+	—	1	1	—
Pupilla muscorum (Linné)	3	1	5	2	5	3
Acanthinula aculeata (Müller)	—	1	2	—	—	—
Vallonia excentrica Sterki	4	5	39	11	15	11
Clausilia bidentata (Ström)	—	+	2	1	1	—
Cepaea hortensis (Müller)	—	—	—	1	1	—
Cepaea spp.	1	2	7	15	11	6
Monacha granulata (Alder)	—	—	—	—	—	1
Helicella itala (Linné)	—	—	—	1	1	10
Cochlicella acuta (Müller)	—	—	—	—	—	2
Punctum pygmaeum (Draparnaud)	—	—	—	1	—	—
Discus rotundatus (Müller)	2	3	5	13	9	1
Vitrea crystallina (Müller)	—	2	—	2	—	—
Oxychilus alliarius (Miller)	2	—	6	5	1	1
Retinella pura (Alder)	—	—	1	—	—	—
Retinella nitidula (Draparnaud)	1	3	14	9	3	—

+ = non-apical fragment

TABLE II Towan Head, Newquay—Profile 1

cm	250–265	235–245	205–215	130–140	65–80	0–15
weight (kg.)	0·5	0·5	0·5	0·5	0·5	0·5
Carychium tridentatum (Risso)	—	—	1	—	1	—
Cochlicopa lubrica (Müller)	—	—	—	—	—	3
Cochlicopa lubricella (Porro)	13	5	48	17	—	—
Vertigo pygmaea (Draparnaud)	—	2	8	5	1	14
Pupilla muscorum (Linné)	36	72	231	65	30	2
Vallonia excentrica Sterki	47	14	287	100	8	74
Helix aspersa (Müller)	—	—	—	1	—	—
Monacha granulata (Alder)	4	2	5	—	—	—
Helicella virgata (da Costa)	—	—	—	—	21	9
Helicella itala (Linné)	11	201	685	492	10	2
Helicella spp.	—	—	—	—	48	24
Cochlicella acuta (Müller)	22	53	126	61	54	141
Punctum pygmaeum (Draparnaud)	—	—	—	—	—	6
Oxychilus alliarius (Miller)	—	2	—	3	6	4
Retinella radiatula (Alder)	—	—	—	1	—	—
Retinella nitidula (Draparnaud)	—	—	3	—	—	—
Vitrina pellucida (Müller)	—	—	—	2	—	—

Six samples from this section were analysed for land shells (Table III, Fig. 2). The fauna throughout the sequence is dominated by *Monacha granulata,* a snail of fairly catholic requirements, although in the west of Britain often found in open habitats.

In the buried soil, the fauna is of open-country type, in contrast to the situation at Newquay. As sand accumulated, however, there was an increase in shade-loving species. Subsequently, open-country species became predominant once more, but neither *Helicella itala* nor *Cochlicella,* so prevalent at Newquay, are present. It seems likely, therefore, that this sequence is earlier than the onset of sand accumulation at Newquay.

The presence of man in this area is known from archaeological remains of Mesolithic and Neolithic date onwards (Harding, 1950). This, taken in conjunction with the findings of open-country conditions at the base of the sequence, suggests that man may have been responsible for early deforestation. Then, as sand accumulated and spread landwards, he moved away, allowing scrub or woodland regeneration. This in turn was followed by clearance, perhaps as a result of continued sand deposition, or of renewed human interference.

Gwithian (SW 588 424)

A section was examined through the sands and interspersed occupation levels of Godrevy Towans on the north-east side of St Ives Bay, near Gwithian, Cornwall. This is an area of fixed dune pasture of varying types: incomplete rough grass cover of recent stabilization, and stretches of older downland-type grass.

Section I. East side of Site X, south side of baulk between Sites X and XI (Megaw *et al.,* 1961).

Archaeological layer	Depth below surface (cm)	
1	0–10	Modern grassland turf.
2	10–*c.* 27	Pale sand.

Fig. 2 Perranporth: molluscan histogram

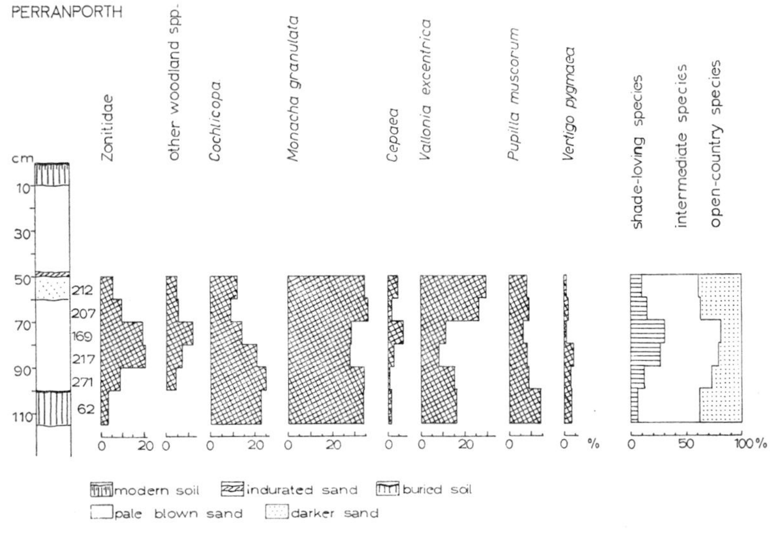

TABLE III Perranporth

cm	100–115	90–100	80–90	70–80	60–70	50–60
Carychium tridentatum (Risso)	—	—	—	2	1	1
Cochlicopa lubrica (Müller)	6	9	14	2	—	4
Cochlicopa lubricella (Porro)	1	4	2	1	—	2
Cochlicopa spp.	7	55	29	21	19	20
Vertigo pygmaea (Draparnaud)	2	8	9	2	4	2
Pupilla muscorum (Linné)	12	24	18	11	19	17
Lauria cylindracea (da Costa)	—	10	6	6	—	1
Acanthinula aculeata (Müller)	—	—	2	1	—	—
Vallonia excentrica Sterki	10	41	18	19	55	61
Clausilia bidentata (Ström)	—	—	—	2	1	1
Cepaea nemoralis (Linné)	1	1	—	—	—	1
Cepaea spp.	—	1	6	12	4	9
Hygromia sp.	—	—	—	—	—	1
Monacha granulata (Alder)	21	93	61	48	75	73
Punctum pygmaeum (Draparnaud)	—	—	—	2	—	—
Discus rotundatus (Müller)	—	—	4	6	8	6
Vitrea contracta (Westerlund)	—	4	4	4	—	—
Oxychilus alliarius (Miller)	—	2	3	5	1	—
Retinella radiatula (Alder)	—	1	1	—	—	—
Retinella pura (Alder)	—	3	2	6	2	1
Retinella nitidula (Draparnaud)	2	15	36	18	17	11
Vitrina pellucida (Müller)	—	—	2	1	1	1

Weight of samples 0·5 kg

Archaeological layer	Depth below surface (cm)	
3	*c*. 27–36	Upper Bronze Age occupation horizon. Dark-brown sand with charcoal fragments.
4	36–*c*. 50	Dark-brown sand.
5	*c*. 50–*c*. 65	Early Bronze Age ploughsoil. Ploughmarks at base.
6	*c*. 65–93	Pale sand.
7	93–115	Pale sand stained with humic material, and becoming darker towards the base.
8	115+	Compressed buried soil on bedrock. Neolithic sherds, shellfish fragments.

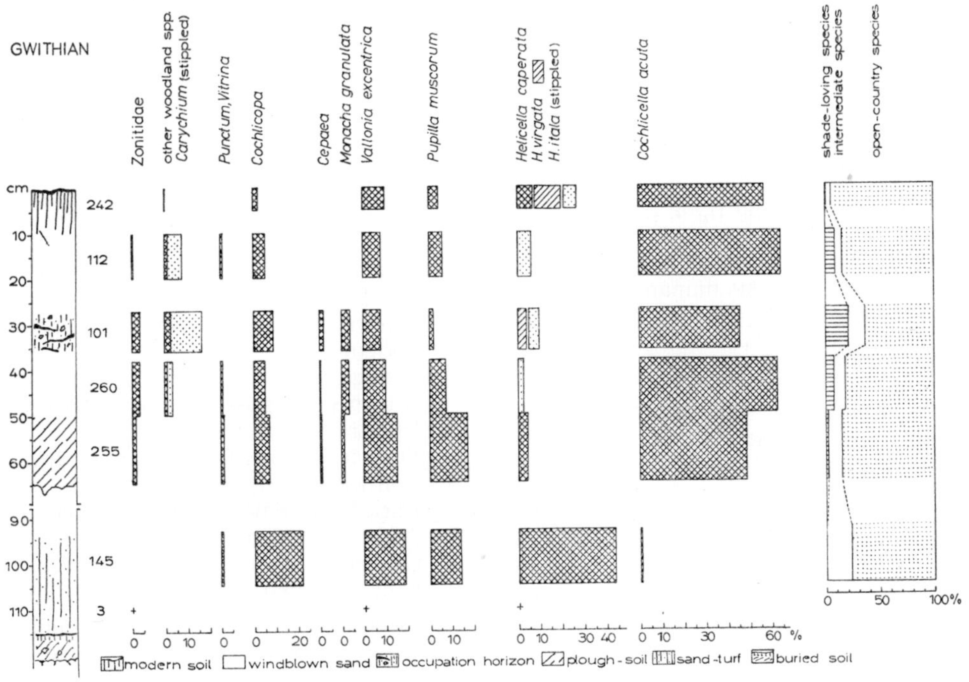

Fig. 3 Gwithian: molluscan histogram

TABLE IV Gwithian

	Section I							II
cm	105–115	93–105	50–65	38–50	27–36	10–20	0–5	50–60
Carychium tridentatum (Risso)	—	—	—	7	14	7	—	—
Cochlicopa lubrica (Müller)	—	32	2	4	—	2	—	—
Cochlicopa lubricella (Porro)	—	—	6	4	—	—	—	8
Cochlicopa spp.	—	—	13	6	9	4	6	—
Pupilla muscorum (Linné)	—	20	44	19	2	7	11	25
Lauria cylindracea (da Costa)	—	—	—	—	—	—	1	—
Vallonia excentrica Sterki	1	27	39	26	8	9	26	41
Clausilia bidentata (Ström)	—	—	—	1	1	—	—	—
Cepaea nemoralis (Linné)	—	—	1	—	—	—	—	—
Cepaea spp.	—	—	1	1	2	—	—	—
Monacha granulata (Alder)	—	—	4	9	4	—	—	—
Helicella caperata (Montagu)	—	27	10	—	—	—	13	—
Helicella virgata (da Costa)	—	—	—	—	4	—	22	35
Helicella itala (Linné)	1	—	—	6	5	7	11	99
Helicella spp.	—	36	1	—	—	—	15	—
Cochlicella acuta (Müller)	—	1	124	163	46	72	137	131
Punctum pygmaeum (Draparnaud)	—	1	3	—	—	1	—	—
Discus rotundatus (Müller)	—	—	—	2	2	2	—	—
Vitrea contracta (Westerlund)	—	—	1	1	—	1	—	—
Oxychilus alliarius (Miller)	—	—	—	—	1	—	—	—
Retinella pura (Alder)	—	—	—	3	—	—	—	—
Retinella nitidula (Draparnaud)	1	—	5	6	3	—	—	—
Vitrina pellucida (Müller)	—	1	1	2	—	—	—	1

Weight of samples 0·5 kg

The interface between layers 5 and 6 has been dated to 1200 ± 103 bc by radiocarbon (Megaw *et al.*, 1961). Nine samples were taken from this profile and analysed for land molluscs (Table IV); two (from layers 6 and 8) were devoid of shells. A sample was also taken from a sand layer dated to the 13th–14th centuries AD (Fowler and Thomas, 1962), further up the hillside of the towans (Section II).

The results of Section I are shown in histogram form in Fig. 3. The fauna throughout the profile is dominated by open-country species. Shade-loving forms occur in the Bronze Age occupation layers and sands, but in small numbers. This is in keeping with the conditions necessary for stabilization and soil formation. The medieval sand (Section II) also shows open-country conditions, similar to those of the present day.

The presence of a totally open-country fauna right at the start of sand deposition, taken with the archaeological evidence for early man in this area (Mesolithic artefacts are frequent in the towans), suggests human interference with the forest vegetation.

It is interesting that *Helicella caperata* is present in a Bronze Age context on this site. The specimens are not quite typical of this species, but of the hellicelids present in Britain today they come closest to *H. caperata*. Otherwise the species is generally thought to have been introduced in medieval times.

Skara Brae (HY 280 188)

A profile in the sand cliff was examined to the west of the Neolithic site of Skara Brae, on the south side of the Bay of Skaill, Orkney (Childe, 1931).

Top part of section Depth below surface (cm)	
0– 20	Modern turf.
20–130	Orange wind-blown sand, with darker humic streaks.
130–160	Iron Age occupation horizon. Dark-brown sand with occasional clay patches, shellfish, bone, and building debris.
160–460	Orange sand with paler and darker streaks.
Bottom part of section (460 above = 0 below)	
0– 30	Pale orange sand with faint humic streaks.
30– 52	Brown compact sand. Soil or occupation horizon.
52– 58	Orange sand.
58– 63	Brown sand, possibly a soil horizon.
63– 68	Pale sand.
68	Surface of buried soil. Gradual transition with overlying sand.
68– 78	Buried soil. Pale-brown clay, becoming darker with depth.
78–103	Orange/brown-mottled stony clay, overlying shattered bedrock.

In parts of the section, a layer of indurated sand, *c.* 3 cm thick, occurred *c.* 10 cm above the buried soil surface.

TABLE V Skara Brae

	Bottom part of Section						Top part of section			
cm	68–71	63–68	58–63	40–50	30–40	10–25	160–170	130–160	120–130	0–20
Cochlicopa lubrica (Müller)	22	8	12	4	6	1	—	—	10	7
Cochlicopa lubricella (Porro)	30	24	27	2	1	—	—	1	8	6
Cochlicopa spp.	104	44	25	13	17	1	—	3	24	31
Vertigo substriata (Jeffreys)	8	20	6	—	—	—	—	—	—	—
Vertigo pygmaea (Draparnaud)	28	38	13	—	—	—	—	—	6	25
Pupilla muscorum (Linné)	14	6	11	—	—	1	1	1	4	21
Lauria cylindracea (da Costa)	89	106	63	3	1	1	—	—	12	42
Vallonia excentrica Sterki	284	213	271	35	34	4	2	5	36	30
Clausilia bidentata (Ström)	18	28	27	—	—	—	—	1	—	—
Punctum pygmaeum (Draparnaud)	48	14	3	—	—	—	—	—	—	22
Euconulus fulvus (Müller)	—	1	1	—	—	—	—	—	—	—
Vitrea contracta (Westerlund)	3	8	1	—	—	—	—	—	—	—
Oxychilus alliarius (Miller)	35	25	12	—	—	—	—	—	—	—
Retinella nitidula (Draparnaud)	14	13	15	—	—	—	—	—	—	—
Vitrina pellucida (Müller)	18	5	1	6	2	—	1	9	3	11

Weight of samples 0·5 kg

Thirteen samples were examined from this section (Table V; Fig. 4). The fauna from the base of the sequence (58–71 cm) shows a pronounced woodland facies, although lacking two species, *Carychium* and *Discus,* most characteristic of woodland and present in the buried soil of the nearby site of Buckquoy (HY 284 243) (Evans, J. G., and Spencer, P. J., unpublished). Moreover, there is a strong open-country element in these lower levels, and this suggests an environment either of open woodland or of scrub with extensive areas of grassland. In the main blown sand deposit an open-country fauna prevails.

The presence of open-country species at the base of the sand suggests a degree of deforestation (if closed woodland ever existed on Orkney) prior to sand accumulation. This is in contrast to the fauna from Buckquoy, which showed no influence of open country.

Knap of Hower (HY 483 519)

This site comprises a Neolithic midden under blown sand on Papa Westray, Orkney (Traill and Kirkness, 1937). The Neolithic age of the midden has been confirmed by recent excavations by Dr Anna Ritchie. The midden lies directly on top of a buried soil containing small quantities of shell sand. Within the overlying blown sand is a layer of freshwater shell marl (Fig. 5). Marine shells from the midden include species of sandy shore habitat (razor shells and cockles) not found in the vicinity today. Detailed snail analysis of the deposits has not been carried out, but the site is an important one in the clear demonstration it gives of environmental change.

The nature of the deposits and the evidence of the land-snail fauna and marine shells indicate the former presence of a sandy beach, with foredunes, dune slacks (shell marl), and a protected area of dune pasture

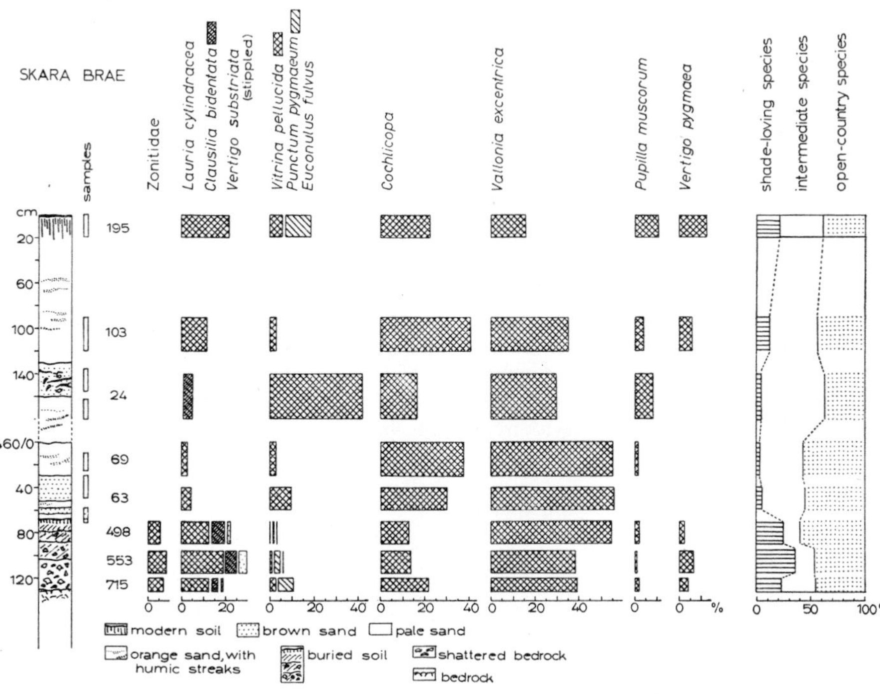

Fig. 4 Skara Brae: molluscan histogram

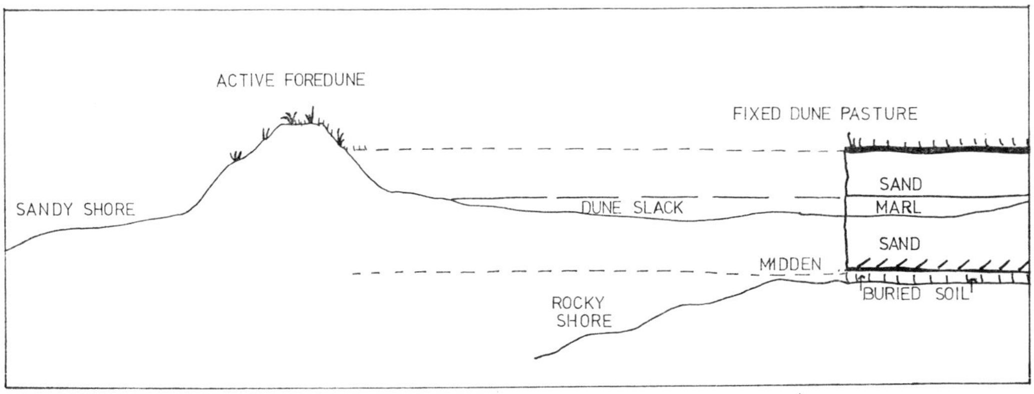

Fig. 5 Knap of Hower: reconstruction of the ancient sand-dune environment

behind (reconstructed in Fig. 5). Erosion of the protective foredune system (by rising sea level or increasing storminess) caused the sea to extend back to the present coastline, while at the same time releasing sand for deposition further inland and burying the soil, midden, and marl deposits.

A similar course of events probably occurred at certain other sites which to-day show no active dune system: for example, Towan Head, Newquay.

DISCUSSION

Most of the sands examined are in areas of currently inactive dune systems, with open stable vegetation of fixed dune pasture. Quite clearly, considerable environmental changes have taken place during the Post-glacial, the most important of which are the destruction of woodland and the deposition of wind-blown sand. In some cases (Knap of Hower and Towan Head) there is today little trace of what were undoubtedly once extensive sand-dune systems.

In talking of the effect of sand and of man on the vegetation of these coastal lowlands, we have often mentioned deforestation, a process clearly demonstrated by land-snail analysis. However, we must also look at other evidence for coastal woodland. In Cornwall there are records of submerged forests and peat deposits offshore (e.g. in Daymer Bay, SW 927 776), indicating that coastal woodland was once present. Pollen analysis in the Scilly Isles (G. W. Dimbleby, personal communication) has shown the former presence of hazel on the coastal sands. In the Outer Hebrides, practically treeless today, the remains of birch and pine are common in peat deposits (Ritchie, 1966). Pollen analysis from the Orkneys shows pollen of mixed oak forest and pine, although this may be derived from the Scottish mainland; at best, the vegetation of these islands was probably birch and hazel scrub (Moar, 1967). None of these areas has coastal woodland today, but it is known on sands at Margam, South Wales, the Culbin Sands, Moray, and on the Lancashire coast. The remains of tree stumps are known from Glenluce Sands, Wigtown (R. J. C. Atkinson, personal communication). It would therefore seem perfectly possible for woodland to have existed on these coastal lowlands prior to sand deposition and, indeed, during stabilization phases of sandy areas as at Perranporth.

The date and method of deforestation and the change to a more specialized open environment seem to vary from site to site. In some cases, as at Towan Head and Buckquoy, clearance may have been coeval with sand deposition. In general, however, open-country conditions were achieved prior to sand accumulation, and the presence of early man in many of the areas investigated suggests that he may have been responsible for this process. On the other hand, many of the areas studied were once inland during the early Post-glacial, in more sheltered situations than they are to-day. The rising Post-glacial sea would have induced stronger winds and brought the woodlands within reach of salt spray, both of which are damaging to tree growth.

The presence of middens and other archaeological material under the shell sands, as the Knap of Hower and Gwithian, helps to date the origin of sand blowing. This probably did not begin before the Neolithic period, as suggested by the absence of any sites where Mesolithic artefacts occur on top of blown shell sand. At Northton in the Outer Hebrides, blown sand was stratified between two Neolithic occupation horizons, the later dated to 2461 $\pm$ 79 bc (Burleigh *et al.*, 1973) and at Borve, Benbecula, also in the Outer Hebrides, wood from intertidal peat deposits, in an area where there is now an active dune system, has been dated to 3750 $\pm$ 170 bc (Ritchie, 1966). However, many former sand deposits may now lie submerged or have been destroyed.

The effect of the build-up of calcareous sand is clear, as demonstrated both by environmental and archaeological evidence and by historical and modern records. The initial effect is to upgrade the soil, both improving it agriculturally and attracting land-snail populations. The initial blows seem to have been slow, soil and sand mixing by faunal activity leading gradually to a calcareous soil. Later, an increased rate of deposition, burial of the soil and destruction of woody vegetation took place. Shell sand, as well as producing a favourable environment for agriculture by its calcareous nature and the creation of open country, also affects man directly by inundating land and settlements. The evidence of cultivation of the sand area during a period of stabilization at Gwithian (Megaw *et al.*, 1961), for example, illustrates the agricultural importance of these areas. It is probable that occupation of the southern Outer Hebrides would have not taken place had there been no blown sand deposits. The attraction of these shell sands thus seems to far outweigh their disadvantages, as is testified by the continued occupation at sites such as Skara Brae, Gwithian, Northton (Evans, 1972) and Brean Down (ApSimon *et al.,* 1961), where man repeatedly returned to the same area over periods of thousands of years despite inundation by sand.

Note on the molluscan faunas

Prior to, or in the very early stages of, sand blowing, shade-loving species (particularly various zonitids, *Carychium* and *Discus*) comprise a significant proportion of the land-snail faunas. Three open-country species, however, are characteristic, namely *Vallonia excentrica, Pupilla,* and *Vertigo pygmaea. Cochlicopa* and *Cepaea* are other important elements, and in Orkney *Clausilia* and *Lauria* are prominent.

As sand accumulation proceeds, the shade-loving element eventually becomes insignificant, while the open-country species already present increase in abundance. At Newquay, *Pomatias elegans* seems, on visual inspection of the sections, to be characteristic in the lowest levels, but this unfortunately failed to come out in the analysis.

Two species, *Helicella itala* and *Cochlicella acuta,* then invade the new habitats and often assume dominance. It is possible that *H. itala* was present in some areas—Harlyn Bay, Cornwall (unpublished) and Northton, Outer Hebrides (Evans, 1972)—slightly earlier than *C. acuta.*

Finally, the introduced species, *Helicella virgata,* appears in the succession, but there is no evidence that this took place prior to the medieval period. *Pupilla* is often rare or absent from the modern fauna.

The only significant exception to this sequence is the occurrence of possible *Helicella caperata* in an Early Bronze Age context at Gwithian. The stratigraphical association is secure but the identification is not. Nevertheless, the shells do not belong to any other species of *Helicella* ever present in Britain, now or in the past, and we are clearly seeing here an isolated introduction in prehistoric times of a species which failed to become widely established.

ACKNOWLEDGEMENTS

I would like to take this opportunity of thanking Dr J. G. Evans for all the help and encouragement he has given me throughout this work and in the preparation of this paper. I would also like to thank Dr Anna Ritchie, Mr David V. Clarke, and Professor Charles Thomas for their help in collecting samples for analysis from Skara Brae, the Knap of Hower, and Gwithian.

REFERENCES

ApSimon, A. M., Donovan, D. T., and Taylor, H. (1961). The stratigraphy and archaeology of the Late-glacial and Post-glacial deposits at Brean Down, Somerset. *Proc. Speleol. Soc.,* 9, 67–136.

Burleigh, R., Evans, J. G., and Simpson, D. D. A. (1973). Radiocarbon dates for Northton, Outer Hebrides. *Antiquity,* 47, 61–64.

Childe, V. G. (1931). *Skara Brae: A Pictish Village in Orkney.* London: Kegan Paul.

Evans, J. G. (1972). *Land Snails in Archaeology.* London: Seminar Press.

Fowler, P. J. and Thomas, A. C. (1962). Arable fields of the pre-Norman period at Gwithian, Cornwall. *Cornish Archaeol.,* 1, 61–84.

Harding, J. R. (1950). Prehistoric sites on the north Cornish coast between Newquay and Perranporth. *Antiq. J.,* 30, 156–170.

Kennard, A. S. and Warren, S. H. (1903). The blown sands and associated deposits of Towan Head, near Newquay. *Geol. Mag.,* (IV), 10, 19–25.

Megaw, J. V. S., Thomas, A. C. and Wailes, B. (1961). The Bronze Age settlement at Gwithian, Cornwall. *Proc. W. Cornwall Fld. Club,* 2, 200–215.

Moar, N. T. (1967). Two pollen diagrams from Mainland, Orkney Islands. *New Phytol.,* 68, 201–208.

Ritchie, W. (1966). The Post-glacial rise in sea level and coastal changes in the Uists. *Trans. Inst. Br. Geogr.,* 39, 79–86.

Traill, W. and Kirkness,W. (1937). Hower, a prehistoric structure on Papa Westray, Orkney. *Proc. Soc. Antiq. Scot.,* 71, 309–321.

Woodward, B. B. (1908). Notes on the drift and underlying deposits at Newquay, Cornwall. *Geol. Mag.,* 5, 10–18, 80–87.

Survival and discovery

J. B. Stevenson

Synopsis

The first part of the paper deals with some approaches to the problem of archaeological distributions and the degree of reliability that may be placed on them. The theory of destruction as the dominant factor in determining archaeological distribution is contrasted with the survival potential and likelihood of discovery of sites. The second half of the paper is given over to the analysis of some archaeological distributions in Perthshire which demonstrate the complexity of the problem and how interpretations of the patterns can modify our overall understanding of the data.

The present interest in field archaeology, particularly the growing awareness of the inadequacy of the field data, has been spurred on from two directions. Amongst the fieldworkers themselves the efforts of the Cornish Archaeological Society have shown how the numbers of sites can be increased enormously by sustained field and documentary research, while the construction of the M4 and M5 motorways has enabled Fowler to demonstrate the unreliability of distributions dependent upon fieldwork alone. The advent of the New Archaeology provided an impetus from another direction, as it is imperative for the application of geographically derived models that the degree of reliability of the data be known. In light of the work of Fowler and the Cornish Parish Check Lists, it is perhaps time to look more closely at the significance of archaeological distributions as a whole.

One method of approach is to regard the present distribution of all archaeological sites and artefacts as a function of the land-use pattern, both past and present. In crude terms, agricultural land is a zone of archaeological destruction and loss of evidence, while unimproved land is a zone of survival. In terms of a distribution map, the greater the variation of land-use in time and space the more difficult any analysis of that pattern becomes. This has greater significance when it is seen in terms of Fox's Highland and Lowland Zones. In fact, one way of redefining the zones may be to see the Lowland Zone as the area with little land-use variation per unit area and a high proportion of agricultural land; while the Highland Zone has much greater variation in land-use and a high proportion of marginal or unenclosed land. Such a definition differs fundamentally from that of Fox, as the country could be broken down into a large number of small units and not into two large blocks. The chalk uplands of Wessex could then be included in the 'Highland Zone' and Strathmore in Perth and Angus in a lowland zone.

At a recent conference, Andrew Sherratt demonstrated a model illustrating the effects of later settlement on a pre-existing archaeological landscape. He was able to show that destruction was not even over the entire area, and that what archaeologists usually discover is only a relict distribution centred around the fringes of the later settlement and not necessarily representative of the real pattern. This type of mechanism forms the basis of the site destruction pattern, and Taylor (1972) has suggested that it is impossible to discover with any degree of certainty a pre-Saxon settlement pattern, as destruction has gone too far. Taylor has proposed a two-fold division of the country as far as evidence for prehistoric and Roman settlement is concerned, based on the Highland/Lowland division, with the uplands as an area of survival and the arable areas as a zone of destruction. This does not imply that a highland distribution is any more valid than one in the lowlands, but merely that it is different, and we have already seen that potentially it is more complex.

So far most workers have only considered the effects of destruction on the distribution of sites. Destruction, even within a limited area, does not have a blanket effect over the whole range of sites. For instance, a bank and ditch can be reduced to a crop-mark, while a small cairn can be totally eradicated. Thus there is another factor affecting our knowledge of archaeological distributions. This is the likelihood that a particular site will be discovered. It is not merely the converse of the destruction factor; it plays an independent and equally important role in the development of the archaeological landscape. One example will make this point more clearly. A flat short-cist located on unimproved land has a very slight chance of being discovered; whereas if it were in agricultural land its chance of discovery would be greatly enhanced. All small sub-aerial features such as cists, post-built structures, and flint scatters will not be located unless the surface is disturbed in such a way as to make them detectable on the ground or from the air. In such cases, discovery is hopefully coincidental with destruction. The effects of this type of mechanism may be particularly marked in areas of contrasting geology, where conventionally the ploughed area is seen as an area of destruction but produces small finds, and the unimproved land, supposedly the zone of survival, produces little or nothing.

Archaeological distributions are generally analysed in terms of destruction and, as has been shown above, the situation is much more subtle than this. Destruction is only one facet; discovery, a far more positive feature, plays as important a role. It would be of greater significance to view each area and its sites in terms of a ratio between the destruction factor (i.e. agriculture, quarrying, etc.) and the likelihood of the discovery of particular types of evidence (i.e. sites). More simply, perhaps what we should consider is the survival value and discovery potential of sites, analysed in their environmental context. This moves away from the

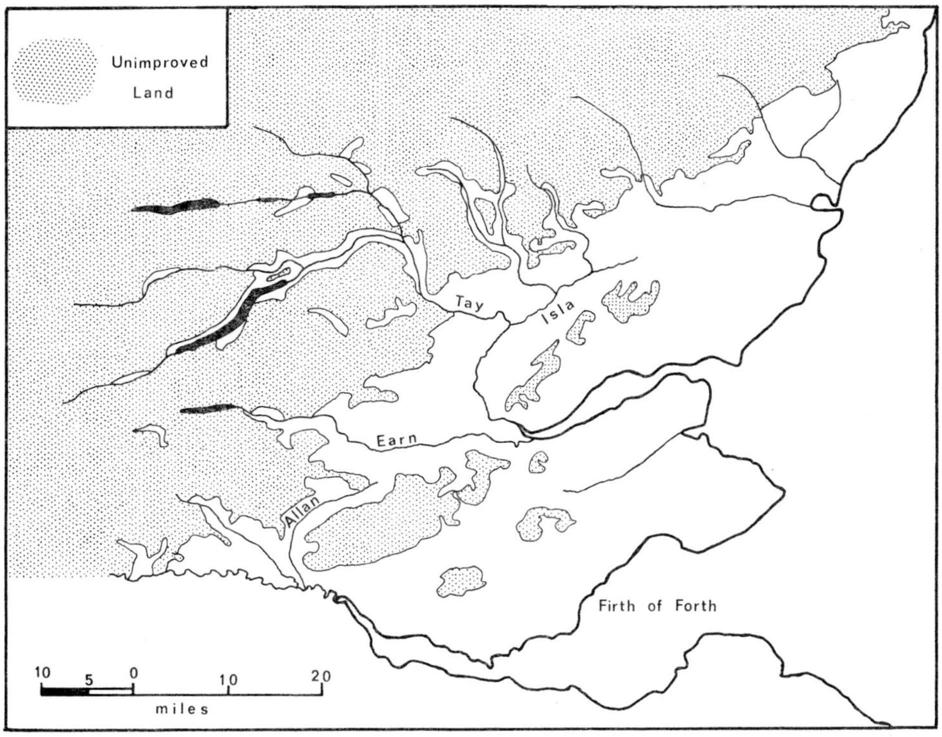

Fig. 1 Unimproved and arable land in the Perth area

blanket concept of the Highland and Lowland Zones, or simple zones of destruction and survival, both of which may mask underlying processes.

The second part of this paper will be concerned with the practical application of some of the ideas already outlined. Instead of taking the best possible examples from geographically disparate areas, a relatively small region centred on the county of Perth has been chosen in order to illustrate how many factors affect distributions, even within a restricted area. It cannot be stressed enough that each area and type of site present must be considered on its own merits, as these will be constantly varying. The conclusions reached are not to be seen as general rules; in fact, one of the features that has become clear is the complexity of the situation and the need not only to see each site as an individual, but also to treat it almost as a special case. This means, unfortunately, that it is practically impossible to produce general maps and diagrams, as there are too many factors involved.

Physically Perthshire can be divided into three types of area: the uplands of the Grampians and Ochils; the wide straths of the Isla, Tay, Earn, and Allan; and the highland glens of the Isla group, the Tay, and the Earn. This three-fold division is reflected in the land-use pattern (*see* Fig. 1), which can be divided between the unimproved uplands, the wide expanses of the improved agricultural straths, and the narrow improved strips of the highland glens.

The situation is, of course, much more complex than this, especially in the highland glens, and this complexity is one of the characteristics of the highland landscape. The wide straths of the Isla, Tay, Earn, and Allan could be seen more as a typical lowland landscape in Taylorian terms, as they contain a high proportion of agricultural land, and the blanket effect of site destruction will be more marked. Although the highland glens contain a proportion of arable land, they are very unlike the straths as they also have a sizeable percentage of pastureland, and their agricultural history is significantly different. In fact the glens consist of a number of zones that are determined by relief. The lowest is the flat U-shaped flood plain of the river; above this is the sloping settlement and agricultural zone, which gives way to the unenclosed mountain and moorland zone. The boundary between the settlement and moorland zone is the head-dyke, which marks the upper limit of cultivation and destruction by ploughing and often forms a conspicuous feature of the landscape, zig-zagging along the hillside above the tree-line. The position of the head-dyke is not constant in time, and only became fixed in its present position in the last century and a half. Formerly it was allowed to wax and wane with pressure on the land. More significant archaeologically, the field immediately below the head-dyke under the old agricultural system was the outfield, and received less attention than the more intensively worked infield, and today is predominantly pasture. So it is hardly surprising that there is a large number of sites close to the head-dyke. In terms of analysis it is necessary to decide whether survival value of the sites solely accounts for this concentration or whether all we are seeing is a relict group.

The distribution of sites in the valley of the Tay poses some interesting problems if viewed along these lines. East of Kenmore (*see* Fig. 2) there is a large number of sites of all ages, but to the west around the shores of Loch Tay there are few. Here the valley widens and in the 18th century supported a large population, but it is now less densely settled than the valley east of Kenmore. This anomaly in the distribution of sites

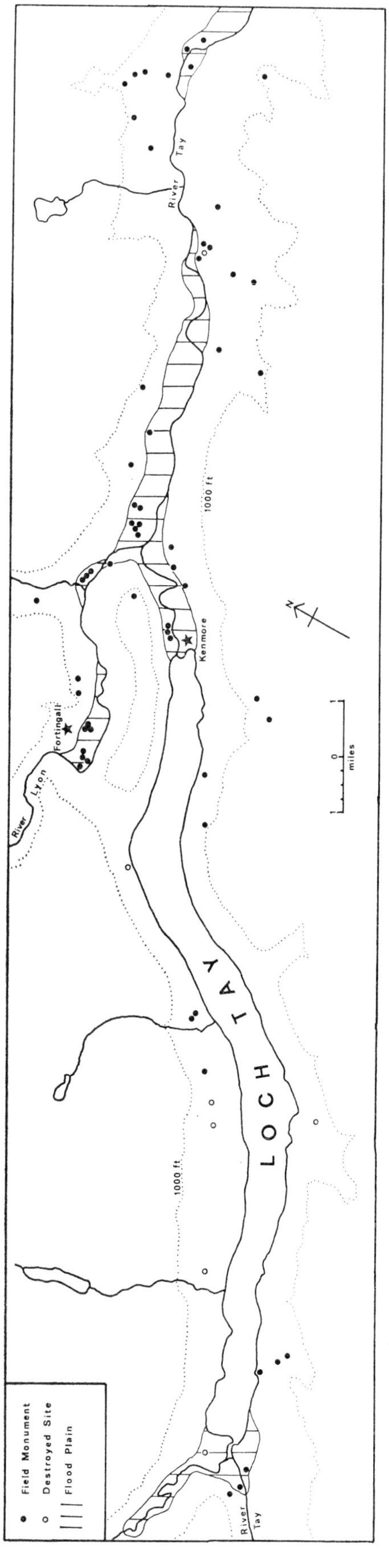

Fig. 2 Archaeological monuments in upper Tayside, Perthshire

along Tayside may then be due to intensive exploitation of the more open parts of Tayside, as early records (Pennant, 1777; Stobie, 1805) indicate that there were a number of ring-forts in the area, only one of which survives today. However, it is not possible to say with any certainty that the lack of sites is a real or merely an apparent feature. Another factor must be considered here. The tripartite division of the valley into moorland, settlement zone, and floodplain has already been mentioned. Over 50% of the sites to the east of Kenmore and Fortingall are to be found in the floodplain. This zone is missing in Loch Tayside, as it is occupied by the loch, so it is not possible to make a simple comparison between the two areas. One reason for the large number of sites in the flood-plain zone is that in many stretches cultivation has not come until comparatively recent times.

A further interesting problem of siting and distribution is that of the ring-forts, which are small stone-walled enclosures, probably representing a farmstead of a single family unit. In Glen Lyon and on Tummelside (Fig. 3) ring-forts are constantly found close to the head-dyke, either in the upper field or just beyond the dyke. One interpretation of the siting of the ring-forts has been based on an economic consideration (Stewart, 1969) i.e. that the ring-fort economy was based on cattle or sheep and that the siting at the junction of the pasture and agricultural zones enabled the occupants to exploit the two zones most economically. This, then, would be a good example of central place theory in action, but an alternative explanation is available. We have already seen that this head-dyke zone is an area of high site-survival, and that it is not possible to say whether a concentration of sites represents a fringe of a once much wider distribution or a real concentration. If the latter explanation is at least in part true, the idea that ring-forts formed the basis for the medieval settlement pattern has greater validity and the low-lying modern farms with the 'dun' element in their names may well in fact be the sites of ring-forts successfully absorbed into the later system. If the ring-forts do form the basis of the later settlement pattern, those that survive are those which were least successful and should not be seen as typical; deductions about the general economy of ring-forts should not be made from the surviving evidence.

The concept of survival value and discovery potential has already been mentioned. A few examples will serve to show how subtle the inter-relationships of the ideas can be. The case of the flat short cists has already been cited, but it is worthwhile to pursue it further. The only way in which a short cist will be discovered is by excavation, whether by ploughing, draining, building, etc. Therefore they will only be discovered in areas where these operations take place. In other words, theoretically they will only be found in the arable zone and in the quarrying areas, and in practice this is largely the case. Although it would be possible to argue that this was the area settled by the cist builders, there are extensive upland areas with hut-circles, fields, and various forms of cairn that might be expected to produce cists. In this case it is discovery potential that is the significant factor, whereas if cairns and barrows are considered it is their survival value that is the more important factor. A far higher proportion of cairns and barrows are found on marginal land and unploughed land than in the improved areas, which is only to be

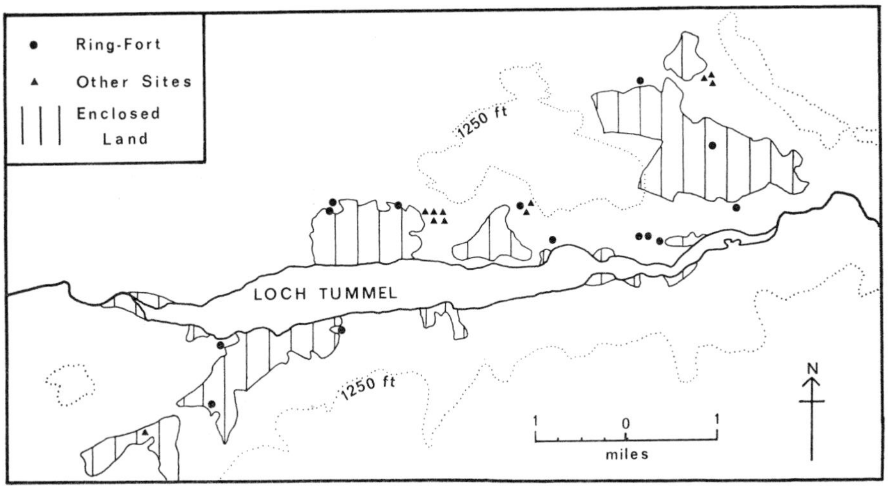

Fig. 3 Surviving monuments and improved land in Tummelside, north Perthshire

expected, but we have no way of knowing whether this represents a true prehistoric bias or is a product of differential destruction. What is more, the proportion of large to small cairns is greater in the agricultural than in the unimproved zone, merely because it is easier to remove the smaller cairns but less economic to shift a large earthen barrow. It would be interesting to know whether the higher proportion of earthen barrows in the arable zone is simply the result of greater availability of top-soil, or whether it is in some way related to the selective robbing of the stone cairns for building. Another minor point is the incidence of large barrows surviving in the parklands of the country houses, and the same might be said of the fine stone circles that are sometimes found in similar positions.

To return to cists and cairns, there are clearly grounds for distrusting the present distributions of both types. It would be of little use to compare the distribution patterns of the two, as in one case discovery potential is the key factor, while survival value is dominant in the case of the barrows and cairns.

The dangers inherent in comparing, or perhaps more importantly in contrasting, the distributions of different types of site can be illustrated by another example involving flat cists and their relationships with flat urn cemeteries. In some respects their survival values and discovery potentials are similar, but they differ in detail. A plough striking a cist will be noticed by the ploughman and he will stop to investigate the obstruction and attempt to remove it. In so doing, the cist will be discovered and one hopes that it will be reported. On the other hand, the plough will go unnoticed through an uncisted cinerary urn. As a result, the ratio of cists to urnfields may be seriously distorted. Moreover, because the types of pot found in association with the two types differ, their ratio will similarly be distorted. Thus, while cists and their associated food-vessels and beakers are well represented, it is by no means certain that in real terms they were more common than urnfields. It would be even more difficult to assess the real importance of the simple pit-grave in any discussion of burial practices in the Early Bronze Age.

Land-use variations in time can profoundly affect the archaeological landscape. These may be more marked in highland regions, where some areas have been abandoned by agriculture since the Bronze or Iron Ages, and give us some of our most reliable data, in that as little destruction as possible has occurred. It is surprising that these areas of houses, field-systems, clearance cairns, and small and large burial cairns of various types have received so little attention in highland Britain. Their remoteness and good state of preservation seems to have made archaeologists wary: they regard them as perhaps exceptional and not at all typical of their period. However, in Perth they are almost invariably found in areas that are only just marginal to the present arable zone; and a slight climatic amelioration would make these areas viable once again. Settlement systems of this type are now totally absent from the arable zone, but 18th century records (Stat. Acc. & NSA.) indicate that their occurrence was once much more widespread, for instance in the valleys of the Tay, Earn, and Isla. Any idea that they represent some peculiar Highland fringe type of settlement should be abandoned. It is rare but illuminating for any type of site to be totally removed from a particular zone, but this may be an example in which 18th and 19th century improvements have been responsible for such a wholescale destruction.

In another field the improvements of the agricultural revolution resulted in the discovery of a large number of souterrains as a result of draining and bringing marginal land under the plough. Our picture of souterrain distribution dates only from this period, roughly 1770, there being virtually no records prior to that date. This raises two points: first, the importance of discovery potential, and secondly, the relevance of that distribution pattern, remembering that it is a function of the 18th and 19th century improvements. Wainwright (1963) made much of the siting of the souterrains but it is questionable whether this can be done. The best sites may have been occupied at a later date and the souterrains destroyed without record. The situation is similar to that of the ring-forts and any analysis of the pattern should be approached with caution.

A somewhat similar situation arises in the case of the Iron Age settlements. Before 1950 hill-forts were largely confined to the unimproved zone (Christison, 1900). Since then aerial photography, a new discovery factor, has shown that in the arable zones of the Tay, Earn, and Isla comparatively large numbers of enclosed settlements exist. Some of these are palisaded and, with their lowland setting, contrast with the more normal upland setting for this type in the Southern Uplands. Here the sites are discovered because of the nature of the turf and not directly by aerial photography. The contrast in siting between the Southern Upland and Perth sites is in itself interesting, but may only be a function of the discovery factor. Taken individually, the choice of siting could have been used to draw conclusions about the sites that are not necessarily valid.

The archaeological data contained in a distribution map are the product of two processes: first, those that determined the original (i.e. real distribution), and, secondly, the factors that have affected the real distribution since its formation and have resulted in its present form. The influence of land utilization is a major consideration in the latter, and it is necessary to understand how the present distribution has developed in order to assess that pattern. The concept of survival value and discovery potential is one way of approaching the problem. It is especially useful in a highland context, where the effects on the archaeological landscape of variations in land-use are most pronounced.

REFERENCES

Christison, D. (1900). The forts, 'camps', and other field-works of Perth, Forfar and Kincardine. *Proc. Soc. Antiq. Scot.*, 34, 43–120.

N.S.A. (1845). *The New Statistical Account of Scotland.*

Pennant, T. (1777). *A Tour of Scotland.*

Stat. Acc. (1791–1799). *The Statistical Account of Scotland.*

Stewart, M. E. C. (1969). The ring-forts of central Scotland. *Trans. Proc. Perthsh. Soc. Nat. Sci.*, 12, 21–32.

Stobie's *Map of Perthshire* (2nd edition), 1805.

Taylor, C. C. (1972). The study of settlement patterns in pre-Saxon Britain. *In* Ucko, P. J., Tringham, R., and Dimbleby, G. W. (eds.). *Man, Settlement and Urbanism.* London: Duckworth.

Wainwright, F. T. (1963). *The Souterrains of Southern Pictland.*

The evidence of air-photographs

D. R. Wilson

Synopsis

Aerial reconnaissance is of particular value in supplementing archaeological fieldwork on the ground: (i) in remote and inaccessible regions; (ii) when surviving earthworks are too poorly preserved or too widely scattered to be readily identified or interpreted; (iii) when former earthworks have been levelled by agriculture, leaving little or no surface trace. The techniques of air-photography are summarized, and various types of prehistoric settlement are illustrated by air-photographs. Field-systems and settlements identified from the air must usually be dated by excavation or by documentary evidence; but some other monuments recorded on air-photographs (for example henge monuments, Roman camps) have distinctive forms allowing them to be dated approximately on typology alone. The distribution of dated agricultural sites provides a rough index of the progress of forest clearance. The presence of large datable monuments can also be significant, precisely because of the large areas which they cover. The outstanding instance of this is afforded by Roman camps, whose size may reach as much as 65 ha.

In the study of landscape, air-photography is acknowledged to be an indispensable tool. In no other way can such a rapid, accurate and complete record be obtained of the details of a landscape; and as an aid to general interpretation the comprehensive field of view afforded by an aircraft is unrivalled. The photographic record, however, preserves a picture of the surface of the ground as it exists at one particular time, when the photographs themselves are taken. This is its great virtue, but for the purposes of the present enquiry it is an obvious limitation. The buried soils and pollen samples described in other papers are actual fossils of the age to which they relate; inevitably our photographs shows us the landscape as it is today. What, indeed, would we not now give for an air-survey of part of Britain in the early Neolithic, or under Roman occupation, or even in the 19th century? In reality the serious use of air-photography is little more than half a century old, and we must deduce the development of the landscape from a study of its most recent phase.

The principal difficulty here is one of dating. The effects of past human activity on the landscape are often plain enough to see, while their age still remains obscure. There is nothing in the technique of air-photography as such which is capable of furnishing a date, though limited conclusions can sometimes be drawn from the degree of weathering discernible. An absolute date, however imprecise, can only be derived from an assessment of historical and archaeological data, supported as necessary by palaeobotanical and radiocarbon determinations. To take an example: air-photography helps us to appreciate the extent of tip-heaps in the Taff valley close to Merthyr Tydfil, but their modern date has to be established by reference to the known history of exploitation of the South Wales Coalfield. Without a detailed historical framework in which to put them, remains of this kind

Fig. 1 The upper Teifi valley, looking east-north-east over Cors Tregaron Nature Reserve (Dyfed), 27 October 1971: extensive forest clearance took place here at the end of the 5th century bc

Fig. 2 Low-level view of the Carse of Forth near Kippen (Stirlings.), looking south-east from Flanders Moss to the Gargunnock Hills, 14 July 1955: there was an episode of extensive clearance here about ad 200

Fig. 3 Prehistoric settlements and fields near Halton Gill (N. Yorks.), seen under snow, 14 February 1973: a line of settlements follows the foot of Potts Moor on the left margin of the Skirfare valley

Fig. 4 Settlement and fields on Begin Hill, Crosby Garrett Fell (Cumbria), looking north-west, 2 January 1967

Fig. 5 Enclosed homestead, Crymlyn, south-west of Aber (Gwynedd), 20 May 1965: the overgrown walls of fields, closes, and hut-circles are revealed by parching of grass in pasture

Fig. 6 Hill-fort beside the Earnscleugh Water at Burncastle, north of Lauder (Berwicks.), looking south, 27 July 1967: two main periods of defences are visible, partly as earthworks and partly as crop-marks

Fig. 7 A row of four circular timber houses beside the river Isla at Mudhall, Bendochy (Perths.), picked out by crop-marks of their foundation-trenches and drainage-gullies, 22 July 1960

Fig. 8 Ridge-top settlement at Grizzlefield, north-east of Earlston (Berwicks.), looking west-south-west, 27 July 1967: the ploughed-down defences are again made visible by transient crop-marks of two broad ditches

would be virtually unassignable to period. Should we suppose, for instance, that the tin-workings seen along the streams of north Dartmoor belong to the Bronze Age, like adjacent prehistoric settlements with hut-circles, or that they are medieval, as their comparative freshness of appearance would suggest? A plausible solution would combine both possibilities, surmising that prehistoric exploration had been followed by re-working in the Middle Ages, but it would require excavation to obtain a definitive answer.

Some activities have been so widespread and their effects so permanent that we cannot expect to judge by mere inspection the time at which they happened. The most obvious case is that of forest clearance. If we compare air-photographs of the upper Teifi valley in Carmarthenshire (Fig. 1) and the Carse of Forth above Stirling (Fig. 2), there is nothing in the photographs themselves which implies that extensive clearance took place half a millennium earlier on the one site than on the other. For that we have to turn to the work of Turner (1965), at Tregaron Bog and Flanders Moss respectively, using pollen analysis and radiocarbon dating to work out the vegetational history of both areas.

It is in relation to forest clearance, nevertheless, that aerial reconnaissance proves to be of value. The extent of clearance at any particular period will roughly correspond with the distribution of contemporary settlements and field-systems. Archaeological remains of settlement and agriculture survive as earthworks on unploughed moorland and other areas of permanent pasture. Their traces may also be found concealed beneath the plough-soil on cultivated ground. Sites of both kinds, ploughed and unploughed, can be detected from the air, so that air reconnaissance becomes a powerful tool of archaeological exploration. The resulting photographs, besides recording the position of the new discoveries, assist in the interpretation of individual sites and in the planning of fieldwork and excavation on the ground.

Extant earthworks of prehistoric settlement and agriculture are most likely to occur on ground that is relatively remote and inaccessible (Fig. 3). It is, in fact, their situation which has contributed most to their survival. Ground survey in such terrain is laborious, inconvenient and protracted. If the survey is to approach completeness, broad tracts must be traversed that are almost entirely unrewarding. The work of the Archaeology Division of the Ordnance Survey is the prime example of a survey team tackling this very problem, but the area to be covered is vast, and they would be the first to admit that progress is inevitably slow.

Air reconnaissance can never replace ground survey, but it can supplement it very effectively, and in doing so it brings considerable advantages. Access is no problem, except in so far as the sites themselves are overgrown or concealed within woodland. Large areas can be searched in a relatively short time and if they prove unfruitful, they can be abandoned in favour of pastures new. Exploration is, however, dependent on the weather. The location and photography of all save the larger earthworks requires bright sunshine and good visibility. Earthwork sites are made visible by their shadows, which are seen at their best when there is strong side-lighting. This is achieved when the sun is within 20° of the horizon. Thus, in the winter months effective photographs can be taken even at mid-day if there is sufficient light, whereas in June a similar effect can only be obtained before seven in the morning or after seven in the evening (Summer Time). In these conditions, when the sun is low, the effect of atmospheric haze is much increased, reducing the clarity with which earthworks can be seen and photographed. For good results a visibility of at least 20 km is needed, though it is possible to work down to a minimum of 10 km. It will be appreciated that freedom from cloud and absence of haze are not available to order, and the reconnaissance of any given area depends on the ability of an air-photographer to take advantage of those opportunities which do occur. In upland areas, such as the Scottish Highlands or the Pennines, one of the principal limiting factors is the development of cloud; but account has also to be taken of the direction of the wind in relation to major sources of industrial smoke, such as Bristol, South Wales, and Birmingham in the south, and Lancashire, Tees-side, and Glasgow in the north.

Reconnaissance is most rewarding if it can be repeated at different seasons of the year. There are some settlements on northward-facing slopes which can be seen in oblique sunlight only in high summer, when the sun sets well to north of west. Other sites, already photographed in one set of conditions, will yield new details when further photographs are taken with the shadows falling in a different direction. Special mention should be made of the value of a light covering of snow (Fig. 3), which affords brilliant highlights, a smooth even-toned surface to display the shadows, and enough reflected light to yield satisfactory photographs, even when the sunshine is rather weak.

When photographic flights can be made in suitable conditions, the surviving remnants of the prehistoric and medieval landscapes are revealed in astonishing profusion. The fields and settlements near Grassington (W. Yorks.) provide a classic example, but are far more extensive than appears from the published plan (Raistrick, 1937; cf. St Joseph, 1969). The general distribution of Iron Age settlement in this region of the Pennines, from Wharfedale to Lonsdale and from Craven to Wensleydale, has been established by Raistrick (1939), but little of the evidence (e.g. Fig. 3) has been planned in detail. The remains are particularly dense along Wharfedale and on Malham Moor, where Malham Tarn has yielded a pollen profile indicating that the first major clearance took place early in Zone VIII, or in archaeological terms about the beginning of the Iron Age (Pigott and Pigott, 1963). Further north another area of abundant prehistoric earthworks exists on the Westmorland fells (Fig. 4). These have been well recorded in the Royal Commission's *Inventory* (1936); but flights along the Cross Fell escarpment, which partly lies in the same county, have revealed scattered settlements and enclosures in an area where none had previously been recorded. It is less easy to find sites that have slipped through the net of the Royal Commission for Wales in their recent *Inventories* (1937; 1956; 1960; 1964), but even here it *can* be done where the earthworks are inconspicuous.

Thus, near Aber in Caernarvonshire a homestead with fields (Fig. 5) has been discovered from the air, but its denuded remains were revealed by the parching of grass over tumbled stonework more than by any visible relief. This emphasizes the point that it is always worthwhile, when the opportunity offers, to fly over known areas of prehistoric settlement, however well recorded and published they may happen to be. We can never be sure that certain sites will not have been missed completely, and others previously concealed by trees or undergrowth may have been newly brought to light. Even on Dartmoor, which has been extensively explored on the ground (Radford, 1952; Fox, 1954; 1964; Simmons, 1969), enclosures containing hut-circles can appear within 400 m of the nearest earthworks marked on the Ordnance Survey map.

These examples are cited not to belittle the excellence of the published surveys concerned, but to show that air reconnaissance has a part to play, even in areas for which comprehensive information is available. It is evident *a fortiori* that in areas where the basic data are still being assembled, such as central and southern Wales, the Lake District, and much of south-west Scotland, not to mention the Highlands, air-photography has a significant contribution to make to the picture that will eventually emerge.

Not all of the Highland Zone consists of mountain and moorland, however. There are considerable areas of arable land, in which few earthworks survive, and the identification of ancient field and homestead depends almost entirely on the aerial observer. On sites where all surface traces have been ploughed away, there may still be an intermittent chance of discovery from the air, provided that archaeological features have caused disturbance of the subsoil. The sort of archaeological features in question will depend partly on the actual depth of soil, but they can include ditches, post-pits, palisade-trenches, rubbish-pits, graves, and quarries. These, even though now completely filled with soil, form local reservoirs of moisture available to crop-plants growing immediately above, which may therefore, in some conditions, show a precocious development in relation to the remainder of the field. When this occurs, an archaeological plan becomes written in the crop, as differences of growth along the lines of ancient features are picked out by local variations in the general tone or colour. This effect is seasonal, transient and sporadic, but at its best it reveals archaeological sites in remarkable clarity of detail (Fig. 6).

The development of crop-marks in this way is dependent on a complex combination of variables, including soil-type, choice of crop, methods of cultivation, and the type of weather at different stages of the growing season. Each field may behave differently from the next, and it cannot be predicted with certainty in which years and on what days any particular site will become visible. There are, however, general indications. Cereal crops are the most useful, and these reach a sensitive stage of growth in the early summer. The exact time will depend on the part of the country, the weather pattern for the year concerned, and whether it was a spring or winter sowing. Sugar beet is also good for crop-marks, which usually come into view a few months later. Reconnaissance is therefore maintained throughout April to July and again in September and October, and crop-marks are recorded as they develop. The records from any particular year are likely to be fragmentary and scattered, but when the results from many years are put together a substantial body of information is achieved.

There are important areas in the Highland Zone for which the evidence of crop-marks now constitutes the principal source of information about prehistoric agricultural settlement. North of the Forth these are the coastal plain on the south side of the Moray Firth, known as the Laich o' Moray, the great vale of Strathmore bordering the Highland massif on its south-east side, and Fife. In much of the Scottish Lowlands the situation is symbolized by a photograph of the partly levelled hill-fort at Burncastle in Lauderdale (Fig. 6): part of the defensive circuit survives as earthworks, but the remainder has been recorded while briefly visible as crop-marks. In the Lowlands generally many earthworks survive, but many more have disappeared beneath the plough. Crop-marks are of particular importance in the Lothians, in the Merse, and in the great river valleys of Clyde, Tweed, Nith, and Annan. South of the Border there are the Northumberland and Cumberland plains; in Wales, the valleys of Dee, Severn, and Wye, and the Vale of Glamorgan; in the South-West, the Exe valley—all of them regions in which air-photography of crop-marks plays an important role.

Crop-marks of agricultural plots and fields seldom appear in the Highland Zone, presumably because field-boundaries were normally walls of stone, and ditches were superfluous. On ground that has been more or less continuously cultivated since prehistoric times, the extent of early agriculture has to be inferred from that of early settlement. At best, however, the evidence for settlement is both clear and detailed. Thus an unenclosed homestead near Forres (Morays.) (St Joseph, 1970) displays the site of several timber round-houses up to 12 m in diameter, of a type dated in the Lowlands to the last centuries BC. Similar homesteads or isolated houses are known in the Laich o' Moray from Elgin almost to Inverness, in the Dee valley where it emerges from the Grampians, and in Strathmore (Fig. 7). Other settlements appear to have smaller, more irregular huts, sometimes only marked by terracing of the hut-platform, as seen in Angus in the valley of the Lunan Water and in Fife near Leuchars (St Joseph, 1967). In exceptional conditions even stockaded enclosures can appear. Unenclosed settlements of circular houses have also been rarely seen in Wales, as in the Severn valley near Caersws (Montgom.) (St Joseph, 1970). Elsewhere in Wales, as in the region from Forth to Tyne, enclosed settlements are the general rule, usually surrounded by one or more broad defensive ditches. They occur most frequently on the crest of a ridge (Fig. 8) or at the end of a spur, and they obviously correspond to the many small hill-forts still surviving in both these regions. In the Northumberland plain a local type of settlement with a rectangular plan looking like a poorly executed Roman fortlet has been identified by McCord and Jobey (1968; 1971) and dated by excavation principally to the period of Roman occupation. Contemporary settlements on the other side of the isthmus in the Cumberland plain, however, show the oval and rectangular single-ditched enclosures also typical of the Welsh Marches.

The evidence of air-photography for ancient settlement, whether recorded in the form of earthworks or of crop-marks, must be integrated with the results of excavation and of fieldwork on the ground before it can realise its full value as a source of archaeological information. In particular, the dating of all but the most distinctive types of settlement must depend on ground investigation. This does not detract, however, from the value of air reconnaissance as a means of exploration, supplementing more traditional methods. Its greatest virtue obviously lies in the detection of archaeological sites on ground that has been levelled by medieval and modern agriculture, thereby correcting gaps previously apparent in many distribution-maps.

A note may be added here of the implications of one particular class of sites, not hitherto considered, whose special features give them direct relevance to the enquiry. These are the marching-camps of the Roman army, especially those falling in the largest size-range, which lies between 45 and 65 ha. Roman forces of considerable size spent the night in leather tents within these temporary fortifications, and their progress can be followed from Melrose on the Tweed, up Lauderdale, and on to Musselburgh, and again from north of Stirling all through Strathmore, northwards past Aberdeen to the Moray Firth near Fochabers (St Joseph, 1973). The layout of these great enclosures, many of which have been revealed by air-photography, is often irregular, partly perhaps because of difficulties of survey encountered by the Roman engineers, but principally because of the need to adjust to the local terrain and vegetation. The fact that such extensive enclosures could be laid out at all and filled with tents tells us a good deal about the state of the local vegetation in the areas concerned in the 1st and 2nd centuries AD.

ACKNOWLEDGEMENTS

Figure 3 is a Ministry of Defence (Air Force Department) photograph and Crown Copyright. The other plates are copyright, the University of Cambridge, and are from the University's Collection.

REFERENCES

Fox, A. (1954). Celtic fields and farms on Dartmoor, in the light of recent excavations at Kestor. *Proc. Prehist. Soc.*, 20, 87–102.

Fox, A. (1964). *South West England.* London: Thames and Hudson.

McCord, N. and Jobey, G. (1968). Notes on air reconnaissance in Northumberland and Durham: 1. Tyne to Wansbeck, Northumberland. *Archaeol. Aeliana,* 4th series, 46, 51–67, pl. vi–ix.

McCord, N. and Jobey, G. (1971). Notes on air reconnaissance in Northumberland and Durham: II. *ibid.*, 4th series, 49, 119–130, pl. xi–xvi.

Pigott, C. D. and Pigott, M. E. (1963). Late-glacial and Post-glacial deposits at Malham, Yorkshire. *New Phytol.*, 62, 317–334.

Radford, C. A. R. (1952). Prehistoric settlements on Dartmoor and the Cornish Moors. *Proc. Prehist. Soc.*, 18, 55–84.

Raistrick, A. (1937). Prehistoric cultivations at Grassington, W. Yorks. *Yorkshire Archaeol. J.*, 33, 166–174.

Raistrick, A. (1939). Iron-Age settlements in West Yorkshire. *ibid.*, 34, 115–150.

Royal Commission on Ancient and Historical Monuments in Wales and Monmouthshire (1937, 1956 and 1960). *Inventory of Caernarvonshire.* London: HMSO.

Royal Commission on Ancient and Historical Monuments in Wales and Monmouthshire (1964). *Inventory of Anglesey.* London, HMSO.

Royal Commission on Historical Monuments (England) (1936). *Inventory of Westmorland.* London: HMSO.

St Joseph, J. K. (1967). Air reconaissance: recent results, 10. *Antiquity,* 41, 148–149, pl. xx.

St Joseph, J. K. (1969). Air reconnaissance: recent results, 17. *ibid.*, 43, 220–221, pl. xxxv.

St Joseph, J. K. (1970). Air reconnaissance: recent results, 22. *ibid.*, 44, 308–310, pl. xliv.

St Joseph, J. K. (1973). Air reconnaissance in Roman Britain, 1969–1972. *J. Roman Stud.*, 63, 214–246, pl. xv–xviii.

Simmons, I. G. (1969). Environment and early Man on Dartmoor, Devon, England. *Proc. Prehist. Soc.*, 35, 203–219.

Turner, J. (1965). A contribution to the history of forest clearance. *Proc. Roy. Soc., B,* 161, 343–354.

Economic influences on land use in the military areas of the Highland Zone during the Roman period

W. H. Manning

Synopsis

An examination of the documentary and archaeological evidence from various parts of the Roman Empire indicates that military garrisons were supplied with grain from the closest available source and that the movement of supplies for long distances overland was avoided wherever possible. Although the majority of Roman forts in Britain are in the Highland Zone, they usually lie on or near areas of good agricultural land which could have been incorporated into their territoria. *The customary view that local supplies of grain were of little importance in supplying the Roman garrisons in Britain is therefore likely to be incorrect.*

The effect of the Roman Conquest of Britain was to weld a large number of tribes into a single province under a government which was accustomed to operating an elaborate economic and fiscal system. The conquest phase lasted for about 50 years, until, at the end of the 1st century AD, there began a period of uncertainty on the northern frontier which was ended by the building of Hadrian's Wall. Although changes were still to take place, these did not alter the fundamental fact that the Roman army was established almost entirely in the Highland Zone (in Wales, the Pennines, and on or beyond the Tyne–Solway line) and was to remain there for almost 300 years. The presence of this army might be expected to have had a considerable effect on land use within the Highland Zone, but it has generally been held that this was not the case. The aim of this paper is to suggest that there are good reasons for doubting this conclusion.

The size of the Roman army in Britain cannot now be established with certainty, but it was very large. Frere has estimated that at the end of the 2nd century it had reached 63,000 men, of whom 45,000 were auxiliaries (Frere, 1967, 310). The position in Wales at the beginning of that century is known with unusual exactness as a result of the survival of three discharge diplomas (Nash-Williams, 1969, 15). The auxiliary garrison of South Wales, the Caerleon command, numbered 8,280, of whom 2,760 were cavalry, to which must be added the 5,300 men of the II Legion. At the same time the Chester command, which covered part of the Pennines as well as North Wales, consisted of the XX Legion and 8,240 auxiliaries, including 3,120 cavalry. The total garrison for Wales must, therefore, have been around 20,000 men.

The provisioning of this army will have been a major administrative problem for the Roman government at all periods. The basic items needed by the men were meat, usually pork or mutton according to the Theodosian Code (7.4.6), although animal bones from fort sites suggest that beef was preferred to mutton in Britain (Applebaum, 1972, 203); grain, normally wheat, barley being regarded as distinctly inferior (Watson, 1969, 126); and wine (Davies, 1971; Jones, 1964, 628). Of these the most important was grain. In addition barley and hay were required for the cavalry and draught animals. Before the 3rd century, the state purchased grain for the army at a fixed price, which might be below the market value, with the amount to be bought in any one area being assessed by the government (Rickman, 1971, 271); once assessed, this amount had to be provided by the provincials. In the 3rd century, the system of *annona militaris* was introduced (Rickman, 1971, 278). This was a tax in kind, with the grain being received directly by the state. In addition to the army, supplies were required for the governor and procurator's staffs and for the imperial posting system.

It is possible to produce an approximate figure for the amount of grain required by the army in Britain. Polybius records that in the 2nd century BC the Roman soldier was issued with 11 bushels of wheat in the course of a year (Polybius vi, 39, 13), which would give a daily ration of about 2 lb. In the 6th century in Egypt, Roman soldiers were supplied with 3 lb of bread per day (Jones, 1964, 629). The link between the two is given by the Elder Pliny who states that "army bread is heavier by one-third than the grain" (Pliny *N.H.* xviii, 67), which almost raises Polybius's ration to that of the Egyptian garrison. In view of this, we may assume with a high degree of safety that an issue of around 2 lb of grain per day per man was normal throughout the Roman period. Given this, we can calculate that an army of 63,000 men would need 20,000 tons of grain a year, and that the Trajanic garrison of Wales would consume 6,500 tons of it. How much land would be required to grow this amount depends on what one accepts as a suitable average yield for Romano-British agriculture. Rivet (1969, 196), following Piggott, suggested 10 bushels/acre, approximately one-third of the modern yield on chalk. But it may be noted that in the late 18th century in Wales, an area regarded by contemporary agricultural writers as exceptionally retarded, this yield would have been thought quite abnormally low. In the more fertile parts of Montgomeryshire, for example, "a wheat crop . . . . . generally yields 20 to 25 streaks per acre"—i.e. 25–30 bushels (Kay, 1794, 17). If this is accepted, however, the Roman garrison would need the produce of 72,000 acres (28,800 ha), to which should be added another one-third to allow for the following year's seed-grain, making a total of 96,000 acres (38,400 ha). If the average yield is assumed to be 15 bushels/acre, a not impossible figure, the total falls to 64,000 acres (25,600 ha).

In the past, British archaeological opinion has generally held that most of this grain came from the Lowland Zone (Wheeler, 1954, 27; Piggott, 1958; Rivet, 1969, 189). The reasons for this are twofold. Firstly there is a generally unstated, but none the less widely held, opinion that few areas within the Highland Zone were suitable for cereal production, an opinion which is clearly incorrect. Within the general area of the Highland Zone there are quite large stretches of excellent arable land, as is shown by the farming regions of Wales, for example, in the Tudor period, when agricultural techniques were not vastly improved in comparison with classical ones (Thirsk, 1967, 128) (Fig. 1). Even in the hills there are still many places where cereals could be and were grown. Often, it is true, these areas are quite small, lying in valleys or on the more sheltered slopes, but in total they can be considerable. In Breconshire, more than half of which lies above the 1000ft contour, it was said in the late 18th century that one-quarter of the county, some 128,000 acres (51,200 ha), was good land suitable for cereal production (Clark, 1794A, 11), while in Radnorshire at the same date there were 86,000 acres (34,400 ha) of tillage land (Clark, 1794B, 17). As late as 1866 over 90,000 acres (36,000 ha) of Montgomeryshire, another rugged county, was arable land (Stamp, 1942, 354).

The second argument is based on the assumption that there was no tradition of cereal cultivation in the Highland Zone. It has been suggested that the absence of storage pits and Celtic fields, together with the heavy emphasis on cattle in the Celtic literary sources, indicated a society based on stock raising, with arable farming playing at most a very minor part (Wheeler, 1954, 27; Piggott, 1958; Rivet, 1969, 189). Neither of these arguments carries the weight that it did a few years ago. The relevance of storage pits and Celtic fields can be much exaggerated (Fig. 2). Storage pits are only one way of storing grain, and one which was not universal even in the Iron Age of southern England, as their absence from large parts of the south-east shows (Piggott, 1958, 10, Map 2). Celtic fields are not completely absent from the Highland Zone, of course (Piggott, 1958, 8, Map 1); quite large areas are known and others are being discovered. What is too often forgotten is that they represent only those parts of the Iron Age and Romano-British arable lands that have escaped medieval and later ploughing. The great bulk even within the Lowland Zone was destroyed centuries ago, as the distribution of settlements shows. Within the Highland Zone, areas of good agricultural land have always been at a premium and therefore liable to ploughing. If an absence of Celtic fields today is taken to mean an absence of arable land, we must cease to regard Roman villas as farms, for scarcely any can now be shown to have an associated field system. Professor Leslie Alcock long ago suggested that it is in the valleys of Wales that many of the Iron Age settlements should be sought, pointing out that the distribution of hillforts within the Principality looks like the distribution of communities interested not exclusively in pastoral farming but rather in mixed arable and stock raising

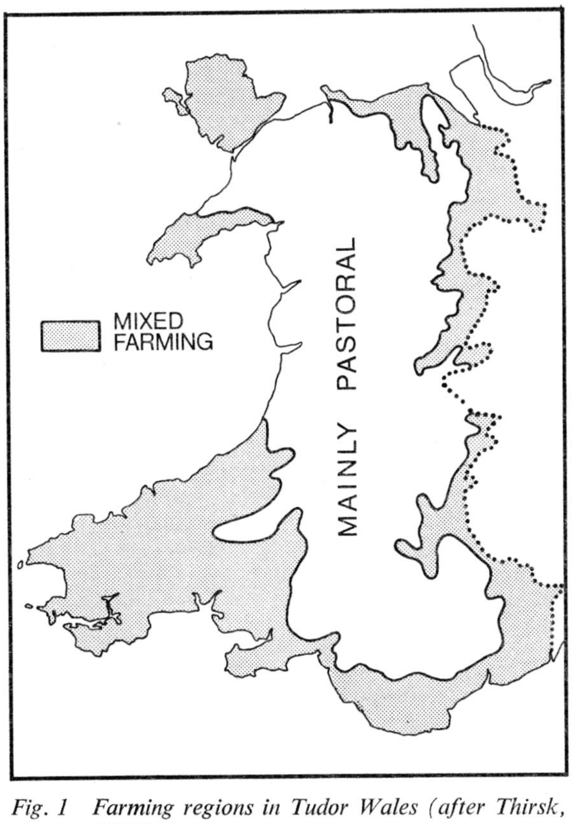

Fig. 1 Farming regions in Tudor Wales (after Thirsk, 1967)

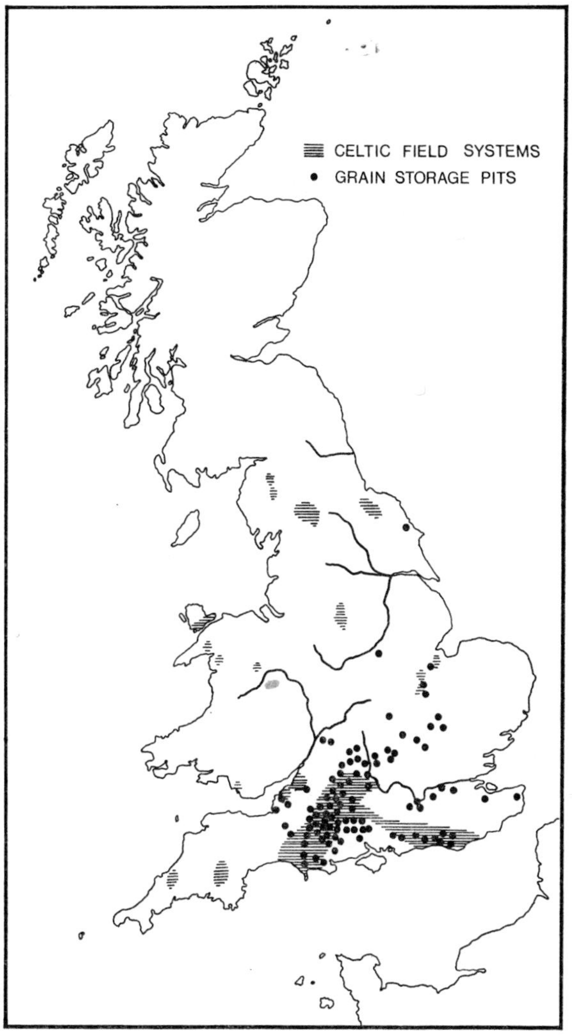

Fig. 2 Distribution of Celtic fields and grain storage pits (after Piggott, 1958)

(Alcock, 1965, 186). Certain evidence for ploughing in the Highland Zone during the Iron Age is provided by the ard fragments from Milton Loch Crannog and Lochmaben (Kirkcudbrightshire) in Scotland (Guido, 1974, 54), and the oak foreshare of a plough (originally identified as a spearhead) from Dr G. J. Wainwright's excavation of the Walesland Rath in Pembrokeshire (Wainwright, 1971, 94). Equally interesting has been the demonstration by Dr M. G. Jarrett that the small Roman villa at Whitton in the Vale of Glamorgan began as an Iron Age farmstead with round huts of the type so familiar in the Lowland Zone (Wilson, 1969, 201).

It may be argued that the population of the Highland Zone was in any event too small in the Roman period to provide any useful part of the grain supplies needed by the army. Estimates of the native population of Roman Britain are inevitably less precise than those for the army, and may indeed be highly inaccurate. Frere has estimated that the total population of the Roman province at the end of the 2nd century was around two million (Frere, 1967, 311). Of these he suggested that between 50,000 and 100,000 will have been in Wales. Jarrett, working from the lower total of one million, thought that the Silures were unlikely to have exceeded 40,000 at the time of the conquest (Jarrett, 1965, 36). Such figures are no more than intelligent guesses, but some comparison with the medieval populations may be helpful. Between 1086 and 1545 the population of Wales varied between 100,000 and 250,000, which was equivalent to 9·1% and 5·4% of that of England (Russell, 1948, 235 and 319). If this ratio is applied to Frere's figures, it would suggest that his upper estimate is more likely to be correct, and it is possible to see some support for this in the size of the Roman army in Wales. A total population of 100,000 is unlikely to contain more than about 40,000 men capable of bearing arms, and a smaller number would certainly not seem to justify an occupying army of 20,000 men. It appears, therefore, that a population for Wales of between 100,000 and 150,000 is quite likely in the 2nd century AD. The advent of the Roman garrison would be equivalent to a rise in population of between 13% and 20%.

But even if it is accepted that grain could be and was grown in the Highland Zone, is there any evidence to suggest that the Roman government would wish to utilize this source rather than rely on the far greater resources of the more fertile Lowland Zone? To this the answer must be yes, for there is a considerable body of evidence from documentary sources and from other provinces showing that it was the aim of the Roman government to avoid moving supplies over long distances wherever possible. This is stated most clearly and authoritatively in an instruction of the Emperors Valentinian and Valens to the praetorian prefect in 369 which is preserved in the Theodosian Code: "Just as We, by Our beneficial foresight, have commanded to be done throughout all frontiers, you shall order supplies of subsistence allowances to be brought to the camps by the provincials nearest to the borders." (7.4.15). There were economic and military reasons for this. Extended supply lines, fanning out to individual forts, would be a source of weakness in those areas such as Wales or the Pennines where the forts were intended to keep the natives in check rather than to defend a frontier against an external enemy. If every cartload of food had to have a military escort over long distances it would pin down large bodies of troops who could be better employed elsewhere. But perhaps more relevant was the cost of transport. As a result of Diocletian's Price Edict we know something of these costs at the end of the 3rd century. The standard vehicle for land transport in the western empire was a wagon with a team of two oxen; the normal load was 1200lb, the maximum 1500lb (Jones, 1964, 831), and the charge per mile for such a load was 20 *denarii*. At that time 20 *denarii* bought 4lb of wheat (Jones, 1964, 841), which meant that a wagon journey of 300 miles doubled the price of wheat.

The Roman state was not unduly concerned with the cost when it felt that necessity justified it, but it could not ignore realities. The provincials, on whom most of the cost and labour will have fallen, might not have the transport; as Tacitus records, they would certainly object to carrying supplies excessive distances (*Agricola* 19). Nor was it the policy of the Roman government to provoke unnecessary trouble, or to raise the burden on the provincials to excessive levels; the duty of the shepherd was to shear his sheep, not flay them, as Tiberius succinctly put it (Suetonius, *Tiberius* XXXII). The organizational problems involved in moving vast amounts of grain over long distances would be immense. The army in Britain would need 38,000 wagon loads each year, most of which would have to be moved after the harvest but before winter. The result of failure would be to put the entire military situation in jeopardy. There is indeed a great deal of literary evidence to show that the transport of supplies overland for what seem today quite short distances was rare. The Emperor Julian, for example, took great pride in the fact that he had corn carried 100 miles to relieve a famine at Antioch in Syria, one of the greatest cities in the empire (Jones, 1964, 844). Water transport was far cheaper. Wheat could be carried from Alexandria to Rome for less than it would cost to move it overland from Cranborne Chase to Caerleon (Jones, 1964, 842). It is, of course, largely for this reason that the three legionary fortresses of Britain—Caerleon, Chester, and York—were in places which could be supplied from the sea by water. Professor A. H. M. Jones has indeed suggested that the establishment of the great chain of Roman frontier forts along the Rhine and Danube was probably dictated as much by logistics as by strategical considerations (Jones, 1964, 844). For the same reason the logical destination for much of the surplus grain of eastern England was not the northern frontier but the Rhineland, and there, at least in the 4th century, we know from classical writers it went (Jones, 1964, 844). Similarly, the garrisons of the Lower Danube were supplied by fleets sailing from the Mediterranean through the Bosphorus (Jones, 1964, 844). But few of the auxiliary forts in Britain were well placed to receive their supplies by water. Highland rivers are in general unsuited for long-distance transport, although in some areas they could have been used locally. When a fort was on a major river or the coast, as at Caernarvon, there is good evidence that this was taken advantage of (Nash-Williams, 1969, 59).

On the Continent we know that supplies acquired from the local population were supplemented (in some cases possibly replaced) by those produced on land attached to the fort or fortress itself, and inscriptions recording such *territoria* come from many provinces.

The most detailed study of this question is that of Petrikovits for the fortress of Vetera (Xanten) on the Rhine (Petrikovits, 1960, 63). From a considerable body of archaeological evidence, including the distribution of stamped tiles and inscriptions, he has concluded that the *territorium* covered not less than 8,645 acres (3,500 ha) and was capable of producing sufficient grain for the legion. Others are known to have contained pasture, orchards, woods, quarries and mines (Rostovtzeff, 1957, 244). In short, the aim was to make the legion independent of outside sources in as many ways as possible. Britain in the main lacks the inscriptional evidence for such *territoria,* but they must have existed. A boundary stone from the sea-defences at Goldcliff Priory, 3 miles south of Caerleon (Collingwood and Wright, 1965, 132, No. 395), shows that this lay within the *territorium* of the II Legion, and it may have extended as far as the site of the earlier fortress at Usk, 6½ miles to the north, where stamped tiles (Nash-Williams, 1969, 118) and the tombstone of a legionary's son indicate some connection with Caerleon (Collingwood and Wright, 1965, 133, No. 396). Archaeological evidence for the edge of the *territorium* around the Flavian fortress at Inchtuthil in Perthshire is probably to be seen in the Cleaven Dyke, which lies almost 2 miles to the north of the fortress and which Richmond thought ran for some 9 miles from the Tay to the hills (Richmond, 1940, 40). The legionary tileworks at Holt on the River Dee about 8 miles south of Chester (Grimes, 1930) strongly suggests that the *territorium* of the XX Legion extended at least that far.

Evidence for the *territoria* (or *prata*) of auxiliary forts is less common but it is provided for the fort at Chester-le-Street, Co. Durham, by an inscription (Collingwood and Wright, 1965, 348, No. 1049). The *territoria* of auxiliary forts need not have been vast. The majority of these forts held garrisons of about 480 men, which, if we accept the low yield of 10 bushels/acre and add an additional one-third for seed grain, means that an area of about 700 acres (280 ha), little more than 1 square mile, would provide all their grain requirements.

Actual evidence of cultivation outside forts is, of course, rare, if only because it has rarely been looked for. It can, however, be shown at Usk, Monmouthshire, where plough furrows containing early Samian ware and following the line of a Roman boundary ditch were found outside the Neronian fortress. In this case there can be no doubt that at least part of the area around the fortress was under the plough, and this in what at the time must have been essentially a frontier station.

With the notable exception of Hadrian's Wall, the majority of Roman forts in Britain are set in valleys, often at the junction of two rivers. One effect of this distribution, and it is probably not accidental, was that the forts almost invariably lie on or close to some of the best agricultural land in the area. Cereal production in their own *territoria* would thus often be a practical proposition. The labour would probably come from the inhabitants of the *vicus* which grew up around every long-established fort, even those as bleakly situated as Housesteads (Bruce, 1957, 128), supplemented by specialists from the garrison itself.

The effect of a fort on local agriculture is likely to have been two-fold. More grain would have to be produced, if any was grown at all to begin with, in order to replace that lost by compulsory purchase, while at the same time the *vicus* around the fort might provide a market for any surplus and for fresh foods, including meat. An additional market would be provided in many parts of Wales and the north by the considerable development of the mining industry; the only industry other than agriculture which flourished in the Highland Zone. The net effect should, therefore, be a marked increase in the area under cultivation. This need not, however, have meant any great increase in the wealth of the peasantry, for they were at best selling in a highly restricted market. Substantial profits which might be reflected in the farm buildings, as in the Lowland Zone, will occur only when a considerable market was near at hand, hence the almost invariable correlation of town and villa distributions (Rivet, 1969, 178). In Wales this occurred to some extent on the southern coastal plain (Nash-Williams, 1969, 2), where the towns of Caerwent and Carmarthen and the great *vicus* at Caerleon will have provided stable markets, while the proximity of the Bristol Channel may have opened up the markets of Gloucestershire. But even here the villas, with the exception of Llantwit Major, which is significantly near the coast, are scarcely luxurious.

Outside the zone which lay within easy reach of a fort the cost of transport increased no doubt by the terrain, probably meant that the pressure for additional grain production did not exist, except for any local increases in population which resulted from the cessation of tribal warfare with the *pax Romana.* As sections of the Highland Zone became pacified and their garrisons were withdrawn, these areas will have increased. If we could plot the grain production of large parts of Wales or the Pennines in the Roman period, we would almost certainly find that there was a steep rise during the last years of the 1st century, followed by a marked decline as the garrisons were removed in the 2nd century. In Wales, for example, it appears that the number of occupied forts fell from about 28 in the early years of the 2nd century to around half that number by *c.* AD 130, and was halved again by the end of the 2nd century (Nash-Williams, 1969, 19).

The demand for cattle, pigs, and sheep, which were also needed by the state for feeding the army and for their hides, is likely to have fluctuated less. They could walk to their destination and, provided that the *territorium* contained sufficient pasture to fatten them again, they would lose nothing by the journey. It is clear from Tacitus that cattle, like grain, were subject to compulsory purchase in areas where they were bred in large numbers (*Annals,* IV, 72).

It would be a mistake to imagine that the problem of supplies was uniform throughout Britain or that the solutions were invariably the same. In some areas the *territorium* of a fort might be so situated that it could provide all the necessary supplies; more often it will have supplemented the grain collected from the provincials farming in the area. When the army occupied an area in depth, their forts were spaced at intervals of ten miles or rather more when the situation allowed. Each fort could, therefore, draw on an area of at least 100 square miles, no part of which would be much more than 5 miles as the crow flies from the fort itself. Under these circumstances it is most unlikely that the military commissariat would refrain from taking their tithe of the local grain. Even in areas where barley rather than wheat was grown, the crop might be taxed, if only for feeding the unit's animals, although it is not improbable that Celtic auxiliaries did not regard barley with the same dislike as the Italian legionaries to whom most of the literary evidence applies. In those cases where neither compulsory purchase nor the *territorium* could provide sufficient supplies for the year, these must have been imported from the nearest convenient source, which may not have been the closest. Wherever possible this will have been done by water, if necessary via one of the legionary fortresses which had docks capable of handling large cargoes. One wonders what the ships which returned to Caerleon ballasted with Preseli slate had carried on their outward journey (Boon, 1972, 52). Only in the event of the greatest necessity will long overland journeys have taken place, although these will certainly have been normal during the conquest phase and in the years which followed before a local system could be organized.

These arguments will apply with equal validity to Wales, the Pennines, and those parts of southern Scotland which were under Roman control for reasonable periods of time. The exception would seem to be Hadrian's Wall with its close-set forts following a line that was certainly chosen on strategic grounds. But even this is never far from reasonably fertile soil, and it may be noted that at Housesteads, surely the bleakest fort of all, there is the remains of a field system on the slope below the fort itself (Birley, 1961, 184). The work of George Jobey has shown that Northumberland supported a flourishing native population during the Roman period, who will doubtless have contributed to military requirements (Jobey, 1966, 8). Admittedly the Wall could be supplied by sea, at least at its ends, but there is little evidence that this was done regularly and on a large scale. The stores base at South Shields, which at once springs to mind in this context, was short-lived and apparently concerned with the export rather than the import of grain.

In short, until we can prove the contrary, I suggest that we should accept that a considerable part of the requirements of the military establishment in the Highland Zone was locally produced, with all that that involves for the expansion of agriculture and its effect on the landscape; further, that supplementary supplies will have been moved by water wherever possible and that the large-scale movement of grain overland to standing garrisons, as opposed to field armies, was no more normal in Britain than it appears to have been elsewhere in the Roman Empire.

REFERENCES

Alcock, L. (1965). Hillforts in Wales and the Marches. *Antiquity,* 39, 184–195.

Applebaum, S. (1972). Roman Britain. *In* Finberg, H. P. R. (ed.). *The Agrarian History of England and Wales. Vol. I Part II A.D. 43–1042.* Cambridge: University Press; 1–277.

Birley, E. (1961). *Research on Hadrian's Wall.* Kendal: Wilson.

Boon, G. C. (1972). *Isca.* Cardiff: National Museum of Wales.

Bruce, J. C. (1957). *Handbook to the Roman Wall.* (Ed. Richmond, I. A.) Newcastle upon Tyne: Reid.

Clark, J. (1794a). *General View of the Agriculture of the County of Brecknock.* London: Smeeton.

Clark, J. (1794b). *General View of the Agriculture of the County of Radnor.* London: Macrae.

Collingwood, R. G. and Wright, R. P. (1965). *The Roman Inscriptions of Britain, I.* Oxford: Clarendon Press.

Davies, R. W. (1971). The Roman Military Diet. *Britannia, 2,* 122–142.

Frere, S. (1967). *Britannia.* London: Routledge and Kegan Paul.

Grimes, W. F. (1930). Holt, Denbighshire. *Y Cymmrodor,* 41, 1–235.

Guido, M. (1974). A Scottish Crannog Redated. *Antiquity,* 48, 54.

Jarrett, M. G. (1965). Early Roman Campaigns in Wales. *Archaeol. J.,* 121, 23–39.

Jobey, G. (1966). Homesteads and Settlements of the Frontier Area. *In* Thomas, C. (ed.). *Rural Settlement in Roman Britain.* London: CBA.

Jones, A. H. M. (1964). *The Later Roman Empire 284–602.* Oxford: Blackwell.

Kay, G. (1794). *General View of the Agriculture of North Wales: Montgomeryshire.* Edinburgh: Moir.

Nash-Williams, V. E. (1969). *The Roman Frontier in Wales* (ed. Jarrett, M. G.). Cardiff: University of Wales Press.

Petrikovits, H. von (1960). *Das römische Rheinland: Archäologische Forschungen seit 1945.* Köln und Opladen: Westdeutscher Verlag.

Piggott, S. (1958). Native Economies and the Roman Occupation of North Britain. *In* Richmond, I. A. (ed.). *Roman and Native in North Britain.* London: Nelson; 1–27.

Richmond, I. A. (1940). Excavations on the Estate of Meikleour, Perthshire, 1939. *Proc. Soc. Antiq. Scot.,* 74, 37–48.

Rickman, G. (1971). *Roman Granaries and Store Buildings.* Cambridge: University Press.

Rivet, A. L. F. (1969). Social and Economic Aspects. *In* Rivet, A. L. F. (ed.). *The Roman Villa in Britain.* London: Routledge and Kegan Paul; 173–216.

Rostovtzeff, M. (1957). *The Social and Economic History of the Roman Empire.* Oxford: Clarendon Press.

Russell, J. C (1948). *British Medieval Population.* Albuquerque: University of New Mexico Press.

Stamp, L. D. (ed.) (1942). *The Land of Britain. Part 36: Montgomeryshire.* London: Land Utilisation Survey of Britain.

Thirsk, J. (1967). *The Agrarian History of England and Wales.* Vol. IV 1500–1640. Cambridge: University Press.

Wainwright, G. J. (1971). The excavation of a fortified settlement at Walesland Rath, Pembrokeshire. *Britannia,* 2, 48–108.

Watson, G. R. (1969). *The Roman Soldier.* London: Thames and Hudson.

Wheeler, M. (1954). *The Stanwick Fortifications.* Oxford: Society of Antiquaries.

Wilson, D. R. (ed.) (1969). Roman Britain in 1968. *J. Roman Stud.,* 59, 198–234.

Dry bones and living documents

L. Alcock

Synopsis

It is generally agreed that specialist reports, for instance on animal bones, should not be buried in an appendix to an excavation report, but should be integrated in the overall history of the site. In historical periods, the synthesis must take account of the abundant literary evidence for farming practices. When this is done, an unconformity may appear between the biological evidence, as interpreted, and the documentary evidence. A striking unconformity of this kind, published in 1963, has been ignored by writers in the biological field. It is therefore re-examined, along with parallel and contrasting cases, as a basis for discussion.

The purpose of this paper is to examine some of the ways in which documentary evidence can be used to breathe life into the animal bones found on archaeological sites, so that the zoological evidence from an excavation may be rescued from a specialist appendix, and integrated into the full historical account. The paper also looks at some of the problems which can arise when this integration is attempted—problems which concern the bone specialist as much as the economic historian. Its inspiration is twofold: an early training in the documents of medieval agrarian economy, and the discovery of well preserved animal bones at the early medieval fortification of Dinas Powys, Glamorgan. This site also yielded a great variety of other evidence on which to base a picture of its economic life. Since medieval Wales has abundant documents to illustrate its economy, it therefore seemed worthwhile attempting a synthesis of the archaeological and literary evidence. What follows here is concerned only with the pastoral aspects of the economy at Dinas Powys.

The principal data, and some discussion of the problems which they raise, have been in print since 1963 (Alcock, 1963). The reason for calling attention to them now is that the problems have been ignored by economic historians making use of the data, and both the data and the problems have been overlooked by students of excavated animal bones.

The most important period in the history of the Dinas Powys site fell in the 5th to 7th centuries AD. At this time, the place was a small and feeble fortification; but its middens yielded an extraordinarily rich collection of pottery and glass, silver, bronze and iron, worked bone, and utilized stone. The limestone bedrock favoured the preservation of animal bones, and consequently great quantities, principally from domestic animals, were recovered. Indeed, within the very limited resources of the excavation, these quantities were an embarrassment, and it was possible to retain only a portion of the bones. Although this was a matter of expediency, the actual selection was based on reasoned principles. Advice was taken from appropriate specialists, and questions about the animal husbandry of Dinas Powys, which the bones might serve to answer, were formulated as a basis for this selection. In particular, it seemed that we might hope to determine the order of frequency of species, the age of slaughter of the stock, and the stature of the beasts. With this in mind, we normally kept only jaws and teeth, and those long bones which retained their articular surfaces, a sample which amounted to about one-third of all the bones discovered.

Small though this initial sample was, in the circumstances of the late 1950s it was not possible to find anyone competent and willing to examine the whole of it. In the event, Dr I. W. Cornwall kindly agreed to examine some 1,600 bones, about one-seventh of those which had been retained on site. For this purpose, a further selection was made on archaeological grounds. All the bones from one particular midden deposit, with much associated pottery of the 5th–7th centuries AD, were studied as a group. It is believed that this represents a fair sample of the bones from that period. The remainder of the original sample still awaits identification.

One outcome of the original method of selection was to make it difficult to determine the actual table meat favoured at Dinas Powys. In his report, Dr Cornwall comments: "Though the remains are clearly of food-animals in the main, the identifiable parts represented are strikingly of the less edible parts of carcasses. The few main long bones are almost all deliberately broken and many, even, of the vertebrae are caudals, representing, if anything, rather oxtail soup than sirloin cuts. The collection looks like waste from the kitchen thrown direct on to the midden, never having been to table at all." (Alcock, 1963, 192). This may require modifying to the extent that oxtail—like cows' heels, pigs' trotters, or sheeps' brains—is perfectly edible in itself, without needing to be made into soup. Moreover, it is difficult to see how top-quality cuts of beef would be represented, except perhaps by T-bone steaks. Leg and shoulder of mutton were certainly present.

The numerical analysis of the animal bones by Dr Cornwall and Mrs Haglund-Calley is reproduced here as Table I. This provides evidence for the interpretation of the age at which domestic animals were slaughtered, which is conveniently presented in a series of histograms for cattle (Fig. 1), sheep (Fig. 2), and pig (Fig. 3). What immediately emerges is the relatively early age of slaughter: all of the sheep, and all but 2% of the pig, at under 2 years of age, and 70% of the cattle at less than 30 months.

If these figures are accepted, they raise an immediate problem about the viability of stock-raising at Dinas Powys. Given such a drastic slaughtering policy, could the stock be maintained at all? It is not easy to determine the age of puberty, the minimum breeding age, for ancient domestic animals. Figures for modern methods of intensive breeding, from animals on a high-nutrition diet, may provide some kind of baseline, to which we must add an uncertain number of months

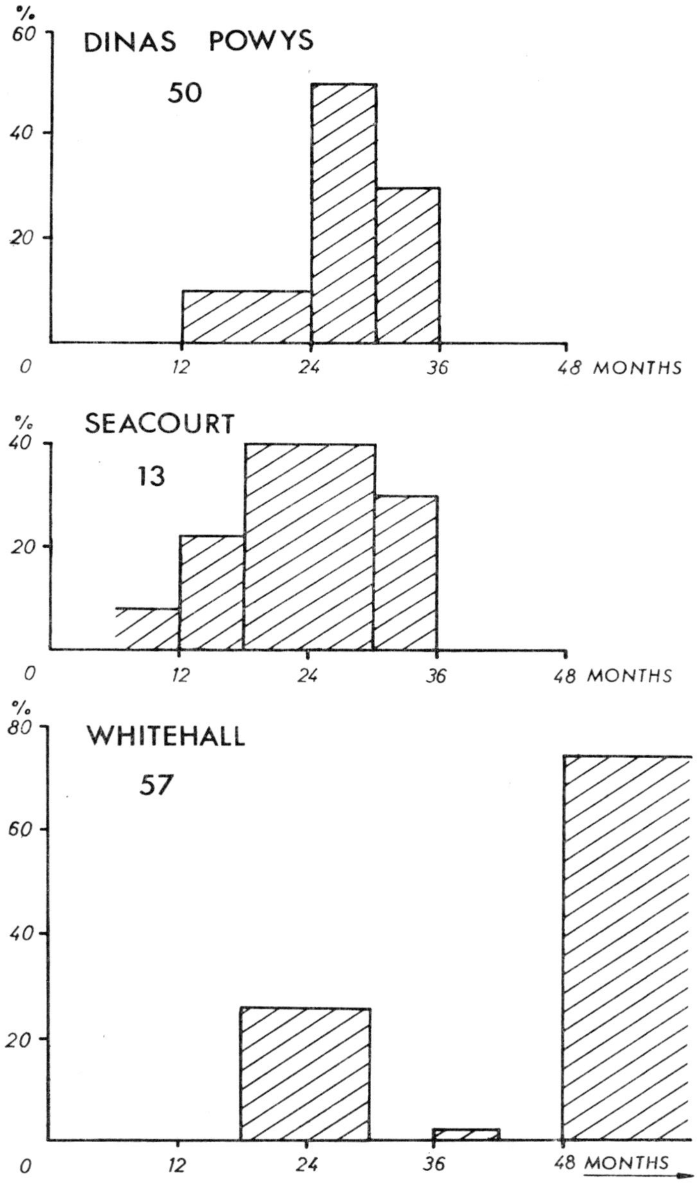

Fig. 1 Age of slaughter of cattle on three medieval sites. For references, see text. The figure below the site name is the total number of animals represented. Note that the methods of calculating these numbers differ from site to site

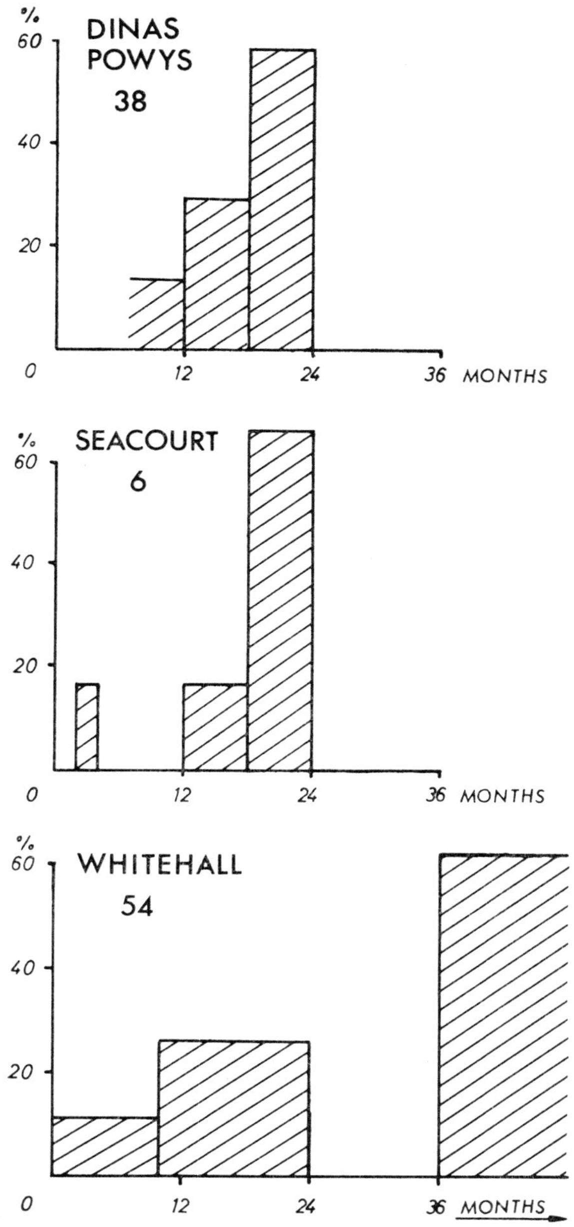

Fig. 2 Age of slaughter of sheep on three medieval sites

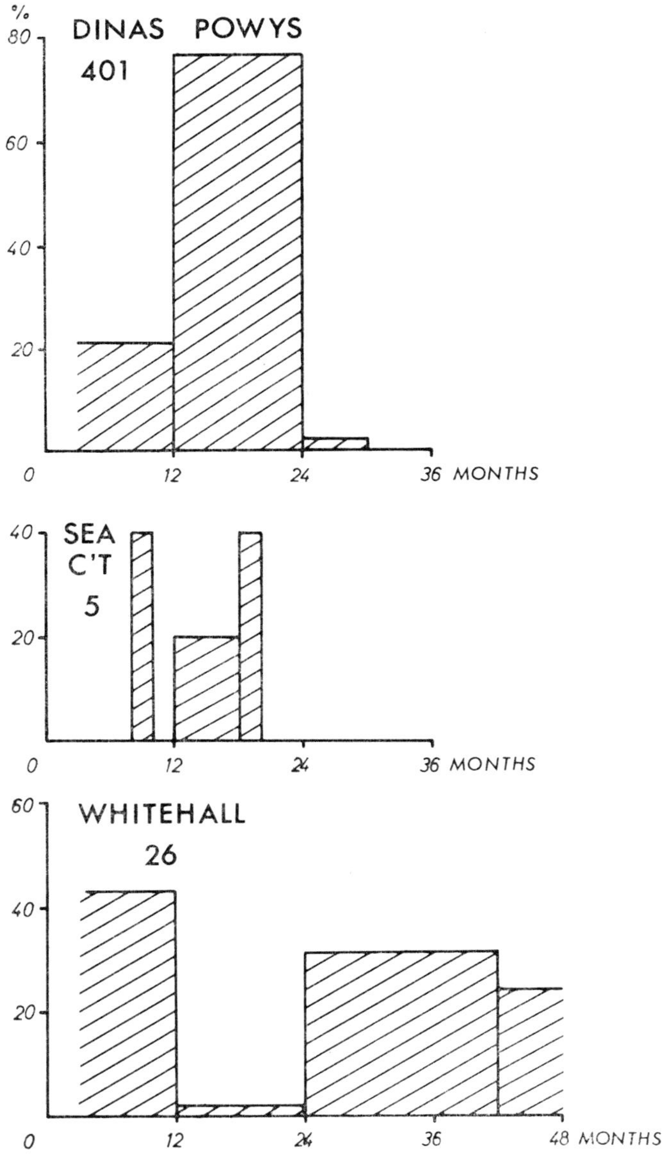

Fig. 3 Age of slaughter of pig on three medieval sites

TABLE I Numerical analysis of animal bones (by Dr I. W. Cornwall and Mrs L. Haglund-Colley)

Group of bones	Cattle				Sheep				Pig					Remarks
		Age				Age				Age				
	sum	1–2	2–2½	2½–3½	*sum*	1	1–1½	1½–2	*sum*	<1	1–2	>2	Others	
Skull fragments					1		1		28	2			1	1 of horse.
Horn-cores	11				10									cattle: 5 long, 5 short.
Maxilla/ mandible	23	5	5	10	39	4	9	16	228	8	106	4		pig: few worn, probably mainly *c.* 2 years old. sheep: the rest probably *c.* 2 years old. cattle: none very worn, adult, but young.
Loose teeth	126		7	2	132		1	6	435	72	100	3	16	4 of horse, very old. 12 of deer, adult. pig: 7 newly born. sheep: mainly young beasts. cattle: 1 calf, 2 very worn (probably one animal), the rest *c.* 2½ years old or less.
Axial skeleton	16				18									sheep: 15 caudal vert., probably sheep or cattle.
Shoulder and hip-girdles	6	1			5				1				4	4 of bird. cattle: 1 fragment, calf.
Long bones	12		2	3	6	1			11	3	2		29	28 of bird. 1 of deer, fairly young. pig: all young, 2 newly born. sheep: 1 lamb. cattle: 3 cut open with sharp tool.
Extremities	146	4	11		13				322		101		10	1 of Homo. 2 of deer (some under 'cattle' may be deer). 7 of bird (1 with spur). cattle: the rest *c.* 1½ years old or more. 2 phal. fused through physical damage, not illness. 1 metapod., definitely calf. 7 metapod. out of 18 split open with sharp tool.
	340	10	25	15	224	5	11	22	1,025	85	309	7	+4	?
													+21	other fragments of bird.
		2·94 %	7·35 %	4·4 %		1·12 %	2·46 %	4·92 %		8·71 %	31·6 %	0·72 %	+2	skulls of rodents.
													+1	concretion.
	340				224				1,025				88	
	21·5 %				13·4 %				61·2 %				5·26 %	

Grand total: 1,677

or years (information from P. G. Hignett, MRCVS). In the case of sheep, it might be suggested that the ewes would normally lamb at the end of their second year, so each of the Dinas Powys sheep can have produced at best one lamb. When allowance is made for rams, barren ewes, and lost lambs, it is clear that this is quite insufficient to maintain a flock.

In the case of cattle, we may find some guidance on the age of calving in the early medieval Welsh laws, which contain a great deal of virtually unquarried evidence for agrarian economy and farming practices. One passage details the rising value of a cow from 6 pence at birth to 30 pence towards the end of its third year. In May of the fourth year "the attributes of a heifer are to be required of it . . . . . an increase of 16 pence is added, namely the value of her milk . . . . and 4 pence for her calf" (Richards, 1954, 87). The implication would seem to be that, by May of the fourth year, the first calf had been weaned, the calf itself being born late in the cow's third year. By this time, according to Fig. 1, the majority of the Dinas Powys cattle were dead.

Only in the case of pigs does there seem some hope of maintaining the stock. Medieval writers on husbandry thought that pigs should farrow two or three times a year, having a litter of at least seven each time. Under modern conditions, puberty might begin at 5 months. Even if we adjust this to a year, it is clear that the stock of pigs could have been kept up, despite the fact that the overwhelming majority had been slaughtered by the end of their second year. But on the available figures, the flocks of sheep and herds of cattle could not possibly have been maintained.

Several explanations for this discrepancy may be offered and examined. The most obvious are: that some bias towards young animals was created by the method of sampling on the site; that there is some bias in the technique of ageing domestic animals from bones and teeth (Silver, 1969); or that social choice had brought to Dinas Powys a collection of animal carcases which in no way represents the normal age pattern of the stock or the normal pattern of slaughtering. These hypothetical explanations can be partially tested by comparison with the animals from other sites and by reference to early economic documents.

Starting with the last of these hypotheses, there is a *prima facie* case that Dinas Powys was a special site. The existence of defences, combined with the site evidence for such prestige activities as fine metal working, argue that it was a chieftain's or prince's defended homestead—a likely place, therefore, for specially selected cuts of meat. But before this line of thought is taken further, it is necessary to examine the evidence from sites for which no such claims can be made: more lowly farms or peasant villages.

Aldwick, Barley (Hertfordshire), would seem to represent such a site in the Iron Age. There "some 65% of sheep were killed at ages less than two years" (Ewbank *et al.,* 1964). Although this rate of slaughter raises problems about the maintenance of the flocks similar to those at Dinas Powys, it does not appear to have been questioned or commented on. A similar problem appears at Old Sleaford (Lincolnshire), in both the Iron Age and the Romano-British period. The sheep which can be aged to greater than 24 months comprise only about one-third of the specimens recovered (Higgs and White, 1963). Again there is a curious silence about the implications of this for the survival of the flock.

Even more directly comparable with Dinas Powys is the medieval village of Seacourt in Berkshire, where animal bones from the late 12th to late 14th centuries AD have been studied by Jope (1961/2). A table showing "approximate ages of animals based on average periods of eruption of teeth" may be converted into histograms which in their terminal ages parallel the Dinas Powys pattern almost exactly. This might suggest that we are observing a normal pattern of slaughter, common to both lords and peasants. If this were really so, it might well inspire serious doubts about ageing criteria. It might appear necessary to recalibrate the age scale on the histograms so as to allow the animals to breed sufficiently often to maintain the stock. As a corollary, it might be necessary for bone specialists to review their ageing techniques.

So drastic a solution may not, in fact, be necessary. Turning from the table of ages at Seacourt to the body of the animal report we find: in Period I, "immature animals were present as well as fully adult ones. The only immature bone apart from jaws was one ox phalanx." In Period II "a sheep metatarsal was the only immature bone apart from jaws". In other words, the use of tooth eruption as a principal criterion of age tips the interpretation in favour of young animals. But this observation does not provide relief from the dilemma at Dinas Powys. There, the teeth and jaws were examined for wear as well as for the degree of eruption. As the Remarks column of Table I shows, only two 'very worn' cow molars provide evidence for an animal that was older than 'adult but young'.

To emphasize the oddity of the Dinas Powys evidence, it is useful to consider the pattern of slaughtering at the early medieval farmstead at the Treasury site, Whitehall, London. Here the fusion of the epiphyses of the limb bones was used as the criterion for age at death, but tooth eruption and wear does not appear to have been taken into account. It is immediately apparent from the histograms that a goodly proportion of both cattle and sheep survived to breed more than once. With pig the proportion was smaller, but no doubt sufficient. It has been well observed that the marked peaks on the histograms demonstrate that "selective killing on an age-related basis was practised on these animals"; and further "the picture presented is one of rational husbandry" (Chaplin, 1971).

Faced with the Whitehall evidence, it is necessary to reconsider the possibility that the explanation for the curious pattern of the Dinas Powys animal bones lies in the high social status of the site. A modern commentator, with a taste for veal or spring lamb, might expect the 6th century lords of Dinas Powys to have had similar tastes, backed by the means to gratify them. The Welsh laws suggest, however, that this expectation may not be justified. These laws are preserved in manuscripts of the late 12th–13th centuries AD, but they claim to have been promulgated by king Hywel Dda (Howell the Good) who died *c.* AD 950. There is agreement that the laws are in fact highly stratified, and that the earliest strata represent the customs of Wales in the centuries before Howell (Emanuel, 1967, 82; Jones, 1972, 300; Pierce, 1972, 353). Among the more primitive elements are those which list the renders- (or taxes-) in-kind owed by both freemen and bondmen to the prince. If Dinas Powys was a princely homestead, these renders should be directly relevant to the animal remains found on the site. Some typical examples may therefore be quoted. It has been claimed that the bondmen "were to present the king with young animals whenever he came to the court" (Jones, 1966-67), but the full text refers to sheep or lambs or kids or cheese or butter or milk, according to the ability of the bondmen (Owen, 1841, 95).

More generally in the laws, however, the emphasis is on mature beasts, and sometimes the degree of maturity is spelt out with great care. For instance, the summer render paid by the freemen comprised four 'food-gifts'. Three of these included a cow—in one case, specifically the 'carcase of a fat cow without skin and entrails'—while the fourth included "a fat wether three years old and a sow of three winters three fingers thick". From the bondmen, the prince was to have two food-gifts a year, including "a sow three fingers thick in her hams, her ribs and her gammons." Another food gift included "a bacon three fingers thick in its gammons, in its ribs and in its hams, or a sow of three years fattening". For three winter food-gifts the carcase of an ox was to be paid (Richards, 1954, 73).

The wider aspects of this emphasis on mature beasts must be considered later, but first we must return to Dinas Powys. In an integrated account of the site, three elements should be capable of correlation: (a) the interpretation of the site as a prince's stronghold; (b) the documentary evidence for the character of food renders to a prince; (c) the interpreted age of slaughter of food animals. As we have seen, the expected correlation does not exist. It may therefore be necessary to question elements (a) and (c). As it happens, one reviewer has rejected the excavator's interpretation as the court of a prince and has suggested: "if on this secluded and safe hill-top there was a nest of robbers, might not one find . . . . . the bones of the most succulent animals belonging to the stock-breeding farmers of the district?" (Gresham, 1965). It is difficult to believe that such a hypothetical robber-band would have preferred a scrawny lamb or calf to a fat wether three years old, or that young beasts are easier to rustle than mature ones. In any case, the interpretation of Dinas Powys as a nest of robbers has not found favour with other commentators, whereas the hypothesis that it was a prince's stronghold has been widely accepted.

It follows, then, that the apparent age of slaughter of the Dinas Powys animals cannot be reconciled with a reasonable interpretation of the social function of the site, nor with a sensible policy of animal husbandry. It is therefore necessary to ask again whether the age-pattern has been distorted by the concentration on jaws and teeth as dating criteria. Table I shows that, out of 50 cattle for which an age estimate is given, only 20 are aged from the limb-bones, but there are no fewer than 138 limb-bones for which no age is given. Among the pigs, limb-bones account for 103 examples aged between 12 and 24 months, but there are also 227 unaged limbs. Could a significant proportion of these belong to mature beasts? At present this question can only be asked, not answered. But similar questions about the true age-span of domestic animals need asking about the stock at Seacourt, Aldwick, and Sleaford, and no doubt about other sites as well.

So far the documentary evidence has been used in an essentially critical or negative manner. Some examples of a more positive use may now be cited. The peaks in the histograms from the Whitehall site have already been quoted as evidence for good husbandry and a rational slaughtering policy. This was on a Saxon farmstead of the late 9th century AD. About four centuries later, Walter of Henley wrote a treatise on husbandry and estate management. Three extracts on the sorting out of animals for slaughter are relevant here:

> "Sort out your cattle once a year between Easter and Whitsuntide—that is to say, oxen, cows, and herds—and let those that are not to be kept be put to fatten; if you lay out money to fatten them with grass you will gain."
>
> "Sort out your sheep once a year, between Easter and Whitsuntide, and cause those which are not to be kept to be sheared early and marked apart from the others, and put them in enclosed wood or in other pasture where they can fatten, and about St John's Day sell them, for then will the flesh of sheep be in season. And the wool of these may be sold by itself with the skins [of those] which died of murrain. And when the sheep are sold, for them and their wool and the skins aforesaid replace as many head."
>
> "Sort out your swine once a year, and if you find any which is not sound take it away. Do not have boars and sows unless of a good breed. Your other female swine cause to be kept, that they do not farrow; then shall their bacon be worth as much as that of the males."
>
> (Lamond, 1890; Oschinsky, 1971)

It is clear that Walter thought of the animals destined for the table as those whose usefulness in other ways was at an end. This is another aspect of that maturity of table meat which we have already seen in the Welsh laws. But it also warns us how far our picture of ancient animal husbandry is distorted by the nature of our own confrontation with it. The archaeologist recovers the refuse of kitchen and table. With the aid of specialist colleagues, he attempts to infer what had actually been on the table, in terms of carcase-weight or even of nutritional value. But only rarely can he calculate all that the animals would have provided in life as well as in death. Here the documents, and especially the medieval manuals of husbandry, are an invaluable source of information.

Among the animals which Walter would have put out to grass to fatten up, the ox, for instance, would already have given years of service at the plough, and probably at the waggon as well. The cows would obviously have yielded calves and milk. An anonymous *Husbandry* tells us that each cow ought to answer for a calf a year, and each ewe for one lamb a year; "and if there be a cow which has not calved or a ewe which has not lambed in the year, let it be enquired whose fault this is". Walter of Henley, in a section entitled 'How much milk your cows should yield' states:

> "If your cows were sorted out, so that the bad were taken away, and your cows fed in pasture of salt marsh, then ought two cows to yield a wey of cheese and half a gallon of butter a week. And if they were fed in pasture of wood, or in meadows after mowing, or in stubble, then three cows ought to yield a wey of cheese and half a gallon of butter a week between Easter and Michaelmas."
>
> (Lamond, 1890; Oschinsky, 1971)

Turning now to the sheep, we may first recall the "fat wether, three years old" of the Welsh laws. He would have yielded three shearings of wool before he was brought to the prince's table. It used to be normal practice, at least in the upland regions of Britain, to keep the wethers for several years for the sake of their wool before they were slaughtered—the taste for lamb is a product of the affluent society. As we have seen, the ewes were required to produce one lamb a year, but twins were not expected in medieval husbandry (Trow-Smith, 1957, 151). Less obvious today is the early importance of the sheep in terms of milk and its products. After his passage on the milk yield of cows, Walter continues:

> "And twenty ewes which are fed in pasture of salt marsh ought to and can yield cheese and butter as the two cows before named. And if your sheep were fed with fresh pasture or fallow, then ought thirty ewes to yield butter and cheese as the three cows before named. Now there are many servants and provosts and dairymaids who will contradict this thing, and that is because they give away and waste and consume the milk!"
>
> (Lamond,1890; Oschinsky, 1971)

It is evident that all these products of the living beast must be taken into account when we attempt to reconstruct the husbandry and agrarian economy represented by the animal bones on archaeological sites. But it is equally important to stress that the dead beast provided more than just a supply of table meat. Sometimes the by-products are demonstrated by actual site evidence. The use of horn, for instance, is well shown by the great numbers of horn-cores, interpreted as workshop debris, from a medieval site in Well Street, Coventry (Chaplin, 1971, 138). But with more perishable organic substances (sinew, gut, and above all hides) the archaeological evidence may fail us, and we must then depend on the hints provided by literary documents.

Some examples may now be quoted at random from the Welsh laws (Richards, 1954, 31–43). The steward of the Royal court was "to have the skins of a hart to make vessels to keep the horns of the king and his cups . . . . . The chief groom is to have an ox hide in winter and a cow hide in summer to make halters for the king's horses." Whereas the king had leathern hose, the summoner of the court had "the legs of the cattle slaughtered in the kitchen to make untanned shoes that are not to be higher than his ankles". On the uses of horn: the chief huntsman blows his horn when the king goes to foray; and for performing this duty he has "a hornful of liquor from the king, and another from the queen, and the third from the steward".

In conclusion, this paper has attempted to indicate how documentary sources can amplify, illuminate, or in some cases cast doubts on the interpretations which we base on the animal bones recovered from archaeological excavations. The documents available are numerous, and have been little quarried even by economic historians. But we might hope for the future that they will not be overlooked by archaeologists and their biological colleagues.

REFERENCES

Alcock, L. (1963). *Dinas Powys: An Iron Age, Dark Age and Early Medieval Settlement in Glamorgan.* Cardiff: University of Wales Press.

Chaplin, R. E. (1971). *The Study of Animal Bones from Archaeological Sites.* London and New York: Seminar Press.

Emanuel, H. D. (1967). *The Latin Texts of the Welsh Laws.* Cardiff: University of Wales Press.

Ewbank, J. M., Phillipson, D. W., and Whitehouse, R D. with Higgs, E. S. (1964). Sheep in the Iron Age: a method of study. *Proc. Prehist. Soc.*, 30, 423–426.

Gresham, C. A. (1965). Review of Alcock, 1963. *Antiq. J.*, 45, 127–128.

Higgs, E. S. and White, J. P. (1963). Autumn killing. *Antiquity*, 37, 282–289.

Jones, G. R. J. (1966—67). Review of Alcock, 1963. *Welsh Hist. Rev.*, 3, 75–76.

Jones, G. R. J. (1972). Post-Roman Wales. *In* Finberg, H. P. R. (ed.). *The Agrarian History of England and Wales, Vol. I-ii, AD 43–1042.* Cambridge: University Press; 279–382.

Jope, M. (1961–62). The animal remains. *In* Biddle, M. The deserted medieval village of Seacourt, Berkshire. *Oxoniensia*, 26–27, 70–201. (bone report: 197–201).

Lamond, E. (1890). *Walter of Henley's Husbandry.* London: Longmans, Green.

Oschinsky, D. (1971). *Walter of Henley.* Oxford: Clarendon Press.

Owen, A. (1841). *Ancient Laws and Institutes of Wales.* London: Commissioners on Public Records.

Payne, S. (1972). On the interpretation of bone samples from archaeological sites. *In* Higgs, E. S. (ed.). *Papers in Economic Prehistory.* Cambridge: University Press; 65–81.

Pierce, T. J. (1972). *Medieval Welsh Society: Selected Essays.* Cardiff: University of Wales Press.

Richards, M. (1954). *The Laws of Hywel Dda.* Liverpool: University Press.

Silver, I. A. (1969). The ageing of domestic animals. *In* Brothwell, D. and Higgs, E. (eds.). *Science in Archaeology.* London: Thames and Hudson.

Trow-Smith, R. (1957). *A History of British Livestock Husbandry to 1700.* London: Routledge and Kegan Paul.

Comments on Professor Alcock's paper

R. E. Chaplin

This paper raises a great many interesting questions, and some comments from the archaeozoological point of view on both general and specific points may be helpful.

The comparison and synthesis of the data from different sources is fundamental to the study of the animal bones and other items found on archaeological sites (Chaplin, 1971). It is not acceptable to publish the bone data as an appendix unrelated to the rest of the report. Publication of the bones found requires the presentation of the data plus an interpretation and discussion of this in relation to other evidence.

Archaeozoology is a relatively recent and very much a cinderella field of study in this country. As recently as 1956 *Bones for the Archaeologist* (Cornwall, 1956) was a pioneer work in this field. Knowing of the lack of specialists then compared even with now, one must sympathize with the problems facing an excavator who, recognising the importance of his finds of bones, could ultimately get less than 5% of it studied.

Most of the difficulties of reconciling the bone data from Dinas Powys stem from this selectivity and from the procedures and data used in their study. Any selection of the bones biases the results and only expert knowledge can determine which fragments have nothing significant to contribute to the parameters selected for study.

It is clear from the tables that the majority of the pieces that were examined contributed nothing to our knowledge of anything except their occurrence. The proportion of the 1600 fragments that gave, for example, age data was so small as to make it unwise to draw any conclusions from it at all.

Most specialists now agree that for a proper interpretation of the results bones must be studied in terms of minimum numbers and not by fragments. The methodology and presentation of the results in the Dinas Powys report would not now be considered entirely appropriate. What is needed is the basic bone data in a concise form that can then be subjected to interpretative manipulation. This is most important in regard to age estimation, where the criteria and categories are required rather than the suggested age in months, etc. The latter is interpretation, not fact.

Silver (1969) has reviewed the techniques and problems of telling the age of domestic animals from their teeth. It is clear from this that in sheep, pig, and cattle the timetable of dental development has changed over the last 300 years. The Dinas Powys timetable is a modern one, and the use of timetables for 19th century stock would bring the findings more into line with the documentary evidence and the time scale for the Treasury site data.

There is no valid reason for assuming that the Dinas Powys sample is representative of the site, and even less for assuming that it reflects the husbandry of the region. Dinas Powys is probably a consumer site. But until this has been established by a frequency analysis of bone types it would be misleading to attempt any interpretation of this data, let alone to extrapolate it into social and cultural contexts. I would suspect, however, that in any large establishment the few lordly specialities would be only a very small part of what was eaten. Agriculture has its long-term cycles and trends as well as short- to medium-term problems. You cannot average the contents of a midden spanning two centuries to determine what was happening at any given point.

The animal bones from Dinas Powys would repay further study. The sample is quite small but should be sufficient to give a broad view of the dietary habits and some hints as to the husbandry practices as well as stock types of early medieval Wales.

REFERENCES

Chaplin, R. E. (1971). *The Study of Animal Bones from Archaeological Sites.* London: Seminar Press.

Cornwall, I. W. (1956). *Bones for the Archaeologist.* London: Phoenix House.

Silver, I. A. (1969). The Ageing of Domestic Animals. *In* Brothwell, D. R. and Higgs, E. S. (eds.). *Science in Archaeology.* London: Thames and Hudson.

During discussion of this paper I referred to the publication of the results of the long-term study of the primitive Soay sheep on St Kilda carried out under the auspices of the Nature Conservancy. This will now be published in June 1974 as the following:—

Jewell, P. A., Milner, C., and Morton Boyd, J. (eds.). (1974). *Island Survivors, The Ecology of the Soay Sheep of St. Kilda.* London: Athlone Press.

The impact of landscape on prehistoric man

Frances Lynch

Synopsis

A short footnote to the study of man in the landscape draws attention to the fact that prehistoric builders had an appreciation of the natural beauty around them and used this backdrop effectively to enhance their own monuments. Some natural features such as the Bluestone outcrops on Preseli even suggest that their visual impact may have won them their magical reputation. This contrasts with the traditional medieval attitude.

The aim of this short paper is to add a footnote—perhaps personal, certainly subjective—to the study and appreciation of certain prehistoric monuments, mainly in the Highland Zone, because it is only here that we can be reasonably sure that we see them in the context in which they were built. The premise is that early man had a very real and sensitive appreciation of the landscape around him, that his relationship to his environment was not simply one of economic exploitation and struggle but was also one in which the beauty and grandeur of the rocks and mountains and the broad views over valleys and plains had an importance and value in their own right.

There are two main points that I would like to raise for consideration, not for proof, because this is an area of discussion which is not susceptible to proof in any logical or scientific sense. The first of these is the effect that certain natural features appear to have had on prehistoric man's thinking, as reflected in the way he used them, incorporating them into his monuments. One may suspect that there was a very strong religious or magical element in this. The second point concerns the more strictly aesthetic attitude which uses the setting, the landscape, to enhance the drama of a man-made structure. Here one is on very subjective and even emotional grounds and, moreover, one must not forget that both the monuments and their settings might have been changed quite seriously in the time that separates the modern observer from the original builder. However, in the Highland Zone where we are dealing with stone structures and with large-scale rocky landscapes, it is reasonable to suppose that we can recapture some of the original impact of the architecture.

The first site that I would like to comment on is Carn Meini, the outcrop that is the source of the Bluestones at Stonehenge. The fact that the Bluestones were brought from Pembrokeshire has been known (with some minor interruptions in belief) for many years, but there has been surprisingly little interest in why that particular rock was chosen. There are three stone circles in that part of Pembrokeshire but none is made from the Bluestone rock (Grimes, 1963); it is used for making stone axes, but these axes are in no way remarkable (Stone and Wallis, 1951; Evens *et al.*, 1962). However, the appearance of the outcrop itself is very remarkable, an amazing coronet of stone which dominates the landscape for miles around. Whenever you are in sight of it your eye is drawn towards it with a fascination that is uncannily compelling. It is scarcely possible to convey the peculiar power of that dramatic natural feature through words, or even through photographs, because it has a lot to do with size and distance and the feeling for the country, which can only be experienced on the spot, but I would suggest that it is the character of the outcrop itself which gave to the rock its magic qualities and made worthwhile the tedious and dangerous journey to Wiltshire. Such a suggestion is by its very nature impossible of proof, but one can show how smaller less magnificent rocks were decorated and incorporated by contemporary man into ceremonial sites in which the presence of the living rock must have been a significant factor.

The decoration of living rock surfaces with inexplicable patterns of cups and rings is a phenomenon that is well known in the Bronze Age. Although one may occasionally find this art on moveable slabs incorporated into burial and other monuments (Simpson and Thawley, 1972), in the majority of instances it is carved on living rock unconnected with any man-made structure or habitation. Without prejudice to any interpretation of the meaning of these symbols, it is clear that here we have another instance of the involvement of prehistoric man with the natural features of his environment although the choice of particular rocks, which in some instances are quite inconspicuous, is less easy to explain.

Natural boulders *in situ* also feature to a quite significant extent in the design and construction of ring cairns, the rather enigmatic Bronze Age monuments which lie midway between the stone circles and the burial cairns (Lynch, 1972). At Cefn Caer Euni (Merioneth) and at Caerloggas I (Cornwall), the natural stone was a central and presumably focal feature of the monument; in the first case it was a sharp thin slab protruding through the yellow clay subsoil to a height of just over 30 cm (F. M. Lynch, excavated 1972), in the second it was a tor, around which the ring had been built, this ring incorporating two more tall natural boulders (Mrs H. Miles, personal communication). At Circle 278, Penmaenmawr (Caernarvonshire), Stanton Moor T2 (Derbyshire), and at Banniside Moor near Coniston the natural boulders were incorporated into the kerb of the ring, where they are conspicuous for their size and, in the first two instances, their importance was emphasized by the presence of cremation burials tucked in beside them (Griffiths, 1960; Heathcote, 1930; Collingwood, 1910). It is impossible to be certain of the status of boulders at unexcavated sites, but one may suspect the presence of naturally set stones at Graigllyscwmllorwg (Glamorgan), Moel Goedog (Merioneth), and at the rather doubtful site, Beudy Cae'rgwyddel (Caernarvonshire) (RCAM Glamorgan; Bowen and Gresham, 1967; RCAM Caernarvonshire, 1960). This list is by no means comprehensive and I am sure that many other instances may spring to the minds of readers; for example, I would imagine that many recumbent stone circles may contain natural boulders in significant positions. But I think it is reasonable, from this list alone, to suggest that the earthfast boulder was a feature of some importance in the ritual thinking served by these monuments.

Ring cairns illustrate another aspect of the power of nature in primitive religious thinking, for they are very often sited near springs and at the sources of streams and rivers, sometimes standing out at the edge of the high moorland where the river begins its descent to the valley. This fascination with bogs and springs is well known in the later periods, when rich Celtic sanctuaries were established at places like the source of the Seine and at the small Anglesey bog, Llyn Cerrig Bach. This interest in water deities was not new, for Late Bronze Age swords and shields and cauldrons are found in similar watery situations, but it is less easy to demonstrate this interest in the earlier periods unless one can suggest that this very broad group of monuments, ring cairns, stone circles, and their arguable predecessors, the henges, show the beginning of this trend.

The Celtic interest in rivers, springs, and wells and their use of natural groves as sanctuaries is well known and I will not reiterate the evidence here, except to point out that in this better documented period we have a good deal of information to show that man's religious thinking was closely bound up with the landscape around him, either through his appreciation of its beauty or through fear of its potential destructive power over his life. This attitude is not confined to Europe and instances could be cited from all over the world, while in the contemporary Mediterranean cultures one can quote the famous oracles at Delphi and Cumae and the numerous caves, such as the Cave of Zeus on Mount Ida, all natural features which form the centre of elaborate sanctuaries.

Professor Thom has drawn attention to the way in which many prehistoric monuments are sited in relation to dramatic views over conspicuous natural land formations and, whether or not one agrees with his complex astronomical explanations for this, one must admit that many monuments do command exceptionally fine views (Thom, 1967). And this applies equally to some low flat structures which could scarcely have been used as siting markers and only indicate in the most general way the appropriate spot on which to stand.

One such monument is the low flat-topped mound in the pass above the Brenig Valley, Denbighshire (Lynch *et al.,* 1974). This in fact should scarcely be described as a mound since it is basically a scarped promontory, and it is almost certainly not a burial site since neither the recent total excavation nor two previous diggings in the centre found any trace of human bone, although there was evidence for activity in the form of charcoal on the old ground surface. However, the one remarkable thing about this monument is the view that it commands; southwards and westwards across the Denbigh Moors to the mountains of Snowdonia and northwards along the Clwyd Valley to the sea at Prestatyn with the imposing bulk of Moel Hiraddug above it. This view encompasses two ecological zones and the mound is almost on the boundary between them; the Brenig Valley itself and the moors beyond are bleak heather-covered, and acid while the Clwyd Valley is rich and green and must at that time have been densely wooded. It seems reasonable to suggest that it was in this dramatic siting between these two such different territories that the significance of this structure lay; that it was some kind of marker, whether of an actual political or tribal boundary or of an emotional religious one, one cannot know. In South Wales a similar pattern of distribution can be recognized at the heads of the valleys where exceptionally large standing stones, such as the Maen Llia (Breconshire), and often cairns as well, are set in the passes with a regularity which suggests a system of demarcation rather than simply a series of signposts.

The siting of the low mound in the pass at Brenig is dramatic, not only in this broad regional context, but also in a smaller scale within the cemetery group to which it belongs, for it provides an apex to the triangular setting of barrows on either side of the valley. In this sense it acts as a bridge between the two aspects of this subject that I want to discuss, for with the question of cemetery planning one enters an area of aesthetics on a more human scale.

Because of the way monuments and their settings have changed through the centuries, the scope of this discussion is necessarily limited. The Neolithic stone tombs are architectural masterpieces which retain a strong dramatic impact even today. But we most often see them as skeletons, perhaps more impressive than their original covered form, so they are not ideal subjects for consideration. It is obvious that the tall entrance stones and monstrous capstones of the Portal Dolmen and the rather theatrical facades of the Court Cairns were designed for dramatic effect but the settings are not unusually spectacular and, since many are on low ground, one cannot be certain how closely the monument might be surrounded by trees. In the Lowland Zone, where not only is it more difficult to judge the contemporary landscape but also the monuments were themselves made from wood and survive only as post-holes, it is almost impossible to get a reliable idea of original architectural quality. The surviving remains of earthen long barrows are very sad indeed and even reconstructions must inevitably show all wooden uprights as telegraph posts rather than the elaborately carved and painted pillars they no doubt were.

It is only in the west where stone is available and moreover, only on the higher moorlands which pollen analysis is showing were already by the Bronze Age denuded of trees (F. A. Hibbert, preliminary results from the palaeobotanical survey of Brenig, personal communication) and where the monuments have not been extensively robbed of stone, that it is possible to judge the monuments as originally designed and see them in their intended setting. This means that we are confined almost exclusively to the Early Bronze Age with its barrows and cairns and more complex circular monuments of the stone-circle/ring-cairn class.

In this class is Bryn Cader Faner (Merioneth), one of the finest, perhaps *the* finest, prehistoric monument in Wales (Bowen and Gresham, 1967). It is a cairn circle, a low stone cairn through which rises a ring of spaced uprights, in this case tall slate slabs inclined outwards so that the final effect is of a spiky crown or of a sunburst. This monument is set on the flat top of a rocky ridge which emerges from an area of bog surrounded by a swirling mass of crags and mountains. Passing through this complex and rather awesome landscape is a trackway certainly prehistoric in origin, for a string of monuments lines its route, beginning close to Harlech and culminating in the exciting and awe-inspiring view of Bryn Cader Faner, outlined against the sky on its isolated ridge. The trackway passes beneath it, but as you draw near the monument disappears, and equally if you approach from the north you may never see it, because it is set in the centre of the flat-topped ridge which conceals it from below. Obviously the siting was carefully contrived to provide a concentrated dramatic impact to those coming up the track from the south. In this monument we have a wonderfully simple yet sensational design coupled with a most skilful choice of site, the two complementing each other in a way that is entirely satisfying.

One can cite other examples of this type of monument which are carefully placed in relation to their background and their visibility from certain aspects. For instance, Moel Ty Uchaf, Llandrillo (Merioneth), can be seen against the sunset from Ffordd Gamelin, and the Druid's Circle, Penmaenmawr, is silhouetted against the sky for those who are walking up to that important plateau from the valley below. But on the other hand there are certain monuments which seem to be almost deliberately hidden until the visitor is only a few yards away, which suggests an equally careful consideration of the siting with a different architectural impact in mind. Two instances of such hidden monuments are the small ring cairns, Circle 278, at Penmaenmawr which is separated from the Druid's Circle by a fold of the moor, and the Hengwm Circle, Llanaber (Merioneth), a low monument set back from the edge of a flat terrace so that it is quite invisible from any distance.

The careful siting of the architecturally simple round barrows of the Bronze Age on false crests and ridges so that they present a striking profile when viewed from the valleys below is a well known feature of all areas where these monuments still survive. This phenomenon has been noticed and commented upon by many archaeologists and I will not go over the same ground again here beyond drawing attention to perhaps the most spectacular example of this large-scale planning of an interrelated group of barrows, the Dorset Ridgeway Group with its fourteen foci comprising 233 barrows in all (RCHM Dorset, 1970). These mounds are quite variously sited in relation to the main ridge and the valleys emanating from it, but this siting is so designed as to create a complex system of intervisibility which must be the result of deliberate planning. The same sort of thing can be seen on a much smaller scale in the Brenig Valley (Denbighshire), where the barrows converge from either side of the valley towards the small mound in the pass. Nowadays, the heather-covered mounds are quite difficult to pick out, but originally the effect must have been very striking, as each mound was capped with a deliberate layer of yellow clay which would have made them extremely conspicuous.

The recognition that many barrow groups are the result of deliberate planning rather than, or perhaps as well as, natural accretion has many social implications beyond the realisation that Bronze Age man had an interest in landscape architecture. Problems of social and political control and of chronology and the role of the cemetery in the life of the community can be raised, but they are outside the scope of this short essay. Suffice it to say that such problems will not be illuminated except by excavation on a broader front than has normally been the case hitherto, when the individual barrow has been considered as a separate entity rather than as part of an interrelated group.

The aesthetic question of appreciation of landscape could also be approached from the point of view of settlement, the choice of position for a house. However, although one can see a varying taste in landscape reflected in the siting of houses of the Classical Revival and of the Romantic Movement, such an analysis is virtually impossible in the context of the prehistoric farmstead, although it is a factor which may not have been entirely ignored. For in contrast to medieval houses, which normally huddle under the lee of the hill, many prehistoric settlements seem absurdly exposed but do command some very beautiful tracts of country.

With farms there are so many practical considerations in siting, such as fertility, water, aspect, and accessibility, that one cannot hope to make a convincing argument for the attraction of the view, but religious monuments do not suffer from the same constraints and, moreover, we have a much fuller picture of their distribution and density, so I would suggest that we may legitimately use the detail of their siting and their relationship to striking natural features to illuminate that elusive aspect of prehistoric man, his sensibility.

REFERENCES

Bowen, E. G. and Gresham, C. A. (1967). *History of Merioneth. Vol. I.*

Collingwood, R. G. (1910). An exploration of the circle on Banniside Moor, Coniston. *Trans. Cumberland Westmorland Antiq. Archaeol. Soc.*, 10, 342–353.

Evens, E. D., Grinsell, L. V., Piggott, S., and Wallis, F. S. (1962). Fourth report of the sub-committee of the south-western group of museums and art galleries (England) on the petrological identification of stone axes. *Proc. Prehist. Soc.*, 28, 209–266.

Griffiths, W. E. (1960). The excavation of stone circles near Penmaenmawr, North Wales. *ibid.*, 26, 303–339.

Grimes, W. F. (1963). The stone circles and related monuments of Wales. *In* Foster, I. Ll. and Alcock, L. (eds.). *Culture and Environment.* Routledge and Kegan Paul; 93–152.

Heathcote, J. P. (1930). Excavations at barrows on Stanton Moor. *Derbyshire Archaeol. J.*, 51, 1–44.

Lynch, F. M. (1972) Ring-cairns and related monuments in Wales. *Scottish Archaeol. Forum*, 4, 61–80. (This volume contains other articles on ring-cairns in the Highland Zone).

Lynch, F. M., *et al.* (1974). Brenig Valley excavations: interim report. *Trans. Denbighshire Hist. Soc.* 23, 9–64.

RCAM Caernarvonshire (1956–1964). *An Inventory of the Ancient Monuments in Caernarvonshire.* London: HMSO.

RCAM Glamorgan. (Forthcoming).

RCHM Dorset (1970). *Royal Commission on Historical Monuments, England. Vol. II. S.W. Dorset, Pt. 3.* London: HMSO.

Simpson, D. D. A. and Thawley, J. E. (1972). Single grave art in Britain. *Scottish Archaeol. Forum*, 4, 81–104.

Stone, J. F. S. and Wallis, F. S. (1951). Third report of the sub-committee of the south-westeı n group of museums and art galleries on the petrological determination of stone axes. *Proc. Prehist. Soc.,* 17, 99–158.

Thom, A. (1967). *Megalithic Sites in Britain.* Oxford: Clarendon Press.

Summary and general conclusions

G. W. Dimbleby

THE CONCEPT OF THE HIGHLAND ZONE

In deciding to treat the history of landscape in terms of Highland and Lowland Zones, those planning the conference were only concerned to divide the growing body of knowledge on this theme into a suitable framework for two conferences. Some participants seemed to think we were meeting to justify concepts, whether instituted by Fox, Mackinder, or whoever, which they deemed to have ceased to be useful in their particular fields. The concept of Highland and Lowland Zones is a form of shorthand, with recognized limitations, which ecologists, geographers, and climatologists still find useful, and the study of landscape is in essence a study of human ecology and geography.

Several papers specifically dealt with the Highland/Lowland contact zone, in order to establish unity of the whole field. Dr Campbell* showed how the two regions were related in the Upper Palaeolithic and how their interrelationships fluctuated during warm and cold phases. In the Mesolithic the economic contacts between upland and lowland in North Yorkshire were discussed by Dr Simmons, and Dr Tutin showed similar connections in the Neolithic in the Lake District. Perhaps this relationship was most strongly demonstrated in the Roman period: Dr Manning showed how military forces on active service in Wales were serviced both from the distant lowlands and by local production in the valleys.

CHARACTERS OF THE HIGHLAND ZONE

Though Dr Campbell showed diagrams of the fluctuations in the ice sheets through the Würm, nobody, surprisingly, discussed the very considerable effects of glaciation in rejuvenating the land, and the considerable effects this had on geomorphology, soil development, etc.

Several speakers favoured definitions of the Highland Zone in terms of pluviality, related to the high relief and its proximity to the sea. Dr Ball described the non-weathering rocks, often with ice striations still clear, and generally of low base status, and gave a sketch of the common soils developed in the region. Low evaporation led to wet soils and overcast weather to low temperatures, resulting in low microbiological breakdown. Professor Estyn Evans pointed out that in Northern Ireland there are only a few spring days each year when the humidity is low enough to allow the use of fire, an ecological factor of great importance anthropogenically.

*Paper not published in proceedings

THE FOREST OF THE CLIMATIC OPTIMUM

Though nobody specifically discussed the ecological features of this forest, the many pollen diagrams shown gave a repeated picture of an all-embracing cover of mixed oak forest, with oak, alder, and elm as important components. The soils accompanying this forest cover were brown forest soils (Dr Tutin, Mr Romans) or brown podzolics at lower altitudes, with podzols at higher elevation. There was some discussion of what the forest was like in the far north, where pine would replace deciduous forest, at least on north-facing slopes, and probably more generally at higher altitudes.

A good deal of hill fog seemed to enshroud our concepts of the level of the tree line of this period; brave estimates of over 2000 ft (610 m) were vouchsafed for Wales, but workers in other areas were more coy. Professor Manley made a plea for detailed study of the tree-line on Cross Fell (2930 ft, 893 m) which he thought was at a critical height OD. At the other extreme of altitude, evidence was produced by Miss Spencer, supported by several other speakers, of some form of oak forest along the coast.

It is important to have some impression of this extensive forest, even though imprecise in detail, for it seems that in the Climatic Optimum there was no very sharp difference in the forest cover between the Highland and Lowland Zones. Perhaps that is why some prehistorians do not find the distinction into zones useful—it hardly existed at first. But from the Neolithic onwards the two zones have emerged as distinct from each other. Archaeologists have to fit man into this development as a cause, a victim of inexorable change, or both.

THE EARLY PHASES OF MAN'S INFLUENCE

Several speakers produced evidence of pre-elm decline clearance in the Lake District (Dr Tutin), on the North York Moors (Dr Simmons), and in Northern Ireland (Professor Alan Smith). Professor Smith pointed out that the radiocarbon dates of some clearances are no earlier than the earliest Neolithic dates in the territory, from which upland Mesolithic seems to be absent, and suggested this might also apply to the Lake District examples. Obviously, questions of terminology will need to be settled soon. Where there are definite microlithic remains, there may be clear evidence of forest destruction, and Dr Simmons suggested that habitat manipulation by fire may have been practised as part of a husbandry of the large wild herbivores, notably the red deer. Mr Chaplin's paper on the ecology of the deer gave support to this idea, and Mrs P. Evans suggested that the aurochs might be favoured by opening up the forest. Dr Simmons paid particular attention to the above-forest belt, saying that fire could more easily be employed there than in the dense deciduous forest.

On the other hand, Professor Smith felt that some of the early clearings in the forest would have been so small that slash-and-burn could hardly have been used, especially in pluvial Ireland. In the Lake District, however, Dr Tutin showed with great ingenuity that the clearances following the elm decline were associated with man and in particular the use of fire.

On acid soils in many parts of Britain there is little evidence of Neolithic settlements, though surface traces of hunting turn up. This may explain why in some areas the *Landnam* effect is late. Dr Turner showed, again with an ingenious application of pollen analysis, that a series of *Landnam* phases could be detected in a raised bog in lowland Ayrshire, ranging in age from 1400 to 1000 bc.

Fire seems to have been used for a number of purposes in prehistory: to favour herbivores and no doubt to make them accessible for hunting, to clear forest for agriculture, and to provide ash for field dressing. It was mentioned that 10 acres of forest have to be burned to provide the ash dressing for 1 acre of arable. Professor Estyn Evans described the early 'lazy-beds' which are now being discovered below peat in Ireland and pointed out that it is usual practice to stack the turf and burn it in order to provide an ash dressing for new beds.

Other forms of land-use in the uplands were described by Mr Feachem,* showing different types of plot systems combined with hut-circles, clearance cairns, etc. Such systems persist in the Highland Zone because the subsequent deterioration of the land (see below) precluded further cultivation.

RELIABILITY OF EVIDENCE

At this point it is useful to mention the papers dealing with the location and interpretation of field evidence of sites. Mr Stevenson discussed the difficulties of interpreting the spatial distribution of sites because of the uncertainties about (a) destruction and (b) discovery. However, Mr Wilson's paper indicated the value of air photography as a means of reducing such uncertainty. From time to time in the conference the reliability of evidence was questioned on various points. Perhaps the most interesting was the conflict between the pollen analysts who find that the northern extremities of Britain—Caithness, Orkney, and Shetland—have not been wooded since the Climatic Optimum and the Norse sagas which say that ships were being built in Caithness well into historic time. There are other examples of discrepancies between bog pollen sequences and independent evidence, and the subject as a whole would seem to be worth investigating further.

*Paper not published in proceedings

ENVIRONMENTAL TRENDS

Vegetation

There is some evidence of forest regression (e.g. falling tree-lines) before the Neolithic (i.e. following the Climatic Optimum), but it is from the elm decline onwards that forest destruction gathers pace. The elm decline itself was not discussed in detail, though Professor Smith contributed good evidence of the barking of elm trees by cattle. Both he and Dr Tutin accepted the decline as being more or less synchronous over Britain, though dates fluctuate through several hundreds of years. Professor Smith showed two pollen diagrams from Northern Ireland, one from an upland and one from a lowland site. Each showed a succession of clearance phases associated with archaeological periods up to the Iron Age, but whereas in the lowland site each clearance was followed by regeneration of the forest back to its previous dominance, in the upland site the returning waves of the forest were progressively weaker. Dr Tutin was able to show similar trends in different situations in and around the Lake District.

There was some concern by Romanists and Medievalists that pollen analyses indicated that the forest would have been destroyed by the period they were interested in, but this continued regeneration, except on highly degraded soils or land which has become peat-covered, allays their concern. Forest clearance is rarely a once-and-for-all episode in these earlier periods of human activity.

The vegetation arising from clearance, unless carried out for arable, was usually grassland, or sometimes bracken. Later heather became abundant on acid soils or as soils acidified. Professor Evans drew attention to the traditional attitudes to flowering shrubs, such as whitethorn, which were venerated, and to the properties attributed to the flowers of the pastures. Herbs are known to provide cattle with trace elements they do not get from grass alone, so there may be some justification for such traditions. It is interesting that our pollen analyses often show a long list of herb types in clearance phases.

Climate and Microclimate

Not surprisingly, at a conference on a subject covering a long timescale, the question of climatic change arose from time to time. Dr Tutin produced evidence of more pluvial conditions about 5000 bp, which coincided with the Neolithic *Landnam*, and Professor Smith thought he could see evidence of increased atmospheric wetness in Ireland at about 2000 bc, again coinciding with early clearance. Dr Turner also found evidence of bog growth, which she attributed to greater climatic wetness.

Microclimatic changes would follow forest destruction on an extensive scale, and Mr Taylor pointed out the effect these would have on the terrain as a habitat for Mesolithic man. He also drew attention to the effect of such changes on the soil; a pluvial climate impinging directly at ground level could lead to peat formation.

Soils

Soil degradation as a concept came in for some semantic discussion. Dr R. Smith defended the concept as applied to soils resulting from human activity, but Dr Ball preferred to think of these changes as natural processes accelerated by man, himself a part of the natural system. Dr Tutin, however, suggested that most ecologists use the term and know what they mean by it. Mr Romans elegantly demonstrated by thin sections that soil changes followed slash and burn; fragments of oak charcoal were surrounded by orientated clay. He gave evidence from Scotland of brown forest soils under oakwood 5,000 years ago now appearing as peaty gley podzols. It may be asked whether a peaty gley podzol is ever found apart from human influence; could it not be an example of a man-made soil not found in the 'natural' retrogressive sequence?

Peat is a special soil type associated with wet climates. Following forest clearance and land use, surface wetness, gleying (with or without an iron pan), and loss of soil structure may in due course initiate peat formation. Professor Estyn Evans vividly described how a heavily grazed sward ceases to absorb water in the wet climate of Ireland, allowing water to stand on the surface or to run off. He remarked that peat is found where man has operated. It was interesting to hear an uninhibited discussion of whether the initiation of blanket peat might be the result of human activity. Dr Simmons suggested that Mesolithic man might contribute to such an effect, and Professor Smith was undecided whether this was so in Northern Ireland or whether an increased wetness of the climate at 2000 bc would have brought this about in any case. It is perhaps relevant that on Gough Island, in the South Atlantic, peat has formed in the absence of human influence.

ECOLOGICAL CONCLUSIONS

The trends exemplify a problem which is characteristic of the Highland Zone. Ecological retrogression is seen in both soils and vegetation, and ecologists are still undecided whether these changes would have happened in any case, though admittedly at a very much slower rate. The archaeologist, however, can be clear that even if man did not initiate these processes he accelerated them so rapidly that the natural rate (if there is such a thing) is of academic interest only. It is surprising that the actual rate of such processes was not discussed by any speaker.

In view of these conclusions, it was slightly disconcerting to see, in a diagram used by Mr Stevenson, the conventional descriptions of upland moor as 'unimproved land'. This is certainly true, but what it does not imply is that this land is highly degraded (no apologies) from its original condition. As Professor Pearsall used to say, our uplands have been converted, in terms of food production, into the equivalent of semi-desert.

OTHER PAPERS

There were two papers which did not fit into the theme of landscape development followed here, but which raised some lively audience participation. Professor Alcock presented a paper in which he questioned the interpretation of skeletal remains of food animals from the site of Dinas Powys. A lively discussion, liberally sprinkled with mixed metaphors ranging from kettles of fish to dead ducks, elicited some very helpful guidance from Mr Chaplin on the question of animal breeding and butchery.

Finally, Miss Lynch gave an enchanting evening lecture drawing attention to the aesthetic appeal of our ancient monuments and their settings. Her suggestion that the CBA should submit some of these for attention in European Architectural Heritage Year 1975 was widely approved.